About Island Press

Island Press is the only nonprofit organization in the United States whose principal purpose is the publication of books on environmental issues and natural resource management. We provide solutions-oriented information to professionals, public officials, business and community leaders, and concerned citizens who are shaping responses to environmental problems.

In 1999, Island Press celebrates its fifteenth anniversary as the leading provider of timely and practical books that take a multidisciplinary approach to critical environmental concerns. Our growing list of titles reflects our commitment to bringing the best of an expanding body of literature to the environmental community throughout North America and the world.

Support for Island Press is provided by The Jenifer Altman Foundation, The Bullitt Foundation, The Mary Flagler Cary Charitable Trust, The Nathan Cummings Foundation, The Geraldine R. Dodge Foundation, The Charles Engelhard Foundation, The Ford Foundation, The Vira I. Heinz Endowment, The W. Alton Jones Foundation, The John D. and Catherine T. MacArthur Foundation, The Andrew W. Mellon Foundation, The Charles Stewart Mott Foundation, The Curtis and Edith Munson Foundation, The National Fish and Wildlife Foundation, The National Science Foundation, The New-Land Foundation, The David and Lucile Packard Foundation, The Pew Charitable Trusts, The Surdna Foundation, The Winslow Foundation, and individual donors.

Modeling the Environment

To Amy

Modeling the Environment
An Introduction to System Dynamics
Models of Environmental Systems

Andrew Ford

ISLAND PRESS
Washington, D.C. • Covelo, California

Cover design by Greg Turner-Rahman.
Cover photo of the Sierra Nevada by Fred Ford.

The following figures have been reproduced from previously published sources:

Figure 1.2 from *Eye and the Brain: The Psychology of Seeing,* by Richard Gregory, Oxford University Press, New York, 1998, p. 183, by permission of Oxford University Press.

Figures 4.1 and 4.2 from *Mono Lake: Endangered Oasis. The Position Paper of the Mono Lake Committee,* 1993, p. 29, reprinted by permission.

Figure 12.1 from *Toward Global Equilibrium: Collected Papers by Jorgen Randers,* edited by D. L. Meadows and D. H. Meadows. Copyright © 1973 by Productivity Press, P.O. Box 13390, Portland OR 97213-0390, (800) 394-6868, reprinted by permission.

ISBN 1–55963–600–9 (cloth)
ISBN 1–55963–601–7 (paper)
Library of Congress Card Catalog Number: 99–18909

Printed on recycled, acid-free paper

Manufactured in the United States of America
10 9 8 7 6 5 4 3 2 1

Contents

Part V.   Management Flight Simulators

Part VI.   Conclusions

Review

Software

Special Topics

Preface

Modeling the Environment is designed for college students with an interest in systems and the environment. It introduces the use of system dynamics models to understand and manage environmental systems. The book provides material suitable for two semesters of study at the undergraduate level. It can also be used for a graduate course in computer simulation applied to environmental systems.

Getting Started

The book was written based on the assumption that you have learned introductory algebra and that you have learned how to combine units of measurement. However, it may be useful to refresh your memory in these areas at the outset. Appendix A reminds you how units are defined and combined. Appendix B describes exponential growth and decay, two of the more important topics from your previous study of mathematics.

You need not know calculus or differential equations to use this book. Rather, you'll learn how to build mathematical models on the computer. Your job is to concentrate on the structure of the model; the tedious job of numerical simulation will be left to the computer. Computer simulation is made easier by software such as Stella (appendix C), Dynamo (appendix D), Vensim (appendix E), and Powersim (appendix F). Stella is used in this book, so you will find the most direct match between your work and the book if you use Stella. However, you can use any of the software packages with this book. Each is easy to learn, and each can be used to build powerful models of environmental systems.

Part I. Introduction

Chapter 1 introduces the general topic of modeling and the specific field of system dynamics. Chapter 2 explains stocks and flows, the fundamental building blocks of system dynamics models. The models are simulated numerically on the computer, as explained in chapter 3. The first opportunity to build and use a model of a real environmental system appears in chapter 4. It describes a model of water flows in the Mono Basin of Northern California.

Chapters 5–9 complete the introductory material. Chapter 5 describes the equilibrium diagram, a variation of the stock-and-flow diagram to show the flows that maintain a system in dynamic equilibrium. Chapter 6 describes two models of seemingly different systems that both exhibit s-shaped growth over time. The similarity in their behavior arises from the similarity in their structure. Chapter 7 introduces a different way to look at the structure of a system. It explains causal loop diagrams and demonstrates how these diagrams draw our attention to the feedback structure of a system. Chapter 8 provides an opportunity to put the new diagrams to use to explain homeostasis. Chapter 9 concludes the introductory material with "bull's-eye" diagrams, a convenient way to portray the boundaries of a model.

Part II. Simulating Material Flow

Material flows are of special interest to environmental scientists and managers, and system dynamics is well suited to simulate material flows because of the clarity of the stock-and-flow approach. Chapter 10 describes the methods most frequently used to simulate material flow through a system. Chapter 11 draws our attention to the fast-moving flows and explains how they influence the selection of DT, the "step size" in the numerical simulations.

The book then presents three applications to real environmental systems. Chapter 12 describes the flow of the pesticide DDT through the soil, the air, and the ocean and into the bodies of fish. Chapter 13 describes the salmon smolts' spring migration down the Snake River, the Columbia River, and into the ocean. Chapter 14 describes the lifecycle of the salmon born in the Tucannon River in eastern Washington.

Part III. The Modeling Process

Chapter 15 describes the process of building and testing a model. This is a trial-and-error process involving a combination of all the skills learned from the previous chapters. You'll read that experienced modelers concentrate as much on the process of model building as the model itself. Chapter 15 concludes with cases in which the iterative nature of the modeling process was the key to project success.

Chapter 16 demonstrates the iterative process of modeling with a concrete example of the deer herd on the Kaibab Plateau in northern Arizona. After several iterations, chapter 16 arrives at a model to explain the rapid growth and subsequent collapse of the deer herd in the 1920s. The Kaibab example is a vivid illustration of the "overshoot" pattern of behavior that can be observed in a wide variety of systems.

Part IV. Simulating Cyclical Systems

The next three chapters turn our attention from systems that grow over time to systems that oscillate over time. The oscillations may be extremely volatile and pose serious problems, or they may be highly stable and provide the key to the system's longevity. Chapter 17 explains the fundamentals of oscillatory behavior by drawing on the examples of s-shaped growth from chapter 6. You'll read how the introduction of delays can change the stable systems from the previous chapter into highly oscillatory systems.

Two examples are provided to allow you to build and test models of oscillatory behavior. The first example, predator-prey cycles, is one of the most widely discussed topics from ecology. Chapter 18 describes cyclical patterns in a population of cougars and deer on the Kaibab Plateau. The second example, commodity production cycles, is one of the more important topics from economics. Chapter 19 describes a model of production cycles in the world aluminum industry.

Part V. Management Flight Simulators

The next two chapters are devoted to management flight simulators. These are highly interactive models designed for ease of experimentation. The first example deals with the persistent problem of urban air pollution. Chapter 20 places you in the role of "feebate" manager. By charging fees on the sale of dirty vehicles and allowing rebates for the purchase of clean vehicles, a state might reduce vehicle emissions within the urban airshed. Chapter 20 challenges you to learn whether a feebate program could be designed to operate in a financially prudent manner.

The second example deals with the Gaia hypothesis and the parable of Daisyworld. Chapter 21 provides a brief review of the Gaia hypothesis and the purpose of the mathematical model of an imaginary planet with black and white daisies. You'll use the flight simulator to design a world with the best possible prospects for sustaining life on Daisyworld.

Part VI. Conclusions

The two concluding chapters deal with the topics of model validation and model use. Chapter 22 introduces opposing points of view on the controversial topic of model validation. It adopts a pragmatic point of view and explains five concrete tests that can be used to bolster confidence in a model.

Of course, the ultimate test of a model's usefulness is whether it is put to use. System dynamics models have been put to extensive use in the electric power industry. Chapter 23 reviews the history of this industry, and it describes how system dynamics has contributed a unique perspective on the industry's problems. The lessons from this industry will help you anticipate how the knowledge from this book might be used in your own field.

Appendices

The appendices provide important material that is not normally read in sequential fashion. You should pick and choose which appendices will best support your own learning. The first two appendices are review material. Almost every reader will benefit from a quick review of units (appendix A) and mathematics (appendix B).

The next six appendices deal with software. Stella is described in detail in appendix C because it has been selected for the examples in the book. But you will quickly see the close similarity between Stella and the other stock-and-flow programs by reading appendices D, E, and F. If you are familiar with spreadsheets, you will benefit from the description of spreadsheet modeling in appendix G. Appendix H concludes the software material with an introduction to some of the special functions that expand the power of models beyond the normal stocks and flows.

The final three appendices cover special topics of interest to students of the environment. Environmental scientists and managers often pay close attention to spatial arrangements, and appendix I illustrates how the spatial dimensions can be included in a system dynamics model. The illustration shows the spread of nitrogen in a catchment. Appendix J is of special interest to environmental managers using models with many highly uncertain parameters. It explains how we may calculate the confidence bounds for model simulations. It then illustrates how the feedback structure of a system causes the confidence bounds to grow or shrink over time. Appendix K concludes with the Idagon, a management flight simulator that allows you to experience the challenges of managing a complex river system. You'll see a summary of the river system in this appendix. The detailed description and the flight simulator are on this book's home page (see below).

Exercises and Home Page

Each chapter concludes with a list of exercises designed to be completed between class meetings. You'll see that many of these are verification exercises, so you will know when you get the right answer. Answers to some of the more complicated exercises are posted on a home page <http://www.islandpress.org/ford>. The home page is designed as a supplement to the book to provide:

- expanded background to selected cases (e.g., Mono Lake)
- links to other pages with case information
- links to related pages on system dynamics
- links to the companies that provide system dynamics software
- models and flight simulators to be downloaded for exercises

The main purpose of the home page is to expand the collection of exercises in the book. It includes several short exercises that are similar to the exercises found at the end of each chapter. It also includes a collection of longer exercises that are suitable for class projects. You'll discover opportunities for modeling projects from the following fields:

- anthropology (the Tsembaga clan and their pigs)
- epidemiology (spread of yellow fever)
- genetics (industrial melanism)
- limnology (cultural eutrophication)
- management (self-imposed limitations to growth)
- physics (equilibrium temperature)
- physiology (simulating the shivering response)
- resource economics (exploration and production of natural gas)

Note to Instructors

This book is intended for use in a college course for undergraduate students interested in systems and the environment. It is arranged for a "typical" course with students meeting three hours per week for sixteen weeks. But courses come in all shapes and sizes, so you should take advantage of the book's modular design to shape the material to your situation. For example, if you are limited to four weeks of instruction, I recommend the following sequence:

1st week: Introduction and review (chapter 1 and appendices A and B)
2nd week: Software (select from appendices C, D, E, or F)
3rd week: Build and simulate (chapters 2 and 3)
4th week: First major application—the Mono Basin (chapter 4)

This material is stand-alone and it concludes with a realistic application to an important environmental system. If you are using the book in an eight-week course, I recommend you add the following sequence:

5th week: Equilibrium diagrams and s-shaped growth (chapter 6)
6th week: Causal loop diagrams (chapters 7 and 8) and bull's-eye diagrams (chapter 9)
7th week: Introduction to material flow (chapter 10) and step size (chapter 11)
8th week: Select one of the examples from chapters 12, 13, or 14.

The Tucannon example in chapter 14 might be the best selection because it concludes with an interactive model to allow students to assume the role of fishery manager. At the end of eight weeks, the students will have mastered the fundamentals of modeling and studied two major applications.

If you are teaching a twelve-week course, you could add the following four-week sequence:

9th week: The modeling process (chapter 15)
10th week: Illustrating the process with the Kaibab deer herd (chapter 16)
11th week: Fundamentals of oscillations (chapter 17) and an example (chapters 18 or 19)
12th week: Management flight simulators (chapters 20 or 21)

At the end of the twelve weeks, students will have acquired a strong foundation to experiment with their own models. I believe a class project is the best way to conclude a one-semester course. I recommend you allow four weeks for students to build a new model or to improve one of the models in the book.

Acknowledgments

This book would not have been possible without support from colleagues at the University of Southern California (USC) and at Washington State University (WSU) who encouraged my teaching of system dynamics and shared their ideas for the classroom and the book. I particularly appreciate the encouragement from Peter Gardiner at USC and from Bill Budd and Eldon Franz at WSU. I also appreciate the many interesting ideas, exercises, and class projects from students at USC and WSU.

Several of the chapters grew out of lessons first presented to me by Dennis Meadows and Donella Meadows, two superb professors who taught system dynamics in the Program on Public Policy and Technology at Dartmouth College in the 1970s. Their classrooms were a special place to learn and think about systems, and I am forever in their debt.

Like most system dynamics practitioners, I have benefited greatly from professional interactions through the System Dynamics Society. I am particularly appreciative of the professional support from David Andersen of the Rockefeller College of Public Policy at the State University of New York at Albany and from John Sterman of the Sloan School of Management at the Massachusetts Institute of Technology.

I wish to acknowledge several teachers who contributed by reviewing drafts or by experimenting with early versions of the book in their classrooms. They include Ted Bjornn from the College of Forestry at the University of Idaho, Donella Meadows from the Environmental Studies Program at Dartmouth College, Fahriye Sancar from the College of Architecture and Planning at the University of Colorado, Krys Stave from the Environmental Studies Program at the University of Nevada at Las Vegas, and Robert Wilkinson from the Environmental Studies Program at the University of California at Santa Barbara. The book has also benefited from my many interesting discussions with Mike Bull from the Bonneville Power Administration and from suggestions by Charles Pretoskowi from the Idaho Fish and Game Department.

Several of the case studies in the book have been taken from research projects that applied system dynamics to energy and environmental problems in the West, and I acknowledge the financial support from the Bonneville Power Administration, the California Institute for Energy Efficiency, and the Idaho National Engineering and Environmental Laboratory. The book has also benefited from financial support from the Weyerhaeuser Environmental Education Project and from the WSU Center for Teaching and Learning.

The logistics of this text are quite formidable. Todd Baldwin, my editor at Island Press, helped to shape the early drafts and prepare the final manuscript for production. Peg Collins and Greg Turner-Rahman, both from the WSU Center for Teaching and Learning, helped with the interactive exercises. I concluded my work on the book during a sabbatical at the

London Business School, and I appreciate the support from Derek Bunn and John Morecroft to make the sabbatical possible.

I close with thanks to Amanda and Emilee, two daughters with the unfailing ability to brighten the day and to challenge the mind. And to Amy, my wife and best friend, my gratitude for your support, your ideas, and your sense for what is important.

PART I

INTRODUCTION

Chapter 1

Overview

A model is a substitute for a real system. Models are used when it is easier to work with a substitute than with the actual system. An architect's blueprint, an engineer's wind tunnel, and an economist's graphs are all models. They represent some aspect of a real system—a building, an aircraft, or the nation's economy. They are useful when they help us learn something new about the systems they represent.

Many of us have built and used models. Our first experiences might have involved physical models such as a paper airplane or a cardboard glider. These models were easy to assemble and easy to use. They made it fun to conduct experiments. We tried our experiments, watched the results, and tried again. Along the way, we learned about the dynamics of flight. If your experiences were like mine, you learned that you can't make a paper airplane fly farther by simply throwing it harder. We also learned that each airplane seemed to follow a natural glide path through the air. Through experimentation, we learned the extent to which the plane's natural trajectory could be improved.

This book focuses on mathematical models of environmental systems. Mathematical models use equations to represent the interconnections in a system. We will concentrate on a special category of mathematical models, which are "simulated" on the computer. They are called computer simulation models because the tedious calculations are turned over to the computer. Our job is to think about the best way to construct a model to describe an environmental system. If we do our job well, we can then use the model to conduct experiments. We will try our experiments, watch the results, and try again. Along the way, we will improve our understanding of the natural trajectories of environmental systems. Through experimentation with the computer model, we'll learn the extent to which the system's natural trajectory could be improved.

Informal Models

We use models all the time, but we work mostly with informal models. The images we carry in our minds are simplified representations of a complex system; they are sometimes called "mental models." Senge (1990, 8) describes mental models as "deeply ingrained assumptions, generalizations, or even pictures or images that influence how we understand the world and how we take action." We use mental models constantly to interpret the world around us, and we usually don't realize that we are doing so.

To understand how quickly and subconsciously we use mental models, try two simple experiments. First, take a look at figure 1.1 and explain to yourself what you see. Then take

3

Figure 1.1. What do you see in this diagram?

Figure 1.2. What do you see in this cartoon? In particular, is the curved line at the bottom a circle or an ellipse?

a look at figure 1.2 and explain what you see.

If you react like others, you will "see" a white triangle superimposed on figure 1.1. You might conclude that the white triangle has to be there—it's the simplest way to explain the entire drawing in a consistent manner. When asked about the cartoon, many respond that the curved line is a circle. When asked to explain why, they often come up with a rather elaborate theory—for example, that someone is playing a trick on the speaker by sawing a hole in the floor, and the most efficient way to saw the hole is in a circle. When told that the curved line in figure 1.2 is actually an ellipse, many immediately respond that they are viewing the circle in three dimensions. Such discussions reveal our amazing ability to form theories to explain the world around us. These theories are mental models.

Thinking About the Environment

Although we are clever in thinking about geometric shapes, we often seem baffled when thinking about serious problems in the environment. Whether it's a localized problem like urban air pollution or a global problem like the accumulation of greenhouse gases, our mental models seem inadequate to the task. We hear multiple and conflicting explanations of the problem, and we are not sure what to believe. If given the authority to act, we might not know what action to take. Our first instincts about complex systems may lead us in the wrong direction. We may think that the answer is to "push harder" by expanding a particular program that has worked in the past, but the system may respond like the paper airplanes from our youth. Pushing harder may be like throwing the airplane harder—it may make the situation worse than before. You'll see an example in the salmon harvesting exercise in chapter 14. You'll read about a salmon population that seems to follow its own "natural trajectory" over time, and you'll discover that the population can support a large harvest year after year. But if you try to increase the total harvest by "pushing harder," that is, by harvesting more, you'll discover that you actually lower the harvest in the long run.

You'll see other examples of unexpected behavior as each new environmental system is introduced in the book. Some systems will surprise us with an unusually sluggish response. (An example is DDT accumulation in chapter 12.) Others will exhibit unexpectedly rapid responses that seem to spin the system out of control. (An example is the cash flow from fee-bates in chapter 20.) The purpose of each new chapter is to allow us to learn about the system's natural tendencies by computer experimentation.

Learning through computer experimentation reminds me of my first experiences learning to steer a boat. The first time I took the controls of the motor at the rear of a fishing boat my instinct was to point the motor handle in the direction I wanted to travel. To steer the boat to the right, I pointed the motor handle to the right. But this caused the boat to pivot and start traveling to the left. My next reaction was to point the handle even farther to the right, and, of course, the boat turned even farther to the left. When I finally sensed that a correction was needed, I swung the motor handle too far to the left and watched anxiously as the boat pivoted too far to the right. With time and practice, however, I developed a feel for the system and was able to steer a fishing boat on a true course. I practiced steering that fishing boat on a calm lake, where errors in thinking could be tolerated and observed. But with complex environmental systems, we seldom have the luxury of practicing with the actual system. So how might we develop an instinctive feel for the natural tendencies of a complex environmental system?

The premise of this book is that computer simulation models can help us develop our instincts for managing environmental systems. We build a mathematical model to capture the key interrelationships in the system; then we conduct experiments with the computer model to sharpen our instincts for managing the simulated system. But you should understand that computer models require a tightly disciplined approach. They require us to be clear and explicit about our assumptions. A well-documented model will allow others to appreciate the assumptions and the conclusions drawn from our experiments. Careful documentation will also permit others to challenge our underlying assumptions and to build improved models with more realistic assumptions.

System Dynamics

The fundamental ideas in this book are not new. They come from the field of system dynamics that originated in the 1960s with the work of Jay Forrester and his colleagues at the Sloan School of Management at the Massachusetts Institute of Technology. Forrester and his colleagues developed the initial ideas by applying concepts from feedback control theory to the study of industrial systems. Their early ideas are described in Forrester's *Industrial Dynamics* (1961). The models were implemented with Dynamo, the software described in appendix D.

One of the best-known applications of the new ideas during the 1960s was Forrester's *Urban Dynamics* (1969). It explained the pattern of rapid population growth and subsequent decline that has been observed in cities like Manhattan, Detroit, St. Louis, Chicago, Boston, and Newark (Schroder and Strongman 1974, 201). Forrester constructed a model to portray a city as a system of interacting industries, housing, and people. The city could grow rapidly under favorable conditions. But as its land area fills, the simulated city shifts into a stagnation mode characterized by aging housing and declining industry. His primary audience was the planners dealing with the challenges of revitalizing an aging city: "Reviving blighted areas is a task forced on us by earlier failures in urban management" (Forrester 1969, 105). Through experimenting with the model, Forrester discovered that "pushing harder" on familiar programs could make the situation worse. Constructing additional premium housing, for example, could lead to increased stagnation because less land would be available for new industries. Forrester then experimented with a demolition program to remove a fraction of the "slum housing." This time, the overall result was beneficial. Housing demolition created the "space" for new industries, permitting a renewal that led to improvements in the mix of industries and workers within the urban boundary.

Forrester recommended that cities adopt demolition programs, even though this proposal ran counter to planners' conventional thinking. His critics charged that his recommendation was based on an imperfect model. Forrester replied that all models are imperfect because they are, by design, simplified representations of a system. He acknowledged that his recommendation ran counter to most planners' intuition, but he suggested that our normal way of thinking about complex systems is often limited and misguided. Models are most useful when they lead to "counterintuitive" results, which force planners to reexamine their intuitive understanding of the system. Forrester believes that counterintuitive results are to be expected in all systems, not just in urban systems. He argued that:

the human mind is not adapted to interpreting how social systems behave. Our social systems belong to the class called multiple-loop nonlinear feedback systems. In the long history of human evolution, it has not been necessary for man to understand these systems until very recent historical times. Evolutionary processes have not given us the mental skill needed to interpret properly the dynamic behavior of the systems of which we have now become a part. (1973, 5)

Urban Dynamics highlighted the field's expansion outside the industrial area. Its approach came to be known as system dynamics because it became evident that the ideas were spreading well beyond the initial focus on industrial systems. One of the most widely known applications of system dynamics appeared a few years later in a best-selling book entitled *The Limits to Growth* (Meadows et al. 1972). The *Limits* study looked at the prospects for growth in human population and industrial production in the global system over the next century. A computer model was used to simulate resource production and food supply needed to keep pace with a growing system. The model also simulated the generation of persistent pollutants that can accumulate and remain in the environment over many decades. The simulations led the authors to conclude that the world system could not support present rates of economic and population growth much beyond the year 2100, if that long, even with advanced technology. The authors concluded that the "most probable result will be a sudden and uncontrollable decline in both population and industrial capacity" (Meadows, Meadows, and Randers 1992, p. xiii).

Many interpreted this initial conclusion as a prediction of doom and gloom. But *The Limits to Growth* was not about a preordained future. It was about making choices to influence the future. The authors examined simulations with changed attitudes toward population growth and industrial growth. The new simulations led them to conclude that "it is possible to alter these growth trends and to establish a condition of ecological and economic stability that is sustainable far into the future" (Meadows et al. 1972, 24). They argued that the sooner the world's people began working toward the goal of a sustainable world, the greater would be their chances of success. You can learn more about this intriguing study in the collection of "Global Equilibrium Exercises" on the home page. You'll read about the world model and some of the supporting models developed in the early 1970s. And you will read about the intense debate that erupted following the publication of *Limits* in 1972. The home page concludes by challenging you to improve the world model. You may then use the improved model to draw your own conclusions about the sustainability of the global system.

Statics and Dynamics

Mathematical models are often divided into two categories: static models and dynamic models. Static models help us learn about the behavior of a system at rest. For example, engineering students (in "statics" courses) use static models to calculate the forces needed to keep an object at rest. Economics students use such models to calculate the price of a product that will motivate producers to make exactly what the consumers wish to buy. When the forces of supply and demand are in balance, market prices will be held constant over time.

Dynamic models are quite different. They help us think about how a system changes over time. A dynamic model may explain the physical forces needed to cause a rocket to accelerate or the economic forces needed to cause a nation's economy to grow over time. Dynamic models can also help us understand why some systems oscillate over time. For example, an ecologist might use a dynamic model to explain if the oscillations in predator populations will remain stable over time.

Growth, decay, and oscillations are the fundamental dynamic patterns of systems. They will be the focus of the examples appearing throughout the book. Consequently, it's useful to become familiar with each of these patterns at the outset.

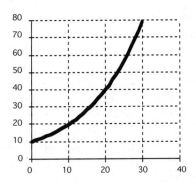

Figure 1.3. Example of exponential growth.

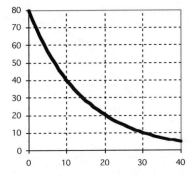

Figure 1.4. Example of exponential decay.

Growth and Decay

One of the most important and fundamental patterns in nature is exponential growth. Figure 1.3 shows an example. This chart portrays a hypothetical animal population of 10 million at the start of the time period. The population grows to 20 million in the first decade and to 40 million after the second decade. By the thirtieth year, the population has climbed "off the chart."

The exponential pattern is characteristic of systems whose growth is in proportion to their size. For example, animal populations grow exponentially when more births lead to more adults and more adults lead to more births. A forested area grows in a similar manner when more trees lead to more seeds, and more seeds lead to more trees. Companies can grow exponentially when they reinvest part of their earnings in productive capacity, and the national economy may grow exponentially when a sufficient portion of economic output is reinvested in new capital. The pattern of exponential growth is so fundamental to all systems that it may well be the most important topic to review from your previous study of mathematics (see appendix B).

Exponential decay is also one of nature's fundamental patterns, and figure 1.4 shows an example. In this illustration, the hypothetical animal population starts at 80 million and declines to 40 million within the 1st decade. The population falls to 20 million in the 2nd decade and to 10 million by the end of the 3rd decade. Exponential decay is characteristic of systems whose rate of decay is proportional to the current size of the system. Exponential decay plays a role in many of the systems in this book, especially the DDT system explained in chapter 12.

Growth and Limits

The exponential growth chart shows the animal population growing off the chart within three decades. If we expand the vertical scale, we would see the population reaching 160 million by the 40th year. And if we thought this rate of growth would continue unabated, the population would become staggeringly large. If the growth continued unabated to the 100th year, for example, the population would exceed 10 billion. Now, you probably known intuitively that no system continues to grow unabated forever. Such growth would be profoundly unnatural. Even the cancerous growth of a malignant tumor encounters limits. All growing systems must eventually deal with limits, and figure 1.5 shows one possible pattern of accommodation. This chart portrays the hypothetical animal population starting at 5 million and growing rapidly during the early decades. The population nearly doubles in the 1st decade, but a slowdown in growth is evident by the end of the 2nd decade. Let's assume that a limit such as food supply prevents the population from continuing to grow at the rapid rate that was possible at the start of the time period. The slowdown is particularly evident around the 40th

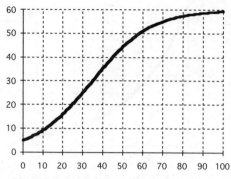

Figure 1.5. Example of s-shaped growth.

year as the population curve begins to approach the eventual limit of 60 million.

The pattern in figure 1.5 is characteristic of a wide range of systems such as plant and animal populations whose growth is limited by food or nutrients. The same pattern characterizes the way a company may grow as it captures a larger and larger share of a fixed market. You'll read more about this pattern in chapter 6, where it is given the general name of s-shaped growth. A fundamental feature of s-shaped growth is the gradual accommodation of the growing system to its limits.

But not all systems find such a smooth accommodation with their limits. In some cases, rapidly growing systems shoot past their limits and reach sizes that are not sustainable. A downward adjustment is then necessary, as shown in figure 1.6. This chart shows the hypothetical animal population doubling in size during each of the first four decades, reaching 80 million by the 40th year. Now, imagine that there is a limit to the eventual size of the population due to a limited food supply. Let's imagine that the food supply could support 60 million, as shown in the previous example. In systems that overshoot their limits, the population does not slow down as the limit is approached. Perhaps the limiting effects of food supply are not felt immediately, or perhaps there is momentum in the growing population that carries it past the limit. Figure 1.6 shows the population reaching 100 million before the corrective decline begins. The population then falls below the 60 million shown previously. This smaller size of the population at the end of the time interval may be due to depletion or damage to the food resources.

You will learn more about this overshoot pattern in chapter 16. It describes the irruption and collapse in the deer population on the Kaibab Plateau. But the overshoot is not just a problem for animal systems, as you've learned from the discussion of Urban Dynamics and The Limits to Growth. The overshoot can also pose serious problems for individual industries. You'll read in chapter 14, for example, that many fisheries around the world have grown to unsustainable levels and declined. Fisheries are only one of many industries that appear vulnerable to a "boom-bust" pattern of behavior (Paich and Sterman 1993). Finally, if we think about our daily lives, we will realize that the overshoot can be a common part of ordinary systems. When we eat or drink too rapidly, for example, we may not perceive the body's signals in time to avoid an upset stomach—another symptom of an overshoot.

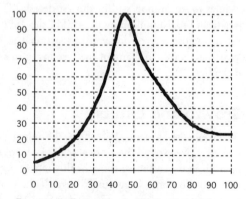

Figure 1.6. Example of overshoot pattern.

Patterns of Oscillation

Figures 1.3–1.6 show four basic patterns that will prove useful later in the book. Each time we study a new environmental system, we will ask ourselves if the system's dynamic behavior resembles one of these basic patterns. If we identify a similarity, we can then ask ourselves if the dynamic behavior in the new system is caused by a combination of factors similar to those we studied in the previous system. The four previous patterns are sufficient to cover a wide range of challenging environmental problems. Our ability to classify systems according to their dynamic behavior will be expanded further if we think about the fundamental patterns of oscillation.

Many systems oscillate over time, and the oscillations may be quite volatile and problematical. Business cycles and commodity production cycles can pose serious challenges, for example. But many systems oscillate in an interesting, repetitive manner that is quite stable and seems to ensure the very longevity of the system. The range of possibilities is best described by four fundamental patterns:

- *Sustained oscillations:* These are oscillations that continue indefinitely without any change in amplitude or period. (*Amplitude* is the height of the variable at its peak. *Period* is the length of time before the oscillation repeats itself.) An example of sustained oscillations is provided by a well-oiled pendulum. If the frictional forces are largely eliminated, the pendulum's oscillations will continue for a very long time with little change in amplitude.

- *Damped oscillations:* Damped oscillations are similar to sustained oscillations in that the oscillations appear with a fixed period. But the amplitude of the oscillations declines over time. If the system is not disturbed, it will eventually come to rest. An example is provided by a normal pendulum with frictional forces that act to dampen the oscillations over time.

- *Growing oscillations:* In an unstable system, the amplitude grows from one oscillation to the next, so the system deviates more and more from the starting position. Growing oscillations are not normally observed in natural systems since the oscillations eventually destroy the system. But they might be observed in selected situations (e.g., when newly associated animal populations are brought together for the first time). The most likely outcome of growing oscillations, however, is that they grow larger and larger over time until they encounter some limitation. At this point, they might turn into a "limit cycle."

- *Limit cycles:* A limit cycle is an example of repetitive oscillations in which the system is limited in its freedom of movement. When the limit is encountered, the cyclical pattern takes on an irregular appearance that no longer resembles the symmetric cycles of a system free to move in both directions. Natural systems are filled with limits, so the logical outcome of inherently unstable oscillations is to grow into a limit cycle. Once the oscillations reach their natural limits, the cycles may continue in an amazingly stable manner, as in the rhythmic beating of your heart. The clearest example of a limit cycle in this book appears in the chapter 19 description of cycles in aluminum production.

These four patterns of cyclical behavior may be combined with the four patterns of growth and decay shown in figures 1.3–1.6 to form a family of fundamental shapes. As we study each new system, we should attempt to classify its dynamic behavior as matching one of the members of the family. In some systems, we might observe a combination of growth and oscillations.

Complexity

Some systems exhibit surprisingly complex patterns of behavior. One example involves a combination of small and large oscillations, which doubles the period of time required to see the cycles repeat themselves. In some systems, further changes can lead to another period doubling, so we would have to wait four times as long to see the cycle repeat itself. Mosekilde, Aracil, and Allen (1988, 27) explain a pattern in which small parameter changes can cause additional period doublings, which eventually result in oscillatory behavior that takes forever to repeat itself. (The cycle has an infinite period.) This intriguing pattern of behavior is called *deterministic chaos.* "Chaos" refers to the apparently random nature of the oscillatory behavior. "Deterministic" refers to the ability of investigators to mathematically replicate the apparently random behavior with a deterministic model.

You may have learned about chaos and other intriguing patterns of behavior if you have read the emerging literature in the field of "complexity" (Gleick 1988; Horgan 1995). System dynamics models are one of many tools to help in the study of chaos and complexity (Mosekilde, Aracil, and Allen 1988). Although chaos is intriguing, it is likely to be a "sparse and elusive" pattern of behavior (Andersen 1988, 7). It will be a better use of our time in an introductory text to concentrate on the fundamental patterns of growth and decay and the more common patterns of oscillations. Chaos and other topics from the field of complexity are subjects for more advanced study.

Modeling for Prediction

The "dynamics" in "system dynamics" refers to the fundamental patterns of change such as growth, decay, and oscillations. System dynamics models are constructed to help us understand why these patterns occur. Our purpose is improved understanding, not point prediction.

Predictive models are quite different. They are constructed to predict the value of an important variable at some point in the future. A weather model may be used to predict whether it will rain tomorrow; a stock market model might be used to predict stock prices several months in the future. These models are sometimes called forecasting models. They are designed around a single task—to provide the best possible forecast of the future state of the system. Since their purpose is clearly and narrowly defined, predictive models are easily evaluated. We simply ask how frequently their predictions turn out to be correct. Predictive models are useful in narrowly defined situations where point forecasts are needed and predictive methods can be evaluated.

But predictive models are not likely to be generally useful to the student of the environment. Let's take ecological models as an example. The questions asked of ecological models are often complex and based on such diffuse problems as "stability" and "trophic efficiency" (Odum 1971, 278). Ecosystems are subjected to highly random inputs, such as weather, so it does not make sense for ecologists to construct models of high predictive power when basic inputs cannot be measured or predicted. Thus, ecological models are more often designed to improve our general understanding or to guide research efforts (Kitching 1983; Hannon and Ruth 1997; Odum 1971; Watt 1968).

Modeling for Learning

System dynamics models, whether they are used in business systems, ecological systems, or any other system, are designed for general understanding, not point prediction. Unfortunately, they are often misinterpreted as predictive models, especially if one is looking for a crystal ball to forecast the future. Misinterpretation often occurs when a time graph shows an important variable displayed into the future. The time graph might be labeled as a "base case simulation," but the reader hungry for a forecast will mentally relabel the graph as "most likely behavior."

To avoid misinterpretation, you should resist drawing any conclusions from a single simulation. A single simulation seldom teaches us much about a system. Its purpose is usually to provide a starting point for comparison with additional simulations. Think of a single simulation as one blade in a pair of scissors. Scissors are not designed to cut with one blade working alone. It's only when the two blades work against each other that the scissors serve their intended purpose. System dynamics simulations should also work in pairs. By comparing one simulation against the other, the model will serve its intended purpose. If you find yourself uncomfortable working with pairs of simulations, you are probably looking for a predictive model. In that case, you should turn to forecasting methods to serve your needs.

Modeling for point prediction is easy to understand because the predictions can be judged as right or wrong. Modeling for improved understanding is more difficult to understand. If we will not learn how to predict the future, what will we learn to do? If you pose this question to experienced practitioners, they will tell you that managers need useful rules of thumb to help manage complex systems. They will argue that the best use of system dynamics is to help managers develop these rules of thumb. To appreciate what they have in mind, think of the "one-car-length" rule of thumb that some drivers use when driving the freeway. If they are driving at 60 miles per hour, for example, they strive to leave six car lengths of space between their car and the car in front. This rule of thumb turns out to be a good summary of a complicated calculation involving their reaction time, the momentum of the car, and the braking power of the tires on the road surface. They don't perform this calculation as they drive the freeway. Rather, they follow the one-car-length rule and hope that it will provide sufficient room if they have to hit the brakes.

Several of the models in this book are designed to teach us about the momentum built into an environmental system. If we discover that the system is in danger, we may decide to "hit the brakes." The model's simulated response will reveal whether our actions will allow the system to recover from a dangerous situation. If the simulations reveal a slow and sluggish response, we can search for more suitable rules of thumb for managing the system. The most obvious example of a model used in this fashion is the DDT model in chapter 12. It shows that DDT will continue to accumulate in fish for several decades after restrictions are imposed on its use as a pesticide.

The Steps of Modeling

A typical modeling project begins with a discussion of the dynamic problem to be studied. To clarify your purpose, you should draw a graph of an important variable that changes over time. (We call this graph the "reference mode.") You and your colleagues should be able to recognize the graph as a summary of the dynamic problem. The general shape of the graph will resemble one of the standard time patterns described in this chapter. For example, your study might focus on growth, decay, or the overshoot. Or you might decide that your problem is best represented as a combination of two of the standard patterns. It's a good idea at the early stage of a project to list policies that might improve the performance of the system. If you are worried about highly volatile cycles in animal populations, for example, you would list policies with some potential to moderate the severity of the cycles.

The next step in a modeling project is to think about the key variables in the system and their interconnections. The important variables in your system will be represented by variables in the computer model. The cause-and-effect connections in the real system will be represented by interconnections in the computer model. As we add more and more interconnections, the model may grow to become quite complex. But, by design, models are simplifications of the system under study. The key to the model's usefulness is our ability to leave out the unimportant factors and capture the interactions among the important factors.

The steps of modeling are explained in full detail later, in chapter 15. For now, you should turn to one of the software appendices to learn about the programs that make it easy to build and test a model. You'll discover that each of the programs is designed to help you build a model as a combination of "stocks and flows." These basic building blocks are described in the next chapter.

Exercises

1. **Classifying dynamic behavior:**

   Draw a graph of a system that exhibits problematical behavior over time. The graph should show time on the horizontal axis and a recognizable and important measure of the system on the vertical axis. Now classify your time graph according to one of the eight fundamental patterns explained in this chapter. Does the graph match one of the standard patterns? Or is it better described by combining two of the patterns?

2. **What is system dynamics?**

   Coyle (1977, 2) defines system dynamics as follows:

   > System Dynamics is a method of analyzing problems in which time is an important factor, and which involve the study of how a system can be defended against, or made to benefit from, the shocks which fall upon it from the outside world.

   or

   > System Dynamics is that branch of control theory which deals with socio-economic systems, and that branch of management science which deals with problems of controllability.

   Describe a problem in your organization that seems to fit Coyle's first definition.

3. **What is a system?**

   You have learned about dynamics in this chapter, and you've read Coyle's definitions of system dynamics. But you might be wondering about the word *system*. A system is usually defined as a combination of two or more elements that are interconnected for some purpose. A bicycle, a car, and a bus are all systems for transportation. And at a larger scale, the collection of freeways, surface streets, and vehicles in an urban area is a system. The distinguishing feature of a system is the impression that the whole is more than the sum of its parts. Describe a system in your organization. Be sure to include at least two elements, some of their interconnections, and an explanation of how the whole is more than the sum of its parts.

Further Readings

- System dynamics instruction is offered mainly in schools of management, and several texts are available (Coyle 1977; Lyneis 1982; Richardson and Pugh 1981; Wolstenholme 1990; Coyle 1996). Richardson and Pugh's *System Dynamics Modeling with Dynamo* is especially useful to the introductory student of management. A forthcoming text by Sterman should also prove useful, as it will include a number of environmental as well as business applications.

- The best place to keep track of current applications is *System Dynamics Review*, the journal of the System Dynamics Society. The inaugural issue appeared in the summer of 1985. The topics in the opening issue illustrated the broad applicability of the approach. They included managing fluid therapy in severely burned patients (Bush et al. 1985) and understanding the "long wave" in the nation's economy (Rasmussen, Mosekilde, and Sterman 1985).

- The best historical perspective on system dynamics is provided by Richardson (1991). He interprets feedback ideas expressed by prominent scientists from biology, economics, engineering, and the social sciences.

- Shortly after Dynamo became available, researchers at the University of Washington used it to construct an interesting model of the Canadian and U.S. salmon fishery. This early study is described by Paulik and Greenough (1966) and by Watt (1968).
- Two texts, both using Dynamo, are available for graduate study of system synamics applied to forestry (Boyce 1991) and to agriculture (Jongkaewwattana 1995).
- Readers interested in the urban study of the 1960s may learn more from Mass (1974); Schroeder, Sweeney, and Alfeld (1975); and Alfeld (1995).
- Readers interested in forecasting methods may turn to a standard econometrics text (Johnston 1972). An interesting discussion of the nearly insatiable demand for predictive forecasts is provided by de Geus (1997).
- Readers interested in chaos and complexity will find plenty to read elsewhere (Andersen 1988; Gleick 1988; Hannon and Ruth 1997; Horgan 1995; Mosekilde and Mosekilde 1991).
- The Kanizsa Triangle in figure 1.1 is discussed by Sterman (1994) and Gregory (1998). The cartoon in figure 1.2 is from Gregory.

Chapter 2

Stocks and Flows

Stocks and flows are the building blocks of system dynamics models. A simple, everyday illustration of stocks and flows is the accumulation of interest in a bank account. Figure 2.1 shows a simple model to keep track of the growth in a bank balance. This diagram shows examples of three types of variables:

stock—the bank balance
flow—the interest added
converter—the interest rate

The double line represents material flow—in this case, the flow of money from a cloud into the stock. The cloud represents the source of the money. A cloud may also be viewed as a stock that is outside the system boundary, so we don't bother to keep track of it. There are two single lines in figure 2.1. One of the lines connects the *interest rate* to the *interest added*. The other connects the *bank balance* to the *interest added*. These are called connectors. Connectors show the flow of information inside the model. In this case, we need to know the value of both the *interest rate* and the *bank balance* in order to calculate the *interest added*. If, for example, the *bank balance* were $10,000 and the *interest rate* were 7 percent per year, the *interest added* would be $10,000 multiplied by 0.07/year, or $700 per year. There are no connectors leading into the *interest rate* converter. When you see converters without any incoming arrows, you know the converter is specified by the model builder. These are sometimes called the model inputs.

It is good practice to double-check the units of every set of stocks and flows. If you are using a model with time measured in years, for example, the flows leading into a stock will be measured in the same units as the stock divided by years. If the *bank balance* in the first model is measured in dollars, the flow should be measured in dollars per year. Figure 2.2 shows another bank balance model, but this one has different units. In this example, the name of the stock variable is *bank balance measured in DM* (DM stands for deutsche marks). Imagine that the model is used to keep track of short-term changes in a German bank account. If time is measured in months, the flow must be measured in DM/month. The long name assigned to the flow in figure 2.2 assures us that we have selected the correct units. You should feel free to use long names wherever they improve communication.

Now consider some examples of simple models to keep track of the growth in a population. Figure 2.3 shows a flow diagram with one stock, one flow, and one converter. Notice the similarity with the bank balance diagrams. Figure 2.3 has the same set of stocks, flows, and converters, and they are interconnected in the same manner. Only the names are different.

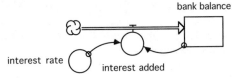

Figure 2.1. Flow diagram of a bank balance model.

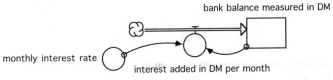

Figure 2.2. Another example of a bank balance model.

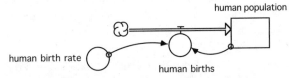

Figure 2.3. Model of human population growth.

When this happens, we say the models have the same structure. You will learn in this book that models with the same structure tend to show the same patterns of behavior when they are simulated over time.

The double line in figure 2.3 stands for the flow of people into the stock called population. If the model were used to project population change over years, the *human births* would be measured in people per year.

The next example expands the model of human population to combine the effect of births and deaths. Figure 2.4 shows two clouds. The cloud on the left represents a source; the cloud on the right is a sink. You may interpret figure 2.4 to mean that this model of population does not represent where people come from when they are born or where they go when they die.

Figure 2.5 expands the population model further by including additional stocks to keep track of the young, mature, and elderly people in the population. The stock of *young people* is increased by *births* and decreased through *maturation*. Similarly, the stock of *mature people* is increased by *maturation* and reduced by *aging*. The final stock of *elderly people* is increased by

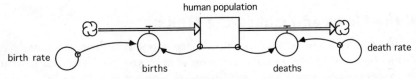

Figure 2.4. Model of population with two flows.

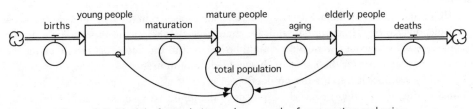

Figure 2.5. Model of population to keep track of maturation and aging.

aging and reduced by *deaths*. The *total population* may now be found by adding the number of people in each of the three stocks.

You will probably find that each of the previous diagrams makes sense, but you might wonder about building a model from scratch. Where do you start?

Where to Start?

What should you do when you face the blank screen? The answer is

start with the stocks!

The stocks are the key variables in the model. They represent where accumulation or storage takes place in the system. In the bank balance examples, the money accumulates in the bank balances. Figure 2.6 shows an example of another stock used to keep track of storage and accumulation. In this case, the stock represents water accumulating and being stored behind a dam.

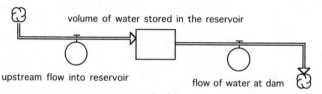

volume of water stored in the reservoir

upstream flow into reservoir

flow of water at dam

Figure 2.6. Illustration of a stock to represent storage in a system.

Another way of deciding on stock variables is to ask yourself what variables would remain at their current values if the flows were to go to zero. For example, you might ask yourself what would happen to the balance in your bank account if the bank were to quit adding interest. Since the balance would remain at the current value, it has the feel of a stock variable. Similarly, the water stored in the reservoir would remain at its current value if the upstream flow and the water release flow were to change to zero.

 Stocks tend to change less rapidly than other variables in the system, so they are responsible for the "momentum" or "sluggishness" in the system. In the bank balance diagrams, for example, the bank balances will change slowly even though the interest added may change abruptly with abrupt changes in the interest rates. In the population examples, the population tends to change slowly even if the births or deaths change suddenly due to a sudden change in the birth rates or the death rates.

Add the Flows and Check the Units

After you've selected the stock variables, the next step is to add the flows. Stocks and flows go together like nouns and verbs. The stocks summarize where you stand today; the flows are the actions to change the system to a new state tomorrow. Remember that the flows DIRECTLY influence the stocks. For example, *deaths* and *births* directly influence the *population* shown in previous diagrams.

It is important to remember that flow variables are measured in the same units as the stock variable, divided by the appropriate unit for time. Once you select the appropriate units for a stock, it will be obvious what units should be assigned to the flows. Let's think about the units of measurement for the model of the world aluminum industry shown in figure 2.7.

Ingot production represents the production of metallic aluminum at smelters. These are stored in the *ingot inventory* to await shipment to the mills that turn the metallic aluminum into products (such as aluminum siding or cans). The mill operators, in turn, maintain an

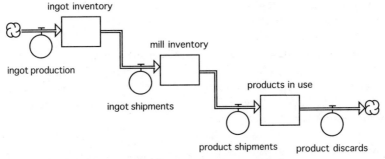

Figure 2.7. Stocks and flows in the aluminum industry.

inventory of products that are to be shipped to the ultimate customers who will put them to use. The final stock is *products in use,* and the final flow is the *product discards.* Now, suppose we measure *ingot inventory* in pounds and time in months. Then the flows of *ingot production* and *ingot shipments* would have to be measured in pounds per month. But let's suppose we measure ingot inventory in million metric tons (mmt) and time in years. Then the units for the *ingot production* and the *ingot shipments* would be mmt/yr. And since the flow of *ingot shipments* feeds into *mill inventory,* the units of *mill inventory* would also have to be mmt. Then you would know that the flow of *product shipments* must be measured in mmt/yr as well.

Figure 2.8 shows a similar combination of stocks and flows. In this example, the stocks represent oil held in inventory at various points from the oil fields of Kuwait to the personal stocks (like the petroleum products stored in the gas tank of your car). Notice that the stocks in the oil industry serve a function similar to that of the stocks in the aluminum industry. They act as buffers in the system. They help the industry ride out the unpredictable variations in supply and demand, hopefully ensuring more efficient operation of the system.

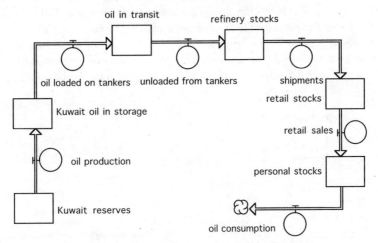

Figure 2.8. Stocks and flows in the world oil industry.

Direction of Flows

The possible directions of any flow are evident from the population model in figure 2.5. Flows can take material from:

- one stock to another (e.g., maturation)

- a stock to a cloud (e.g., deaths)
- a cloud to a stock (e.g., births)

All the flows shown so far are "one-way" flows. The material flows in the direction of a single arrow. But you can also have "two-way" flows. In the bank balance example, we might want to consider a case in which the bank balance falls below zero. Then, instead of interest being added, there will be interest charges. Figure 2.9 shows a revision in the bank balance model to allow for negative as well as positive inter-est. If the bank balance is positive, the flow is positive, and the stock grows larger. (The open arrowhead shows the positive direc-tion.) If the bank balance is negative, the flow is negative, and the stock is drained by the flow. (The darkened arrowhead shows the negative direction.)

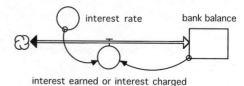

Figure 2.9. Bank balance model with a biflow.

Fill Out the Picture with the Converters

If you design the right combination of stocks and flows, you will have a good foundation for a model. Your next job is to add the converters to help describe the flows. If the stocks and flows are the nouns and verbs of a model, then the converters are the adverbs. They help describe the verbs.

Frequently, converters are used to provide model inputs such as the *interest rate* in the bank examples and the *birth rate* in the population examples. Figure 2.10 illustrates the use of converters to fill out the shape of the model of the aluminum industry. This diagram is similar to the previous diagram in terms of the stocks and flows. The new variables are the times spent in each of the stocks. These time intervals are represented by three converters. Each converter is connected to a flow that drains a stock. The *product discarded*, for example, is the *products in use* divided by the *average life of product*. If there were 160 mmt of aluminum *products in use*, and the average life of those products were 10 years, then the *product discarded* would be 16 mmt per year. Similarly, the flow *product shipments* would be the *mill inventory* divided by the time to mill. For example, if the aluminum in *mill inventory* were 8 mmt and the *time to mill* were 0.5 years, then the *product shipments* would be 16 mmt per year.

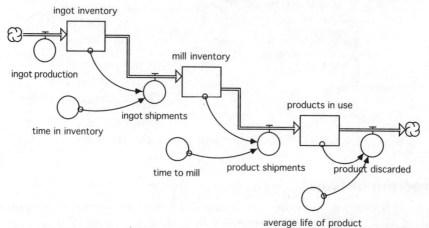

Figure 2.10. Using converters to fill out the model of the aluminum industry.

You may think of converters as variables that don't logically meet your description of a stock or a flow. They are often added to the model to describe the flows. You can add as many as you want to make your explanation of flows as clear as possible. The remaining purpose of a converter is to calculate additional measures of the system performance. If we wanted to know the total amount of aluminum, for example, we would add a converter to figure 2.10 with information connectors from each of the stocks. A similar converter appears in figure 2.5 to show the total population based on stock of young, mature, and elderly people.

Adding to a Model

Now, suppose you wish to add recycling to the previous diagram of the aluminum industry. How do you make additions to an existing model? The answer is the same as when you faced the blank screen—start with the stocks. In this case, we would ask ourselves if the recycling of aluminum introduces important delays or accumulation into the system. If recycled aluminum accumulates for many months before it is returned to the producers, we would add an extra stock. For this example, let's assume that recycled products move back into the production system rather quickly. There would be no need to add any new stocks. The next step is to consider new flows. Figure 2.11 expands the model by adding a new flow: *recycled old scrap*. It moves aluminum from the stock of *products in use* to the stock of *ingot inventory.*

When the new stocks and flows are in position, the final step is to fill out the picture with the converters. As before, their job is to help us describe the flows. In figure 2.11, a *recycle potential* is introduced to clarify the calculation of recycled aluminum. The potential would be calculated as *products in use* divided by the *average life of product*. For example, if there were 160 mmt of *products in use,* and their average life were 10 years, then the *recycle potential* would be 16 mmt per year. The *fraction recycled,* is introduced as a new input. If we set the fraction at 25 percent, for example, 25 percent of the *recycle potential* would be *recycled old scrap,* and the other 75 percent would be *product discarded.*

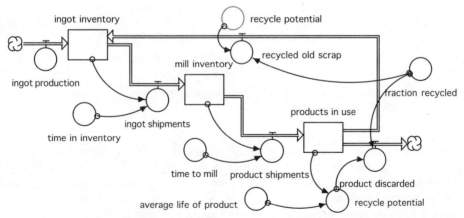

Figure 2.11. Expanding the model to include recycling. (The recycle potential is calculated at the bottom of the diagram. A "ghost" appears at the top of the diagram to avoid a long information connector.)

Material Feedback versus Information Feedback

The recycling example shows a circular flow of material within the system. In this case, aluminum flows from the smelter to the mill, from the mill to the customer, and from the customer back to ingots in inventory. You might have noticed that figure 2.11 is our first example of a model with a circular flow of material. Students of environmental science know that natural systems are designed with circular flows of material (e.g., the carbon cycle and the nitrogen cycle.) Each of these cycling systems can be represented with a combination of stocks and flows similar to that of the aluminum example. The circular flow of material can be traced by following the double lines around the diagram.

Later in the book, you will learn about *information feedback,* and you will read that information feedback is crucial to the design of useful models. The information feedback will not be as readily apparent in the stock-and-flow diagrams, so we will introduce a separate diagramming approach to help us see the information feedback in the system. These new diagrams are called causal loop diagrams, and they are explained in chapter 7.

What About the Equations and the Software?

All mathematical models must eventually appear in the form of equations. Writing equations can be a time-consuming task in some modeling methodologies. But equations should be easy in system dynamics. The key is a well-structured flow diagram. When you become proficient at flow diagrams, the equation writing becomes routine. In the model shown in figure 2.12, for example, the equation for *interest added* is easy to specify. When you click on the ? variable, the software will open an equation window that prompts you to use both the *bank balance* and the *interest rate* in the equation. Like Vensim and Powersim, the Stella software makes it easy for you to write the equation as the product of these two variables.

Appendices D, E, and F explain the Dynamo, Vensim, and Powersim programs that may be used to implement stock-and-flow models. As you read about the different programs, you will encounter other names for the stocks and flows:

- stocks are often called *Levels;*
- flows are often called *Rates;* and
- converters are often called *Auxiliaries.*

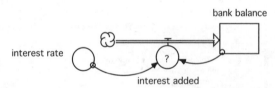

bank balance

interest rate

interest added

Figure 2.12. Bank balance model with a "?" indicating that the equation for interest added has not been specified.

It won't take long to recognize the terminology because all of the software programs are designed to help you follow a similar approach to model building. Start with the stocks; add the flows; then fill out the model with the converters. When you've constructed the diagram and written the equations, you'll be ready to simulate the model. The simulation results are generated numerically, as explained in the next chapter.

Exercises

1. **Find the errors:**

    Can you spot one error in each of the four flow diagrams accompanying this excerise? (Stella won't allow a user to make these mistakes, so the errors were entered with a separate drawing software.)

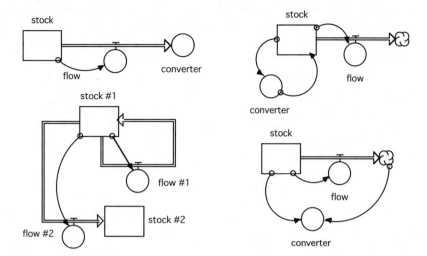

2. **Improper connections:**

Attempt to make the improper connections in the four diagrams using Stella. How does Stella deal with the improper connections?

3. **Find the error:**

This model finds the total number of undergraduates if you specify the number of freshmen, sophomores, juniors, and seniors. The software did not complain when the diagram accompanying this exercise was constructed, but the diagram still suffers from a fundamental error in formulation. What is the error?

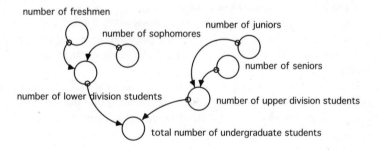

4. **Units:**

Assume that time is measured in months and *Kuwait reserves* is measured in barrels of crude oil. What are the units for each of the remaining variables in figure 2.8?

5. **Controlling the flow that drains a stock:**

Notice that there is an information connection from each of the stocks in figure 2.10 to the flows that drain each stock. Do you think these connections are unique to the aluminum industry? Or should we expect to see similar connections in all systems?

6. **Non-negative stock option:**

Have you noticed the "non-negative" option whenever you open a Stella stock variable in the mapping mode? If you elect this option, the software will impose its own rules to prevent the flows from driving a stock to negative values. This option might make sense in figure 2.11 if we did not want product shipments to drive the *mill inventory* negative. Would you need to rely on Stella's hidden rules to control this flow if you have done a good job in the equation for the *product shipments*?

7. **Complete the diagram**

The diagram accompanying this exercise expands the population model shown in figure 2.5 by adding three new converters. The converters are needed to calculate flow of *births*, but the information connectors are missing. What would you add to the diagram to calculate the *births*?

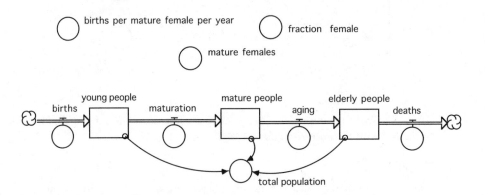

Now, notice that there is no information link from the stock of *young people* to the *maturation* flow that drains this stock. Suppose you were told that the maturation rate is 10 percent per year. How would you expand the diagram to introduce a *maturation rate* and to find the *maturation* flow?

Also, notice that there is no information connector from the stock of *mature people* to the *aging* flow that drains this stock. Suppose you were told that the aging rate is 5 percent per year. How would you expand the diagram to calculate the *aging* flow based on the *aging rate*?

Finally, notice that there is no information connector from the stock of *elderly people* to the *deaths* flow that drains this stock. If you learn that the death rate is 2.5 percent per year, how would you expand the diagram to calculate the *deaths* flow based on the *death rate*?

8. **Advanced exercise—fill the gas tank:**

Your friend Joe pulls his car into the gas station with the gas tank nearly empty. The flow diagram accompanying this exercise shows a model to stimulate the gas in the tank during refilling. The stock is measured in gallons; the *gas flow at the nozzle* is measured in gallons/second; the *capacity of the tank* is 20 gallons; and the *fullness* is the ratio of *gas in the tank* to the *capacity*.

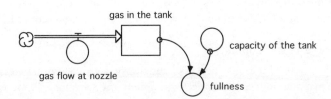

Your job is to complete this model. The maximum flow at the nozzle is 1 gallon/second, so the model will probably show that it will take Joe around 20–30 seconds to fill the tank. The diagram is a good start, but something is missing. There has to be feedback from the *fullness* to the *gas flow at the nozzle*. Without information feedback, there would be no control. The exact form of the information depends on what Joe is actually doing when he fills the tank. Imagine that you have interviewed Joe, and here are your notes:

> My first idea was that Joe watched the meter on the gas pump and adjusted the flow downward when the meter got close to 20 gallons. But Joe said he couldn't see the meter without his glasses. My second idea was that he used a pump with an automatic shutoff valve, but he told me that the pump used manual control. My third idea was that Joe has learned by experience that it takes around 20 seconds to fill the tank, and he counted the seconds before cutting back on the nozzle. But he said he has no idea how long it takes to fill the tank. I asked if he knew that the tank holds 20 gallons. He said he had no knowledge of the tank capacity, nor did he know that the nozzle could deliver 1 gallon/second.
>
> Joe saw that my questions were not leading anywhere, so he told me that he controls the flow at the nozzle based on the sound coming from the gas tank. I pressed for details, but he wasn't very scientific about the nature of the sound. All I could learn was that the sound starts out as a "free-flowing sound." Joe could not describe the volume in decibels or the frequency in cycles/second. He simply said the sound led him to believe that the gas was pouring freely out of the nozzle into the tank. After a few seconds (Joe couldn't remember how many) the sound seemed to change. The new sound led Joe to think that there was some congestion in the top of the gas tank. And quickly thereafter the sound changed again to make Joe believe that he was running out of empty space in the tank.

Now, you may be disappointed that Joe cannot be more scientific in his description, but he has given you valuable information that can be used to simulate the information feedback in this system. Define a *sound index* to take on three values to match Joe's description:

sound index = 1:   stands for "free flowing"

sound index = 2:   stands for "some congestion"

sound index = 3:   stands for "running out of space"

Furthermore, suppose you are able to conduct some controlled experiments to learn that the free-flowing sound occurs whenever the tank is less than 80 percent full. You learn that the sound changes from free flowing to "some congestion" as the volume changes from 80 to 90 percent full. The final change is from "congestion" to "running out of space;" it occurs when the tank moves from 90 to 95 percent full. Joe tells you that he leaves the nozzle at the full open position as long as he hears the first sound. He cuts the nozzle position approximately in half (cutting the flow rate in half) when he hears the second sound. Then he cuts the flow rate to zero when he hears the third sound.

Expand the flow diagram to include the *sound index* and the changes in the *gas flow at the nozzle*. Review the Stella information in appendix C and write the equations. Then use the model to stimulate the volume of gas in the tank over time. Document your work by turning in a copy of your (1) flow diagram, (2) equations, (3) time graph of the *sound index, fullness,* and *gas flow at nozzle* over a 40-second time period.

9. **Discussion exercise:**

The gas tank example is illustrative of many systems in which we quickly identify flow and accumulation of material. And with stocks and flows, we can quickly put together a flow diagram. But the information flows will often prove much more difficult to identify. Once they have been identified, simulating the information flows may involve "softer variables" that appear "unscientific" in a computer model.

As a discussion exercise, draw a flow diagram of an environmental system where you can easily identify flow and accumulation of material. The material can be anything you like—water, soil, nutrients, etc. Now, can you identify the information flows that will control the flow of material?

When you encounter such situations, remember that information feedback is the key to control in a system. Be sure to take advantage of all the information available to you in order to "close the loops" in the system. Until you close the loops, the model will not teach you about the controllability of the system.

Chapter 3

Numerical Simulation

System dynamics models are constructed as a combination of stocks and flows and then simulated on the computer. The simulation results are generated in a simple, step-by-step fashion that will be illustrated with a "pencil-and-paper" example. The numerical calculations are
tedious with pencil and paper, but they are performed in the blink of an eye on today's high-
speed computers. This chapter uses a simple population model to illustrate the numerical
approach. The power of numerical simulation is then contrasted with the "analytical"
approach used before the advent of high-speed computers.

Population Example

Suppose we were to build a model to study the growth in a population shown in figure 3.1.
The population is at 10 million at the start of the time period. After 10 years, it has doubled
to 20 million. At the end of 20 years, it has doubled again to 40 million. This is the characteristic pattern of exponential growth. With a 7 percent/yr growth rate, you know from
appendix B that the population will double in size every 10 years.

Figure 3.2 shows a simple model of the population. It uses a stock to keep track of the
population and a flow to represent the growth in the population. This is a Stella diagram, but
you know that a similar model could be constructed with Dynamo, Vensim, or Powersim. We
would build this model and set the initial population at 10 million and the growth rate at 7
percent/yr. You've learned in appendix C that a time graph of the simulation results of this
model would match the pattern in figure 3.1.

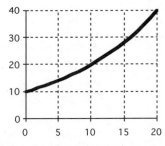

Figure 3.1. Exponential growth in population.

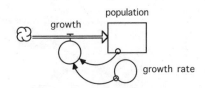

Figure 3.2. Population model.

Numerical Simulation

All of the system dynamics software programs generate the time graphs in a simple, step-by-step manner. To demonstrate the steps, let's imagine that we did not have access to any software. What could we do with pencil and paper to estimate the growth in population over time?

We might begin with the starting population of 10 million and estimate the growth in the 1st year at 0.7 million based on the 7 percent annual growth rate. This would build the population to 10.7 million at the end of the 1st year. These numbers are entered in the first row of table 3.1. The 10.7 million is transferred to the second row, and the growth during the 2nd year is estimated at 7 percent of 10.7 million, or 0.749 million/year. This would build the population to 11.45 million by the end of the 2nd year, as shown in table 3.1.

Table 3.1. Population estimates with pencil and paper.

	Population at start of year	Growth during the year	Population at end of year
1st year	10.00	0.70	10.70
2nd year	10.70	0.749	11.45
3rd year	11.45	0.80	12.25
4th year	12.25	0.86	13.11

Continuing the row-by-row calculations would lead us to estimate the population at 13.11 million by the end of the 4th year. Figure 3.3 arranges these annual estimates alongside the actual values for the animal population; with 7 percent/yr exponential growth, the animal population would reach 13.23 million by the end of the 4th year. The pencil-and-paper estimate of 13.11 million is about 1 percent below the actual value.

The annual estimates appear as a staircase pattern. The width of the stairs is one year, the time interval used to update the population estimates. You can tell from the appearance of figure 3.3 that we might obtain a more accurate estimate by shrinking the width of the stairs. Let's consider how much better we could do if we were willing to update the estimates every 6 months.

The new estimates appear in table 3.2. Each row corresponds to a 6-month interval. The table starts with 10 million as before. Growth is 7 percent/yr, so we would expect an extra 0.7 million during the first year. The estimated growth during the 1st half of the year would be 0.35 million. The value of 10.35 million is transferred to the second row, and the growth during that interval is estimated at 0.36 million. By the end of two intervals, the population would be estimated at 10.71 million.

If we continue this approach for six more intervals, the final population would be estimated at 13.17 million. Figure 3.4 arranges these estimates alongside the actual values of the animal population, showing the row-by-row estimates as a staircase pattern with twice as

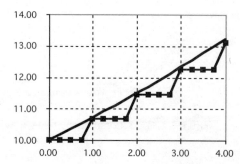

Figure 3.3. Comparison of pencil-and-paper estimates with actual values of the population.

Table 3.2. Pencil-and-paper estimates updated every 6 months.

	Population at start	Growth during interval	Population at end
1st interval	10.00	0.35	10.35
2nd interval	10.35	0.36	10.71
3rd interval	10.71	0.37	11.08
4th interval	11.08	0.39	11.47
5th interval	11.47	0.40	11.87
6th interval	11.87	0.42	12.29
7th interval	12.29	0.43	12.72
8th interval	12.72	0.45	13.17

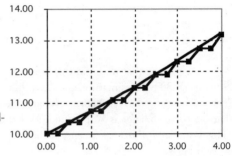

Figure 3.4. Comparison of new pencil-and-paper estimates with the actual values of the population.

many steps as before. The pencil-and-paper estimate of 13.17 million is within 0.5 percent of the actual value.

Discussion of "DT"

The numerical calculations appear tedious, but they are easily performed with today's high-speed computers. All of the stock-and-flow software programs make use of these simple numerical calculations. The approach is sometimes called numerical simulation or computer simulation. The computer does the tedious work. Our job is to formulate the models. When it comes time to simulate a model, we are responsible for setting the step size for the numerical calculations. In this example, a step size of 1 year gives reasonably accurate results; a step size of 0.5 year does even better. If further accuracy were required, we could cut the step size to 0.25 year and try again. This same approach should be followed with any of the stock-and-flow software programs. If you are not sure whether the numerical calculations are accurate, simply cut the step size in half and repeat the calculations. If you get essentially the same results, you know the step size is sufficiently small to provide accurate results.

The step size is often called *DT*, which is short for *Delta Time*. You'll learn more about selecting an appropriate value of DT in chapter 11. For now, think of the staircase pattern and ask yourself how small the width of each step in the staircase must be to provide a reasonable approximation of the time trend you are simulating. Set DT at your best guess and simulate the model. Then cut DT in half and repeat the simulation. If you get essentially the same results, your first guess is a good value of DT.

The Sequence of Numerical Calculations

Let's turn to the population model in figure 3.5 to illustrate the sequence of calculations in a model with several stocks, several flows, and a converter that changes over time. The animal population is described by three age groups. *Births* depend on the number of *mature females*

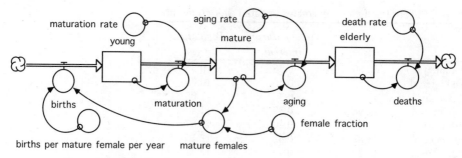

Figure 3.5. Population model to illustrate the numerical sequence.

and the *births per mature female per year.* The *maturation* flow transfers animals from the young category to the *mature* category, while the *aging* flow transfers animals from *mature* to the *elderly.* The final flow is *deaths,* which lowers the number of animals remaining in *elderly* category.

Now imagine that we build this model with the initial values of the stocks set at 50 million young, 30 million mature, and 20 million elderly. Let's set the maturation rate at 10 percent/yr, the aging rate at 10 percent/yr and the death rate at 20 percent/yr. Finally, let's assume that the *female fraction* is 50 percent and that there are 0.5 births per mature female per year. (This last assumption makes sense if the average mature female gives birth to a single youth every other year.)

Table 3.3 shows the sequence of numerical calculations if DT, the step size, is set at 1 year. All of the stock-and-flow programs begin with the user-specified values of the stocks. The initial values of the stocks are then used to calculate each of the converters. The converters column in table 3.3 concentrates on *mature females* since that is the only converter that changes over time. The next step is to calculate each of the flows. (Their values can be determined once we know all the stocks and all the converters.) The maturation flow, for example, is 50 million multiplied by 10 percent/yr, which gives 5 million/year. The final column in Table 3.3 updates the values of each stock. The flows are assumed to apply for one DT (in this case, 1 year). The updated values of each stock are then transferred to the start of the next row, and the programs would proceed to the second step of the numerical simulation.

The approach in table 3.3 would be continued for 100 rows if we wanted to simulate the population changes over a 100-year interval. To check the accuracy of the results, we could

Table 3.3. The sequence of numerical simulation.

	Stocks at start of interval	Converters at start of interval	Flows during the interval	Stocks at end of the interval
1st yr	young 50.0 mature 30.0 elderly 20.0	mature females 15.0	births 7.5 maturation 5.0 aging 3.0 deaths 4.0	young 52.5 mature 32.0 elderly 19.0
2nd yr	young 52.5 mature 32.0 elderly 19.0	mature females 16.0	births 8.0 maturation 5.25 aging 3.20 deaths 3.80	young 55.25 mature 34.05 elderly 18.40
3rd yr	young 55.25 mature 34.05 elderly 18.40	mature females 17.02	births 8.51 maturation 5.53 aging 3.40 deaths 3.68	young 58.24 mature 36.17 elderly 18.12

cut the step size to 0.5 years, and 200 steps would be needed to complete the simulation. If we see important differences in results, we could cut DT to 0.25 years, and 400 steps would be needed to complete the simulation. You can appreciate that there is a tradeoff between accuracy of the simulation results and the number of steps to complete a simulation. Most of the models in this book require fewer than 500 steps, so they can be executed quickly on the computer. You'll learn more about the tradeoff between accuracy and simulation speed in chapter 11.

Differential Equation for Population Growth

Let's turn now to an entirely different way to estimate the size of an exponentially growing population. If you have studied differential equations, you will appreciate that the population in figure 3.1 can be described by a differential equation. And if we find an analytical solution to the differential equation, we can skip all the tedious pencil-and-paper calculations. (If you have not studied differential equations, you might skip to the end of the chapter.)

Let's begin by defining some terms:

- $P(t)$ stand for the population as a function of time.
- $P(0) = 10.0$, the initial value of the population.
- dP/dt, the derivative of $P(t)$ with respect to t, stands for the slope of a curve showing how $P(t)$ will vary with time.

Then, for any position along the curve, the slope will be equal to the growth, and the growth is equal to the growth rate multiplied by the size of the population. If we let r stand for the growth rate, we can write the differential equation:

$$dP/dt = rP$$

This is a first-order differential equation. It also happens to be a linear differential equation, which means we might be able to find a solution. Solving differential equations involves a mix of trial and error, knowledge of some standard solutions, and a willingness to guess the form of the solution based on our intuition about the dynamic behavior. So let's start guessing:

FIRST ATTEMPT
Guess that the solution is $P(t) = 10 + t$. This guess gives $P(0) = 10$ as desired, and $P(t)$ will grow with time. Now differentiate $P(t)$ with respect to time to get:

$$dP/dt = 1$$

But we were hoping to see $dP/dt = rP$, so we need to guess again.

SECOND ATTEMPT
Guess that the solution is $P(t) = 10 + rt$. This gives $P(0) = 10$ as desired. Let's differentiate $P(t)$ with respect to time to get:

$$dP/dt = r$$

THIRD ATTEMPT
Perhaps the solution is $P(t) = 10 + rt + rt^2$. This guess gives $P(0) = 10$ as desired. If we differentiate $P(t)$, we obtain:

$$dP/dt = r + 2rt$$

This line of guesswork doesn't seem to be getting anywhere, so it would be useful to ask ourselves about the shape of the population curve shown in figure 3.1. This curve exhibits the fundamental shape of exponential growth, so our guesswork is likely to be more productive if we work the exponential function into the proposed solutions.

FOURTH ATTEMPT
Let's guess that the solution is $P(t) = 10 + e^t$. This guess gives $P(0) = 11$, which is wrong from the start.

FIFTH ATTEMPT
Suppose we guess that the solution is $P(t) = 10e^t$. This guess gives $P(0) = 10$, and taking the derivative gives

$$dP/dt = 10e^t$$

In other words, $dP/dt = P$. This is encouraging, but we want $dP/dt = rP$.

SIXTH ATTEMPT
Let's guess that the solution is $P(t) = 10e^{rt}$. This gives $P(t) = 10$, and taking the derivative gives

$$dP/dt = 10re^{rt}$$

which is the same as $dP/dt = rP$.

We have confirmed that

$$P(t) = 10e^{rt}$$

is the solution to the differential equation. Now, if you've studied differential equations, you might have found this solution with only one or two attempts. But the preceding example is meant to illustrate what happens when searching for the solutions to more complicated differential equations. There are no hard and fast rules to guarantee that you will find the solution within a few attempts. This example also illustrates another important point: the key to good guesswork is your own intuition. In this example, we knew intuitively that the solution must involve the exponential function. As a general rule, we need to have a preconceived image of the answer before our guesswork is likely to lead to the analytical solution.

Analytical Solutions versus Numerical Solutions

The analytical solution is useful because it gives the value of the population, $P(t)$, for any value of time and the interest rate. Just insert the values of r and t into the equation and you have an exact value of the future population. There is no need to work through tedious numerical solutions like the one shown in table 3.2.

The problem with the analytical approach is that the search for analytical solutions becomes quite difficult as the differential equations become more complicated. If the growth rate depended on the size of the population, for example, the analytical solution would be more difficult. As a general rule, differential equations with nonlinear terms are difficult if not impossible to solve.

You will see examples throughout this book of relationships that are highly nonlinear. (In the next chapter, on Mono Lake, for example, the surface area of the lake is a nonlinear function of the volume of water in the lake.) The ~~analytical approach is simply not productive for these real-world systems. We would be constantly challenged to find ways to approximate a nonlinear world with linear relationships.~~ If we were sufficiently clever to meet this challenge, we would then have to find the analytical solution to the collection of differential equations. Suppose we met this second challenge? Where would we be? Would others understand our results? Would they be able to build from our results?

I believe that modeling in the form of differential equations can be understood by colleagues with advanced mathematical training, but they would not be able to build upon our work. Any significant improvement would entail the addition of a nonlinear relationship, and they would be stuck. This fundamental difficulty was pointed out in forceful manner by Crawford Holling over thirty years ago. Holling was discussing the best strategy for building models of ecological systems. His review of predation models led him to the following conclusion, which is still relevant today:

> It is clear that none of these models include very many of the relevant components. As a result, they are extremely restrictive. However, each has been constructed by borrowing the techniques and mathematical language, largely calculus, of classical physics. This choice was really the only one available before the advent of computers and it imposes major limitations. The more components included, the more obvious this becomes since it becomes progressively more and more difficult to include new components in a differential equation and even more difficult to integrate it. The models therefore tend to be dead ends, preventing future revision and expansion. (Holling 1966, 204)

Summary

With the power of computers that can perform the tedious calculations required in numerical simulation, there is no need to rely on the analytical approach. With the availability of stock-and-flow software programs, we can concentrate our attention where it will do the most good—thinking about the realism of the model, not its "analytic tractability" (Hannon and Ruth 1994, 24). (For these reasons, differential equations are not discussed further unless there is a close correspondence between our model results and a differential equation that has become widely known in the literature.)

The next chapter introduces the first major example of a real environmental system. The Mono Lake system will provide an opportunity to practice what you've learned from chapters 2 and 3 and to apply one of the software programs from appendices C–F.

Exercises

1. **Verify the population numbers:**

    Build the model in figure 3.2 using any of the stock-and-flow programs. Set DT to 1 year and run the model for 5 years to verify the tabular results shown in table 3.1.

2. **DT/2 test:**

    Change the DT from the previous exercise to 0.5 years and run the model to verify the tabular results shown in table 3.2

3. **Numerical accuracy:**

    Continue cutting DT in half until the estimate of population at the end of the 4th year is within 0.2 percent of the actual value of 13.23 million.

4.   **Verify the sequence:**

Build the model in figure 3.5 using any of the stock-and-flow programs. Simulate the model with a step size of 1 year and confirm the tabular results in table 3.3.

5.   **Advanced topic—higher-order integration methods:**

The numerical approach illustrated in table 3.3 is a first-order integration method with fixed step size, sometimes called Euler's method. The method is simple to implement, and it works well as long as DT is sufficiently short. You can use Euler's method for the models in this book. All of the stock-and-flow software programs allow the numerical simulation to be performed with either Euler's method or more sophisticated methods such as second-order or fourth-order integration. Each program comes with excellent documentation about the pros and cons of the integration options (HPS 1993, 12-3; Ventana Systems 1995, 115; Powersim Corporation 1996, 6-2; Pugh-Roberts Associates 1986, 9-1). The "higher-order" methods make extra calculations to obtain a more accurate estimate of the values of the flows to apply during the time step. They provide a more accurate estimate than Euler's method, but the price is extra time to perform the calculations. Check whether you get more accuracy by repeating the first three exercises with "second-order Runge Kutta" integration.

Chapter 4

Water Flows in the Mono Basin

Mono Lake is an ancient inland sea in the eastern Sierra. It is one of the oldest continuously existing lakes in the world, and the land forms reflect the lake's ancient history. Volcanic islands rise in the middle of the lake, and tufa towers rise around the edges. The basin is a land of stark contrasts and spectacular vistas. It's also an oasis for wildlife in the high desert country. Migratory birds use the lake as a stopover location; nesting birds raise their chicks on the islands. The birds are drawn by a simple but extraordinary ecosystem. Microscopic algae thrive in the lake, providing the food supply for brine shrimp and brine flies. These are astoundingly prolific organisms that can provide a virtually limitless food supply for birds under proper conditions.

Mono Lake was selected for your first experience with a "real-world" model because it provides important lessons for policy making as well as simulation modeling. From a policy point of view, Mono Lake is a story of how

> a handful of people began a campaign to save a dying lake, taking on not only the City of Los Angeles, but the entire state government by challenging the way we think about water. Their fight seemed doomed in the beginning, but long years of grassroots education and effort finally paid off in 1994, when the California Water Resources Control Board ruled that Los Angeles's use of Mono Basin waters be restricted. Over time, the lake will return to a healthy condition. . . . The battle over Mono Lake is one of the longest and most fiercely contested conservation battles in US history, and that rare one with a happy ending. (Hart 1996)

Mono Lake is well suited to demonstrate the power of stock-and-flow modeling. By the end of this chapter, you will see a model that may be used to simulate changes in the lake level with different policies controlling water export to Los Angeles. You may then expand the model and test your own policies for controlling the size of the lake.

Background

The Mono Lake story began early in the century when the City of Los Angeles looked to the Owens Valley for new sources of water. Under the direction of William Mulholland, the city completed the Owens Valley aqueduct in 1913. Los Angeles was a city of 100,000 in the year 1900. By the year 1930, the population had reached 1 million, and the city was looking

Aqueducts Serving Los Angeles

Los Angeles Aqueduct System
California Aqueduct System
Colorado River Aqueduct System

Figure 4.1. Location of Mono Lake and the aqueducts serving Los Angeles.

beyond Owens Valley. By 1941, the Colorado River Aqueduct was completed. And in the same year, the Los Angeles Aqueduct was extended to reach the Mono Basin. Figure 4.1 shows Mono Lake and the aqueducts that serve Los Angeles.

The city began diverting water from the Mono Basin in 1941. Stream flows toward the lake were diverted into a tunnel running beneath the Mono Craters to reach the northern Owens River. The journey to Los Angeles is nearly four hundred miles, and the water flows by gravity and siphons the entire way, producing hydroelectric energy en route. By the 1970s, diversions averaged around 100 KAF/yr (thousand acre-feet per year).

The impact of the diversions is evident from the chart in figure 4.2. The lake's surface was measured at 6,417 feet above sea level in 1941. The lake held around 4.3 million acre-feet of water, and its surface area spread across 55 thousand acres. Salinity, a crucial factor for the brine flies and brine shrimp, was around 55 g/L (grams per liter). Then the diversions began. Figure 4.2 shows the steady decline in the lake's elevation during the next four decades. By

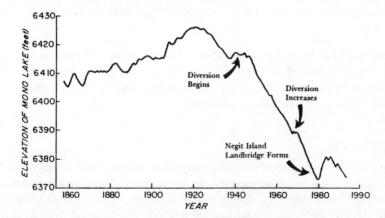

Figure 4.2. Historical elevations of Mono Lake.

Photo 4.1. The Northwest corner of Mono Lake with the land bridge connected to Negit Island. Source: Mono Lake Committee Collection.

the year 1981, the lake's volume had been cut approximately in half, and its salinity had climbed to around 100 g/L. The lake stood at 6,372 feet, 45 feet below its position when diversions began. As the lake shrinks, salinity climbs, and higher salinity can reduce algae production and lower the survivability of brine flies and brine shrimp. When these herbivores decline in number, the nesting birds may not find adequate food to raise their chicks. The migrating birds may not be able to add sufficient weight for the next leg of their migration. A declining lake level poses other dangers as well. When the lake receded to 6,375 feet, for example, a land bridge was formed to Negit Island (see photo 4.1), and a once secure nesting habitat became vulnerable to predators.

Reversing the Course

Environmental science students studied the lake during the 1970s. They were alarmed at what they found and fearful for the future of the lake. For example, they feared that higher salinity could lead to serious declines in brine shrimp population and a subsequent loss of suitable habitat for the bird populations. In 1978, one group of students formed the Mono Lake Committee, a grassroots education and advocacy group. Mono Lake also drew the attention of the National Audubon Society, which filed suit against the City of Los Angeles in 1979. The California Supreme Court responded in 1983. It held that the public trust mandated reconsideration of the city's water rights in the Mono Basin. The court noted that Mono Lake is a scenic and ecological treasure of national significance and that the lake's value was diminished by a receding water level. The court issued an injunction later in the 1980s limiting the city's diversions while the State Water Resources Control Board reviewed the city's water rights.

The Control Board considered a variety of alternatives for the future. One extreme was the "no restriction" alternative, in which the city would be free to divert water as in the past. With no restrictions, the Control Board expected the lake to decline for another fifty to one hundred years and reach a dynamic equilibrium at around 6,355 feet (Jones and Stokes Associates 1993, 2–17). The opposite extreme was the "no diversion" alternative. If all of Mono Basin's streams were allowed to flow uninterrupted to the lake, the Control Board expected the lake to climb over a period of one hundred years, eventually reaching dynamic equilibrium at around 6,425 feet.

The Control Board issued its decision in 1994. It concluded that the appropriate balance between the city's water rights and the public trust would be served by allowing the lake to rebuild to a higher elevation. The target elevation is marked with a small plaque next to the boardwalk leading to the shore of the lake. The plaque explains that the lake stood at 6,392 feet back in the year 1963. The lake will now be allowed to rebuild toward that level.

Water Flows in the Basin

The preceding background provides the context for the modeling exercises in this chapter. If you wish to learn more, turn to the book's home page. It includes information on the Mono Basin and how the diversions fit within the water supply system for the City of Los Angeles. It also includes additional background, photographs, and links to related home pages. Figure 4.3 shows one of the sketches to be found on the home page. It depicts water flows in the basin in an average year. These flows will help us appreciate why the lake has declined historically.

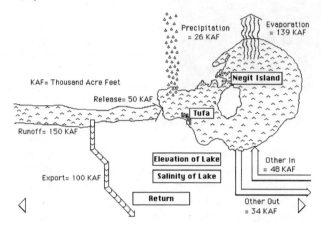

Figure 4.3. Illustrative flows in an average year.

The principal flow into the basin is the runoff from five streams that drain the Sierra Nevada. (Photo 4.2 shows Rush Creek, the largest of the five streams, during high runoff.) Vorster (1985) reviewed measurements of the five streams over the years 1937–83 and concluded that they amount to 150 KAF/yr with average weather. The City of Los Angeles operates diversion points on the gauged streams, and figure 4.3 depicts diversions of 100 KAF/yr. This leaves 50 KAF/yr to reach the lake. Precipitation and evaporation can vary from year to year depending on weather and the size of the lake. Evaporation is, by far, the largest flow out of the basin. The "Other Out" is a combination of several smaller flows such as evapotranspiration and exposed lake bottom evaporation, The "Other In" is a combination of several flows such as ungauged sierra runoff and municipal diversions. The total of all inflows in figure 4.3 is 224 KAF/yr. The outflows total 273 KAF/yr. The net result is a loss of around 50 KAF/yr.

Now imagine what would happen if this annual loss were sustained year after year. There

Photo 4.2. This photo shows flow in Rush Creek, one of the five gauged streams that drain the Sierra Nevada and flow toward Mono Lake. Source: Mono Lake Committee Collection.

would be less and less water stored in the lake. After twenty years, the lake would have lost 1 million acre-feet. If the loss continued for forty years, the lake would lose 2 million acre-feet. This simple arithmetic is sufficient to illustrate how a lake with 4.3 million acre-feet could be cut approximately in half with forty years of diversions. Let's turn now to computer simulation modeling to look at this problem in more detail.

Purpose of the Model

It is crucial at the outset of any project to specify the purpose of the model as clearly as possible. Our purpose is to project the future size of the lake given different assumptions about the amount of water exported to Los Angeles. We expect to use the model to make projections that resemble the graph shown in figure 4.4. This initial graph is called the *reference mode*. It serves as a target pattern of behavior that you expect the model to generate. The reference mode is normally drawn based on our understanding of the fundamental patterns of growth, decay, overshoot, or oscillation explained in chapter 1. In each new problem area, we should ask ourselves if our dynamic problem corresponds to one of the standard shapes. When classifying the Mono Lake problem, the best shape is decay. If there were no influx of water each year, Mono Lake would decay to zero. But nature provides precipitation and runoff each year, so our intuition tells us that the lake will probably decay to a smaller size, but not all the way to zero.

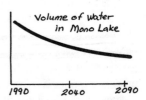

Figure 4.4. The reference mode for the Mono Lake model.

The reference mode begins in the year 1990. (This is the year when one of my students did a class project on the lake, but you may equally well imagine starting the analysis in the current year.) Figure 4.4 shows the reference mode extending from the year 1990 to the year 2090. This long time period seems reasonable given the Control Board's assessment of the time needed for the lake to reach dynamic equilibrium. The length of time appearing on the horizontal axis of the reference mode is often called the *time horizon* of the model.

With such a long time horizon, we can now begin to make useful decisions on what to include and what to exclude from the model. When looking forward one hundred years, let's ignore daily or monthly variations in the lake volume. Notice that figure 4.4 is a smooth line that shows a gradual decline in the volume of water in the lake. It makes it clear that we are ignoring seasonal variations. The shape of the reference mode also reminds us that we are ignoring year-to-year variations in the weather. One year may be particularly wet; the next, particularly dry. These variations could be important in a short-term model, but they can be ignored in a long-term model. For now, let's assume that every year is an average year as far as the weather is concerned.

One final feature of figure 4.4 should catch your attention—there are no numbers on the vertical axis. You might have wondered why we don't show the lake volume at around 2 million acre-feet at the start and show estimates of the final volume in the year 2090. You should feel free to include or exclude numerical detail when sketching the reference mode. If the numbers are available and they improve communication among members of the team, include them in the sketch. If not, feel free to leave them out. It's the general shape of the diagram that counts at this stage of the process.

Drawing a reference mode before building the model may seem like "rigging" the analysis. Some would say that you should wait until the model is done and then see how it behaves. Don't let this thinking divert you from this first step. Think about the process that you went through the first time you built a model airplane. You didn't build the model blind, thinking that you would learn its likely pattern of behavior once you threw it into the air. You built it with a predetermined image of the behavior. You probably envisioned that the model could glide through the air for five to ten feet, maybe longer if you were clever with the design. Building a system dynamics model is similar; you start with a predetermined image of the model's likely behavior over time. Drawing a reference mode is key to the dozens of decisions you must make later in the model building process. Your choice of a reference mode will guide which factors are included (and which factors are excluded) from the model.

List the Policies and Start Simple

Specifying policies at the outset is also important because it guides our decisions about what to exclude from the model. For our purposes, there is one key policy variable: the amount of water exported from the Mono Basin. Our purpose is to learn how the size of the lake varies with variations in water exports. In this example, we must be sure that *exports* are included explicitly in the model. Other policy variables (like the demand for water or the price of water in Los Angeles) are not on our list, so they may be excluded from the model.

Building a model is an iterative, trial-and-error process. The best approach is to begin with the simplest possible model that could explain the reference mode. You should build, test, and reflect on the first model before moving to a more complicated model. The worst thing you can do is try to build the "perfect model" right from the start. You will make more progress in the long run if you start simple and learn as much as you can from each new model. Now, before reading ahead, ask yourself what you would do next. What are the stock variables for a model of Mono Lake, and what are the flows that directly influence those stocks? What units would you use to measure the stocks and flows? Then think of the converters you would use to fill out the picture.

An Initial Model of Mono Lake

Figure 4.5 shows a first cut at a model. A single stock is used to keep track of the volume of *water in lake*. The volume of water has the feel of a stock variable because it changes more slowly than other variables. If there was zero runoff this year, for example, there would still be some water in the lake next year. Also, the water in the lake seems to make sense as the main place where accumulation takes place in the system. Let's measure the stock in KAF (thousand acre-feet). We may set the initial value of the stock at 2,228 KAF to represent the water stored in Mono Lake in 1990. The model is specified to run in years, so the units for each of the flow variables must be KAF/year. To keep the units consistent, the area of the lake will be measured in thousands of acres, and the annual rates of precipitation and evaporation will be measured in feet per year.

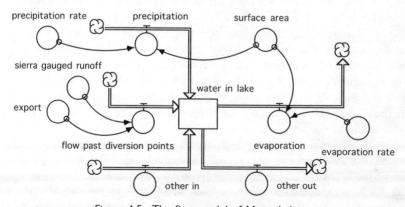

Figure 4.5. The first model of Mono Lake.

You've seen in figure 4.3 that the main flow into the basin is the runoff from the sierra streams. To match the names used by Vorster (1985), let's name this converter *sierra gauged runoff.* The *export* stands for the amount of water diverted into the tunnel to leave the basin. We would subtract export from the gauged runoff to get the *flow past diversion points,* the flow that actually reaches Mono Lake. The model includes *evaporation* and *precipitation* flows as well. The *evaporation* is the lake's *surface area* multiplied by the *evaporation rate,* while the *precipitation* is the surface *area* multiplied by the *precipitation rate.* Let's set the area at 39 thousand acres based on the area in 1990, and let's assume that the evaporation rate is 3.75 feet/yr and the precipitation rate is 0.67 feet/yr in an average year. Other flows are the collection of *other in* flows and a collection of *other out* flows. The numerical values will be set at the average year values shown previously. The equations for this first model are listed in figure 4.6.

Now, what do you expect to see from this initial model? Will it generate the reference mode? Figure 4.7 shows the simulation result. Flow past the diversion points is constant at 50 KAF/yr. The evaporation is at around 146 KAF/yr. The water in the lake declines in a linear fashion throughout the simulation. Indeed, the volume reaches zero by the year 2030, and it

```
water_in_lake(t) = water_in_lake(t - dt) + (flow_past_diversion_points +
other_in + precipitation - other_out - evaporation) * dt
INIT water_in_lake = 2228
INFLOWS:
flow_past_diversion_points = sierra_gauged_runoff-export
other_in = 47.6
precipitation = surface_area*precipitation_rate
OUTFLOWS:
other_out = 33.6
evaporation = surface_area*evaporation_rate

evaporation_rate = 3.75
export = 100
precipitation_rate = 0.667
sierra_gauged_runoff = 150
surface_area = 39
```

Figure 4.6. Equations for the first model.

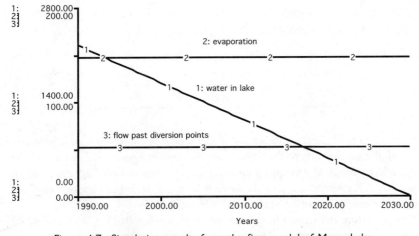

Figure 4.7. Simulation results from the first model of Mono Lake.

would continue to decline if we were to extend the simulation further. These results are clearly spurious. Not only do they not match the reference mode, but it makes no sense to see the *water in lake* become negative.

At this point, you might be tempted to invoke the "non-negative" option on the stock variable. But this would simply be covering up a fundamental problem with the model. Also, you might wonder if the spurious behavior is the result of the particular parameters. Perhaps we should try a simulation with lower *export* or a simulation with a different estimate of the *surface area* of the lake. Do you think these experiments would change the linear pattern? Would they ever allow the model to generate the reference mode?

You can give these experiments a try. You'll soon discover that this model will never generate the target pattern. No matter what set of input parameters you try, the pattern will turn out to be either linear decline or linear increase. The problem with this first model is not the input parameters; it's the structure. It's time to expand the stock-and-flow diagram to improve the structure.

Second Model of Mono Lake

If Mono Lake were shaped as a cylinder, its surface area would remain constant as the volume falls. But the lake looks much more like a shallow cup than a cylinder. Its surface area tends to shrink as the volume falls. For the second model, let's change the *surface area* to an internal variable that will decline with a decline in the volume of water in the lake. To introduce some new terminology, one might say that we have changed the area from an *exogenous* variable to an *endogenous* variable. The challenge is to represent the *surface area* as a function of the volume of the lake. Perhaps we could write the equation for the surface area of a cone as a function of the volume of water stored in the cone. This approach is not likely to be realistic, however, because the shape of the lake bottom is complicated due to islands and volcanic structures. Fortunately, geologic and bathymetric surveys have been completed to provide all the detail we need. The survey results are reported by Vorster (1985, 261) and are summarized in table 4.1 in terms of volume, area, and elevation of the lake.

Table 4.1. Survey results.

Volume of water in lake (KAF)	Surface area (Kacres)	Elevation (feet above sea level)
0	0	6,224
1,000	24.7	6,335
2,000	35.3	6,369
3,000	48.6	6,392
4,000	54.3	6,412
5,000	57.2	6,430
6,000	61.6	6,447
7,000	66.0	6,463
8,000	69.8	6,477

To incorporate the survey information in the model, we would use an information connector from the *water in lake* to the *surface area* as shown in figure 4.8. Then invoke "become a graph"; select *water in lake* to appear on the horizontal axis and ask for 9 points on the horizontal axis. Set the lower bound of the horizontal axis at 0 and the upper bound at 8,000; then enter the nine values of surface area from the survey table.

The results from the second model are shown in figure 4.9. They are certainly different from those of the previous model. The *surface area* begins the simulation at 39 thousand acres

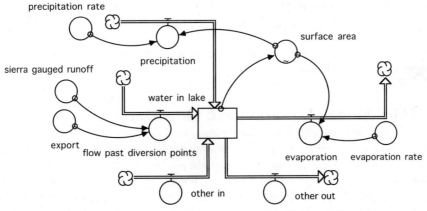

Figure 4.8. The second model of Mono Lake.

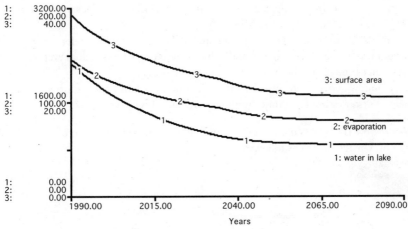

Figure 4.9. Simulation results from the second model of Mono Lake with export held constant at 100 KAF/year.

and declines as the volume of water declines. *Evaporation* is around 146 KAF/yr at the start of the simulation, but it declines over time as the lake shrinks in size. The pattern in figure 4.9 is just what we are looking for. We see a gradual decline to dynamic equilibrium.

This is good progress; we have a relatively simple model that generates the reference mode. But a serious limitation of this model is that it provides no indication of whether the lake's ecosystem is in danger. What can be done to represent the state of the ecosystem without having to simulate the complexities of the food web? One approach is the "proxy approach." We search for a variable that would be easy to include and allow the new variable to serve as a proxy for the state of the ecosystem. Most discussions of the threats to Mono Lake's ecosystem rely on elevation as a proxy. For example, several investigators have cautioned that we should be watchful for different categories of problems if the lake falls to the following elevations:

6,380 feet—severe dust storms

6,375 feet—general ecosystem decline

6,372 feet—major loss of gull nesting habitat

6,363 feet—critical salinity levels

6,352 feet—general collapse of the ecosystem

For the next iteration, let's add elevation to the model. And while we are making changes, let's elaborate on the description of some of the flows.

A Third Model: Elevation and Flow Details

Since the elevation is reported in the survey data, we may add elevation as a converter that is linked to the volume with a connector. Then invoke the "become a graph" feature with the volume of water on the horizontal axis. Design the axis for nine entries and enter the nine values of elevation from the survey table. Figure 4.10 shows the new diagram. The other changes appear at the bottom of the diagram where we have more detail on the other flows in and out of the basin. *Other out* is now the sum of four separate flows, each of which has been estimated by Vorster (1985) as follows:

- Net evaporation from Grant Lake, a small lake upstream from Mono Lake, is 1.3 KAF/yr.
- Evapotranspiration from irrigated land, riparian vegetation, and vegetation such as salt grass, greasewood, and willows is 13 KAF/yr.
- Exposed lake bottom evaporation is estimated at 12 KAF/yr. (This refers to the evaporation from residual pools of water stranded by the receding lake as well as evaporation from groundwater brought to the surface by capillary action.)
- Some groundwater is intercepted by the underground conduit and exported south to Los Angeles. Vorster estimates "groundwater export" at 7.3 KAF/yr.

The *other in* flow is now calculated as the sum of four separate flows, each of which has been estimated by Vorster (1985) as follows:

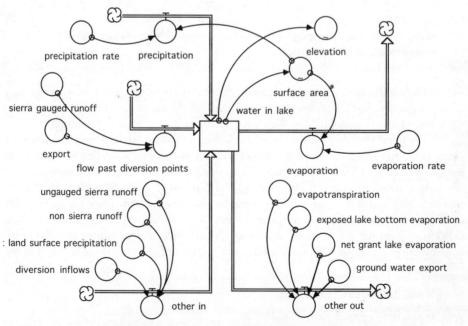

Figure 4.10. The third model of Mono Lake.

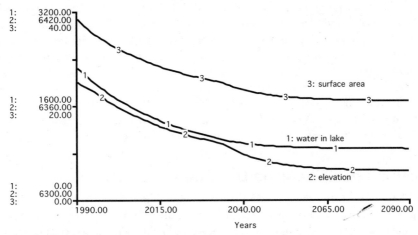

Figure 4.11. Results from the third model.

- Ungauged sierra runoff from small and intermittent watersheds is expected to be 17 KAF/yr.
- Nonsierra runoff from watersheds to the north, east, and south are estimated to yield 20 KAF/yr based on a soil moisture surplus method.
- Vorster refers to precipitation falling on the basin (but not on the lake) as "net land surface precipitation," and he estimates it at 9 KAF/yr.
- The small municipalities divert water from Virginia Creek (outside the basin) and allow the used water to flow toward Mono Lake, creating what Vorster calls "diversion inflows" of 1.6 KAF/yr.

You can double-check the sums to ensure that the new model has the same flows as before. We are not expecting the new model to show different behavior. Rather, we are looking for more clarity in communicating the nature of the flows.

The results of the third model are shown in figure 4.11. The water in the lake follows the same downward path as before. *Elevation* is the new variable, and we see that it follows an irregular downward path, especially around the year 2040. The lake has a complex shape, and there is a so-called nick point at around 6,368 feet where the topographic relief changes markedly. But the irregular pattern of *elevation* in figure 4.11 is probably not showing us the "nick point." The irregularities are probably due to the crude representation of the elevation with only nine survey points. By the end of the simulation, Mono Lake has declined to under a million acre-feet of volume, and its elevation is below 6,320 feet.

Checking the Model

One way to check the model is to set the initial value of the stock of water in the lake to match the volume back in 1941. We could then set the model inputs to match time series information during the four decades of diversions. Our confidence in the model would be bolstered if it could simulate the 45-foot decline in lake elevation that occurred during the interval from 1941 to 1981. Another test would be to check year-by-year variations in the simulated size of the lake with recorded variations. For example, if we simulated the unusually wet conditions in 1983, we would look to see if the simulated lake rose by 6 feet. We would also check the model by comparing it with more detailed models of the lake. One of the best is Vorster's (1985) water balance model. Vorster's thesis is exemplary because of the careful documentation, the independent estimates of each flow, and the historical comparisons to check accuracy. Since Vorster's model has been carefully checked against historical records, we might proceed on the assumption that it provides a good benchmark for the future. Furthermore, many of the parameter values in the third model are taken from Vorster's documentation, so we should expect to see similar results when the models are simulated under similar hydrologic scenarios. Vorster calculates the dynamic equilibrium of the lake under average climatic conditions with differing values of export. For a constant export of 100 KAF/yr, he expects the lake to equilibrate at 6,335 feet. This result is more than 15 feet higher than the elevation at the end of the simulation in figure 4.11. Something is missing from the model.

Fourth Model: Changing the Evaporation Rate

The missing factor is the change in the rate of evaporation as Mono Lake's water becomes more and more dense over time. The increased density arises from a fixed amount of dissolved solids held in solution in a shrinking volume of water. Highly saline waters tend to evaporate more slowly than fresh water due to a reduction in the vapor pressure difference between the surface of the water and the overlying air. But we don't need to add vapor pressures to the model to represent the change in evaporation. Rather, we can take advantage of evaporation studies documented by Vorster (1985, 90) and tabulated in table 4.2. This table uses specific gravity to measure the density of the water. (A value of 1.0 corresponds to fresh water; a value of 1.1 means the lake's water is 10 percent heavier than fresh water.) The second column reports a "multiplier" to summarize the impact of higher salinity. If Mono Lake's water is 10 percent heavier than fresh water, for example, its evaporation rate would be 92.6 percent of the evaporation rate for fresh water.

Figure 4.12 shows the flow diagram of a new model that includes the missing factor. The specific gravity depends on the *water in lake*, the *total dissolved solids*, and the *mass of fresh water*. The *mass of fresh water* is 1.359 million tons per KAF; the *total dissolved solids* is 230 million tons. The specific gravity is the mass of the actual water (with its dissolved solids) divided by the mass of the same volume of fresh water. For a lake with 2,228 KAF of *water in lake*, you should verify that the specific gravity would be 1.076. In other words, the water in the lake is 7.6 percent heavier than fresh water.

Table 4.2. Summary of evaporation studies.

Specific gravity of water in the lake	Evaporation rate multiplier
1.00	1.000
1.05	0.963
1.10	0.926
1.15	0.880
1.20	0.883
1.25	0.785
1.30	0.737
1.35	0.688
1.40	0.640

The *specific gravity* is then used to determine the *evaporation rate multiplier from specific gravity*, and the multiplier is used to find the actual evaporation rate. The multiplier takes on the value 1.0 when the specific gravity is at 1.0. Under this benchmark condition, the model would multiply the *fresh water evaporation rate* by 1.0 to get the actual *evaporation rate*. As the *specific gravity* increases above 1.0, however, the multiplier will decline below 1.0. If the *specific gravity* increases to 1.076, for example, the multiplier will turn out to be 0.94. In other words, the evaporation rate is 6 percent slower than the *fresh water evaporation rate*. The equation for the evaporation rate would multiply 0.94 times the *fresh water evaporation rate* of 3.75 feet/year to obtain the actual *evaporation rate* of 3.54 feet/year. Then, as in previous models, the *evaporation rate* is multiplied by the *surface area* of the lake to obtain the *evaporation*.

Figure 4.13 shows the simulation results of the new model with export held constant at 100 KAF/yr. The time graph shows volume, area, and elevation, the same measures shown before. It also shows the *specific gravity*. It begins the simulation at around 1.076, as you would

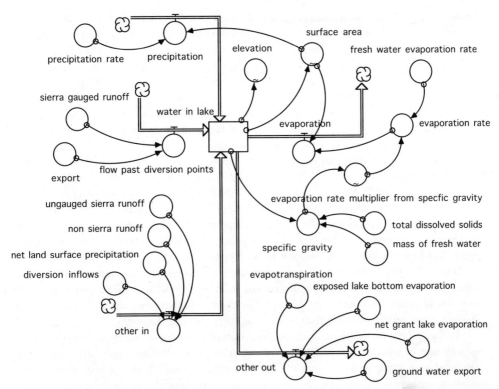

Figure 4.12. Stella flow diagram of the fourth model of Mono Lake.

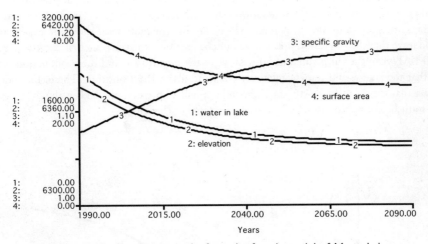

Figure 4.13. Simulation results from the fourth model of Mono Lake.

expect. It ends the simulation at 1.163. By the end of the simulation, the lake has declined to an elevation of 6,336 feet. The general pattern is the same as before—a gradual decline, eventually reaching dynamic equilibrium. And it's gratifying to see the equilibrium value within 1 foot of the corresponding result by Vorster (1985, 225).

Testing the Model

Now let's see what we might learn by testing the model. You've learned previously that system dynamics simulations should be used in pairs (like the blades of a pair of scissors). It takes at least two simulations to arrive at useful conclusions, so let's compare some simulations. For the first test, let's imagine that we allow the 100 KAF/yr of export to continue for the first half of the simulation period. Then we'll cut the export to zero for the second half. This is a crude but simple test to learn how responsive the lake is to a change in exports. Since water export was designated as a "policy variable" at the start of the chapter, this simple test might be called a "policy test" of the model.

Figure 4.14 shows the results of this first policy test. Elevation follows the same downward trajectory seen previously for the first half of the simulation. By the year 2040, the lake stands at 6,341 feet. After that year, the lake grows in size, eventually reaching an elevation of 6,398 feet. This test reveals that the slope of the recovery is somewhat steeper than the downward slope during the first half of the simulation. Because of the steeper recovery, the lake requires only around fifteen years to recover to the starting elevation. Then the recovery slows somewhat as the lake becomes larger and larger. This slowdown in the recovery is caused by the growing surface area of the lake. As the area increases, the lake's evaporation increases, and the lake's recovery is slowed. (And to a lesser extent, the slowdown in the recovery arises from the reduced specific gravity of the water in the lake.)

The policy test in figure 4.14 is meant to illustrate the type of tests you should conduct when first testing a model. It is simple and easy to interpret. But you should understand that this simple policy does not match the specific policies proposed or adopted in the Mono Basin. (These policy tests are left as exercises at the end of the chapter.)

Let's conclude the testing with an example of multiple simulations to portray the impact of a change in water export policy from the start of the simulation. Figure 4.15 shows the results of a sensitivity analysis of the importance of water export. This is a comparative graph showing the *elevation* from six different simulations of the model. Each simulation assumes a constant export from the beginning to the end of the simulation. The first run sets the export to zero, and the *elevation* climbs slowly over time. It reaches 6,410 feet by the year 2090 and is still growing at the end of the simulation. The sixth run sets export to 100 KAF/yr, and we see the same pattern as shown before. Two of the intermediate tests show the export that would leave the lake's elevation pretty much unchanged over the time interval. Exports are set to 40 KAF/yr in the third run and 60 KAF/yr in the fourth run, and these simulations suggest that the lake would remain relatively constant at the 1990 position. These simulations suggest that export must be cut approximately in half to preserve the lake at the 1990 level; they must be cut further to rebuild the lake to a higher elevation.

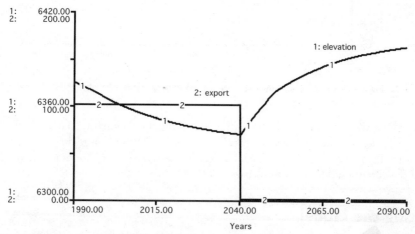

Figure 4.14. Simulated recovery after a change in export midway through the simulation.

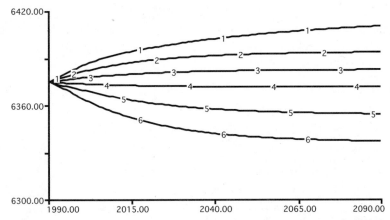

Figure 4.15. Simulated elevation of Mono Lake in a sensitivity analysis with export ranging from 0 (run 1) to 100 KAF/yr (run 6).

Conclusion

The fourth model is an excellent model of the water flows in the Mono Basin. Its main advantages are simplicity and clarity. Take a close look at the flow diagram in figure 4.12 and think of this way of describing a computer simulation model. This small diagram is sufficient to show every variable and every interconnection. The names are simple, and the units are clear. The simulations show the reference mode, and the results have been checked against a more detailed model. We now have a model that may be used to test the impact of different export policies.

Now, what do you think are the main problems with this model? Are you worried about the "average year" assumption? the lack of seasonal variation? the lack of precision in describing the geometry of the lake? Does it bother you that all five of the gauged sierra streams are combined into a single flow? These are some of the potential problems that may be addressed in student projects to improve the mode. As you add "improvements" to the model, use the policy results from the original model as a guide to whether your improvements are important. If your new model shows essentially the same policy results as the previous model, then you know your improvement is important only if it adds clarity and bolsters confidence in the model.

Perhaps the principal limitation of the Mono Lake model is that it is limited to hydrological factors. The model does a good job of simulating the change in the size of the lake. But it does not simulate the vulnerability of the ecosystem to changes in volume. Rather, it relies on elevation to serve as a proxy for the health of the ecosystem. You may deal with this limitation in the "model merger" exercise at the end of the chapter.

Exercises

1. **Verification:**

   Build the fourth model, set DT to 0.25 years, and simulate the model to verify that it matches the results in this chapter. Document your work with a printed copy of the flow diagram and time graphs to match the results in figure 4.13. If you are not sure about all the equations, double-check your equations against selected equations below. For example, here are the equations describing the evaporation and the specific gravity:

```
evaporation = surface_area*evaporation_rate
evaporation_rate =
fresh_water_evaporation_rate*evaporation_rate_multiplier_from_specfic_gravity
specific_gravity = (water_in_lake*mass_of_fresh_water+total_dissolved_solids)/
(water_in_lake*mass_of_fresh_water)
```

Here are the various constants:

```
diversion_inflows = 1.6
evapotranspiration = 13
export = 100
exposed_lake_bottom_evaporation = 12
fresh_water_evaporation_rate = 3.75
ground_water_export = 7.3
mass_of_fresh_water = 1.359
net_grant_lake_evaporation = 1.3
net_land_surface_precipitation = 9
non_sierra_runoff = 20
precipitation_rate = 0.667
sierra_gauged_runoff = 150
total_dissolved_solids = 230
ungauged_sierra_runoff = 17
```

Here are the three graphs for the nonlinear relationships:

```
elevation = GRAPH(water_in_lake)
(0.00, 6224), (1000, 6335), (2000, 6369), (3000, 6392),
(4000, 6412), (5000, 6430), (6000, 6447), (7000, 6463), (8000, 6477)

evaporation_rate_multiplier_from_specfic_gravity = GRAPH(specific_gravity)
(1.00, 1.00), (1.05, 0.963), (1.10, 0.926), (1.15, 0.88), (1.20, 0.833), (1.25, 0.785),
(1.30, 0.737), (1.35, 0.688), (1.40, 0.64)

surface_area = GRAPH(water_in_lake)
(0.00, 0.00), (1000, 24.7), (2000, 35.3), (3000, 48.6), (4000, 54.3),
(5000, 57.2), (6000, 61.6), (7000, 66.0), (8000, 69.8)
```

2. **Check the dynamic equilibrium:**

    Look at the numerical values for each of the flows at the end of the simulation in the previous exercise. Add the flows into and out of the stock. Is the lake in dynamic equilibrium?

3. **Simulate a buffer policy:**

    Modify the model to allow it to simulate a "buffer policy." The idea is to specify a target range for the lake elevation where you are confident that the ecosystem is "safe" as long as the elevation is confined to the range. (A similar policy was advocated by the Mono Lake Committee.) For this exercise, assume a 10-foot buffer zone as shown below.

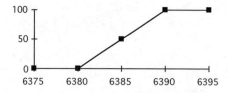

    Expand the model to allow exports to depend on the elevation of the lake. If the *elevation* is below 6,380 feet, *export* must be zero. If the *elevation* exceeds 6,390 feet, *export* is set at the "historical" value of 100 KAF/yr. If the elevation is somewhere inside the buffer zone, the *export* should change in a linear manner. Simulate the model over the time period from 1990 to 2010. Document your work with a copy of the flow diagram, the equations, and a graph of *elevation* and *exports*.

4. **Monthly version of the buffer policy model:**

   Change the interpretation of "time" from years to months and repeat the previous test of the buffer policy. Let time run from 0 to 240 months (month 0 corresponds to the year 1990 in the previous simulation). Retain the convention of measuring model inputs in KAF/yr or in feet/yr, but make sure your equations have the correct units. Set the DT to 1 month; simulate the model; and turn in a time graph of *elevation* and *exports* with the same scales as in the third exercise. You should get the same results as before.

5. **Buffer policy with seasonal changes in runoff:**

   Expand the monthly model from the fourth exercise to allow the *sierra gauged runoff* to vary from one month to another within the year. Use the "monthly counter" (see appendix H) to represent the months of a year. Most of the runoff occurs from melting snowpack during the spring and summer, so set these monthly flows to higher than average. Set the fall and winter flows to lower than average. Don't forget to make sure that the average over all 12 months turns out to be 150 KAF/yr or 12.5 KAF/month. Next, you need to make sure that the model does not export water that may not be flowing down the streams in the fall and winter months. So change the export buffer policy to a fraction of the *sierra gauged runoff.* Document your work with a copy of the flow diagram, the equations, a time graph showing elevation and exports with the same scales as in the previous exercises.

6. **Control Board policy:**

   Hart (1996, 171) describes some of the details of the State Water Resources Control Board's 1994 policy to rebuild the lake toward an elevation of 6,392 feet. He explains that the city is allowed no diversions until the lake reaches 6,377 feet. Then it would be allowed 4.5 KAF/yr until the level reaches 6,390 feet. It would be allowed 16 KAF/yr until the lake reaches 6,391 feet. If the lake reaches higher levels, the city could divert all water in excess of fish flows (which are expected to be 30.8 KAF/yr). Draw an export/elevation chart similar to the chart in the third exercise to approximate the Control Board policy. Then simulate the policy. Document your results with a time graph of elevation and exports. How long does it take for the lake to reach the target elevation? How much water is the city able to export once the lake reaches dynamic equilibrium?

7. **Advanced exercise—model merger from home page:**

   It is often useful to merge two models dealing with different aspects of a system because the combined model may teach us something new. That is, we gain insights that could not be gained from operating the two models separately. After you have learned about the use of "conveyors" in models of animal populations (see figure 14.2), turn to the home page to read about a model of the brine shrimp population of Mono Lake. You are to imagine that the new model has been developed independently of the hydrology model in this chapter. Your job is to merge the two models to provide an internally consistent simulation of size of the brine shrimp population as well as the size of the lake.

   You will discover what many modeling teams discover when working in large organizations: independently developed models do not necessarily fit together just because they deal with the same topic. You may need to make some adjustments in one or both of the models in order to combine them into a holistic picture of the lake and its shrimp. After you succeed in merging the models, use the combined model to examine the Control Board policy tested in the previous exercise. Can you design an export policy based on the observed brine shrimp population rather than the observed elevation? Does your new policy allow the city to export more water from the basin?

Post Script

The focus of this chapter is the Mono Basin and the need for reduced diversions in order to rebuild the lake. But many readers will wonder about the wider implications of reducing the diversions. Where will the extra water come from—

- the Colorado River?
- new reservoirs in Northern California?
- desalinization plants along the ocean?

I believe the most attractive supply of new water to compensate for reduced diversions from the Mono Basin is hidden in the homes and businesses of the City of Los Angeles. The inefficient methods of water use within the city provide an investment opportunity for the water department. Rather than investing in new reservoirs hundreds of miles away, the department could commit its financial resources to help its own customers invest in water efficiency. In my opinion, the saved water could more than compensate for the reduced diversions from the Mono Basin. Moreover, efficiency programs can lead to reductions in the customer's average water bill. Chapter 23 explains how conservation programs can be advantageous to electric utilities, and many of the advantages to an electric utility apply to a water utility as well. Regarding the city's plans, the department has announced that it intends to "meet increased water demands created by growth through a combination of water conservation and recycling programs." The department has invested over $50 million in demand-side management between 1990 and 1995, and it plans to continue demand-side program spending at around $10 million per year between 1995 and 2005 (LADWP 1995, ch. 5).

Further Readings

- Information on Mono Lake is given in several reports by academics (Winkler 1977; NRC 1987; Botkin et al. 1988; Hart 1996), by the City of Los Angeles (LADWP 1987, 1988a,b) and by the Mono Lake Committee (1989, 1997).
- The most extensive single collection of information is the Environmental Impact Report prepared for the State Water Resources Control Board's review of the Mono Basin Water Rights of the City of Los Angeles (Jones and Stokes Associates 1993).
- Much of the modeling information is taken from the water balance model developed by Peter Vorster. The model is thoroughly explained and tested in his thesis (Vorster 1985).
- Supplemental information may be found on this book's home page.

Chapter 5

Equilibrium Diagrams

System dynamics is the study of how systems change over time. Our focus is on dynamics, but dynamics are often difficult to understand. In watching students and professionals work with dynamic models, I have noticed that the moments of equilibrium provide an opportunity for great progress. If we see a system reach equilibrium at some point in a simulation, it is tremendously helpful to study the counterbalancing forces that produce that equilibrium. An equilibrium diagram is a simple but effective technique to help us pay closer attention to the key moments in a simulation. An equilibrium diagram is the same as a stock-and-flow diagram except that you write the numerical values and the units for each variable directly onto the diagram. The numerical values are found by simulating the model over time and picking a year in which the system is in equilibrium. Simply take note of the numerical values in that year and write them on the diagram. The diagram will help you verify that the flows in and out of each stock are in balance. The diagram will help us to become more familiar with the numbers and to spot obvious inconsistencies in the model.

Mono Lake Example

Let's begin with an example from the previous chapter. The model shows that Mono Lake could rise or fall over time depending on the value of water export. But if we watch the simulation long enough, the lake eventually reaches a certain size and remains at that size for the remainder of the simulation. The lake may be said to be in dynamic equilibrium. *Equilibrium* in this case means that the lake's conditions remain constant over time. *Dynamic* means that there are flows in and out of the system. You discovered in chapter 4 that the lake changes size over time until it "finds" the size that causes the flows in and out of the basin to balance. Figure 5.1 shows the balancing flows in a simulation with the export held constant at 100 KAF/yr. The lake volume is 1,048 KAF. For the stock to remain at this value, the inflows must balance the outflows. Let's check whether this is true:

- total inflows: 50.0 + 16.8 + 47.6 gives   114.4 KAF/yr
- total outflows: 82.0 + 33.6 gives   115.6 KAF/yr

You can tell that the volume of *water in lake* is slowly declining. The slow decline will lead to a smaller volume, a smaller surface area, and a somewhat smaller evaporation. For example, if you run the model until the year 2190, the next one hundred years will show that the lake would decline by an additional 10 inches. At the somewhat smaller size, the inflows and outflows would be in balance at 114.2 KAF/yr. The lake eventually finds its equilibrium position.

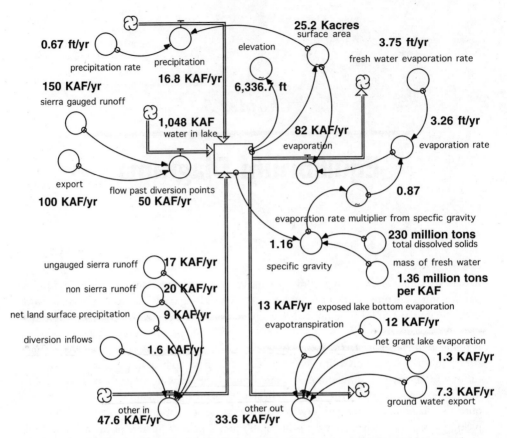

Figure 5.1. Equilibrium diagram for the Mono Lake model at the end of a simulation with export held constant at 100 KAF/yr.

An equilibrium diagram can also help us check the numerical values. In this example, there are only three converters that make use of a graph function (~). Every other converter and every flow are either an input or some simple, algebraic combination of other variables. So, we should be able to verify the logic behind the numbers in this diagram. An equilibrium diagram can also help you to verify that the units make sense. For example, it should make sense to you that evaporation is measured in KAF/yr, given the units for surface area and the evaporation rate, and you should be able to explain why the specific gravity turns out to be a dimensionless variable.

Two-Bottles Example

The Mono Lake model has only one stock, and the equilibrium diagram allows us to check that the flows in and out of the stock are in balance. In systems with multiple stocks, the flows in and out of each stock will be in balance. Figure 5.2 illustrates with an example from the "two-bottles" exercise in appendix C. If you constructed this model correctly, your simulation would show that the volume of water in the first bottle reaches equilibrium in around 15 seconds. The overflow from the first bottle then begins to fill the second bottle, and it reaches equilibrium around 20 seconds later. After that time, the volume of water and the height of water in both bottles remain constant over time. But we still have water flowing in and out of the system. In other words, we have dynamic equilibrium. The two-bottles exercise assumes that fluid flows into the first bottle at the constant rate of 5 cc/sec. The fluid gradually fills the first bottle (a cylinder with a surface area of 5 square centimeters). The fluid would reach an equilibrium height of 15 cm, filling the bottle to 75 cc, before causing the overflow to reach 5 cc/sec. The 5 cc/sec of overflow adds to the volume in the second bottle, causing the

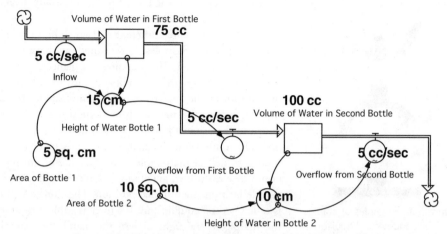

Figure 5.2. Equilibrium diagram from the two-bottles exercise.

water level to climb to an equilibrium height of 10 cm, filling the bottle to 100 cc. At this height, the overflow from the second bottle reaches 5 cc/sec, and the flows are in balance.

These two diagrams are easy to understand because it is easy to visualize the fluid flow and the fluid storage in the systems. But you should realize that all models may be checked in this manner, regardless of the nature of the flows. For example, you will see equilibrium diagrams later in the book to show a dynamic balance between:

- growth and decay in flowered areas (chapters 6 and 21),
- application and degradation of DDT (chapter 12),
- births and deaths of deer (chapter 16), and
- production and consumption of aluminum (chapter 19).

The diagrams are also useful to check your understanding of a system even if the model has not reached dynamic equilibrium. If you find a prominent point during the simulation where portions of the system are in dynamic balance, freeze the simulation and take note of the values. By simply writing the results on top of the flow diagram, we learn a lot about the relative magnitude of flows within the system. An example of such a diagram appears in the Yellow Fever exercise on this book's home page. It highlights the flows of infected mosquitoes and infected humans at the peak of a simulated epidemic. Other examples include Verburgh's (1994, 139) diagram of patient flows through the Dutch health care system and Barney's (1974, 37) description of worker flows through an urban system.

Dynamic Equilibrium and Stability

Equilibrium diagrams help us picture the forces that keep a system in dynamic equilibrium. In some cases the variety of forces may be quite complex, and we may be surprised by what we see. Stephen Forbes's (1887) essay from the previous century is illustrative. He selected a lake as a microcosm of life: "A lake forms a little world within itself—a microcosm within which all the elemental forces are at work and the play of life goes on in full." Forbes described the food chain of the black bass, and his description revealed a great diversity of creatures pitted against each other in severe competition. He was struck by the remarkable ability of nature to achieve dunamic equilibrium. "Perhaps no phenomenon of life . . . is more remarkable than the steady balance of organic nature, which holds each species within the limits of a uniform average number, year after year, although each one is always doing its best to break across boundaries on every side."

Figure 5.3. Examples of stable, unstable, and neutral equilibrium.

Let's turn now to the related topic of stability, beginning with the simple illustration in figure 5.3. It shows a marble resting on three different surfaces. The marble is at rest in all three examples, so we would say that the system is in equilibrium. But you know at a glance that these are very different types of equilibria. With the marble at the bottom of the cup, the equilibrium is stable. If you were to deflect the marble from its position, it would return to the original position. The middle example is an unstable equilibrium. A small disturbance is all that is needed to deflect the marble from the equilibrium position. Once disturbed, gravitational forces would take the marble far from the original position. The third example is called neutral equilibrium. If a force is applied to move the marble to the right or left, the marble will simply remain at the new position once the force is removed.

The stability of the equilibria in figure 5.3 are obvious to you because you have spent your whole life becoming familiar with gravitational forces. But the stability properties of environmental systems are not so easy to discern. An equilibrium diagram can show the balance of flows that create a dynamic equilibrium, but it does not teach us whether the equilibrium would be stable.

Testing for Stability

There is a simple test that can help us anticipate the stability properties of a system. Imagine that you have constructed a model, and the simulated system reaches equilibrium. Since the system "found the equilibrium" on its own, your first instinct should tell you that the equilibrium is stable. You can test your instinct with a "stability test" that introduces a disturbance into the system. If the system returns to the original position after the disturbance is removed, you know that the equilibrium is stable. If the disturbance sets loose a chain of events that drives the system away from the original equilibrium, the equilibrium is unstable.

Figure 5.4 shows a simple way to introduce the disturbance. The *stock variable* is any stock in the model that you wish to test. The *regular flow in* and the *regular flow out,* illustrate the flows that are part of your existing model. The new flow is the *disturbance flow,* which is added for the test. You may set the fraction to any amount and the Tyear, or test year, to the year in which the system will have reached the equilibrium.

The following equations, for example, disturb the system by adding 20 percent of the stock in the 10th year of a test simulation:

Fraction = .2
TYear = 10
disturbance_flow = IF((time>TYear) and (time<TYear+1)) then
Stock_Variable*Fraction else 0

To learn whether the equilibrium is stable, simply watch the simulated behavior after the 10th year. After the 10th year, the disturbance flow returns to zero, and the future values of the stock will be governed by the "regular" flows in the model. If they return the stock to the original value, you know the equilibrium is stable. Stability tests are useful to double-check

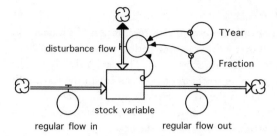

disturbance flow

TYear

Fraction

stock variable

regular flow in

regular flow out

Figure 5.4. Addition of a disturbance flow to permit a stability test.

your understanding of the system. But, as a general rule, you can guess whether the equilibrium is stable. If you notice, for example, that the system seems to find the equilibrium position "on its own," then the equilibrium is probably stable. The Mono Lake and two-bottles examples are illustrative. Each of these systems "found its way" to the equilibrium conditions, so we should expect that they are stable situations.

Exercises

1. **Stability of Mono Lake:**

   Introduce a disturbance in the Mono Lake model to learn if the equilibrium in figure 5.1 is stable. Since the system is approximately in equilibrium by the year 2090, you may set TYear to 2090 to expand the volume of water in the lake by, say, 20 percent. Extend the time of the simulation to allow several decades after 2090 to see the simulated response to the disturbance.

2. **Stability of two bottles:**

   Introduce a disturbance flow in the two-bottles model to learn if the equilibrium in figure 5.2 is stable. Since the system reaches equilibrium after 50 seconds, you might set the TYear (better to call it TSec) to 50. Set the disturbance to remove 40 percent of the fluid from the first bottle.

3. **Missing numbers for Silver Lake:**

   The diagram accompanying this exercise shows an incomplete equilibrium diagram for a model of Silver Lake. The lake is fed by two creeks and drained by Silver Creek. The *net evaporation* represents the evaporation minus precipitation and is based on a *net evaporation rate* of 4 feet/yr. The diagram shows the creek flows into the lake and out of the lake.

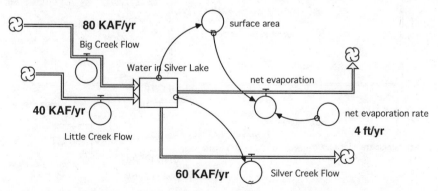

What are the missing value and the units for the *net evaporation*?

What are the missing value and the units for the *surface area*?

5. Missing numbers for carbon flows:

Huggett (1993) describes a model of carbon flows in a tropical forest. His model was implemented in Stella and simulated over a 50-year time period with the *carbon flowing into the system* fixed at 30 GT/year (gigatons per year). The carbon influx is split into four directions, with 20 percent going to the roots, 30 percent to the leaves, 20 percent to the branches, and 30 percent to the stems. For example, the *flow to stems* is 30 percent of 30 GT/year, or 9 GT/year. The transfer rates are all expressed as a fraction/yr. For example, the *humus to charcoal transfer rate* at the bottom of the diagram is 0.01/yr or 1 percent/yr. Working from top to bottom, the diagram accompanying this exercise shows the flows of carbon to litter on the forest floor, to the humus stage, and eventually to charcoal. By the end of the simulation, all stocks reached dynamic equilibrium except for one—the stock of *carbon stored as charcoal*. It continues to grow slowly over time. The six question marks stand for missing entries in this equilibrium diagram. Replace the six question marks with the numerical values and the units. Then describe how the *carbon stored as charcoal* will grow over time. Will the growth be exponential? linear? oscillatory?

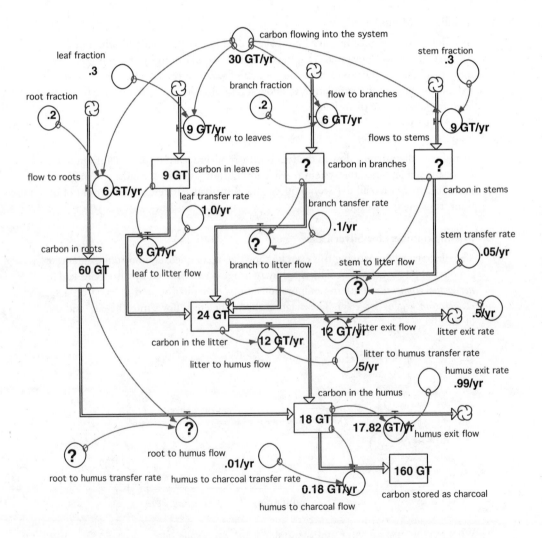

6. **New equilibrium in forest:**

   Suppose we were to simulate Huggett's model with the *carbon flowing into the system* fixed at 60 GT/year. Do you think it would reach dynamic equilibrium (except for the charcoal)? If so, how much carbon would be stored in the litter on the forest floor when the forest reaches equilibrium?

7. **Forest management in equilibrium:**

   The equilibrium below is adapted from Stephen Boyce's (1991) model to simulate the impact of forest harvest policies. The diagram portrays a hypothetical area of 1 million acres with over half the area covered by mature reserves. Boyce focused on the harvest policy, and the diagram shows a *harvest* of 14,280 acres/year in dynamic equilibrium.

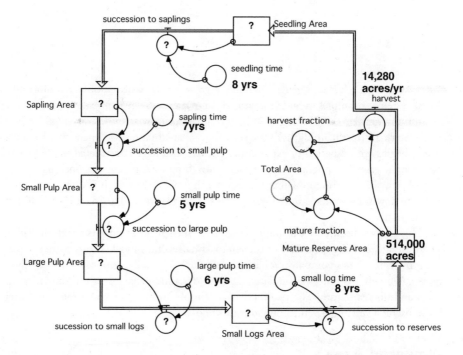

Each of the remaining five flows is governed by the size of the stock divided by the relevant time interval. What are the values (and the units) for each of the flows? Each of the remaining five stocks is governed by the action of the flows. What are the values (and the units) for each of the stocks?

Chapter 6

S-Shaped Growth

S-shaped growth refers to a general pattern of growth that has been observed in a wide variety of systems. Examples include the growth in certain animal populations (Ricklefs 1990), the spread of epidemics (Hastings 1997), and the diffusion of innovations (Bass 1969; Porter 1980; Sterman [forthcoming]). You've seen the s-shaped pattern in chapter 1, so you know that it begins with a period of exponential growth. You have constructed models to explain exponential growth (appendix C), so you know how to simulate the opening phase of s-shaped growth. You also know that no system can grow forever, so it is useful at this stage to simulate how some systems find a way to slow their growth and arrive at a state of dynamic equilibrium.

This chapter begins with a simple example of the spread of flowers across the landscape. Then, to illustrate the generality of the approach, a second model is constructed to simulate the growth in a sales company. You'll see that the two models generate remarkably similar results. We will attribute the similarity in their dynamic behavior to the similarity in their stock and flow structure. The two models are simple and easy to understand, and they will prove useful again and again throughout this book.

Flowered Area

Suppose we wish to simulate the spread of flowers in an area. Let's start with only 10 acres of flowers, but say 1,000 acres of land is considered suitable for the flowers. Figure 6.1 shows a simple model to simulate the change in the flowered area over time. Figure 6.2 gives the equations. A stock is used to keep track of the acres of land occupied by flowers. This seems like a good choice for a stock variable because it will tend to change more slowly than variables like growth and decay. If there were no growth in the area this year, for example, we would still have some area covered by flowers next year because it will take some time before the old flowers decay. The *decay* will be based on a constant decay rate of 20 percent/yr. This makes sense if a newly flowered area will remain occupied with flowers for an average of around 5 years.

Notice that there are two growth rates in figure 6.1. The *actual growth rate* determines the *growth* at the current point in time. The *intrinsic growth rate* is the rate of spread in the flowered area when the flowers occupy only a small fraction of the suitable area. The *intrinsic growth rate* is set at 100 percent/yr. This rate applies when the area is nearly empty, so the flowers do not encounter any space limitations. As the flowers fill the space, the *fraction occu-*

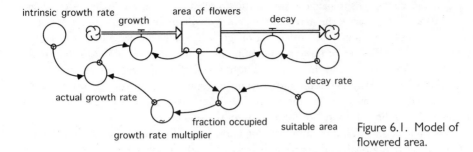

Figure 6.1. Model of flowered area.

```
area_of_flowers(t) = area_of_flowers(t - dt) + (growth - decay) * dt
INIT area_of_flowers = 10
INFLOWS:
growth = area_of_flowers*actual_growth_rate
OUTFLOWS:
decay = area_of_flowers*decay_rate
actual_growth_rate = intrinsic_growth_rate*growth_rate_multiplier
decay_rate = .2
fraction_occupied = area_of_flowers/suitable_area
intrinsic_growth_rate = 1
suitable_area = 1000
growth_rate_multiplier = GRAPH(fraction_occupied)
(0.00, 1.00), (0.2, 0.8), (0.4, 0.6), (0.6, 0.4), (0.8, 0.2), (1.00, 0.00)
```

Figure 6.2. Equations for the flower model.

pied will increase, and the *actual growth rate* will decline. The downward adjustment in the growth rate is achieved with a multiplier.

You've seen a multiplier previously in the Mono Lake chapter, so you would expect the multiplier to take the value of 1.0 at a benchmark position. In this situation, the multiplier is equal to 1.0 when the *fraction occupied* is zero, and the *actual growth rate* will be identical to the *intrinsic growth rate*. As the *fraction occupied* increases, the multiplier falls below 1.0, and the *actual growth rate* is adjusted downward. Let's assume that the downward adjustment follows the linear trend shown in figure 6.3.

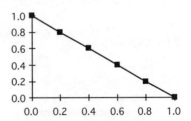

Figure 6.3. The growth rate multiplier as a function of fraction occupied.

Results of the Flower Model

What would you expect this simple model to show over time? At the beginning of the simulation, the flowers fill only 1 percent of the area, so the growth rate will be quite close to 100 percent/yr, the intrinsic rate. You would probably expect the flowered area to grow rapidly, filling up the space. According to figure 6.3, the *growth rate* would be reduced completely to zero if the flowers fill 100 percent of the area. Do you think they will eventually fill the entire area?

Figure 6.4 shows the simulated spread in the flowered area over a 20-year period. There are only 10 acres of flowers at the start, but their area grows rapidly, covering around 500 acres by the 6th year of the simulation. Notice that the growth exceeds the decay by a large margin during this year, so the area of flowers is climbing quite rapidly at this point of the simulation. The growth peaks around this time and begins to decline. But the growth still exceeds decay, so the area of flowers continues to grow until around the 12th year. By this time, the growth has fallen into balance with the decay. The system has reached dynamic equilibrium, with the flowers filling 800 acres, or 80 percent, of the suitable area.

It's useful to check the equilibrium situation at the end of this simulation, as shown in figure 6.5. We see that growth and decay are balanced at 160 acres/yr and that the growth rate and the decay rate are balanced as well. The decay rate is fixed at 20 percent/yr throughout the simulation. The system appears to be growing to a level at which the growth rate will end up at 20 percent/yr, exactly the value needed for growth and decay to be in balance. You might describe the system as having found equilibrium "on its own." When this happens, our intuition tells us that the equilibrium is stable.

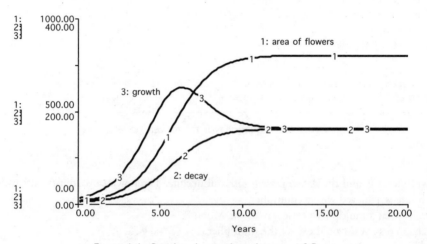

Figure 6.4. Simulated growth in the area of flowers.

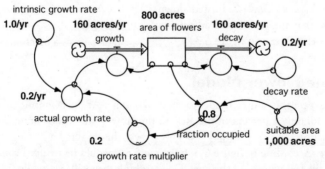

Figure 6.5. Equilibrium diagram from the end of the simulation.

Variations in the Density-Dependent Relationship

The *growth rate multiplier* in figure 6.5 is an example of a density-dependent relationship. It moves from 1 to 0 as the density of the flowers increases from 0 to 100 percent of the area. The linear relationship was selected for mathematical simplicity, but there is no need to limit ourselves to the linear relationship. For example, we could simulate the flower growth using all three relationships in figure 6.6. If the flowers did not "feel the effect" of limited space until they covered 50 percent of the area, for example, we could use the upper curve. If the reduction in growth was quite pronounced as soon as the flowers filled 20 percent of the space, the lower curve would be more suitable. All three curves adopt the same starting and ending points. This means that the same intrinsic growth rate applies with only a few flowers and that no growth is possible when they occupy 100 percent of the area.

The variations in the density-dependent relationship lead to the variations in the simulated spread of flowers shown in figure 6.7. This chart compares the flowered area in simulations with each of the three assumptions for the growth multiplier. The three simulations are quite similar for the first three years because the growth is dominated by the 100 percent/yr intrinsic growth rate. The first simulation (with the upper curve) shows that the flowers would rapidly reach an equilibrium of 900 acres. The second simulation is the same as the previous example; the flowers grow to cover 800 acres. The third simulation shows the growth slowing down considerably by the 5th year, and the flowers reach dynamic equilibrium with only 400 acres occupied. In all three cases, the flowered area seems to find the equilibrium situation in which the growth rate is 20 percent/yr, exactly the amount needed to counter the rate of decay.

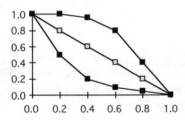

Figure 6.6. Three assumptions on the change in the growth rate multiplier as a function of fraction occupied.

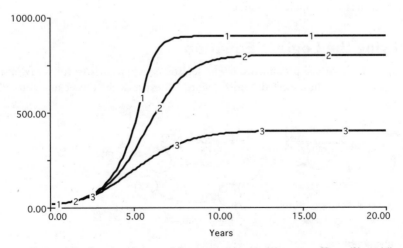

Years

Figure 6.7. Simulated area of flowers with the (1) upper curve, (2) middle curve, and (3) lower curve from the previous figure.

The Logistic Equation

The middle trajectory in figure 6.7 is a special case that could have been derived using differential equations. Suppose we let $A(t)$ stand for the area of flowers as a function of time. To match the explanation found in standard texts (Odum 1971, 184; Hastings 1997, 84), we would let K stand for the maximum possible area covered by flowers and r for growth rate of flowers when A is zero. K is sometimes called the "carrying capacity," but the term can be misleading. In this example, K would be set to the 800 acres that is the maximum value that the flowered area would reach over time. The r stands for the net increase rate that would apply when A is at zero. In this example, r would be 100 percent/yr minus 20 percent/yr, or 80 percent/yr. With these definitions, we could write the following differential equation:

$$dA(t)/dt = r * A(t) * M(t)$$

where M is the "multiplier," $M = (K - A)/K$.

Notice that M is a linear function of A and that M has the correct extreme values. We could now rewrite the differential equation:

$$dA/dt = r * A * (K - A)/K$$

which you can solve using the trial-and-error approach explained in chapter 3, or you might turn to Hastings (1997, 85) to learn that the solution is

$$A(t) = \frac{A_0 e^{rt}}{1 + A_0(e^{rt} - 1)/K}$$

This equation is sometimes called the logistic equation, and you may have read about it if you've studied ecology. Ricklefs (1990, 329) explains that the logistic equation was the "first equation in ecology to generate research that would provide the data to test a mathematical model." He explains work on the growth of humans, yeast, fruit flies, water fleas, and flour beetles in which different investigators attempted to match observed data with the logistic equation. He concluded, "By and large, they were successful, and the logistic equation took a permanent place in population biology."

Verifying the Logistic Equation

Because of the historical prominence of the logistic equation, it is worth verifying that the flower model yields the expected results. Figure 6.8 expands the flower model to allow the

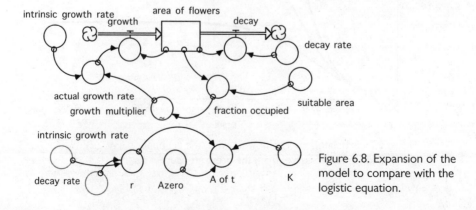

Figure 6.8. Expansion of the model to compare with the logistic equation.

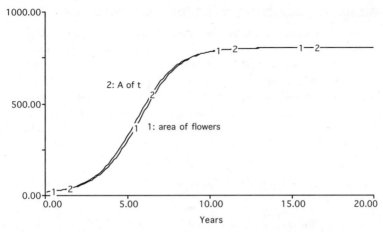

Figure 6.9. Simulated area of flowers compared to the logistic equation.

logistic equation to be calculated over time. The model assumes that *Azero* is 10, that *K* is 800, and that *r* is the difference between the *intrinsic growth rate* and the *decay rate.*

The comparison of *Aoft* in figure 6.9 with the simulated *area of flowers* verifies that the two approaches give the same pattern of growth over time. If you look closely, however, you will notice that *Aoft* is slightly higher than numerical simulation results during the years of rapid growth. This small difference arises from the numerical step size. The step size (DT) is intentionally set at 0.25 year so that there would be small differences visible in figure 6.9. You may verify that these differences will disappear if the simulation is repeated with a smaller step size.

Limitations of the Logistic Equation

The logistic equation is explained because you are likely to encounter it in your courses on ecology and population biology. But you should be aware of three limitations in applying this equation:

1. First, the logistic equation is simply one example of a possible pattern of s-shaped growth. In this book, the term s-shaped growth refers to any pattern of growth that starts out looking like exponential growth and ends up with a gradual approach to equilibrium.

2. Next, you should not necessarily expect the forces that slow the growth of natural systems to apply themselves in a linear manner. Odum (1971, 185) cautions us that "the simple situation in which environmental resistance increases linearly with density seems to hold for populations of organisms that have very simple life histories, as for example, yeast growing in a limited space."

3. A third problem is ambiguity in the carrying capacity. When thinking of the flower growth example, your first instinct was probably to set *K* to 1,000 acres. For the logistic equation to work properly, however, *K* must be set to 800 acres, the upper asymptote in figure 6.4. At this point, you might be asking yourself how one knows in advance that the flowered area will stop growing at 800 acres. This unanswered question is the third and final obstacle to applying the logistic equation. Some scientists try to work around this obstacle by drawing several logistic curves with different values of *K*. They then select the value of *K* that positions the curve for the best possible fit to the time series data that is currently available. This "curve fitting" approach is not likely to teach us much about the nature of s-shaped growth (Odum 1971, 185).

Suggestions for Studying S-Shaped Growth

The logistic model has proven useful largely because it provided a convenient mathematical expression to allow scientists to report their empirical evaluations of population systems during an era prior to the use of computer simulation techniques. As you take advantage of computer simulation to study systems that exhibit s-shaped growth, you should move beyond the logistic equation. You will make more progress if you follow the approach illustrated with the flower example. Use the regular stock-and-flow building blocks of system dynamics to represent the structure of the system; use numerical simulation to learn the dynamic behavior over time; and use equilibrium diagrams to verify that the equilibrium conditions make sense.

S-Shaped Growth in a Company

These suggestions apply to any system that is likely to exhibit s-shaped growth, not just to ecological systems. To illustrate the generality of the approach, let's turn to an example of a growing company. Figure 6.10 shows a model to simulate the growth in the sales force of a company selling widgets (a hypothetical product). The initial sales force is 50 people, and it is subject to a 20 percent annual *exit rate*. The company recruits new people based on the *budgeted size of the sales force*. The department budget is 50 percent of the company's annual revenues from the sale of widgets.

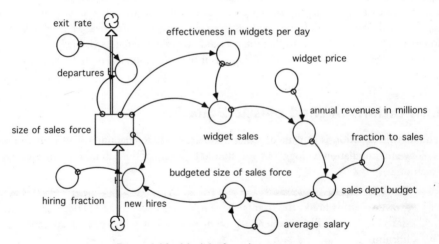

Figure 6.10. Model of a sales company.

Widget sales depend on the number of salespeople and their individual effectiveness. Let's assume that each salesperson can sell 2 widgets/day if they have the market area to themselves. But if there are too many salespeople working the same market, individual effectiveness is expected to decline. The decline may arise from the ratio of salespeople to potential customers, or it might arise from problems back at the company. In our hypothetical example, the effectiveness of each salesperson will fall below 2 widgets/day once the sales force climbs above 400 people. If there are 1,200 people in the sales force, their individual effectiveness will fall to only 0.4 widgets/day.

The flow diagram in figure 6.10 is more complicated than the flower diagram because the growth of the sales force is not controlled by a simple "growth rate." Rather, the growth rate is implicit in the collection of assumptions about the sales force. It is useful to work through the numbers to find the implicit growth rate that would apply at the start of the simulation:

For each salesperson selling 2 widgets/day at $100/widget for 365 days/yr, the company would collect $73,000 in annual revenues. Half of this goes to the sales department, so one person's contribution to the department budget would be $36,500. The *average salary* is $25,000, so the department could budget for 1.46 sales people based on the earnings from each existing person. Since the *hiring fraction* strives to meet the budgeted workforce target within 1 year, the initial growth rate would to be 46 percent/year. So the workforce should grow rapidly during the early years of the simulation.

The equations for the sales company model are listed in figure 6.11, and the simulation

```
size_of_sales_force(t) = size_of_sales_force(t - dt) + (new_hires - departures) * dt
INIT size_of_sales_force = 50
INFLOWS:
new_hires = hiring_fraction*(budgeted_size_of_sales_force-size_of_sales_force)
OUTFLOWS:
departures = size_of_sales_force*exit_rate
annual_revenues_in_millions = widget_sales*widget_price/1000000
average_salary = 25000
budgeted_size_of_sales_force = sales_dept_budget*1000000/average_salary
exit_rate = .2
fraction_to_sales = .5
hiring_fraction = 1
sales_dept_budget = fraction_to_sales*annual_revenues_in_millions
widget_price = 100
widget_sales = size_of_sales_force*effectiveness_in_widgets_per_day*365
effectiveness_in_widgets_per_day = GRAPH(size_of_sales_force)
(0.00, 2.00), (200, 2.00), (400, 2.00), (600, 1.80), (800, 1.60), (1000, 0.8), (1200, 0.4)
```

Figure 6.11. Equations for the sales company model.

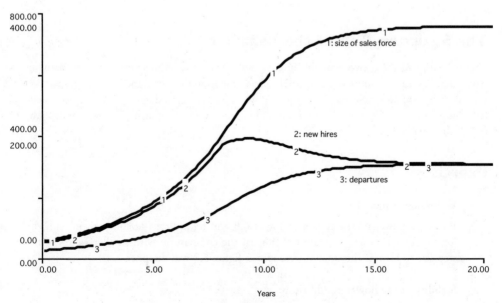

Figure 6.12. Simulated growth in the sales force.

results are reported in figure 6.12. The familiar pattern of s-shaped growth appears when this company is simulated over a 20-year period. The sales force grows from 50 persons to over 400 persons by the 8th year of the simulation. New hires are well above departures in this year, so the sales force is growing quite rapidly. But new hires peak around this year and begin to decline. The decline arises from the inability of the sales force to maintain the 2 widgets/day of sales achieved in previous years. Lower individual sales means that revenues do not grow as quickly. The department budget does not grow as quickly, and the company must slow the flow of new hires. Figure 6.12 shows that the flow of new hires into the company will decline after the 8th year. New hires fall gradually into equilibrium with departures around the 16th year of the simulation. The company is now in dynamic equilibrium with a sales force of just over 750 people.

Similarity of the Growth Patterns

At first glance, growth in a company may strike you as entirely different from growth in a field of flowers. But the simulations show that the two systems exhibit essentially the same dynamic behavior. Both systems begin the simulation growing rapidly. The growth is made possible by a high flower growth rate and by a high financial return to each salesperson's efforts, respectively. Both systems face limits, so they cannot grow forever. Both systems show a gradual decline in growth as they "fill" the space available. And both systems eventually "find" the size at which the dynamic forces are in balance. In both cases, the system appears to find the equilibrium "on its own." (We didn't insert explicit targets for the flowers to grow to cover 800 acres or for the sales force to grow to 750 people.) The s-shaped growth patterns are also similar in that:

- Both the flowers and the sales force grow to a value that is sustainable year after year after year. In other words, both of these systems are simulated to avoid the "overshoot pattern." You'll read about the overshoot in chapter 16.
- Both the flowers and the sales force find their way to the equilibrium value in a gradual manner. In other words, both of these systems are simulated to avoid oscillations above and below the eventual equilibrium position. You'll read about oscillatory tendencies in chapter 17.

The Structure Causes the Behavior

The similarity of these two growth patterns arises from the similarity in their underlying structures. You can see some of the similarity by comparing the stock-and-flow diagrams. But the similarity will become even more apparent when we draw new diagrams to reveal the feedback loop structure. The new diagrams are called causal loop diagrams, and they are the subject of the next chapter.

Exercises

1. **Verify flower model:**

    Build the flower model shown in figure 6.8 and reproduce the comparison with the logistic model shown in figure 6.9. Repeat the comparison with smaller values of the step size to learn if the small differences in figure 6.9 will disappear.

2. **Stability of the flower equilibrium:**

    Introduce a disturbance to remove 20 percent of the flowers in the 15th year of the sim-

ulation. Run the model over a 30-year time period and turn in a graph similar to figure 6.4 to show whether the equilibrium is stable.

3. **Importance of the initial conditions:**

    Conduct a sensitivity test of the flower model with the starting value of the stock set to
    5, 10, 15, and 20 acres. Turn in a comparative time plot of the acres of flowers in the
    four simulations to document your results. Is the initial value of the stock important to
    our understanding of the eventual size of the flowered area?

4. **Verify and test the sales force model:**

    Build the sales force model from figure 6.10 and verify that it behaves as shown in
    figure 6.12. Then introduce a disturbance in the 15th year of the simulation in which
    an additional 40 percent of the sales force departs abruptly. Run the model over 30
    years and turn in a graph similar to figure 6.12 to show whether the equilibrium is
    stable.

5. **Build a bigger company:**

    Use the sales force model from the previous exercise to learn if you can build a bigger
    company by devoting a larger fraction of company revenues to the sales department
    budget. Conduct a sensitivity test with the fraction of revenues allocated to the sales
    department set at 45, 50, and 55 percent. Turn in a time graph showing the company's
    total revenues from each of the three simulations.

6. **Matching structure and behavior:**

    Imagine that you are presented with the four diagrams accompanying this exercise. You
    are told that you can simulate any of the fundamental dynamic patterns of exponential
    growth, exponential decay, and s-shaped growth. You simply select the appropriate

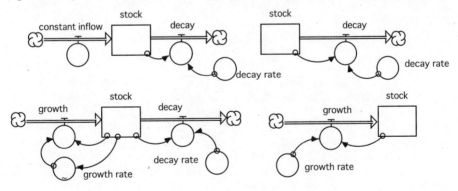

    structure and set the parameters to represent the rates of growth or decay in your par-
    ticular system.

    Exponential decay : Which of these structures would you select if you were asked to sim-
    ulate a system that decays to zero?

    Exponential growth: Which would you select to simulate a system that is expected to
    grow exponentially over time?

    S-shaped growth : Which would you select to simulate a system that is expected to show
    s-shaped growth?

Approach equilibrium: Which would you select if you were asked to simulate a system that decays toward an equilibrium value that is different than zero (e.g., Mono Lake)?

Further Readings

- The sales model in this chapter is similar to the "market growth model" described by Forrester (1975). He demonstrates that a company with tremendous potential can see its growth stunted by poor delivery delays. Peter Senge (1990) tells the story of "WonderTech," a company that has a virtual lock on its market niche but that creates its own market limitations by allowing long delivery delays to persist over time. You may learn more about the market growth model from this book's home page. It includes an interactive version of Forrester's model along with a collection of modeling exercises.
- Sterman (forthcoming) provides a detailed account of how system dynamics may be used to understand s-shaped growth in a variety of systems from the fields of business and public health.

Chapter 7

Causal Loop Diagrams

System dynamics helps us to analyze complex systems with special emphasis on the role of information feedback. This chapter describes causal loop diagrams, a technique to portray the information feedback at work in a system. The word *causal* refers to cause-and-effect relationships. The word *loop* refers to a closed chain of cause and effect. Let's begin with some simple examples. Then we'll discuss guidelines for drawing the diagrams.

Examples

Two flow diagrams from chapter 2 are shown in figure 7.1. They portray the accumulation of money in a bank balance stock and the accumulation of people in a human population stock. The causal loop diagrams are shown immediately below each flow diagram. Think of the new diagrams as simply "word-and-arrow" diagrams. The words represent the variables in the system; the arrows represent causal connections. The arrows are drawn in a circular manner to draw our eye to the closed chain of cause and effect.

The words in a word-and-arrow diagram represent any variable in the system. Regardless of whether the variable is a stock, a flow, or a converter, it will appear in the causal loop diagram by name only. The arrows stand for the causal connections between the variables. For example, the arrow from *interest added* to the *bank balance* stands for the fact that adding interest builds the balance in the bank account. This arrow is labeled with a + at the tip of the arrow to designate positive polarity. The arrow from the bank balance to the interest added stands for the fact that a higher balance causes more interest to be added in the future. This arrow is also labeled with a + at the tip of the arrow. The important thing to observe is the closed chain of cause and effect—a larger bank balance leads to higher interest, and higher interest leads to a higher bank balance. This is an example of positive feedback. We label positive feedback loops with a (+) in the middle of the loop. The population diagram is similar. It shows a closed chain of cause and effect in which a higher population leads to more births, and more births lead to still higher population in the future.

Figure 7.2 shows another example from chapter 2. The flow diagram shows a population stock that is fed by the flow of births and drained by the flow of deaths. The causal loop diagram shows two feedback loops. The loop on the left is the positive feedback loop shown previously. The loop on the right shows the causal links between *deaths* and *population* and population and deaths. The arrow from deaths to the population is labeled with a − to stand for negative polarity. This means the deaths will reduce the size of the population. The arrow from the population to the deaths is a positive arrow. It stands for the fact that a larger pop-

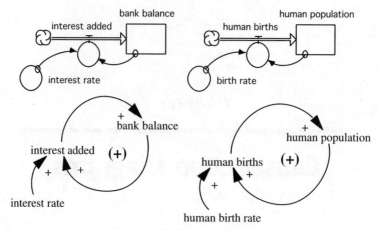

Figure 7.1. Flow diagrams along with the corresponding causal loop diagrams.

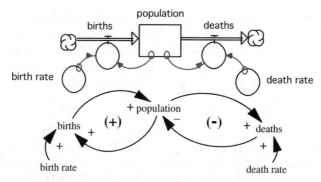

Figure 7.2. Flow diagram and corresponding causal loop diagram.

ulation will tend to have a greater number of deaths (given a fixed value of the death rate). The closed chain of cause and effect is labeled with a (–) to stand for negative feedback.

As a third example, consider your home heating system. It probably uses thermostat control to maintain the indoor temperature at a comfortable level. You haven't seen a stock-and-flow diagram of this system, but you will appreciate the causal relationships shown in figure 7.3. The arrow from energy content to temperature is a positive arrow because these variables change in the same direction. (If energy content increases, the temperature increases. If energy content declines, the temperature declines.) Moving around the loop to the right, the next arrow connects the temperature to the heat loss. This arrow stands for the fact that a higher indoor temperature causes greater heat loss through the walls and windows of the house. The next arrow connects heat loss to the energy content. This is labeled as negative because the heat loss will reduce the BTUs of energy stored in the house. The closed chain of cause-and-effect relationships forms a negative feedback loop. If left to act on its own, this loop will work to remove the energy from the house until the indoor temperature falls into balance with the outdoor temperature.

Now, let's look at the loop on the left. The heat added to the room by the furnace over the course of an hour depends on the capacity of the furnace and the fraction of time that the furnace is operating. The operation is controlled by the temperature of the room at the location of the thermostat. When the inside temperature goes up, the thermostat turns the furnace off. In other words, a higher inside temperature means less heat production from the fur-

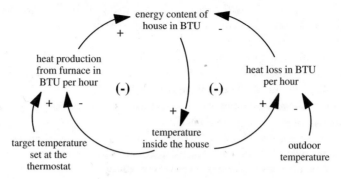

Figure 7.3. Feedback loops in a home heating system.

nace. The furnace loop is a negative feedback loop that strives to move the inside temperature close to the target temperature.

Now, what about the combination of the two loops? You may think of your home heating system as two, coupled negative feedback loops that are striving to reach different goals. If the house is equipped with a large furnace capable of delivering more BTUs per hour than are lost on a cold day, the heat production loop will dominate the system. It will succeed in driving the indoor temperature to the target. If the furnace is inadequate to the task, the heat loss loop will dominate, and the indoor temperature will fall over time.

Guidelines

The arrows in causal loop diagrams are labeled + or – depending on whether the causal influence is positive or negative. We use the + to represent a cause-and-effect relationship in which the two variables change in the same direction. In figure 7.4, for example, the arrow can mean that an increase in A causes an increase in B. It could also mean that a decrease in A causes a decrease in B. This is the meaning of the + arrow connecting the birth rate and the births in figure 7.2, for example. A higher birth rate means higher births; a lower birth rate means lower births. The two variables change in the same direction.

Figure 7.4. Causal arrow with positive polarity.

A positive arrow can also stand for the causal link between a flow and the stock that accumulates the inflow. In figure 7.1, for example, the positive arrow from interest added to bank balance stands for a flow into the stock. The positive arrow from births to population stands for a flow into the stock. In both cases, the flow tends to build the value of the stock over time.

We mark the tip of the arrow with a – when the two variables change in opposite directions. In figure 7.5, for example, the arrow could mean that an increase in *X* causes a decrease in *Y* or that a decrease in *X* causes an increase in *Y.* This is the meaning of the – arrow connecting the outdoor temperature and the heat loss in figure 7.3. A higher outdoor temperature means less heat loss; a lower outdoor temperature means higher heat loss. The two variables change in the opposite directions. A negative arrow can also stand for the causal link between a flow and the stock that is drained by the flow. In figure 7.2, the negative arrow from deaths to population stands for a flow that drains the stock.

Figure 7.5 Causal arrow with negative polarity.

When assigning the + or – to each arrow, focus your attention on one causal connection at a time. Try to imagine a situation where every other variable is held constant; only the variable under consideration is allowed to vary up or down. Suppose, for example, we are consid-

ering whether to assign a + or – to the arrow linking *C* to *X* in figure 7.6. We should consider
the impact of *C* on *X* if the values of *A* and *B* are held constant, *ceteris paribus* ("other things
being equal").

It's sometimes difficult to force ourselves to hold other
variables constant because we immediately see the consequences of a change in our mind's eye. Consider what goes
through our mind when labeling the arrow from target temperature to heat production in figure 7.3. For purposes of
labeling this arrow, we should think of the temperature
inside the house as held constant. Then we ask if an increase
in the target temperature would cause an increase in the heat
production. Since it does, we label that arrow with a +.

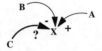

Figure 7.6. Hold A and B
constant in your mind when
thinking about the polarity of
the arrow linking C to X.

But we would immediately recognize
that higher heat production leads to more energy content and a higher temperature inside the
house. This may seem like a contradiction—weren't we supposed to hold the inside temperature constant? Don't let this apparent contradiction bother you. We are merely holding variables constant for purposes of assigning a label to a diagram. The labels are a communication
device to help us identify the feedback in the system. The actual simulation of whether temperatures are likely to go up or go down is reserved for the computer model.

Positive and Negative Feedback

The examples of positive feedback in figure 7.1 are similar. The loops describe a situation
where the system reinvests in itself to make itself grow over time. This is the most common
form of positive feedback. It tends to make the system grow bigger and bigger over time. You
can identify a loop as positive if it appears to perform the same function as the loops in figure 7.1. If a loop acts to reinvest in the system and make it grow, it's probably positive feedback. In some cases, the function of the loop will not be obvious. When that happens, you
can simply count the number of negative arrows around the loop. If there are no negative
arrows, it's a positive feedback loop. If you count two, four, six, or any even number of negative arrows, it's positive feedback.

The feedback loop involving deaths in figure 7.2 is typical of negative loops that appear
in many systems. Their function seems to be to wear down the system over time. We may see
a population declining due to deaths, a workforce declining due to retirements, a lake shrinking due to evaporation, or assets falling because of depreciation. If you encounter a loop that
appears to be wearing down a system over time, it's probably a negative feedback loop. There
will be cases where you won't be able to discern the function of the loop. When this happens,
you can simply count the number of negative signs around the loop. If you count an odd
number of negative signs, it's a negative feedback loop.

Now turn to the negative feedback loops in the home heating system. They seem to play
a somewhat different role in the system. Their purpose is to control the energy content of the
room so that the temperature approaches a goal. The goal of the outdoor loop is to equilibrate the indoor and outdoor temperatures. The goal of the furnace loop is to bring the
indoor temperature into agreement with the thermostat target. When you encounter a loop
that appears to be striving for a goal, it's probably negative feedback. As before, you can check
your intuition by counting the number of negative signs around the loop.

Examples of Coupled Loops

You've seen two examples of loops working in tandem with one another. The two loops in figure 7.2 show the interplay of births and deaths working through population as a common

variable. Figure 7.3 shows the interplay of heat production and heat loss. This coupling of loops is quite common, so it is worth looking at additional examples.

Figure 7.7 shows two loops controlling the interplay of supply and demand in a market for automobiles. Car production by automobile manufacturers builds the inventory of cars at the dealers. A higher inventory leads to a lower market price for cars, and lower market prices cause less car production in the future. There is only one negative arrow in the production loop on the left side of figure 7.7, so we know that this is negative feedback. This loop characterizes the "supply response" in a market for cars.

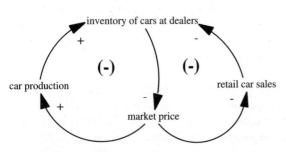

Figure 7.7. Coupled loops in a market for cars.

The loop on the right side of figure 7.7 characterizes the "demand response." If the price were to increase, the sale of cars at retail would tend to fall (all else being equal). Retail car sales drain the inventory of cars held in stock at the dealership. And a decline in the inventory will cause the dealers to raise their prices in the future. There are three negative arrows in the demand loop, so we know that it is negative feedback.

The two-bottles exercise from appendix C provides another example of two loops working in tandem. Recall that the first bottle receives a constant inflow of 5 cc/second (as shown previously in figure 5.2). This builds the volume of water in the first bottle until it reaches the overflow position. A higher volume means a higher height, and a higher height means greater overflow. The overflow from the first bottle drains the first bottle and adds to the second bottle. In figure 7.8 we have two loops that are connected by the overflow from the first bottle. The loops do not have an explicit goal, but the implicit goal seems to be to bring the heights of the fluid to the overflow position in each bottle.

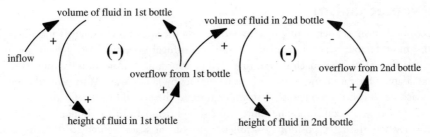

Figure 7.8. Causal loop diagram of the two-bottles system.

Negative Loops Act to Negate Outside Disturbances

Several of the examples are revealing a basic property of negative loops—they appear to act over time to negate the impact of outside disturbances. In the home heating system, for example, the furnace loop acts to negate the impact of changes in outdoor temperature. If it gets colder outside, there is more heat loss and a drop in the indoor temperature. But the furnace then comes on more frequently, and indoor temperature is returned to the target value. In the automobile market, both the production and the sales loops act to negate outside disturbances. Let suppose, for example, that a hail storm destroys 20 percent of the cars held in inventory. The market price would increase; higher prices would spur more production; and higher production would build inventory. Higher prices will also reduce demand, which will also help to build inventory. Once again, the negative loops lead to a closed chain of cause and effect that feeds back to negate the impact of the original disturbance.

The "hail storm" illustrates a useful way to think about the polarity of a loop. Pick any variable in the loop that is suitable for a simple "thought experiment." Invent a disturbance (like the hail storm) and ask yourself if the closed chain of cause and effect will end up negating the impact of the disturbance. If it does, you have negative feedback. Let's try such an experiment with the two-bottles system. Suppose we were to spill some coffee into the first bottle. This would increase the height of the fluid in the first bottle, causing greater overflow. The overflow would then exceed the inflow, so the volume of fluid in the first bottle would be reduced over time. The effect of the first loop in figure 7.8 is to negate the impact of the outside disturbance.

Positive feedback loops have the opposite effect. They lead to changes over time that amplify the impact of the disturbance. Suppose, as an example, the bank balance in figure 7.1 receives an extra deposit of $10,000. This adds to the balance, which means that more interest is earned in the future. When the higher interest is added to the bank balance, the $10,000 becomes even larger over time. The effect of positive feedback is to magnify or reinforce the impact of an outside disturbance.

By this point, you can appreciate that the terms *positive* and *negative* do not carry any judgmental meaning. Positive loops are not called positive because they deliver good results. Negative loops are not expected to deliver poor results. The terms originate from the field of control engineering, where the term *positive feedback* might refer to runaway growth (e.g., a poorly designed microphone and loud speaker system that creates an ear-shattering sound). Control engineers use the term *negative feedback* when designing devices to achieve stable control of electromechanical systems. These devices are sometimes called servomechanisms. The early history of system dynamics is linked with control engineering (Richardson 1991), so it is instructive to consider an example of a servomechanism.

Servomechanism

A servomechanism is a self-acting machine to control the operation of a larger machine. One of the most famous servomechanisms is the "centrifugal governor" or "flyball governor" shown in figure 7.9. This machine was first used in flour mills to control millstone operation. It was adapted for automatic control of steam engines by James Watt. Watt wanted a self-acting machine to control the speed of steam engines so they would be a safer part of a larger machine such as a steamship. The illustration shows steam from the boiler approaching a chamber where the valve position controls the amount of steam vented to the atmosphere. Most of the steam is allowed to reach the turbine, which will spin the shaft and deliver power to the ship. But the same shaft is connected to the governor. Now, imagine what would happen if the steam engine were running "too hot." Too much steam would flow toward the chamber and some of it would reach the shaft, spinning it more rapidly. But the governor would also spin more rapidly, and the centrifugal force would drive the flyballs farther out and lift the valve in the chamber. The rising valve would vent more steam to the atmosphere, and less steam would reach the shaft. The rotation speed of the shaft that drives the ship is thereby controlled by the design of the governor as well as the steam that happens to be produced at the boiler.

The centrifugal governor operates through the negative feedback loop shown in figure 7.10. Steam generation is an input to the system, but only a fraction of the steam is allowed

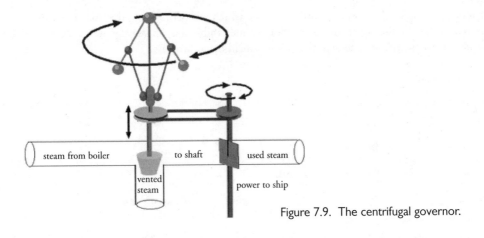

Figure 7.9. The centrifugal governor.

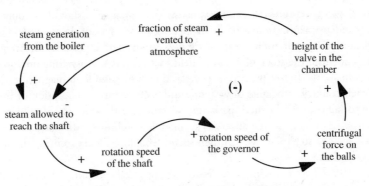

Figure 7.10. Negative feedback in the centrifugal governor.

to reach the shaft. This fraction is controlled by the height of the valve in the chamber. Let's work our way around the loop with a thought experiment in which the shaft is spinning too slowly. A low speed means lower speed of the governor, less centrifugal force on the balls, and a lower height of the valve in the chamber. A lower height lowers the fraction of steam vented to the atmosphere. This means that more steam will reach the shaft, and more steam to the shaft will correct for our original thought that the shaft was spinning too slowly.

Look for the Big Picture

Feedback ideas may be new to you, so you may not immediately recognize the feedback loops that control the systems around us. You will come to see the loops more readily if you ask yourself about the "bigger picture." To illustrate, let's consider the causal loop diagram in figure 7.11. It shows a stock of weapons held by country A. This variable might represent the dollar value of the nation's stockpile of conventional and nuclear weapons. The stockpile held by country B is shown as an input to the system. Country A builds its stockpile by spending federal dollars to acquire new weapons. The positive arrow from spending to the stockpile represents the flow of weapons into the stockpile. As the stockpile grows higher over time, it will be possible for country A to reduce its spending. The negative arrow from the stockpile to the spending represents the reduction in spending that may occur when the nation reaches its goal. (We might assume that country A's goal is to have the same number of weapons as country B.) Figure 7.11 is a goal-oriented loop, which will act to bring the stock of weapons into balance with the target. Any growth or decline exhibited by this system will be attributed primarily to growth or decline in the weapons held by country B.

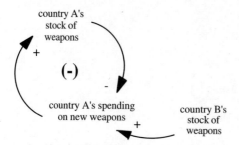

Figure 7.11. Weapons-spending loop.

   The single loop in figure 7.11 is one part of a bigger picture. One way to open our eyes to the bigger picture is to think of the inputs to the system. We should ask ourselves if the inputs vary independently from what is happening in our system. In the weapons example, we would think about variations in the stock of weapons held by country B. Are those variations independent of the stock of weapons held by country A? Answering questions like this will lead us to see the bigger picture, as portrayed in the causal loop diagram in figure 7.12. It shows each country's stockpile of weapons and each country's perception of the stockpile held by the other country. Desired "parity ratios" represent the thinking of military experts in each country. Knowledge of the adversary's stockpile combined with our parity goal gives a target value for our stockpile. We can then spend federal resources to bring the stockpile up to the target value.

   We now have a system with three feedback loops. Each country's weapons spending is directly governed by a goal-oriented, negative feedback loop. Thinking narrowly, each coun-

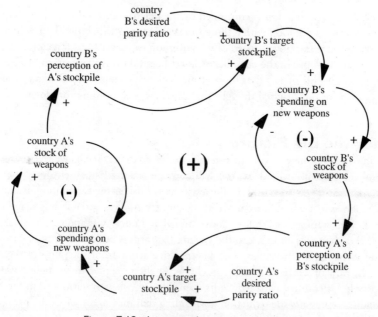

Figure 7.12. Loops in the arms race system.

try might reason that it should be able to reach its goal. But when we think more broadly about the system, we see that a major positive feedback loop could create runaway growth in the system. Now, at this point, you are probably already thinking of many additional factors that influence weapons spending and possibly the retirement of weapons. Perhaps the additional considerations create even more of a destabilizing situation. Or perhaps they act to stabilize or limit the extent of an arms race. As you think more broadly about this system, you will see the additional feedback loops that influence its dynamic behavior.

The arms race loop is an example of a "vicious circle," in which a situation gets progressively worse and worse over time. Vicious circles will appear from time to time in complex systems, but they are not as common as the more familiar examples of positive feedback that involve "reinvestment" in the system (like the population growth and bank balance growth examples). If you do encounter a vicious circle in a system, the causal loop diagram should reveal a positive feedback loop.

Creating Causal Loop Diagrams from Flow Diagrams

This chapter began with examples of flow diagrams before we looked at the causal loop diagram. You will learn later, in chapter 15, that it is useful to build the flow diagram prior to drawing the causal loop diagram. This a pragmatic suggestion based on observing that most people "see" the stocks and flows more easily than they "see" the loops. They find it easier to build the flow diagram first. Now, suppose we have a good flow diagram, and we wish to draw the causal loop diagram. How can we make sure we find all the loops? And how can we avoid drawing a diagram that ends up looking like a plate of spaghetti?

When drawing the loop diagrams, our best staring point is the same as when we first constructed the stock-and-flow diagrams:

start with the stocks!

The best way to begin is to write down the names of the stocks and leave room for the other variables to appear later. Then add the arrows to represent each flow. Inflows are labeled with a +. Outflows are labeled with a −. Then work your way from one flow to another, adding the necessary arrows to explain each flow. By the time you're done, you will have found every loop in the model.

Let's try this approach with the population model from the exercises at the end of chapter 2. If you did the exercises correctly, you would arrive at the flow diagram shown in figure 7.13. Figure 7.14 illustrates the first step toward a causal loop diagram. It shows the three stocks and the four flows. The arrows represent the impact of each flow on the stocks.

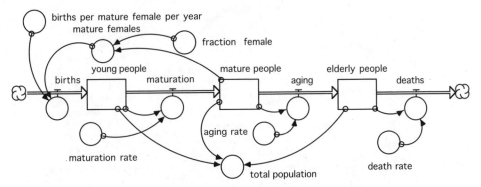

Figure 7.13. Flow diagram of a population model.

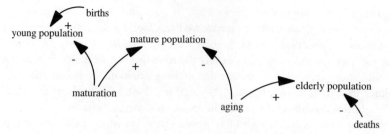

Figure 7.14. The first causal diagram of the population model: begin with the stocks and flows.

At this stage, you won't see a single feedback loop in the diagram. They appear later when we add the arrows to explain each of the flows.

Figure 7.15 shows how the diagram would appear after we explain the deaths, aging, and maturation flows. Deaths is shown to depend on the size of the elderly population and the death rate. Adding these arrows reveals a negative feedback loop in the lower right corner of the diagram. The next flow is aging. Aging is shown to depend on the size of the mature population and the aging rate. Adding these arrows reveals a second negative loop in the middle of the diagram. The maturation flow depends on the young population and the maturation rate. Adding these arrows closes the third negative loop in the figure. At this point, you'll notice a trend developing—each of the loops works its way through one of the stocks.

Figure 7.16 completes the causal loop diagram by explaining births, the final flow in the model. Births depend on the number of mature females and the births per mature female per year. The mature females depend on the size of the mature population and the fraction of the population that is female. Adding these arrows allows us to see the positive feedback loop in the system. This loop involves two of the stocks—the stock of young people and the stock of mature people.

Figure 7.16 is sufficient to show the feedback loops in the system. The one positive loop gives the system the power to grow. The three negative loops act to "wear out" the system over time. The only variable from the original flow diagram that does not appear in the final dia-

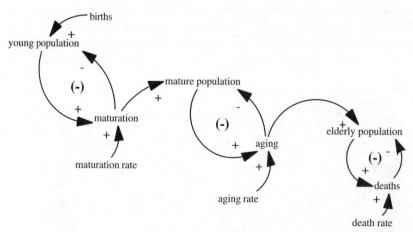

Figure 7.15. Explaining deaths, aging, and maturation adds three negative feedback loops.

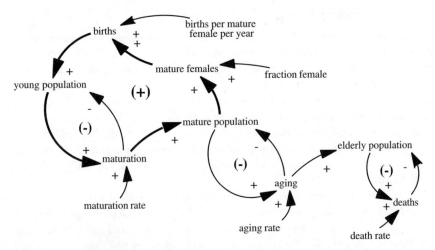

Figure 7.16. Expanding the diagram to explain births reveals the positive feedback loop in the system.

gram is the total population. If you pencil in the total population, you will discover that its inclusion adds no new feedback to the system. At this point, you may choose to include the total population or leave it out, depending on the purpose of the diagram. If your goal is to show each and every variable, go ahead and add the extra arrows. More commonly, however, our goal is to discover the feedback loop structure. In this case, it would be better to leave out the extra arrows to avoid cluttering up the diagram.

Software Support for Loop Identification

You can also turn to the software to support your investigation of the feedback loops once you've constructed the stock-and-flow diagram. Appendix E shows an example with Vensim. You simply click on Vensim's "loops tool," and the software responds with a listing of all the loops along with the names of the variables appearing in the loop.

The Stella loops tool is also quite convenient. Simply click on the loops tool, and the software responds by opening a dialog box to ask you which of the stock variables are of interest. You select a stock, and Stella responds with a list of loops that work their way through that particular stock. Figure 7.17 shows an example for the population model. This diagram was obtained by selecting the *young people* as the relevant stock and asking for the loop that involved *births*. Stella responds with all the loop's variables interconnected with arrows in a circle. It then allows you to label the loop with a C or R. "C" stands for "counter-act," as when negative feedback loops act to counteract the effect of disturbances from outside the system. The "R" stands for "reinforce," as when positive feedback loops act to reinforce the effect of outside disturbances.

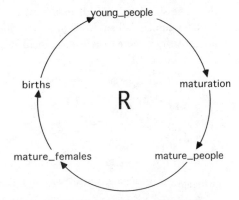

Figure 7.17. The positive feedback loop portrayed with Stella's loops tool.

A Stock in Every Loop

The loops tool is organized around the principle that there ~~must be at least one stock in every loop.~~ You might be wondering why this is true. You can verify that the principle applies for the population model and the two-bottles model. But suppose you were to build a stock-and-flow diagram of the arms race in figure 7.12. Would you end up with at least one stock appearing somewhere in each of the three loops? You would probably elect to use one stock to keep track of country A's weapons stockpile and a second stock to keep track of country B's weapons stockpile. Each country's spending to increase the stockpile would then be represented as flows. The remainder of the variables might be treated as converters. As in each of the previous examples, you would end up with at least one stock appearing in each of the feedback loops.

Of course, you know that three examples do not prove a fundamental principle. Suppose you were to try an experiment to contradict the principle. Construct the population flow diagram in figure 7.13 and attempt to close a feedback loop that does not involve one of the stocks. Suppose, for the sake of argument, that the *births per mature female per year* depends on the fraction female. Then, to close a loop without involving a stock, suppose that the *fraction female* depends on the *births per mature female per year*. Give this a try. You'll discover that you can't make the closing connection because Stella will respond with: "Sorry, but that would create a circular connection."

This warning may seem surprising since the system dynamics approach is predicated on the need to understand circularity in systems. Why should we be afraid of a circular connection? The purpose of this warning is to prevent "lazy thinking" about circularity. If you encounter this warning, take it as a challenge to think more deeply about the system. Previous students typically encountered this warning when attempting to mimic a set of simultaneous, algebraic equations from a textbook description of a system. When you find yourself in this predicament, think about the stocks and flows that are "hidden" behind the textbook description. In many cases, if you add a stock, you will be able to close the loop in a more realistic manner. In some cases, the flows act almost instantaneously to adjust the stock, so the new stock is not a good addition to the model. In these situations, your best approach is to solve the simultaneous algebraic equations and insert the solution as a converter variable.

Look for Similarity in Feedback Loop Structure

One of the main reasons for drawing causal loop diagrams is to look for similarity in the structure of systems. We are tempted to look for similar structures when two systems exhibit the same dynamic behavior. The s-shaped growth examples from the previous chapter are illustrative. The simulated growth in the area of flowers and the size of the sales company is remarkably similar. When this happens, we should check the feedback loop structure to learn if the similarity is more than just a coincidence. Figure 7.18 shows the feedback loops at work

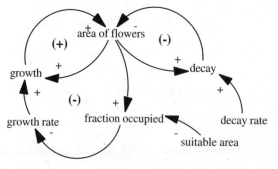

Figure 7.18. Causal loop diagram of the flower-growth model.

in the flower model. The positive loop gives the flowers the power to grow early in the simulation. One of the negative loops involves the decay or wearing out of flowers over time. The other negative loop acts to slow the rate of growth as the flowers "fill up" the area.

Figure 7.19 shows the feedback loops at work in the model of the sales company. We see a positive loop involving the widget sales, revenues, and the budgeted size of the sales force. Recall that this loop gives the system the power to grow early in the simulation because each salesperson is able to generate a large contribution to the departmental budget. Figure 7.19 shows a negative feedback loop involving the departures of employees. This loop is similar to the decay of the flowers. It acts to wear out the system at a constant rate over time. A second negative loop involves the decline in effectiveness of each salesperson as the number of sales people grow over time. This loop acts to weaken the strength of the positive loop as the salespeople "fill up" the area. Eventually, each sales person will be effective only in contributing enough to the departmental budget to cover his or her own salary. The company will stop growing at this point.

The comparison of the flower and sales systems confirms that their similarity in behavior is not a coincidence. These two systems have the same structure. Each is powered by a strong positive feedback loop early in the simulation; each is subject to a constant rate of decay; and the growth in each system is slowed by the actions of a single negative loop as the system fills up the space available. One final conclusion can be drawn from this comparison:

It is not necessary for the feedback loop structure to be absolutely identical for systems to show the same dynamic behavior.

Notice that figure 7.19 shows a negative loop involving the control of new hires to bring the number of employees up to the budgeted number, but this loop is not present in the flower model. The loop makes sense for a company that has established an explicit policy for hiring new employees, but it would not make sense in a flower model since nature does not set "explicit targets" for growth in flowers. The two systems differ in this respect, but their similarity in terms of the other three loops is sufficient to guarantee that they both exhibit s-shaped growth over time.

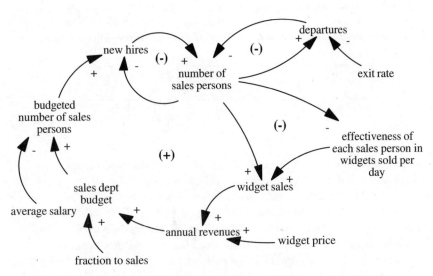

Figure 7.19. Causal loop diagram of the sales company model.

Communicating with Loop Diagrams

Loop diagrams are used as a communication tool, not a simulation tool. They help us think about the structure of the system. They are used extensively in the system dynamics literature because there is a general consensus that understanding the underlying feedback loop structure of a system is key to understanding the system's dynamic behavior.

Although there is a consensus on the fundamental purpose of the diagrams, there is plenty of room for variations in how these loops are communicated. You have seen the letter "R" used in figure 7.17 to communicate that the positive feedback loop acts as a reinforcing loop. The "R" and other symbols that might appear within a positive loop are shown in figure 7.20. The snowball rolling downhill is often used to remind us that a positive loop can lead to a snowballing effect over time. (The snowball and the remaining images are available in Vensim's loop-drawing tool.) Some authors might place the exponential growth graph inside the loop to communicate the likely behavior over time. If you wish to communicate the favorable results from the loop, use the smiling face within the loop. If the loop works against your interests, use the frowning face.

Figure 7.20. Symbols sometimes used for positive feedback.

I have elected not to use these symbols in this book because the (+) provides a neutral symbol that is likely to serve well under a broad range of examples, regardless of the context. But you should feel free to rely on any of the alternative symbols if you feel that they improve the communicative power of the diagram.

A collection of five symbols that might appear in the middle of a negative feedback loop are shown in figure 7.21. The "C" comes with Stella's loop tool; it reminds us that a negative loop acts to counteract the effect of outside disturbances. The teeter-totter reminds us of the balancing acts of negative feedback, as when the furnace loop in the home heating system brings the room temperature into balance at the desired level. The exponential decline graph might be placed in a loop to communicate the expected pattern of behavior, or you might use one of the faces to show your feelings about the loop. I rely on the (–) symbol throughout the book, but that doesn't mean you won't do better using one of the other symbols.

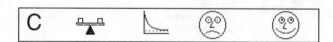

Figure 7.21. Symbols sometimes used for negative feedback.

In reading about system dynamics, you should be prepared to encounter a variety of symbols, both in the middle of the loops and at the arrows in the diagram. Some authors prefer to use an "S" rather than a +. The "S" reminds them that the two variables are likely to change in the *same* direction. With this convention, they are likely to use an "O" rather than a – for a causal arrow linking two variables that are likely to change in *opposite* directions. Some authors will simply leave the arrows without any labels because they believe the accompanying text makes the proper points about the feedback loop structure. Still others will leave the positive arrows unlabeled and will attach a "u-turn" symbol to the negative arrows to denote that the two variables change in opposite directions. If you are speaking the "same system dynamics language," you'll be able to understand their meaning. (Think of the differences as different regional accents that add color to the language of system dynamics.) But you should be cautious when looking at diagrams with similar appearance used within a different field of study. The words may look the same, but the authors may not be speaking the same language. For example, the causal loop diagrams used in system dynamics have an entirely different purpose than the "influence diagrams" used to aid decision analysis (Clemen 1989; Kirkwood 1992).

Beginners' Difficulties

Learning to use causal loop diagrams is like learning a new language. If your experiences are like those of other students, you will probably find it easier to read a diagram from the literature than to create a diagram of your own. Your first attempts may be cluttered with too many arrows, and the loops may not make sense. One way to learn is to review the many examples that appear throughout the book. Another tip is to use multiple diagrams as needed to portray the multiple loops in the system. Finally, it is helpful to avoid the pitfalls of too many arrows and of action words.

Beginning students will often fill a causal loop diagram with so many arrows that the loops are hidden within a plate of spaghetti. When asked why there are so many arrows, they answer that they want the diagram to be "complete." What they have in mind is documenting each and every interconnection in the model. Don't fall into this trap. The causal loop diagram is not the place to document every single interconnection in the model. That is better done in the flow diagrams or the equations. Your goal is to show the loops, not the clutter.

Another useful tip is to avoid action words. The words in a word-and-arrow diagram should be nouns, not verbs. To illustrate the problem with action words, suppose we are thinking about the supply and demand for cars (shown previously in figure 7.7). We might think about the consequences of an increase in the market price. And to communicate this line of thinking, we place "market price is going up" at the bottom of the diagram (see figure 7.22). The positive arrow to car production makes sense because car production would go up if prices go up, and the negative arrow to sales makes sense as well. Then we explain that inventories will go up because of both higher production and lower sales. The problem arises when we connect the arrow from inventories to the price. There is no way to determine whether this arrow is positive or negative because of the apparent contradiction between inventories going up and the market price going up.

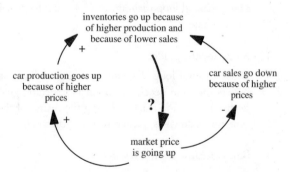

Figure 7.22. Avoid using "action words" in a causal loop diagram. (This is a poorly conceived version of the supply-and-demand loops shown previously in figure 7.7.)

The problem with this diagram is the initial decision to use action words like "is going up." Keep these action thoughts in your head, but limit the words in the diagram to nouns like price, production, sales, and inventory. Remember that the "action is in the arrows, not in the words" (Richardson and Pugh 1985, 28).

Summary

By reviewing the previous examples of positive feedback, you can observe that they have many features in common. To summarize, positive feedback loops:

- act to magnify the impact of changes from outside the loop;
- often show the way the system reinvests in itself to generate exponential growth over time;
- sometimes take the form of "vicious circles"; and
- have an even number of negative arrows around the loop.

But the negative feedback loops are quite different. They tend to:

- act to negate the impact of the change from outside the loop;
- often show the way a system strives to reach a goal;
- sometimes take the form of "wearing out" loops that simply depreciate or retire the stock of resources in a system; and
- have an odd number of negative arrows around the loop.

After building a system dynamics model, you should draw a causal loop diagram to reveal the key feedback loops in the system. The positive feedback loops will give the system the power to grow. The negative loops will reveal its attempt to reach a goal or to wear out over time. And the interaction of the different loops will often explain a system's interesting behavior. But you might be wondering: what if the diagram does not show any feedback loops?

In these circumstances, the system is not likely to show interesting dynamics on its own. Any dynamic patterns will simply be imposed on the system from outside forces. You don't need system dynamics ideas and stock-and-flow software to study these systems. They are probably best studied with spreadsheets (see appendix G).

Exercises

1. **Joe fills the tank:**

   Draw a causal loop diagram to reveal any feedback loops in the gas tank exercise at the end of chapter 2.

2. **Study for the grade:**

   Draw a causal loop diagram to reveal feedback in the study habits of a student who invests the time necessary to reach a specific grade. Assume that the student receives feedback from the teacher during the course of the semester and is able to adjust study time up or down as needed to reach the goal.

3. **Study because it's interesting:**

   Draw a causal loop diagram of a student whose study habits are dominated by a growing interest in the subject. More interest leads to more questions, which lead to more time invested in studying, which leads to further questions.

4. **Combined diagram:**

   Combine the previous diagrams into a causal loop diagram of a typical student who is motivated by a combination of grades and interest. Include a loop in the diagram to control for the fact that there are only so many hours in a day.

5. **Sports talk:**

   Two commentators are arguing over why the team quarterback is in a slump. The first commentator says he needs more confidence before his performance will improve. The second commentator says he needs to complete more passes, and the confidence will follow. You suspect that they are both right because of the circular cause and effect in the system. To clarify your reasoning, draw a causal diagram to reveal the positive feedback loop that influences athletic performance.

6. **Campaign talk:**

   Two political consultants are arguing over why their candidate is not making good progress in the presidential primaries. The first consultant says he needs more voter recognition before his ranking in the polls will improve. The second consultant says he needs more campaign contributions. With more money, he can buy more television time to "get his message out." You suspect that they are both right because of the circular cause and effect in the system. To clarify your reasoning, draw a causal diagram to reveal the positive feedback loop that influences the success of a political campaign.

7. **Monopoly:**

   Draw a causal loop diagram to reveal your growing advantage in the game of monopoly once you are able to place some hotels on blue chip properties like Boardwalk and Park Place.

8. **VCRs:**

   Draw a causal loop diagram to reveal competitive market shares between two types of videocassette recorders, or VCRs—VHS and Beta. Assume that a large market share of VHS leads video outlets to stock more prerecorded tapes in VHS format, thereby increasing the attractiveness of VHS recorders. Of course, the same argument applies to VCRs with the Beta format.

9. **Find an error in each diagram:**

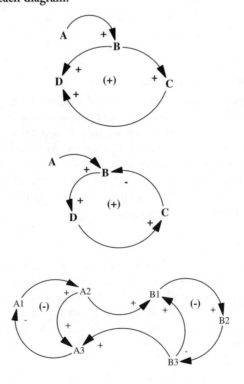

10. **Loops in the first model of Mono Lake:**

Here is the first step in translating the flow diagram of the first model of Mono Lake (see figure 4.5). Water in the lake, the only stock variable, is placed in the middle of the diagram. Each of the flows is included to get you started.

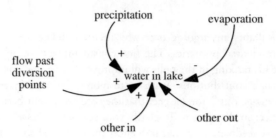

Complete this diagram. Do you see any loops? (Remember that the first model did a poor job of explaining the decline in Mono Lake.)

11. **Loops in the final model of Mono Lake:**

Draw a causal loop diagram of the final model of Mono Lake shown in figure 4.12. You do not need to include every variable in the diagram, just enough to reveal the loops in the model. You should see one negative loop involving evaporation and a second negative loop involving the specific gravity. There is also a curious positive feedback loop arising from the way precipitation is simulated in the model.

12. **Mono Lake export policy:**

Expand the causal loop diagram from the previous exercise to include a policy to control water exports as a function of the lake's elevation. Assume that higher exports are permitted when the elevation exceeds a "safe" level. When the elevation declines, exports must decline. Draw any new loops that appear in the diagram because of this policy.

13. **The exponential growth challenge:**

There are several examples in this chapter of systems that exhibit exponential growth. They each involve a positive feedback loop. A conference speaker once told his audience that you will *always* find a positive feedback loop if there is exponential growth in a system. The word "always" will probably make you nervous. Do you think the speaker is right? If so, bring three new examples of positive feedback loops to class to support his assertion. If not, come to class with a counterexample! That is, describe a system that grows in an exponential manner but lacks a positive feedback loop that contributes in an important manner to the growth.

14. **Spread of forest fire:**

Draw a causal loop diagram of the spread of a fire through a forest based on the account by Botkin and Keller (1995, 36). They note that the wood may be slightly damp at the beginning and not burn well, but once a fire starts, wood near the flame dries out and begins to burn, which in turn dries out a greater quantity of wood, leading to a larger fire. The larger the fire, the more wood is dried, and the more rapidly the fire increases. Your diagram should show the positive loop involving the rate at which damp wood is dried and possibly a second positive loop involving the ignition of dry wood. Show some negative loops as well. One might involve the depletion of damp wood over time. Another might describe how the fire eventually burns out over time.

15. **Positive feedback loop in forest management model:**

    Draw a causal loop diagram of the forest management model depicted in the final exercise of chapter 5. You should see six negative feedback loops associated with each of the flows that drains a stock. You should also see one positive feedback loop that involves all six flows and all six stocks.

16. **Material cycles—a special form of positive feedback:**

    The positive feedback loop in the previous exercise is a special case associated with the flow of the material in a conserved system. The forest model describes 1 million acres of land; there is neither growth nor decay in the total amount of land over time. So you know that the positive feedback loop is different from the growth-generating loops shown in figure 7.1. Systems that cycle a fixed amount of material around and around are special cases of positive feedback. The gain around such loops is zero, so there will be neither growth nor decay in the total amount of material. Can you detect such a loop in the model of carbon flows in the fifth exercise of chapter 5? If not, how would you change the flow diagram to simulate the cycling of a fixed amount of carbon?

Further Readings

- Useful guidelines for drawing causal loop diagrams are provided by Richardson and Pugh (1981, 28) and by Sterman (forthcoming).
- Richardson (1986) explains potential problems in drawing and interpreting causal loop diagrams.
- Causal loop diagrams as an aid to systems thinking within a learning organization are described in Peter Senge's management best-seller, *The Fifth Discipline* (1990). Useful advice in a similar vein appears in "links and loops" in Goodman, Kemeny, and Roberts's (1994) contribution to *The Fifth Discipline Fieldbook* and in Anderson and Johnson's *Systems Thinking Basics: From Concepts to Causal Loops* (1997).

Chapter 8

Causal Loops and Homeostasis

Homeostasis refers to our remarkable capability to maintain a relatively stable physiological state even when the outside environment is varying dramatically. This chapter explains homeostasis with examples from Walter Cannon's classic book *The Wisdom of the Body* (1932). It then turns to general ideas that may be useful beyond physiological systems. The global warming system is used to illustrate the challenge of transferring ideas from physiology to the environment. This chapter provides historical and conceptual support for subsequent chapters dealing with the stability of environmental systems.

There are no models or flow diagrams in this chapter. The main tool of communication is the causal loop diagram. By the end of the chapter, you will appreciate how these diagrams may be used to illuminate the feedback structure of rather complex systems.

Walter Cannon

The term *homeostasis* was invented by Walter Cannon, professor of physiology at the Harvard Medical School. It first appeared in his book *The Wisdom of the Body*. Cannon was intrigued by how the body maintains a stable state. He believed higher organisms had "learned" this ability over eons of time through gradual evolution. Organisms have had large and varied experience in "testing different devices for preserving stability" in the face of potential dangers. As they have grown to become more complex, Cannon believed that it was imperative that they develop more "efficient stabilizing arrangements."

Cannon opened with an example of homeostatic control of blood pressure. This topic deserves special emphasis in physiology because of the danger of blood loss and the need to maintain adequate pressure for the blood to "perform as a common carrier of nutriment and waste and to assure an optimum habitat for living elements" (Cannon 1932, 41). Cannon provided detailed accounts of how the body responds when subjected to major disturbances such as a wound. Figure 8.1 shows a causal loop diagram with blood loss depending on the size of the wound. A larger wound means greater blood loss, and the loss of blood reduces the volume of blood remaining in circulation. (You may think of the volume of blood in circulation as a stock. The blood loss would be a flow.) Blood pressure is influenced by the amount of blood in circulation. A decline in the volume of blood will cause the blood pressure to decline (*ceteris paribus*), and a decline in the blood pressure will cause a decline in the rate of blood loss. This closed chain of cause and effect forms the negative feedback loop on the right side of figure 8.1. The second loop involves the formation of clots as the blood exits the wound. Higher blood loss leads to more clot formation, which serves to reduce the size of the

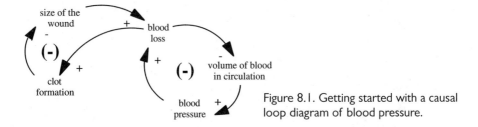

Figure 8.1. Getting started with a causal loop diagram of blood pressure.

wound in the future. These loops were not part of Cannon's description, but they provide the starting point for subsequent diagrams.

Figure 8.2 expands the diagram to illustrate the role of the coagulation time, the time interval observed in a controlled experiment for clots to form. (A longer time interval means the blood has more difficulty forming clots.) Figure 8.2 shows that a higher coagulation time lowers the rate of clot formation. The dark arrows draw our attention to the two loops that Cannon detected in experiments to measure the coagulation time. First, he observed that the coagulation time will become shorter after the body has suffered considerable loss of blood. This is the inner loop in figure 8.2—as blood loss lowers the volume of blood in circulation, the remaining blood has a shorter coagulation time; clot formation is more rapid, and the wound closes more rapidly.

The outer loop involves adrenin secretion. Cannon observed that a drop in blood pressure will lead to an increase in adrenin secretion. He also observed that a higher concentration of adrenin allows the blood to form clots with a shorter coagulation time. The outer loop in figure 8.2 shows another example of negative feedback: blood loss leads to a decline in blood volume, a decline in blood pressure, an increase in adrenin secretion, a reduced coagulation time, a more rapid formation of clots, and a faster closing of the wound.

Cannon described additional physiological reactions working through the muscles and the spleen. These actions are diagrammed alongside the previous actions in figure 8.3. The inner loop involves the muscles that encircle the vascular system. The muscles contract when the blood pressure declines, and their contraction reduces the space inside the vascular system. Lower capacity means higher blood pressure. It appears that the inner loop acts to maintain normal blood pressure in the face of cumulative blood loss. The outer loop in figure 8.3 works through the spleen. The spleen serves as a reservoir of blood, and a drop in blood pressure may trigger the spleen to contract. A contraction releases the stored blood into the gen-

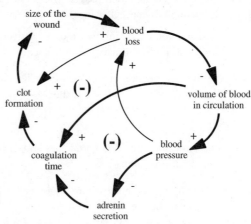

Figure 8.2. Additional loops to control blood loss.

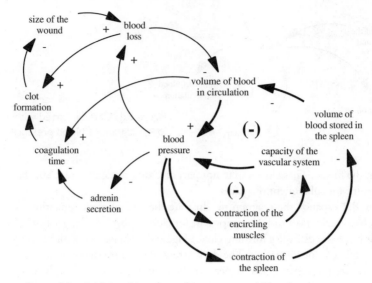

Figure 8.3. Additional loops working to control blood pressure.

eral vascular system. The extra blood builds the volume of blood in circulation and increases the blood pressure.

Cannon's description of blood pressure control is followed by descriptions of systems that control blood sugar, food intake, water intake, and salinity. At first glance, these systems may appear to be entirely different in design and composition, but Cannon saw that they were fundamentally the same when viewed in terms of homeostasis.

Beyond Physiology

Cannon concludes with the suggestion that the physiological mechanisms employed by highly evolved animals may reveal general principles that go beyond physiology, perhaps even to the management of social and industrial systems. The term *homeostasis* is now in wide use to describe systems whose properties seem similar to those of the physiological examples studied by Cannon. Odum (1971, 34) notes that *homeo* means "same" and *stasis* means "standing" and that the term *homeostasis is* generally applied to the "tendency for biological systems to resist change and to remain in a state of equilibrium." It's revealing to turn to *Webster's Dictionary* for alternative definitions. *Webster's* first entry is the narrow, physiological definition. Homeostasis is defined as the

> tendency toward maintenance of a relatively stable internal environment in the bodies of higher animals through a series of interacting physiological processes.

Webster's then lists an alternative definition that shows how broadly the term has come to be used. Homeostasis is also defined as the

> tendency toward maintenance of relatively stable social conditions among groups with respect to various factors (such as food supply and population among animals) and to competing tendencies and powers within the body politic, to society, to culture among men.

When thinking about environmental systems, we should take Cannon's concluding suggestion as a challenge to think about the interacting factors that allow the system to remain stable. His suggestion seems particularly relevant if we come across a system that has managed to survive over a long time period with large variations in the external factors. Cannon's views were predicated on the opportunity for evolutionary change:

> The perfection of the process of holding a stable state in spite of extensive shifts of outer circumstances is not a special gift bestowed upon the highest organisms but is the consequence of a gradual evolution.

Odum certainly reinforces Cannon's point when he states that "really good homeostatic control comes only after a period of evolutionary adjustment." We'll return to this topic in more detail when simulating predator-prey interactions in chapter 18.

A general observation that might be drawn from Cannon's examples is that environmental systems are probably controlled by a combination of negative feedback loops working in tandem. Once you begin to think in terms of feedback, it will be easy to spot one or two loops that govern system behavior. We should challenge ourselves to look beyond the first few loops that jump immediately to mind.

Another observation that will help in our study of environmental systems is to appreciate the extreme difficulty in verifying theories about homeostatic systems, especially if we focus our measurements on the central, controlled variable in the system. By design, homeostatic systems control the central variable (e.g., blood pressure) to erase the impact of outside disturbances. Imagine, for example, that we wanted to verify the workings of the physiological mechanisms that control the body's core temperature at 98.6 degrees. Every time we took a temperature reading, it would be 98.6 degrees! Physiologists appreciate the challenge when dealing with a normal human subject:

> The truth is that in a normal unanesthetized human subject feedback control of body temperature is so extremely effective that precise quantitative characterization of the mechanisms is well-nigh impossible. (Riggs 1970, 398)

A physiologist may deal with the limitations of a "normal" subject by conducting controlled experiments that place the subject in a highly stressed situation. Cannon described several unusual experiments with animals, with himself, and with graduate students. Environmental systems are less amenable to such experimentation. Consequently, we should be prepared for major challenges to verify homeostatic theories of environmental systems.

Look for Positive as well as Negative Feedback

If Cannon's ideas are to prove useful in environmental systems, it is imperative than we expand our thinking beyond negative feedback. Our study of the environment must consider both positive and negative feedback. Cannon did not emphasize positive feedback, but the human body certainly relies on it. The growth of new cells from cell division is an example of positive feedback: More cells lead to more cell divisions, which lead to more mature cells in the future. Also, the body may exhibit positive feedback in the form of "vicious circles." An example in which higher body temperature leads to increased basal heat production is described on this book's home page. Higher heat production leads, *ceteris paribus,* to an increase in the body temperature. Although physiologists are aware of positive feedback, it is negative feedback that dominates the discussion of homeostatic systems. Richardson (1991, 48) observed that "to some in the social sciences, the feedback concept became identified, virtually synonymous, with homeostasis, and that the close association of feedback with homeostasis eliminated completely the consideration of positive feedback loops." You probably appreciate the need to consider both positive and negative feedback from the many examples in the previous chapter. Let's turn now to the example of global warming to reinforce this view.

Global Warming

Global warming generally refers to an increase in the average global temperature of the atmosphere near the earth's surface. The increase may be caused by natural factors, human-made factors or a combination of both. The temperature near the surface of the earth is determined by the amount of sunlight the earth receives, the amount reflected, the retention of heat by the atmosphere, and the evaporation and condensation of water vapor (Botkin and Keller 1995, 432). When sunlight reaches the earth, it warms both the atmosphere and the surface. Water vapor and several other gases such as carbon dioxide warm the atmosphere because they absorb and re-emit radiation. These gases trap some of the heat energy radiating from the atmospheric system. The overall process is somewhat analogous to the way a greenhouse traps heat. You are probably familiar with the term *greenhouse effect,* and you have probably heard the term *greenhouse gases* to refer to carbon dioxide (CO_2), methane, and other gases that act to trap the radiating energy.

Greenhouse effect is a simple term for a staggeringly complex system. One of the best introductions to the complexities of global warming is given by Jon Luoma (1991) in his *Audubon* article entitled "Gazing into Our Greenhouse Future." Luoma begins by concentrating on negative feedback. Two of the feedback loops work through photosynthetic activity, as shown in figure 8.4. Trees and other green plants may respond to warmer air temperature with accelerated growth. Green plant photosynthesis would lead to greater CO_2 absorption, less CO_2 in the atmosphere, less absorbed radiation, and a reduction in air temperature. This is the outer loop in figure 8.4. The inner loop involves an increase in air temperature, followed by an increase in ocean temperature, which could lead to more rapid growth in algae phytoplankton, greater CO_2 absorption by the ocean, less CO_2 in the atmosphere, less absorbed radiation, and a reduction in air temperature.

The third loop involves the water vapor. An increase in air temperature could lead to more rapid evaporation, more water vapor in the air, and a more extensive cloud cover. A wider spread of bright, white clouds leads to greater reflection of short-wave energy, a reduction in absorbed radiation, and a reduction in air temperature.

These three examples of negative feedback are only part of the overall puzzle of global warming. But Luoma argues that they are sufficient for some to make the point that negative feedback could act to keep the problem "under control." He summarizes this possibility as follows:

> It is possible, just maybe, that the Earth has enough built-in self-regulating resistance to atmospheric alteration that the planet will not be devastated. That resis-

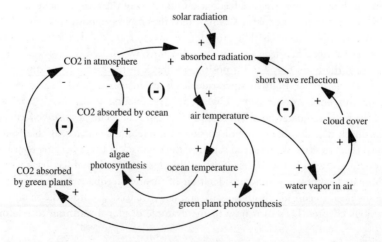

Figure 8.4. Three examples of negative feedback in the global warming system.

tance comes from phenomena called "negative feedbacks." And the notion that negative feedbacks will greatly moderate the effects of greenhouse gases provides the entire basis for argument by those who deny that global warming is an actual threat.

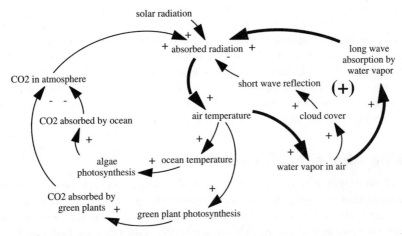

Figure 8.5. Positive feedback acting through long-wave absorption.

Luoma goes on to warn that "the hitch is that there are also positive feedbacks," and he cites three examples to make his point. Figure 8.5 shows a positive loop that involves the increased water vapor that could occur with higher air temperatures. Increased water vapor could lead to greater long-wave absorption, greater total absorbed radiation, and still further increases in the air temperature.

Figure 8.6 shows two additional examples of positive feedback, both of which operate through the permafrost. Enormous amounts of methane (CH_4) are believed to be trapped in the Arctic permafrost. Methane is one of the most potent of the greenhouse gases, and scientists fear that a reduction in the area of the permafrost could release the methane into the atmosphere, where it would lead to an increase in absorbed radiation, further increases in air

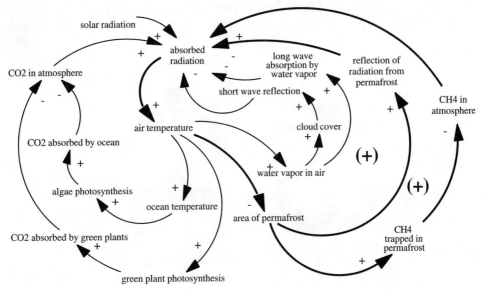

Figure 8.6. Additional positive loops acting through the permafrost.

temperature, and still further reductions in the area of the permafrost. This is the outer loop in figure 8.6.

The inner loop in figure 8.6 involves the reflective power of the permafrost. The ice sheets of the Arctic act to reflect incoming radiation. If these sheets were to shrink due to higher air temperatures, we could see greater absorbed radiation, higher air temperatures, and still further shrinkage of the ice sheets in the future.

Luoma observes that scientists are properly concerned about the growing accumulation of greenhouse gases in the atmosphere and the massive uncertainties about how the various feedback loops will play out over time. He describes their research challenges in using global circulation models to untangle the relative importance of the many feedback loops at work in the climate system. He cautions us to avoid the argument of the "happy Pollyannas" who are "relying almost entirely on negative feedbacks to balance, like magic, not only the straightforward warming itself but all the positive feedbacks as well."

Thinking About the Environment

The global warming system has a high degree of complexity, as do many of the environmental systems described in this book. Our general approach to managing highly complex systems will be guided by our fundamental images of how nature works. Figure 8.7 shows four images that might influence our thinking. Timmerman (1986, 440) refers to these images as the "myths of nature." You have seen three of the images in the chapter 5 discussion of equilibrium. The marble on the flat surface portrays a neutral system. The marble simply comes to rest whenever outside forces stop moving it from place to place. The marble at the top of the cup represents an entirely different view of nature. Timmerman describes the marble posed precariously on the top of the cup as a powerful metaphor for people who hold the myth of "nature malign." The slightest disturbance will pose a problem. He describes the marble at the bottom of the cup as a metaphor for "nature benign." If this image dominates our thinking, we expect natural systems to continue to behave as they have in the past. Outside disturbances are easily erased by the corrective actions within the system.

I believe the fourth image provides the most useful metaphor as we grapple with the complexity of environmental systems. It shows a marble in a stable position, but the marble can be displaced only so far before we have "runaway" behavior. Odum (1971, 35) describes the interval over which the marble will return to a stable position as the *homeostatic plateau.* I use the term *span of control* throughout this book. If the system is pushed beyond the span of control, the positive feedback loops will take over and the system will be altered

Figure 8.7. Four images of nature.

dramatically. Keep this fourth image in mind when we return to the span-of-control concept later in the book (especially in the chapter 21 discussion of climate control on Daisy World).

Summary

The concept of homeostasis can aid our thinking about environmental systems if we expand Walter Cannon's original ideas to include the impact of positive feedback. Causal loop diagrams are an effective tool to communicate the feedback loop structure of complex systems. As we approach the study and management of environmental systems, our actions will be guided by fundamental images of how nature works. A span-of-control image is likely to be the most productive of the simple metaphors.

This chapter shows that causal loop diagrams are an excellent way to depict the feedback loops at work in a physiological system. The diagrams are certainly a good tool for communication, but you are probably wondering about the rest of the system dynamics method? Wouldn't computer simulation help us study the dynamics of physiological systems?

System dynamics is well suited for the study of physiological dynamics because of the emphasis on information feedback, the ability to capture nonlinear relationships, and the clarity of the model diagrams. Many biomedical problems (such as diabetes and hypertension) can be viewed as biological control problems, for which system dynamics is ideally suited (Gallaher 1996). Indeed, several investigators have put system dynamics to use on such problems. Previous applications include the study of burn patient recovery (Bush et al. 1985), bone remodeling and osteoporosis (Smith 1996), and ultradian oscillations in human insulin secretion (Sturis 1991). These and other applications are summarized in the physiology segment of the home page. The home page then demonstrates how a physiological model of body temperature regulation (Riggs 1970) may be constructed and tested in a step-by-step manner.

Exercises

1. **Additional loops:**

    The diagram that accompanies this exercise shows shivering and sweating, two of the physiological responses that control body temperature. Expand the diagram to show additional loops involving layers of clothing or degree of exercise. Each new loop should introduce an additional form of negative feedback.

    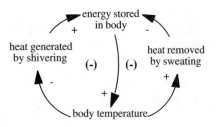

2. **Complete the diagram:**

    Complete the diagram that accompanies this exercise to describe body temperature control by a reptile. The reptile lacks our ability to regulate body temperature internally, so it must resort to behavioral mechanisms like burrowing in the cool sand or basking in the warm sun.

    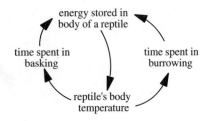

3. **More than two loops:**

    The diagram for this exercise shows the first two loops that spring to mind when thinking about a market economy and the interplay between supply and demand. Expand this diagram to show additional examples of negative feedback. The new loops might be used to keep track of long-term contract prices as well as short-term spot prices. Or new loops might be added to portray the operation of a "black market" alongside the regular market. Finally, you might draw new loops to describe competition on quality and delivery time as well as price of the product.

    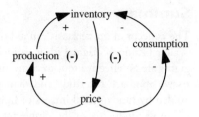

4. **Extra loop in global warming:**

    Draw a causal loop diagram to reveal the additional feedback created during a period of global warming by the increased use of air conditioning. Assume that higher air temperature leads to greater use of electric air conditioners and that the electricity is generated in coal-fired power plants that release carbon dioxide into the atmosphere.

Further Readings

- George Richardson (1991) examines Cannon's ideas and their importance to the spread of feedback thinking within the social sciences and the systems sciences. Capra describes the influence of Cannon's ideas in *The Web of Life* (1996), a book for the general reader.
- System dynamics has been used to simulate both climate systems and physiological systems. Physiological examples may be found on this book's home page. Climate examples may be found in the doctoral research by Fiddaman (1997), the text by Sterman (forthcoming), an instructional booklet by Few (1991), and a model for nonscientists by Bernstein, Richardson, and Stewart (1994).
- Holling (1976) and Timmerman (1986) discuss the fundamental images of nature, which they describe as the "myths of nature."

Chapter 9

Bull's-Eye Diagrams

The structure of system dynamics models may be explained with stock-and-flow diagrams, equilibrium diagrams, or causal loop diagrams. The best way to describe a model is with a combination of all of these diagrams coupled with time graphs of the simulation results.

There is one remaining diagram that can prove useful in describing computer models. It's called a bull's-eye diagram because it's shaped like the bull's-eye used as a target. Endogenous variables are placed in the center of the bull's-eye; exogenous variables are placed in the outer ring. Excluded variables are placed outside the outer ring. These diagrams are a concise way to portray the system boundary of the model. They are particularly useful for describing a model that has grown too complex to be easily displayed with flow diagrams.

Examples

Let's begin with the sales force model used to study the s-shaped growth in the number of people selling widgets. The causal loop diagram is shown in figure 9.1. It shows that the exit rate, widget price, fraction to sales, and average salary are exogenous variables. All the remaining variables appear in feedback loops, so they are endogenous.

A bull's-eye diagram of the sales model is shown in figure 9.2. The seven endogenous variables are placed anywhere within the inner circle. The four exogenous variables are located anywhere in the outer ring. A few excluded variables are listed outside the outer circle. The diagram is used to emphasize that the model does not deal with widget quality, delivery delays, or the color of the widgets. We also ignore the price of competing products and the price of used widgets. At this point. you are probably thinking that we could list hundreds of other variables that are excluded from the model. How many variables should be placed in the diagram? The custom is to list a few variables that might have been included because they are closely related to the model purpose. These might be candidates for inclusion in a future version of the model. Your purpose is to convey a sense for the boundary you have chosen for the model.

The bull's-eye diagram is an extremely concise way to show the model focus and the required inputs. It's also a convenient way to show the relative balance between required inputs and endogenous variables. A quick glance at figure 9.2 confirms that the model has more variables in the center of the bull's-eye. This is a good sign. Models with a large number of endogenous variables are more likely to generate interesting dynamic behavior from "inside the system." This is especially true when the exogenous inputs are held constant over time, as was the case in the sales force simulations in chapter 6.

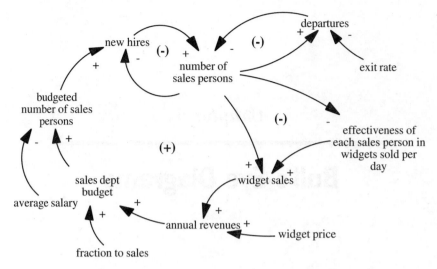

Figure 9.1 Causal loop diagram of the sales model.

Figure 9.2. Bull's-eye diagram of the sales model.

Let's turn now to a somewhat different view of the sales company, as shown by the flow diagram in figure 9.3. This model could be used to simulate the change in the company's cash balance over time. The revenues from widget sales add to the cash balance, and the balance is drained by salary payments and a variety of other payments. Salary payments are based on four categories of salespeople, each earning a different salary. Other payments consist of payments for rent, furniture, utilities, etc. The model shows that widget sales are broken down into black, green, blue, and red, and a separate price is assigned to each color.

Now, suppose you were to construct a bull's-eye diagram for the new model of the sales company. Which of the many variables would you place in the center of the bull's-eye? Some students view the cash balance as an "output" of the model and interpret it as an endogenous variable to be placed in the center of the bull's-eye diagram. This view misses the key point in the definition of endogenous variables. Endogenous variables are not simply "outputs" of a

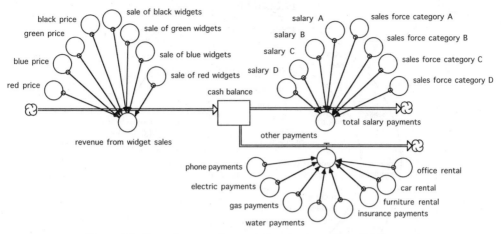

Figure 9.3. Flow diagram of a model to simulate the cash balance.

model. They are variables that appear somewhere in a feedback loop, or they are variables that are influenced by another variable that is in a feedback loop. You can see that there is absolutely no feedback in the model in figure 9.3. All the variables are exogenous, so nothing would appear in the center of the bull's-eye.

The new model appears to be more complex than the previous model, especially if we are interested in the eight categories of expenses, four categories of widgets, and four categories of employees. We would say that the new model is "categorically complex." But is the model structurally complex? Apparently not, because it does not contain a single feedback loop. Since it has no feedback structure, it is not likely to teach us anything about the dynamic behavior of the company. Any changes in the cash balance over time will simply be imposed on the system by the values assigned to the twenty-four converters in figure 9.3.

Models like figure 9.3 are sometimes called "bookkeeping models." Their job is to perform a series of well-defined calculations based on an extensive set of inputs. The interrelationships are often clearly understood or are tautological. If you see a need for a bookkeeping model, you could certainly use one of the stock-and-flow programs to construct a model like the one in figure 9.3. But why bother? The best way to construct bookkeeping models is with spreadsheets (see appendix G). System dynamics models should be reserved for the study of systems with structural complexity, not categorical complexity.

Boundary Diagrams

Bull's-eye diagrams are often called boundary diagrams because they provide a concise summary of the modeler's choices for the system boundary. Boundary diagrams may be used to document a wide variety of models, regardless of their size and regardless of their methodology. Meadows and Robinson use boundary diagrams to summarize nine different models in *The Electronic Oracle* (1985). The models address the formulation of long-term policies dealing with population growth, agricultural production, and economic development in both industrialized and nonindustrialized nations. The models employ a variety of methodologies including system dynamics, econometrics, linear programming, and input-output analysis. Many of the models have grown to become quite complex, both in size and in eclectic combination of methodologies. Nevertheless, Meadows and Robinson were able to summarize each model on a single page with a boundary diagram. Figure 9.4 shows an illustrative example.

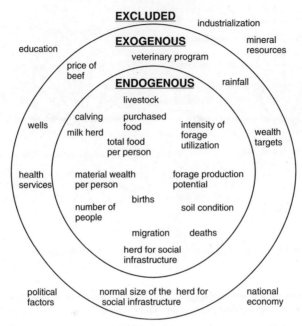

Figure 9.4. System boundary diagram of a long-term model of the people, livestock, and range lands of the Sudano-Sahel area in Africa.

Figure 9.4 is a system boundary diagram of a long-term model of the people, livestock, and rangelands of the Sudano-Sahel area in Africa. The model was constructed by Tony Picardi as part of a project for the United States Agency for International Development (AID). He used the model to simulate the overgrazing and soil degradation that is widespread in the Sahel. The simulations led him to conclude that the pastoral system lacks effective feedback between the range capacity and the human decisions that affect both human population and livestock population. He used the model to simulate various AID proposals (e.g., veterinary programs) and concluded that some of AID's proposals would only intensify the system problem. The model contains almost two hundred equations. Nevertheless, you will be able to appreciate the main thrust of Picardi's work from the boundary diagram in figure 9.4.

Hitting the Bull's-Eye

System dynamics models are used to study systems with feedback, so the bull's-eye diagram should show the key variables in the center of the diagram. A general rule of thumb for an introductory model is to look for at least three or four key variables at the center of the bull's-eye diagram. If the important variables are missing from the center of the diagram, the model won't convey useful insights about the dynamic behavior of the system.

Now let's imagine that you've made a good start with an introductory model. How should you proceed to improve the model over time? A pragmatic approach is to move important variables toward the center of the diagram each time you make a substantial improvement in the model. The Mono Lake models (chapter 4) illustrate the approach:

- First model: The first model did not contain any feedback, so it did not meet the goal for a good introductory model. There were no endogenous variables, and it failed to generate plausible behavior.
- Second model: The next model represented the surface area of the lake as a function of the volume. The area then influenced the evaporation and precipitation, which act to change

the volume. This model had four endogenous variables, and it generated reasonable behavior.

- Third model: The next improvement was to link the elevation to the volume of water in the lake. Elevation became an endogenous variable because it was influenced by volume, which is endogenous. We also used the third model to elaborate on the collection of "other inflows" and "other outflows." These distinctions added eight new exogenous variables to the model.

- Fourth model: The final model represented the evaporation rate as a function of the specific gravity of the lake. This improvement created an additional feedback loop, and two more variables moved to the center of the diagram

- Export policy: The exercises in chapter 4 call upon you to link the export to the elevation of the lake. With these changes, the export joins the other endogenous variables in the center of the diagram.

The pattern of improvements in the Mono Lake model illustrates a useful approach for all system dynamics models. It's certainly useful to add new exogenous variables to elaborate on the inputs to the model. But the best way to learn more about the system's dynamic behavior is to move the key variables to the center of the bull's-eye diagram.

Exercises

1. **Bull's-eye for flowered area:**

   Draw a bull's-eye diagram for the flower model described in chapter 6. Does it end up with the majority of the variables in the center of the bull's-eye?

2. **Bull's-eye for Daisyworld:**

   The Daisyworld model in chapter 21 describes the spread of black and white flowers over the surface area of Daisyworld. Draw a bull's-eye diagram of the Daisyworld model based on the flow diagrams and causal loop diagrams in chapter 21. Are the majority of the variables in the center of the bull's-eye?

3. **Special functions:**

   Review the advice at the conclusion to appendix H on when it is appropriate to use MAX, MIN, EXP, and other special functions. Do you expect these functions to be used for variables at the center of the bull's-eye?

PART II

SIMULATING MATERIAL FLOWS

Chapter 10

Introduction to Material Flow

System dynamics may be used to simulate material flow through a system. The material may take many forms—people, animals, plants, water, cash, cars, heat, or pollutants, for example. The flow of material is represented by flow variables. The accumulation of material is represented by the stocks. This chapter looks at standard combinations of stocks and flows that will prove useful throughout the book. It then describes the conveyor, a special type of stock that will prove useful in simulating tightly controlled flows of material. Environmental systems sometimes exhibit tightly controlled flows, as when a school of fish migrate to the ocean. Conveyors are used to simulate animal populations that move or grow in tightly controlled patterns. Examples include the salmon in the Columbia River (chapters 13 and 14) and the brine shrimp in Mono Lake (exercise 7 in chapter 4).

Introduction

The model in figure 10.1 shows the flow of material from one category to another. The key flow is the *transfer* between the two categories. It is set as the amount of material in the first category multiplied by the *transfer rate*. The flow equation would be written as:

```
transfer = material_in_first_category*transfer_rate
transfer_rate = .0693
```

Let's set the inflow as a time graph to deposit 8 tons of material into the first stock by the 10th year of a simulation. Figure 10.2 shows the material in the first category if the transfer rate is set at 6.93 percent/yr. The material jumps to 8 tons in the 10th year due to the inflow. It then declines over time as 6.93 percent of the material is moved out year after year. The material follows the pattern of exponential decay explained in appendix B. You know from the appendix that a 6.93 percent/yr rate of decay will cause half of the material to be removed after 10 years, as highlighted in figure 10.2. The graph also directs our attention to a longer time interval of 14.4 years. The dashed line is drawn tangentially to the initial rate of decline. It shows that the material would reach zero after 14.4 years if the removal were to continue at the same value that occurs immediately after the material arrives in the stock. But with exponential decline, the slope of the decline becomes flatter and flatter over time as less and less material remains in the stock. This pattern is useful for material flows that are expected to be proportional to the amount of material remaining in the stock.

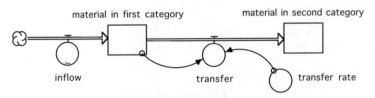

Figure 10.1. Flow of material governed by a transfer rate.

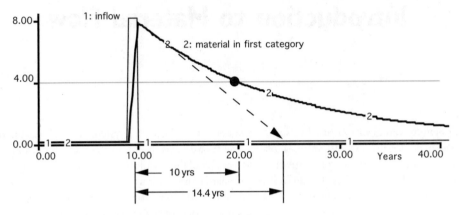

Figure 10.2. Simulated material with a transfer rate of 6.93 percent/year.

You may think of the 14.4-year time interval as the average amount of time that the material spends in the first category. If you wish to specify this interval as an input to the model, you may use the model in figure 10.3 with the transfer flow set as:

```
transfer = material_in_first_category/average_time_interval
average_time_interval = 14.4
```

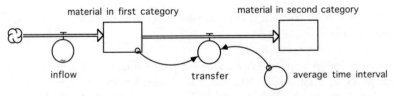

Figure 10.3. Material flow governed by average time interval.

This new model will give the same results because the material divided by 14.4 years corresponds to 6.93 percent of the material transferred per year. In other words, the reciprocal of the transfer rate corresponds to the average time interval that the material remains in the category.

It may be useful in some systems to specify the flows in terms of the half-life. The properties of toxic materials are often summarized in terms of their half-lives, so figure 10.4 shows an example of a material flow model with the half-life as the user input. In this case, the equation for the transfer flow must account for the fact that the average time interval is 1.44 times larger than the half-life. The flow equation would be

```
transfer = toxic_material_in_1st_category/(1.44*half_life)
half_life = 10
```

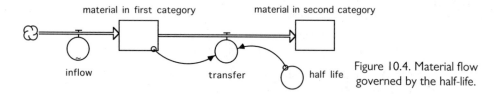

Figure 10.4. Material flow governed by the half-life.

You can tell that a half-life of 10 years corresponds to the previous example of a 14.4-year average time interval spent in the first category. This model will generate the same behavior shown in figure 10.2.

The previous three examples were selected to correspond to a 10-year half-life to match a pattern of exponential decay that you have seen in appendix B. But you can work with any of these three approaches by keeping the parameters in the right proportions. Simply adjust the half-life by 1.44 to learn the average time interval; the transfer rate will be the reciprocal of the average time interval, as in the three examples in table 10.1.

Table 10.1. Equivalent values of time intervals and transfer rates.

Half-lives	Average time intervals	Transfer rates
10 yrs	14.4 yrs	6.93%/yr
20 yrs	28.8 yrs	3.47%/yr
40 yrs	57.6 yrs	1.74 %/yr

Population Examples

You may explain the material flows in a system by using any of the three standard approaches. You might find half-lives to be the most suitable if you are dealing with toxic pollutants (as in the DDT example in chapter 12). Transfer rates and average time intervals tend to be more suitable in other systems. Figure 10.5 shows a combination of transfer rates and average time intervals used in a simple population model. The time intervals are the *average time to mature* and the *average time to age*. These inputs control the flow of people from one stock to the next within the system. The model includes three deaths that remove people from the system. The deaths are based on mortality rates that give the fraction of people in each age category that die per year.

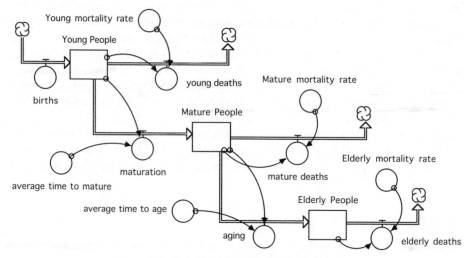

Figure 10.5. Population model with three stocks.

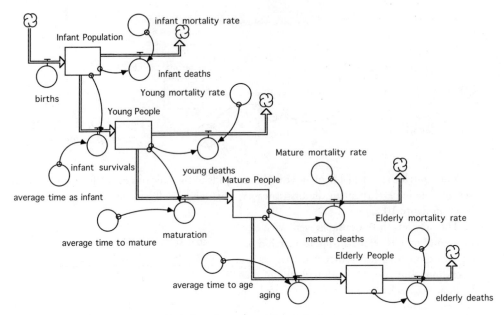

Figure 10.6. Population model with four stocks.

Now suppose we discover that the mortality statistics reveal that there is a greater chance of death during infancy. We could expand the population model as shown in figure 10.6. The *infant population* stock is fed by *births* and drained by *infant deaths* and *infant survivals*.

The population models are meant to illustrate a simple point: You can describe material flow in greater and greater detail by adding more stocks and flows. As the model becomes more complicated, there is no need for the equations to become more complicated. The equations governing each new flow can be quite simple. The standard approach is to write the equation with a transfer rate or an average time interval.

The population examples also show a situation with time intervals that differ by an order of magnitude. In figure 10.6, for example, the average time to mature might be 20 years, and the average time to age could be 50 years. But the time spent in infancy is much shorter. If infants are vulnerable only for the first three months of their life, the average time as infant would be set at 0.25 years. If we compare the 50 years in the mature category with the 0.25 years in the infant category, we have an unusual situation in which the time intervals differ by a factor of 200. This can pose troublesome problems in simulating the model. We'll return to this topic in the chapter 11 discussion of DT, the step size for the simulation.

The preceding examples show the movement of material through a system with accumulation of material represented by the familiar "reservoir" stock. The reservoir requires us to explain all the flows into and out of the stock. The outflows are typically explained by the use of average time intervals, half-lives, or transfer rates. Let's now turn to special examples of material flow that proceeds in a tightly controlled pattern. Examples in the environment include animals who remain tightly grouped during migrations. Examples in our everyday life include our progress through school (as our teachers and administrators keep us tightly grouped for a variety of social and administrative reasons). Simulating these flows is much easier if we turn to the conveyor.

The Conveyor

The conveyor is a special version of the stock variable to help you simulate material moving through the system in a tightly controlled pattern. Think of the way material moves along a

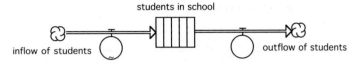

students in school

inflow of students   outflow of students

Figure 10.7. Example of a conveyor stock.

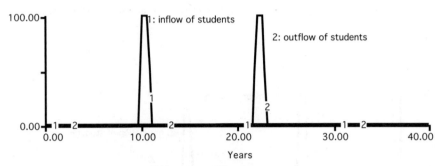

Figure 10.8. Results of the student model.

conveyor belt. If the material flows through your system like material on a conveyor belt, select the conveyor stock rather than the conventional "reservoir" stock. To select the conveyor, open the stock variable and change the designation from a "reservoir" to a "conveyor." The stock icon will change from a normal rectangle to a rectangle with slats, as shown in figure 10.7. You need only write the equation for the inflow; the software automatically writes the equation for the outflow based on the transit time for the conveyor. Think of the "transit time" as how long material spends on the conveyor belt.

Figure 10.8 shows the simulation results if the *inflow of students* is a time-dependent graph set at zero for most of the simulation. But in the 10th year, the inflow increases to 100 students/year for 1 year. The initial value of the conveyor is set to zero, and the transit time is set at 12 years. Figure 10.8 shows that the *outflow of students* will be identical to the inflow except delayed by 12 years.

Figure 10.9 gives an example of a conveyor with a "leakage" flow. The first outflow from the conveyor represents the main flow off the conveyor belt. In this example the *graduation of students* is the first flow to be connected to the conveyor. The graduation will be determined by the transit time of the conveyor. If a second flow is connected to the conveyor, it represents "leakage" or losses from the system. In this example, the second flow is *student dropouts*, which are based on the "leakage fraction" for the conveyor.

Figure 10.10 expands the previous example by adding extra converters to assign names to the transit time and the leakage fraction. In this example, the transit time is set equal to the *average time in school,* and the leakage fraction is set equal to the *dropout rate.*

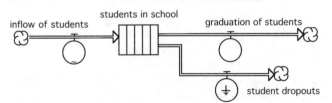

inflow of students   students in school   graduation of students

student dropouts

Figure 10.9. Example of a conveyor with a leakage flow.

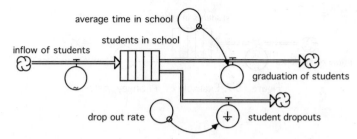

Figure 10.10. Extra converters to name the transit time and the leakage fraction.

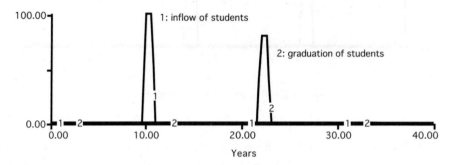

Figure 10.11. Simulation results with leakage.

Figure 10.11 shows how this model would behave if the dropout rate is set to 20 percent. The *graduation of students* is somewhat lower than the *inflow of students* due to the dropouts. But notice that the conveyor delivers the same characteristic pattern seen before—the main outflow takes on the same shape as the inflow, except it is delayed in time by 12 years, the length of the transit time.

Why Use Conveyors?

The conveyor is a convenience, not a necessity. You can construct a model to yield outflow patterns similar to the conveyor by combining several reservoir stocks in tandem. Let's consider the example of student flow through a 12-year educational system. The example will reveal that conveyors may not be necessary, but they are extremely convenient.

Figure 10.12 shows three approaches to simulate student flow through a 12-year educational system. The three inflows stand for the students arriving for the 1st year in their education. The model on the left is the simplest. It uses a single stock to keep track of the number of students *enrolled.* The flow called *out 1* is calculated by dividing the number *enrolled* by the 12 years needed to graduate. The left-side model uses only one stock variable, so it is sometimes called a *first-order delay* in the flow of students.

The middle example uses two stock variables, the first for the students *enrolled 1 to 6,* the second for the students *enrolled 7 to 12.* A 6-year interval is associated with each stock. The *advance* flow moves students between the first two stocks; it is found by dividing the students *enrolled 1 to 6* by 6 years. A similar calculation is used to find the *out 2* flow. The middle example is sometimes called a *second-order delay* in the flow of students.

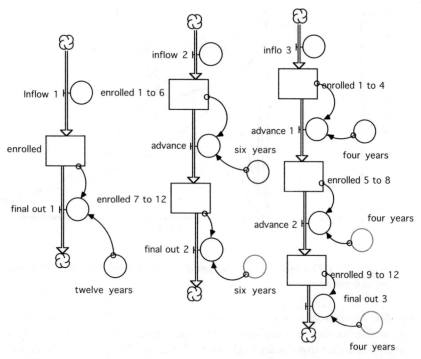

Figure 10.12. Three models to simulate student flows using conventional stocks and flows.

The third example uses three stock variables and could be described as a ***third-order delay*** in the flow of students. The first stock represents students *enrolled 1 to 4;* the second represents students *enrolled 5 to 8;* and the third represents students *enrolled 9 to 12.* The average time in each of the stocks is set at 4 years, one-third of the 12 years needed to graduate.

Figure 10.13 shows the response of the three models. Each model responds to the same *student arrivals.* This input is set to zero until the 10th year. Arrivals jump to 100 students/year in the 10th year and return to zero by the 11th year. This sends a surge of 100 students into the system. Each of the models will graduate all of the students, but the time pattern of graduations is dramatically different:

1. First-order response: The outflow jumps immediately to over 8 students/year after the surge in admissions. This immediate increase is caused by the assumption that one-twelfth of the students will graduate in the 1st year. Then, in the following year, one-twelfth of the remaining students will graduate. The outflow continues to decline over the remainder of the simulation until all 100 students have graduated.
2. Second-order response: There is no outflow immediately after the surge of students because all the students are still located in the first stock. Then, after a few years, some students have progressed to the second stock, and the outflow begins to increase. The outflow peaks around the 15th year and declines throughout the remainder of the simulation.
3. Third-order response: The outflow remains at zero for several years before beginning to grow. Then the outflow grows more rapidly and reaches a higher peak than in the previous example. The outflow peaks around the 18th year of the simulation, and it declines for the remainder of the simulation.

Now let's imagine what would be required to continue this approach. Suppose we were to construct a sixth-order model with each of the six stocks representing the enrollments in two

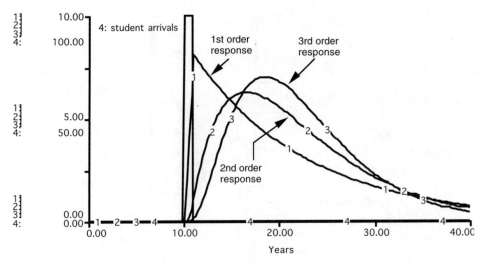

Figure 10.13. Outflows from three models of student flows through a 12-year educational system.

of the grades. The average time spent in each of the stocks would be 2 years, and the flows from one stock to another are calculated in the same manner as before. This model could be said to represent a *sixth-order delay* in the flow of students. You would probably feel more comfortable with a twelfth-order model in which each stock represents the enrollments in one of the grades. The average time spent in each of these stocks is 1 year, and the flows are calculated in the same manner as before. This would be a *twelfth-order delay* in the flow of students.

Figure 10.14 shows the simulated outflows from the sixth-order and twelfth-order models along with the third-order results shown previously. It demonstrates that the higher-order delays cause the peak in the outflow to be delayed further into the future. The higher-order delays also cause a higher peak and a steeper decline. With the twelfth-order delay, the peak outflow occurs in the 22nd year, 12 years after the surge in the inflow. In other words, the

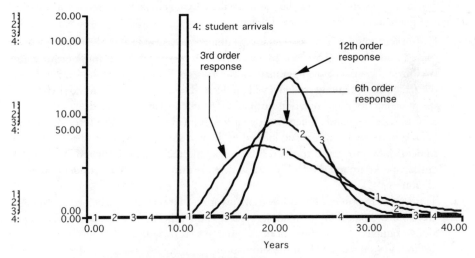

Figure 10.14. Responses of three models to a surge in student arrivals.

majority of the students graduate 12 years after entering the system—just what you would expect. But the twelfth-order delay shows that some students would graduate as soon as the 16th year, only 6 years after starting their education, and that some students would not graduate until around the 28th year, 18 years after starting their education.

Which Model Is Best?

Which of these models would you select as the "best" representation of student flows through primary and secondary school? You might select the twelfth-order model because it assigns a separate stock to each of the grades 1–12, so the names look familiar. Also, the time pattern of graduating students is probably more descriptive of your own school system. The peak in graduations occurs roughly twelve years after the surge in admissions. Also, the response allows for some students to graduate earlier than normal, while other students take longer than normal. However, although the twelfth-order model gives a reasonable response pattern and has easily recognized variable names, it is certainly the most tedious of the models.

Now, suppose the data suggest that the pattern of graduates should be more tightly centered around the 22nd year than shown in figure 10.14. For example, only a small fraction of the students tend to graduate before the 18th year and none of the students will still be in school after the 24th year. In other words, the "schooling pattern" is tighter than shown in figure 10.14.

To simulate a tighter schooling pattern, you could simply turn to a higher-order delay. For example, you might experiment with a twenty-fourth-order delay in which twenty-four stocks are arranged in tandem. Each stock could represent one semester in a two-semester school year. The average time spent in each stock would be set to 0.5 years, and the flows from one stock to another would be calculated in the same manner as in all the previous models. The new model would deliver a tighter pattern of graduates than shown in figure 10.14 while still allowing some students to graduate earlier than normal and other students to take somewhat longer than normal.

Schooling Patterns and the Conveyor

The conveyor stock can be viewed as an extreme example of the trend toward higher and higher order delays. (Indeed, you might describe the conveyor as an *infinite-order delay*.) The conveyor is appropriate if you feel that the material flowing through the system is governed by strict rules that ensure a tight schooling pattern. Educational systems are certainly a prominent example of "schooling" patterns. Migratory animal populations are another notable example.

As a model builder, you have many choices to simulate the pattern of material flows through a system. You may elect to assemble a collection of stocks to form an "*n*th"-order delay. Your job is to select *n* to create a flow pattern to match the pattern observed in your system. If the pattern is diffuse, you might use a third-order delay. If the pattern is rather tight, you might use a twelfth-order delay. And if you encounter an extremely tight pattern of schooling, you may elect to use Stella's conveyor option.

Exercises

1. **Missing connection?**

    The fifth exercise in chapter 2 asks you to check each flow that drains a reservoir stock to make sure that there is an information link from the stock to the flow. If this link is missing, there is the troublesome possibility that the flow could drive the stock below zero. Should we worry that this link appears to be missing in figure 10.7?

2. **Wedding announcement arrivals:**

You deliver 500 wedding announcements to the local post office on the 10th day of the month. The announcements are addressed to your out-of-town friends and relatives. Draw a flow diagram of a model that uses conventional reservoir stocks to simulate the arrivals of the announcements. Assume that the announcements spend about 1 day in the local post office before they are shipped to a central facility. They spend around 1.5 days at the central facility before they are shipped to the post office in the destination cities. They spend around 1.25 days in the destination-city post offices before they are delivered to your friends and relatives.

3. **Initial contents of the conveyor:**

The flow diagram for this exercise shows a conveyor of *overwintering eggs* with an incubation period of 6 months. The conveyor is to be initialized with 120 eggs. If you sim-

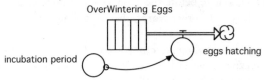

ply enter one initial value of 120, Stella will automatically spread the 120 across all six "slats" on the conveyor. Run the model over a 12-month time period. You should see 20 eggs hatch during each of the first 6 months. Then experiment with placing the ini-

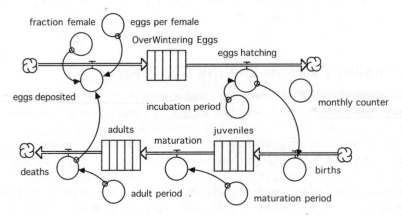

tial value "on different slats" of the conveyor (e.g., 0,0,0,120,0,0). Generate one simulation with all 120 eggs hatching in the 1st month. Then change the initial value so that all 120 eggs hatch in the 6th month.

4. **Extend the eggs model:**

Expand the previous model as shown in the diagram accompanying this exercise.

Then set the *fraction female* to 50 percent, the *eggs per female* at 2, and the transit times as follows:

- *incubation period*—6 months

- *maturation period*—5 months
- *adult period*—1 month

These parameters guarantee a 1-year life cycle and that each generation will be exactly the same size as the previous generation. The model assumes that the females deposit the eggs as the final act of their life cycle. The model will begin with time = 0, which corresponds to early January of the first calendar year. Initialize the *juveniles* at zero, the *adults* at zero, and the *overwintering eggs* so that 100 eggs will hatch in the 4th month of the simulation. Add a monthly counter (see appendix H) to keep track of the month in each new calendar year. Run the model over a 48-month time period to verify that the *eggs hatching* will occur in the 4th month of each new year.

5. **Extend the eggs model to account for egg loss:**

   Expand the previous model by adding a leakage flow to represent egg loss. Assume that 50 percent of the eggs are lost and the other 50 percent result in births. You may assume that the loss occurs evenly throughout the 6-month incubation period. Increase the *eggs per female* from 2 to 4 so that each generation is able to replace the previous generation. Run the model to see if you get the same results as in the previous exercise.

Further Reading

- The response of delays of various orders are described by Forrester (1961, 89, 417) and by Richardson and Pugh (1981, 109).
- The conveyor is a special Stella feature that will not necessarily appear in identical fashion in each of the stock-and-flow programs. Refer to the technical documentation for your software to check how you may generate results similar to the results in this chapter.

Chapter 11

The Numerical Step Size

Chapter 3 explained the numerical approach used to generate the simulation results in system dynamics models. You learned that the calculations are repeated over and over as time is advanced in small increments to cover the entire time interval. The time increment is called DT, which stands for "delta time." This chapter reviews the previous suggestions and provides additional guidelines for arriving at a suitable value of DT. The most important part of this chapter is the simulations to illustrate what you will see when you have selected a poor value of DT.

Introduction

Recall the Mono Lake simulations that ran from 1990 to 2090. The DT was set to 0.25 year, so the simulation required 400 steps. You learned that we can check the accuracy of the numerical results by cutting DT in half and repeating the simulation. The computer would then need 800 steps to complete the simulation. If we get essentially the same results with 800 steps as with 400 steps, we can be confident that the original results are numerically accurate.

At this point in the book, you have seen models of populations, bank balances, water flows, flowered areas, and widget sales. How is it possible that we have come this far without discussing additional guidelines for DT? The answer, quite simply, is that 0.25 time units turns out to be a remarkably good starting value. Each new situation has its own time horizon, but the software gives us the opportunity to describe the units of time to fit our situation. When working with Mono Lake, we chose "years." A DT of 0.25 year means that 400 steps were needed to complete the 100-year simulation. When working with the two-bottles exercise in appendix C, we chose "seconds" and used the model to simulate the fluid flows over an 80-second interval. The computer used 320 steps to complete the simulation. In both cases, we obtained fast and accurate simulations without worrying about the choice of DT.

Not every situation will be as simple as the previous examples, so it is time to take a closer look at the selection of DT. Some additional guidelines are needed to help ensure that our first guess at DT is reasonable.

Time Constants

A useful guideline is to find the shortest "time constant" in the model. Then check to be sure that DT is only half as large as the shortest time constant. In material flow models in the previous chapter, a "time constant" could take the form of the average time interval that material spends in each stock. In an exponentially growing system like the bank balance or population models in appendix C, a time constant can take the form of a doubling time. You'll learn in chapter 17 that time constants can also take the form of lags in the transfer of information from one part of the system to another.

The easiest time constants to identify are the time intervals associated with material flow, so let's consider some examples from the previous chapter. In the three models of student flows in figure 10.12, we saw time constants of 4 years, 6 years, and 12 years. And if we expanded the model of student flows to include a stock for each of grades 1 through 12, we would have twelve stocks, each with an average time interval of 1 year. The shortest time constant in all of these models appears to be 1 year.

Now, recall the population model from figure 10.6, which uses four stocks to keep track of the movement of people through the categories of infancy, youth, maturity, and elderly. The average time in the mature category might be 50 years, while the average time in infancy could be as low as 0.25 year. You were told that this situation can pose unusual problems when it comes to simulating the model. The problems arise from the short value of DT combined with the long time horizon needed to see the pattern of growth of the population. The shortest time constant in the population model is 0.25 year, which suggests that our initial guess at DT should be 0.125 year. We would need 8 steps to complete 1 year of a simulation. Now imagine that we wish to simulate the growth in the population over the course of 200 years, enough time to see the population trend over three or four generations of humans. The computer would require 1,600 steps to complete the simulation. This raises the question of whether we should be willing to wait for the computer to execute 1,600 sets of calculations. With today's high-speed chips, you may not need to wait long. But what if the next example involves 3,200 steps or 6,400 steps? Where should we draw the line?

One Thousand Steps

I recommend that you reexamine the purpose of your model whenever you find yourself with a simulation that requires over 1,000 steps. Take the opportunity to reconsider either the long time horizon or the short DT. In the population example with 1,600 steps, for example, we could begin by asking ourselves if we really need to study the population over a 200-year interval. If the long time horizon is needed, we should turn our attention to the short DT. In this case, the short DT is dictated by the assignment of a separate stock variable to keep track of the infant population. So we would ask ourselves if it is really necessary to assign a separate stock to keep track of the infant population.

The population example is meant to illustrate a general problem that occurs when models contain both long and short time constants. Such models pose special challenges for numerical simulation. They are sometimes called "stiff" by mathematicians working in numerical methods (Pugh-Roberts Associates 1986, 9–11; Shampine and Gear 1979). The short time constants force us to select a small value of DT. The long time constants force us to simulate the model over a long time interval to see the dynamics play out fully over time. Stiff models pose questions as to whether you should use simple integration methods (like the Euler's method mentioned at the end of chapter 3) or resort to integration methods especially designed for stiff systems. But these questions need not interest us, because a better approach is simply to avoid building models that require over 1,000 steps.

Let's consider how this could be done for the infant mortality portion of the model in figure 10.6. We need to eliminate the stock assigned to the infant population, but we know infant deaths are an important part of the population calculations. How can we avoid simulating the stock of infants and still count their deaths? The key is to reformulate the model with its steady-state equivalent. Figure 11.1 shows an example of an equilibrium diagram of the infants portion of the population model.

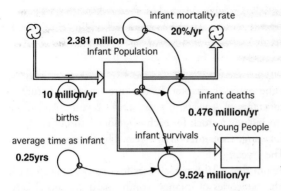

Figure 11.1. Equilibrium diagram for the infant population model.

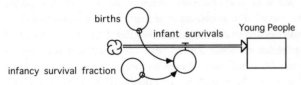

Figure 11.2. Simulating infant survivals.

For purposes of studying the equilibrium tendencies, let's assume that the flow of births is constant at 10 million/yr. Our goal is to learn what fraction of the 10 million births will survive infancy. The model in figure 11.1 is simulated over several years, with DT at 0.125 year (or even smaller). Within a few years or so, we observe the steady-state conditions in figure 11.1. We see that the logical consequence of the model operations is that 95.24 percent of the births will survive to become young people. We can now replace the model in figure 11.1 with the model in figure 11.2 with the infancy survival fraction set at 95.24 percent. Both models require *births* to get started, and they both end up with a stock of *young people* that can be used to build toward a stock of mature and elderly people. The advantage of the model in figure 11.2 is that it will keep track of the infant survivals without the need for an extremely short DT.

Illustrating the "DT Problem"

The most important thing you can learn about numerical simulation is how to recognize when you are looking at inaccurate results. Experienced modelers immediately recognize spurious results—they simply glance at the time graph and announce that there is a "DT problem." Let's look at an example of the flower growth model from chapter 6 so you will be able to recognize the characteristic appearance of a "DT problem."

The flower model flow diagram is shown in figure 6.1. The simulation results are shown in figure 6.4. The time constants in the model are associated with the decay rate and the growth rate. The decay rate is 20 percent/yr, so the implicit value of the time spent in the stock is 5 years. The growth rate is 100 percent/yr (when the flowers are just getting started), so the doubling time is around 0.7 years early in the simulation. The shortest time constant is 0.7 years, so it looks like we can simulate this model quite nicely with DT set at 0.25 year.

Now suppose we change the parameters to represent a new variety that grows and decays much more rapidly. The new variety has an intrinsic growth rate of 400 percent/yr and a decay rate of 80 percent/yr. (Think of this variety as moving through the processes of growth and decay four times faster than the previous variety.) With such rapid response times, we should be careful about the choice of DT. Just because the value of 0.25 year worked for the previous variety doesn't mean that it will work for the new variety.

Figure 11.3 shows the simulation results with DT at 0.25 year. Figure 11.4 shows the simulated growth if the simulation is repeated with DT at 0.125 year. A small difference is evident, especially in the growth during the second year of the simulation. This difference suggests that the default value is too large. If you cut DT in half again, you will learn that a DT of 0.125 year is adequate for this model.

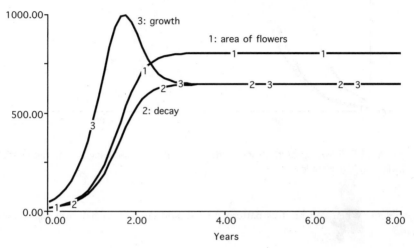

Figure 11.3. Flower growth model with DT at 0.25 year.

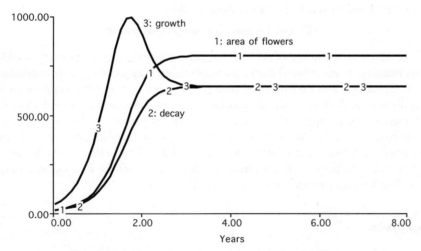

Figure 11.4. Flower growth model with DT at 0.125 year.

Figure 11.5 shows the results that are important for you to recognize. This simulation was created with DT set to 0.5 year. This value is well beyond the guidelines, so we should not expect to see accurate results. The important thing to recognize in figure 11.5 is the appearance of numerical inaccuracy. Notice, for example, that growth and decay oscillate in a sawtooth pattern. These oscillations have nothing to do with the real world. They are caused by errors in the numerical calculations, and they are sometimes called artifactual oscillations or pathological oscillations. Experienced practitioners recognize from the sawtooth pattern that the oscillations are artifacts. They know the "sawtooth" is telling them that the model has a

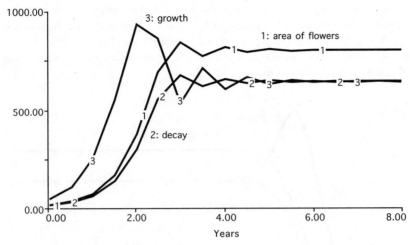

Figure 11.5. Flower growth model with DT at 0.5 years showing the characteristic look of a "DT Problem."

DT problem. When you see this pattern, you should cut DT in half and repeat the simulation.

Final Suggestion

The final guideline for setting DT is to remember that:

DT has NO counterpart in the real world.

A DT of 0.25 year in a model of the sales company does not stand for quarterly bookkeeping, for example. In flower simulations, you might be inclined to interpret the oscillations as realistic, especially if you have observed systems that arrive at an equilibrium position in an oscillatory manner. Perhaps we should associate a DT of 0.5 year with a 6-month delay in the way flowers react to changes in the fraction of area that is occupied. This line of reasoning will only get you into trouble. Not only will you select a poor value of DT, but you will end up with a poorly formulated model. If you want to simulate a delay in the way the flowers react over time, take advantage of the information delays to represent the time lags in an explicit manner. You'll learn how this is done in chapter 17.

Exercises

1.   **Time constants in the Mono Basin:**

     What is the shortest time constant in the model of Mono Lake shown in figure 4.14? (Ask yourself how long a cubic foot of water would remain in the lake if the main outflow is evaporation.)

2.   **Time constants with Grant Lake and Mono Lake:**

     Suppose we were to add Grant Lake to the previous model. The new model might be used to simulate the volume and surface area of Grant Lake as endogenous variables, and net Grant Lake evaporation would remove water from Grant Lake (rather than Mono Lake, as in figure 4.14). Grant Lake is fed by Rush Creek, which averages 60

KAF/yr (Vorster 1985, 72). The capacity of the reservoir is around 48 KAF (LADWP 1987, v–5). What would be the shortest time constant in the new model? (Ask yourself how long a cubic foot of water would remain in Grant Lake.)

3.   **Expanding the simulation of infants:**

Figure 11.2 shows how we could simulate the number of infant survivals without assigning a stock to keep track of the infant population. Now suppose we wanted to know the typical size of the infant population. Use the steady-state conditions from figure 11.1 as a guide and add a converter to figure 11.2 to estimate the size of the infant population as proportional to the births.

Chapter 12

Simulating the Flow of DDT

System dynamics may be used to simulate the flow of material through the environment. The flows can involve multiple media such as water, soil, air, and the bodies of human beings and other animals. The models can help us understand the time delays between the application of a controlled flow and its arrival at "target" or "nontarget" organisms. The models are normally constructed in a step-by-step manner, based on our understanding of material flows in each medium. The goal is to improve our instincts for managing the controlled flows to achieve the desired impacts on the target organism with minimal indirect effects on nontarget organisms. This chapter illustrates a general approach to simulating multimedia flows with an example of DDT. This pesticide is well known to students of the environment, and the example will reveal the usefulness of system dynamics in the field of toxicology. The ideas are useful wherever scientists wish to simulate material flows through several media (e.g., in pharmacokinetic modeling of drug flows in the body).

Figure 12.1 shows a flow diagram of a system dynamics model constructed by Jorgen Randers (1973) to study the long time delays between the application of DDT on crops and the appearance of the chemical in fish. The flow diagram follows the Dynamo conventions explained in appendix D. The DDT model is thoroughly documented in Randers's chapter in *Toward Global Equilibrium*. You can work with the model directly in Dynamo, or you could choose to convert the model into any of the stock-and-flow programs. This chapter explains the DDT model in a step-by-step manner, using progressively more complicated Stella models. By the end of the chapter, you will appreciate the applicability of system dynamics to simulating material flows through multiple media. You will also appreciate some of the challenges that can arise when simulating material flows with a wide disparity in time constants.

Background

The birth of the modern environmental movement is often associated with the publication of Rachel Carson's *Silent Spring* in 1962. Carson described the dangerous side effects of chemicals invented during the 1940s and 1950s, including the insecticide dichloro-diphenyl-trichloro-ethane, or DDT.

DDT is an organic compound, one of the chlorinated hydrocarbons. It is toxic to insects but not to crops, and it is extremely stable. A single application remains toxic to insects for a long time. It was first put to use in the 1940s with spectacular success, and it was thought to be an ideal insecticide. Botkin and Keller (1995, 208) comment that scientists of that time

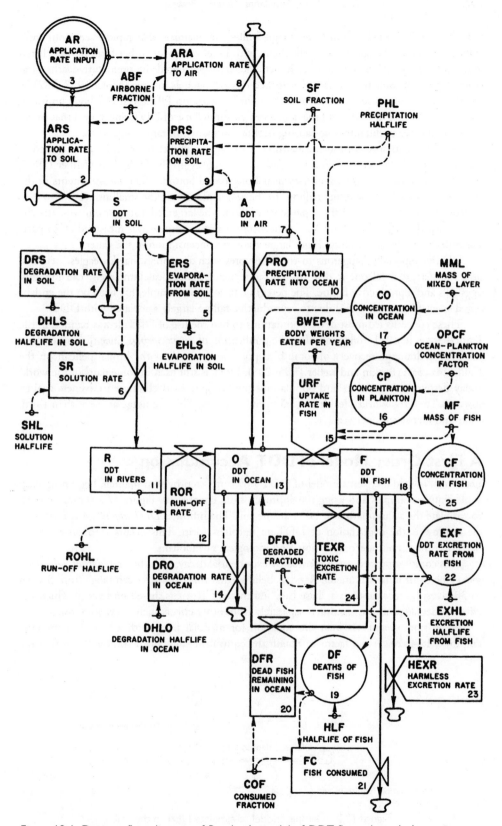

Figure 12.1. Dynamo flow diagram of Randers's model of DDT flows through the environment.

thought they had finally "found the 'magic bullet'—a chemical that rapidly seeks out individuals of a particular species and kills them, with no effect on any other form of life." It has been estimated that DDT and other insecticides have prevented the premature deaths of at least 7 million people from insect-transmitted diseases such as malaria (Miller 1997, 382) In 1948, Paul Mueller received the Nobel Prize for his work on DDT. Carson's book appeared fourteen years later to warn us of the dangers of continued use of DDT. She argued that insecticides and other pollutants were causing declines in many nontarget organisms.

DDT presents special problems because of its high solubility in fat. It becomes stored in animal fat and is subject to bioconcentration as it moves up the food chain. Miller (1997, 385) gives an example from an estuary near Long Island Sound. DDT measurements in the water were around 2.5 parts per trillion. In the zooplankton and the small fish (minnows) its concentration was measured at 0.5 parts per million. The larger fish eat the minnows, and the ospreys eat the larger fish. The DDT concentration in the ospreys was measured at 25 parts per million, around ten million times larger than its concentration in the water.

DDT is especially dangerous to top carnivores such as ospreys, hawks, eagles, pelicans, and the peregrine falcon. It disrupts hormone regulation of calcium levels, causing thin eggshells and reproductive failure. The peregrine falcon, for example, has been on the endangered species list (until 1994) due to reproductive failure largely associated with DDT.

These concerns led most developed nations to ban the use of DDT. It was banned in the United States in 1971, nine years after the publication of *Silent Spring*. Since that time, there has been a dramatic recovery of some bird populations, such as the brown pelican on the California coast (Botkin and Keller 1995, 208). DDT is still used in some parts of the world today despite its impact on bird populations (and despite its declining effectiveness against insects). The UN World Health Organization reports worldwide usage at more than thirty thousand metric tons per year.

A First-Order Model of DDT Accumulation

Let's work toward a systems model of DDT flows in a step-by-step manner, beginning with some simple examples and using the approach from chapter 10. Figure 12.2 shows a model to simulate the accumulation of DDT in the soil. The inflow is *DDT applied to soil*; the single outflow is the degradation of DDT to harmless form. This occurs through chemical decomposition, photodecomposition, and biological metabolism.

This complex process is represented by exponential decay, with the *degradation half-life in soil* as the controlling parameter. Randers believes that this parameter can range from 3 years to 30 years; he recommends a "base case" estimate of 10 years, based on tests in which the effect of degradation was measured separately from other effects such as evaporation.

Recall from chapter 10 that the equation for material flows with a half-life parameter employ a 1.44 conversion factor to obtain the equivalent value of the time interval that the

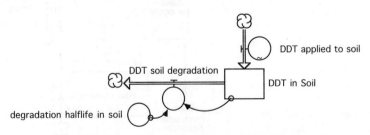

Figure 12.2. A simple model to simulate DDT in the soil.

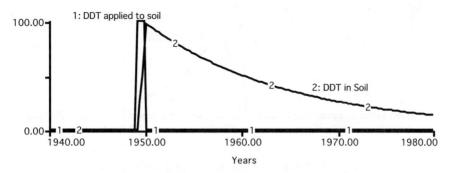

Figure 12.3. Simulated response of the first-order model.

material remains in the stock. Since Randers was working with such highly uncertain esti-mates, he took the liberty of using 1.5 as a conversion factor. Let's follow his example so that our results may be compared to his original results. Using Randers's approximation, the equa-tion for the outflow in figure 12.2 would be written as:

```
DDT_soil_degradation = DDT_in_Soil/(1.5*degradation_halflife_in_soil)
```

Figure 12.3 shows the simulated response of DDT in soil if 100 tons of DDT are applied to the soil in the year 1950. The accumulated amount jumps immediately to 100 tons and then declines in exponential fashion. Ten years after the application, around 50 tons would remain in the soil; after 20 years, around 25 tons would remain.

Figure 12.4 expands the simple model to include two additional outflows. The *DDT evaporation from soil* is controlled by *the evaporation halflife in soil,* which may be set to 2 years. The third outflow represents the removal of DDT as the soil particles are swept away by water erosion. The DDT molecule is only slightly soluble in water, so it is not likely to go into solu-tion. But DDT adheres strongly to soil particles, and these particles may be "washed away" by water erosion. Very little of DDT leaves the soil by this pathway, so Randers sets the *solu-tion halflife in soil* at 500 years.

The simulated response of DDT in soil if 100 tons of DDT are applied to the soil in the year 1950 is shown in figure 12.5. The accumulated amount jumps immediately, but it does not reach 100 tons because evaporation quickly goes to work, removing some of the DDT

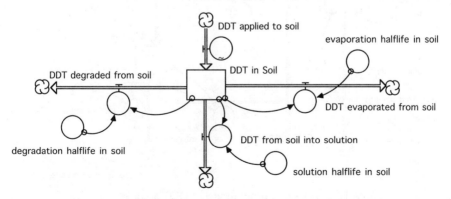

Figure 12.4. Expanding the simple model.

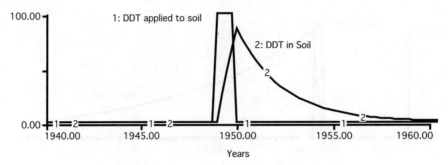

Figure 12.5. Simulated response of the expanded model.

from the soil. This new model suggests that very little DDT would be left in the soil after 10 years.

A Second-Order Model

At this point, you are probably thinking about the fate of the DDT that leaves the soil through evaporation. Once the DDT molecules are in the air, they become highly mobile and can move great distances before they fall to the ground again, mainly through precipitation. If it rains every 2–3 weeks, we might assume that DDT will quite quickly leave the atmosphere. But during the time it is airborne, it might be swept out over the ocean. Figure 12.6 shows a further expansion of the model to keep track of the airborne DDT and the amount of DDT returning to the soil due to precipitation. This is a second-order model, as it uses two stocks to keep track of the accumulation of DDT in the system.

Following Randers's recommendations, the *fraction of airborne DDT above land* is set to 30 percent. The *precipitation halflife* is set to 0.05 years on the assumption that half of the airborne DDT is removed from the atmosphere by precipitation roughly every 2–3 weeks. The

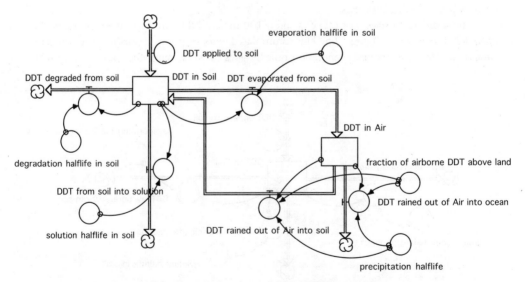

Figure 12.6. A second-order model of DDT accumulation.

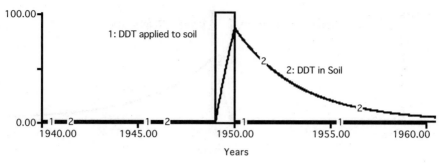

Figure 12.7. Simulated response of the second-order model.

simulated response of the new model is shown in figure 12.7. As before, 100 tons of DDT is applied to the soil in the year 1950. The new model responds in generally the same manner as the previous model because of the rapid removal of DDT from the soil by evaporation. But the quick return of some of the airborne DDT to the soil causes a somewhat slower pattern of decline in figure 12.7.

Now, let's expand the second-order model to account for the possibility that some of the DDT becomes airborne immediately, during its application. *Total DDT application* is now a converter, and the *airborne fraction* is used to split the applied DDT into two flows, as shown in figure 12.8. The airborne fraction is set to 50 percent based on Randers's recommendation.

The simulated response of the new model is shown in figure 12.9. The 100 tons of DDT in 1950 are now split into two flows. Half lands in the soil; the other half becomes airborne, where a fraction can return to the soil by precipitation. The simulated response shows that there would be very little DDT left in the soil 10 years after its application.

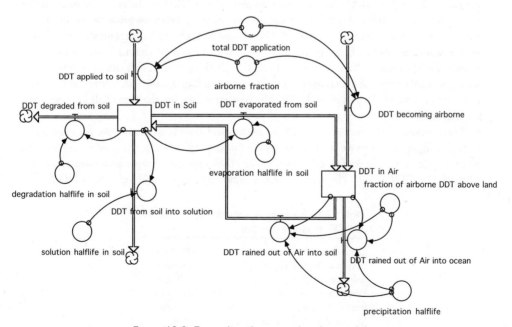

Figure 12.8. Expanding the second-order model.

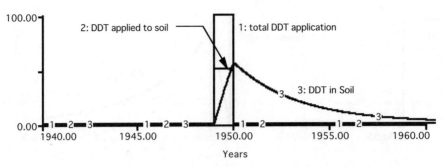

Figure 12.9. Simulated response with DDT inflows split between soil and air.

Randers's Model

The previous four models demonstrate how one may gradually build up a comprehensive simulation of the paths that DDT could follow through the environment. This approach may be continued to arrive at DDT concentrations in the ocean and in the fish. The fish concentration is especially important because the fish are a source of food for many of the birds that experienced reproductive failure.

Figure 12.10 shows a flow diagram of Randers's original model. Five stocks are used to keep track of the DDT accumulation in the system. Each stock is measured in metric tons of DDT; each flow is measured in metric tons/year. Many of the flows use the term "rate" (e.g., *degradation rate in soil*). A rate variable in Dynamo corresponds to a "flow" variable in Stella, so don't be confused about their units. Each and every flow is measured in metric tons/year.

The top portion of figure 12.10 is similar to the model in figure 12.8. DDT enters the system at the top and works its way through two stocks. The pathway to the ocean is either through runoff in the rivers or by precipitation of airborne DDT that has drifted over the ocean. The lower portion of figure 12.10 assigns one stock to keep track of DDT in the ocean and a second for DDT stored in fish. The concentration of DDT in the ocean is based on the mass of water in the mixed layer. The model uses an *ocean-plankton concentration factor* to estimate the concentration in plankton. (McKinney and Schoch [1998] explain the use of bioconcentration factors [BCF] for pollutants that move up the food chain.) The concentration of DDT in plankton is then used to estimate the DDT update in fish. Randers gives "best estimates" and a range of uncertainty for each parameter based on a wide variety of information sources available in the early 1970s. His best estimates for the eight half-lives are presented in table 12.1.

The purpose of the model is to help us understand how long it will take for changes at the top of figure 12.10 to work their way to the bottom. Specifically, the model may be used to test how long it will take for reductions in the DDT *application rate input* to translate into reductions in *DDT in fish*. The *application rate input* represents worldwide use of DDT. This

Table 12.1. Randers's estimates of half-lives of DDT in various media.

Degradation half-life in soil	10 years
Evaporation half-life in soil	2 years
Solution half-life	500 years
Precipitation half-life	0.05 year
Runoff half-life	0.1 year
Degradation half-life in ocean	15 years
Half-life of fish	3 years
Excretion half-life from fish	0.3 year

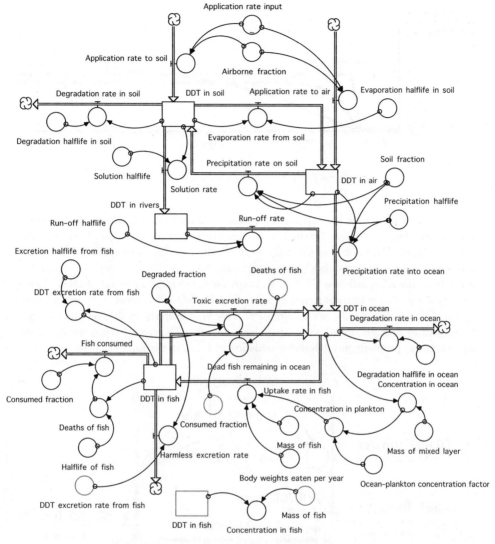

Figure 12.10. Flow diagram of Randers's original model.

is set to around 100,000 metric tons/yr in the 1950s and peaks at around 175,000 metric tons/yr in the 1960s.

Step Test and Equilibrium Diagram

Figure 12.11 shows results of a simple test with the application rate fixed at zero until the year 1950. Then DDT use increases abruptly to 100,000 metric tons/year and remains at that value for the rest of the simulation. The purpose of this "step test" is to allow us to study the responsiveness of the model under simple conditions. The simulated response reveals that DDT in the soil would reach an equilibrium value within the first 10–15 years. This suggests that the "top part" of the model acts rather quickly to reach equilibrium. DDT in the fish, on the other hand, continues to grow decade after decade. It reaches around 300 metric tons and is still increasing at the end of the simulation.

An equilibrium diagram based on the results at the conclusion of the step test is shown in

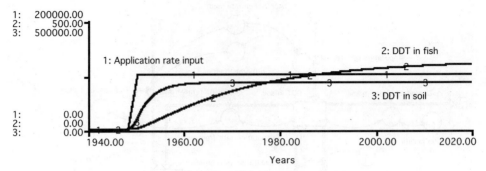

Figure 12.11. Step test of Randers's model.

figure 12.12. The diagram focuses on the top portion of the model, as this is the portion that reaches equilibrium. It shows 100,000 metric tons/year entering the system from the application of DDT. The bottom of the diagram shows the two flows that move DDT into the ocean. One flow is the runoff from rivers. It accounts for only 288 tons/year. The second flow is precipitation of the airborne DDT. It accounts for over 85,000 tons/year of DDT flowing into the ocean. The numerical results in figure 12.12 indicate that roughly 85 percent of the applied DDT will enter the ocean, almost entirely via precipitation that removes airborne DDT drifting over the ocean. Now, what about the other 15 percent? It appears to be leaving the system primarily through the degradation of DDT in the soil.

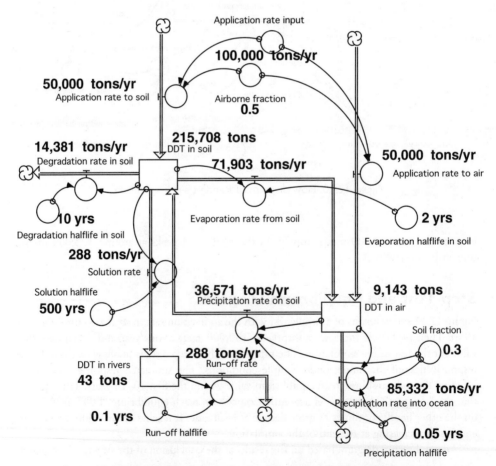

Figure 12.12. Equilibrium diagram for the "top" portion of the DDT model.

Suppose we were to cut DDT use to zero in the year 2021. You know that the flow of DDT into the ocean would not drop immediately to zero. There is a "backlog" of DDT built up in the soil, in the air, and in the rivers. It will take time for this backlog to gradually work its way to the ocean. The total DDT stored in the system in the year 2020 is around 255,000 tons, and the vast majority is stored in the soil. You might expect that around 85 percent of the backlog would eventually work its way to the ocean, primarily via evaporation to the air and then through precipitation into the ocean.

Implications of the Base Case Projection

Figure 12.13 shows Randers's projection of DDT in the soil and in the fish if the application of DDT follows a "best estimate" scenario. It allowed for an increase in DDT use during the 1960s with a peak of around 175,000 tons/year during the 1970s. He reasoned that concern over the adverse impacts would cause a gradual phaseout of DDT use by the year 1998. Figure 12.13 shows that the DDT in the soil would peak shortly after the peak use of DDT as a pesticide. DDT in the fish would continue to grow for several years, reaching a peak in the 1980s. The dashed lines in figure 12.13 are included to draw your eye to the year 1962, when *Silent Spring* was published. The first arrow shows the level of DDT in the fish around 1962, a level sufficiently dangerous to trigger the publication of *Silent Spring*. Now follow the horizontal line to see how long one must wait for the simulated level of DDT in the fish to return to the 1962 value. The simulation reveals that we must be prepared to wait around 50 years for the DDT to return to the level that triggered the publication of *Silent Spring*.

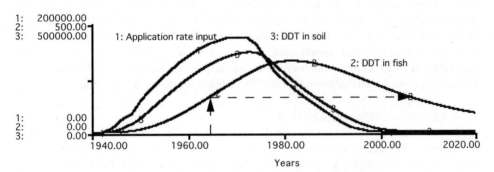

Figure 12.13. Base case results from Randers's model.

Understanding this long delay in the transmission of a persistent pollutant was the main point of Randers's investigation. He used numerous simulations, with variations in the uncertain parameters and with changes in the scenario for DDT use in the future. His findings might be summarized relative to the 50-year return interval in figure 12.13. For example, with consistently optimistic estimates of all the uncertain parameters, the simulation required around 40 years to return to the 1962 level. In a scenario with a complete ban on DDT use around the world in 1971, 35 years would be required to return to the 1962 level. This long time interval reveals the considerable momentum associated with the flows of DDT through multiple media.

An Alternative Model

The numerical step size in Randers's model is set to 0.02 year, so 4,000 iterations are required to simulate the 80-year interval. The model clearly violates the "1,000 steps" guideline from chapter 11. The guideline should challenge us to reconsider the long time horizon or recon-

sider the selection of such a small DT. Randers needed an 80-year time horizon to allow sufficient time to simulate the slow buildup and slow decline of DDT in the fish. If we shorten
the time horizon, we miss the main point of his exercise. So let's turn our attention to the DT.
The short DT is required because of the extremely short time constants such as the precipitation half-life and the runoff half-life. At 0.05 year, the precipitation half-life is the shortest
time constant in the model. You know that we must set the DT to less than half the shortest
time constant, so the value of 0.02 year appears reasonable.

Perhaps we could revise the model if we were to eliminate this short time constant. But
we have to be careful because we have learned from figure 12.12 that precipitation of airborne
DDT over the ocean is the principal pathway for DDT to reach the ocean. The revised model
must maintain the pathway to the ocean, but perhaps we can eliminate the use of the stock
to keep track of the amount of airborne DDT. (Eliminating this stock is similar to eliminating the stock assigned to the infant population in chapter 11.)

The next shortest time constant is the runoff half-life, which is set to 0.1 year. To eliminate this short time constant, we would need to eliminate the stock assigned to DDT in the
rivers. The equilibrium conditions in figure 12.12 indicate that we could eliminate this stock.
Moreover, we could eliminate the pathway, as only a minuscule fraction of the DDT makes
its way to the ocean via the rivers.

Figure 12.14 shows a revised DDT model. The new model uses three stocks instead of
five. It ignores the stock of DDT in the rivers, and it ignores the pathway through the rivers.
The new model does not assign a separate stock to keep track of the airborne DDT. But it
preserves in mathematical form the key pathway that moves DDT to the air and into the
ocean via precipitation. Figure 12.14 shows three clouds clustered in the upper right corner.
One of these is a sink. It represents where DDT goes when it evaporates from the soil. The
other two clouds are sources. They are drawn adjacent to the sink to convey the point that
the model will not lose track (mathematically) of the DDT that evaporates from the soil. One
portion of it goes right back into the soil; the remainder goes into the ocean. This is accom-
plished by the information connections that link the *evaporation rate from soil* to the *precipitation on soil* and the *precipitation on ocean*. The relevant equations are as follows:

```
Evaporation_rate_from_soil =
    (DDT_in_soil/(1.5*Evaporation_halflife_in_soil))
Precipitation_on_ocean =
    (Evaporation_rate_from_soil+Application_rate)*(1-Soil_fraction)
Precipitation_on_soil =
    (Application_rate+Evaporation_rate_from_soil)*Soil_fraction
```

The first equation is the same as the previous model. But the next two equations must represent the flow of DDT via precipitation into the ocean or back to the soil. They do this by
working directly with the two flows that lead to airborne DDT and the *soil fraction*. Figure
12.15 confirms that the revised model gives the same pattern of results as the original model.
The relative timing of the peaks and the long time interval required for DDT in fish to return
to the 1962 level are the same as shown previously. The new model delivers the same important insights as the original model.

The revised model does more than match the general trends in the original model; it
matches the numerical values quite closely as well. Table 12.2 provides a summary taken from
the year 1980, the year with the maximum value of DDT in fish. It shows that the revised
model matches the original model exactly in terms of the DDT stored in the fish, and it
comes quite close to the values in the soil and the ocean.

The revised model results were generated with a DT of 0.125 year. At 8 steps per year, the
80-year simulation requires 640 steps. We are now operating within the suggested guidelines
for numerical simulation.

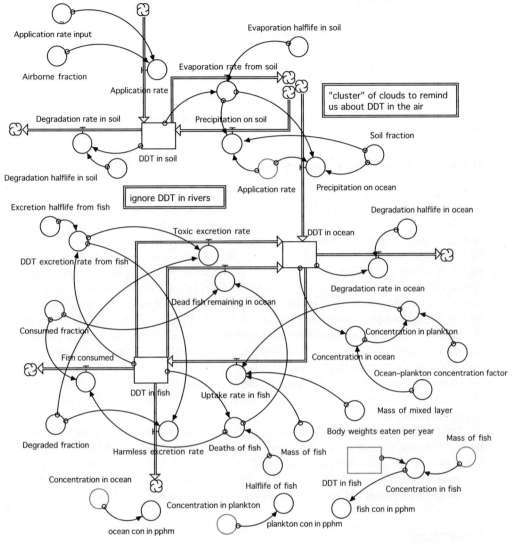

Figure 12.14. Revised model of DDT flows.

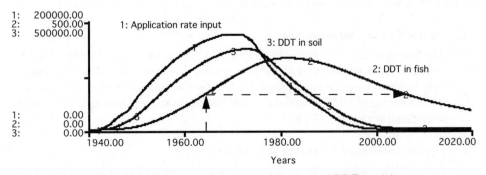

Figure 12.15. Base case simulation of the revised DDT model.

Table 12.2. Numerical results from the year 1980.

	Original (metric tons)	Revised (metric tons)
Soil	268,362	269,301
Air	10,293	n.a.
Rivers	54	n.a.
Ocean	2,014,124	2,016,528
Fish	329	329

Summary and Discussion

This chapter demonstrates with an example of DDT how system dynamics may be used to simulate the flow of materials through multiple media like soil, air, and water. The demonstration makes use of step tests and equilibrium diagrams to help us appreciate which of the many pathways dominate the system. The demonstration also arrived at two versions of a multimedia model. The two models present us with an interesting question: Which of the models is better? The revised model certainly executes more quickly on the computer, and it does so without loss of accuracy. If we intend to conduct extensive sensitivity testing, we could certainly reduce the time in front of the computer with the revised model. But many students find the original model more appealing because it is easier to "see the flows" of DDT through the environment. They understand the logic behind the revised model, and they understand that the two models yield the same numerical results. Nevertheless, they are drawn to the original model, and they are willing to "pay the price" of sitting in front of the computer waiting for a slower simulation to appear on the monitor. Their choice is entirely reasonable, as modeling is more than making calculations—it's also a process to improve understanding and communication.

The DDT example involves material flow through multiple media where the individual flows may be described as a diffuse flow with a characteristic half-life. Not all of nature's flows follow this pattern. Some flows are much more tightly controlled, as when animals migrate to the ocean. You'll see how these flows are simulated in the next two chapters. Appendix I rounds out the treatment of material flows with simulations in the spatial dimensions.

Exercises

The exercises require that you download the DDT models from the book's home page. The flow diagrams should resemble figures 12.10 and 12.14. You should verify that the models generate the results shown in figures 12.13 and 12.15 before starting the exercises.

1. **Update the base case simulation:**

    The base case results in figures 12.13 and 12.15 assume that use of DDT would be gradually eliminated by the year 1998. It appears that worldwide DDT use is higher than Randers's base case assumptions. Update the base case run with current information on the use of DDT around the world. Document the new base case with a graph corresponding to figure 12.15.

2. **Equilibrium diagram for the ocean and fish:**

    Subject the revised model to the "step test" shown in figure 12.11. Allow the test to run sufficiently long for the *DDT in fish* to reach equilibrium. Draw an equilibrium diagram for the bottom half of the model.

3. **Importance of half-life conversion factor:**

   Randers uses an approximate conversion factor of 1.5 in each of the flow equations involving a half-life. Chapter 10 explains that the conversion factor appearing in flow equations should be set to 1.44. Conduct a test with the revised model to learn if the change in the conversion factor leads to significant changes in Randers's base case simulation.

4. **Bar chart for bioconcentration:**

   Repeat the base case simulation shown in figure 12.15 with the bar chart open to see the ups and downs of the relative concentrations. Document your work by pausing the simulation in the year 1980 and printing the bar chart that accompanies this exercise. The three concentrations are measured in parts per hundred million (pphm) to allow for a visual check on the bioconcentration as DDT moves up the ocean food chain.

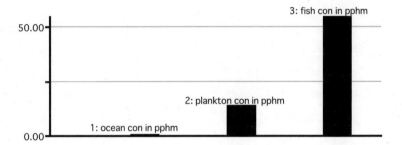

5. **Project exercise—regions A and P:**

   Miller (1997, 388) describes a "circle of poison" involving the production of DDT in the United States for sale to countries that have not adopted the ban. DDT residues may return to the United States by several pathways, such as fruits and vegetables, migrating birds, and airborne DDT. Expand the model to simulate DDT use in two regions. Region A continues to allow DDT; region P prohibits its use. Assume that the principal pathway connecting DDT in the two regions is the drift of airborne DDT. Adopt the same half-lives for both regions. Assume that DDT use is 50,000 metric tons/year in both regions until the year 1970. After 1970, DDT use falls to zero in region P but remains constant at 50,000 metric tons/year in region A. Run the A & P model with a variety of assumptions on the fraction of airborne DDT from region A that drifts over the coastal waters of region P. Use the model to learn how much longer DDT levels in region P will remain above dangerous levels due to the continued use in region A.

Further Reading

This chapter explains a pragmatic approach to reducing the DDT model from a model with five stocks to a model with three stocks. We have changed from a fifth-order to a third-order model. I recommend you follow this "pragmatic" approach whenever you find yourself in a situation similar to the DDT model with extremely short time constants. Now, if you have studied advanced mathematical methods, you will appreciate that order reduction can be addressed more formally.

- Eberlein (1989) describes an approach to model simplification that begins by linearizing the model. He then finds the eigenvalues of the linearized model to reveal which stocks might be eliminated. The method is illustrated by simplifying a fourth-order model of a zebra population to a first-order model.

- Mohapatra (1985) uses modal control theory to simplify a model of factory distribution and ordering. As with Eberlein's approach, Mohapatra must work with a linear system, and he warns us to expect difficult mathematical computations for higher-order systems.

Chapter 13

The Salmon Smolts' Spring Migration

The declining salmon runs on the Snake and Columbia river system is one of the most serious environmental problems in the Pacific Northwest. The salmon have disappeared from 40 percent of their historical breeding ranges despite a public and private investment of more than $1 billion. The annual salmon and steelhead runs have dwindled to 2.5 million, less than a quarter of the run sizes of one hundred years ago. This chapter describes a model that may be used to simulate one piece of the complex and threatened salmon system. It focuses on the spring migration of hatchery smolts to the ocean. It may be used to test the relative merits of barging fish or drawing down the reservoirs to help the smolts reach the ocean.

Background

A smolt is a juvenile salmon that migrates from its stream habitat to the ocean. It undergoes physiological changes called smoltification to adapt from fresh water to salt water. This chapter concentrates on hatchery smolts. The juveniles are raised in the hatchery until they are ready to be released into the river for the spring migration. After two days, the smolts reach the Snake River, where they encounter the slack water behind Lower Granite dam. Lower Granite's location is shown in figure 13.1. It is the first of eight dams the smolts will encounter in their journey to the ocean. The dams are owned and operated by the federal government primarily for hydroelectric generation. (They also provide flood control, irrigation, and transportation.) The reservoirs are connected, one after the other, so the smolts will experience slack water all the way to the Bonneville dam. The slack water slows their migration compared to the era when the Snake and Columbia flowed freely to the ocean.

Speed is important if the smolts are to reach the ocean before their bodies complete the physiological changes for saline conditions. The smolts that remain in fresh water too long will die from the high stress of smoltification. Other threats along the way include predators, disease, and starvation. The smolts are also vulnerable to turbine mortality if they are swept into the currents leading to the turbines.

Model Organization and Policies

The model is organized as a series of "sectors" to keep track of the smolts' progress toward the ocean. The first sector simulates the smolts' release from the hatchery and their travel to the first reservoir. Each of the next eight sectors is associated with a reservoir and dam. The smolts must survive their travel in the reservoir, and they must pass safely through or around each

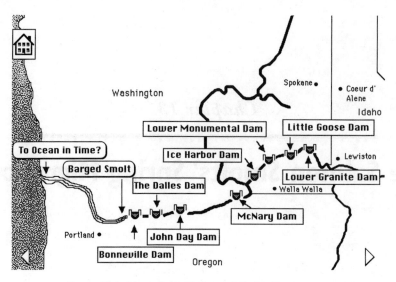

Figure 13.1. Map of the Snake and Columbia river system.

dam. The final sector tracks their progress in the final reach of the river between the Bonneville dam and the ocean. The model assumes that the smolts remain grouped in a relatively tight schooling pattern. So it makes sense to take advantage of the "conveyor" stock, as explained in chapter 10. We will begin the simulation by releasing 10 million smolts in day zero. Stocks will be measured in millions of smolts; flows will be measured in millions of smolts per day. The model time horizon is 40 days, a sufficient time interval for the smolts to either reach the ocean or die from smoltification.

The model will be used to test the two commonly discussed policies to improve the chances that the smolts (see photo 13.1) reach the ocean:

- The first policy is barging, the transport of smolts around many of the dams and reservoirs. Barging allows the smolts to avoid turbine mortality, and it speeds their journey. The model simulates barging at Lower Granite and Little Goose on the Snake as well as McNary on the Columbia. Barging has been used extensively, and you will learn that tag-

Photo 13.1. Migrating Smolts. Source: Courtesy of the Bonneville Power Administration.

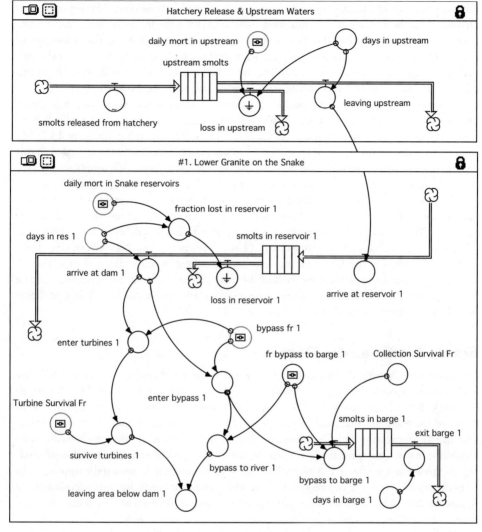

Figure 13.2. The first two sectors of the model.

ging studies yield valuable insights on its effectiveness. We will take advantage of the tagging studies to include the "latent deaths" from barging in the model.

• The second policy is drawing down reservoirs to create higher water flow during the migration period. Draw-down proponents argue that faster water flow will speed the smolts' migration to the ocean, thereby reducing the danger of smoltification. The model accepts travel times as the key inputs. You can set these inputs based on the estimated reduction in travel time to be achieved by a drawdown.

The model may be used to indicate whether barging or a drawdown is better under different weather conditions.

Model Structure

Figure 13.2 shows the first two sectors of the model. The first sector keeps track of the hatchery smolts shortly after their release and prior to their arrival at the slack water in the Lower

Granite reservoir. The model begins with the *smolts released from hatchery*. This input is set at 10 million on the first day of the simulation. All the stocks in the model are initialized at zero. *Upstream smolts* receives the 10 million smolts released from the hatchery. The smolts spend 2 days in this stock, where they are subject to a mortality of 25 percent/day based on the estimate by Olsen (1992). With this assumption, we would expect to lose 5 million smolts in this sector. The other 5 million leave the upstream sector and arrive at the first reservoir.

The arrival at Lower Granite can be represented in either of two ways. We can connect the flow draining the stock of smolts in the upstream sector with the stock of smolts behind Lower Granite. This is relatively easy at the interface of the two sectors in figure 13.2, but similar connections will be quite cumbersome elsewhere in the model. So the approach in this chapter is to use an information link between the corresponding flows. We simply set the flow of smolts arriving at Lower Granite to the value of the flow leaving the upstream sector.

The smolts behind Lower Granite reservoir are represented by a conveyor whose transit time is called *days in res 1*. The time interval is set at 25 percent of the total time on the Snake reservoirs. The total time on the Snake is a key input, which you will set based on flow conditions or your decision about a drawdown. (The 25 percent is based on relative size of this reservoir.) The loss in the Lower Granite reservoir is caused by starvation and predation. A loss of 2 percent/day is assumed for each of the Snake River reservoirs based on the estimate by Olsen (1992). The smolts that survive the reservoir are represented by a flow that drains the stock and arrives at the dam.

Smolt Traffic at the Dam

The home page sketches the various routes of travel through and around each dam. One route is downward through the turbines. Smolts swept in this direction are exposed to 15 percent mortality. A less dangerous route is around the dam via the spillway or the sluiceway. Bypass is a third route at dams that have installed screens to divert the smolts away from the turbines and into a collection system. The losses from bypass and spillways are relatively low compared to turbine losses. Our approach is to keep the simulated traffic as simple as possible by sending the smolts in one of two directions. The "dangerous direction" is toward the turbines. The "safe direction" is into the bypass system. You will control the traffic by your selection of the bypass fraction. The maximum feasible fraction is around 70 percent, based on optimum design of the diversion screens.

To illustrate the calculations at each dam, imagine that 4 million smolts arrive at the first dam, and you have set the bypass fraction to 70 percent. The model would send 2.8 million into the bypass system and 1.2 million to the turbines. The turbine survival fraction is set at 85 percent for all the dams, based on the estimate by Olsen (1992). With this assumption, 1.02 million smolts will survive the turbines. Now, what about the 2.8 million smolts in the bypass system? These are under your control. You may place some or all of them in a barge, and they will be transported around the remaining dams and released in the final reach below Bonneville. Or you may return them to the river to join their schoolmates that have survived the trip through the turbines. The smolts leaving the area below the first dam arrive immediately at the reservoir behind the second dam. Smolt survival in each reservoir is represented in the same manner as in Lower Granite. Smolts that arrive at the Little Goose dam face the same traffic options as at Lower Granite, so the model assigns the same combination of stocks, flows, and converters to simulate the second reservoir.

The smolts that leave the area below the second dam arrive immediately at the third reservoir, as shown in figure 13.3. Lower Monumental does not have barging facilities, so the traffic at the dam is somewhat simpler than the previous dam. The user simply specifies the bypass fraction to match the bypass or spillway fractions at the dam. In this case, a default

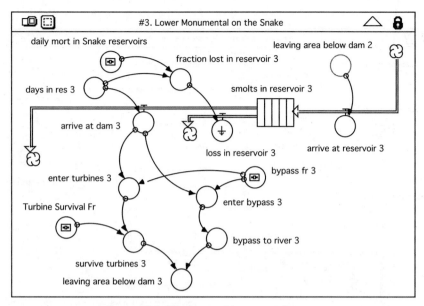

Figure 13.3. The Lower Monumental sector.

value of 30 percent is used to represent 30 percent of the smolts passing over the spillway. (Spillway losses are assumed to be negligible.) The other smolts must pass through the turbines, where they are exposed to 15 percent mortality. The stocks and flows for Lower Monumental are used for each of the five dams without barging. The previous approach is applied to the other three dams.

The smolts that survive the journey through eight reservoirs and dams will arrive at the final reach of the river below Bonneville. Figure 13.4 shows the final sector to simulate their progress to the ocean. Notice the three ghosted variables in the upper right corner. These represent the smolts exiting the three barges. The barge trip survival fraction is set to 98 percent, as only around 2 percent of the barged smolts are observed to die in transit (Olsen 1992).

A far larger fraction of the barged smolts are expected to encounter problems later in their life cycle. A *latent deaths fraction* stands for the fraction of the exiting smolts that will die later in their life cycle because of the disruptive effects of barging. You'll learn shortly that the *latent deaths fraction* is around 50 percent. In other words, only half of the *total smolts exiting the barges* are counted as *barged smolts that we will consider to continue the trip*. They are added to the smolts leaving area below dam 8 to create the flow into a conveyor for the *smolts in final reach*.

The loss in the final reach depends on the *days in final reach* and the *total daily morality in final reach*. The estimated travel time is around 4 days based on 3 days to travel from the barge release point to the Columbia River estuary (Mundy 1994, 108) plus 1 day for the Bonneville smolts to travel to the release point. During the final days in the river, the smolts are subjected to *normal daily mortality in the final reach* (due to predators, disease, and starvation). But they are also subject to the additional mortality effects of smoltification. The *high stress daily mortality in final reach* is found using a graph function (~). The graph assumes zero mortality unless the smolts are still in the fresh water after a threshold of, say, 25 days. This input is called *fresh days before smoltification*. We will assume that the *high stress mortality* increases with each successive day that the smolts have not reached the saline waters of the estuary. A maximum rate of 50 percent/day is applied if they are still in fresh water 5 days later. This plausible combination of assumptions allows the model to match the losses estimated by Olsen (1992).

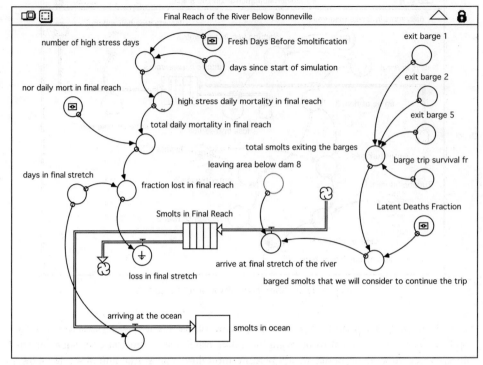

Figure 13.4. Smolts in the final reach below the Bonneville dam.

Travel Time Inputs

The key inputs are the travel times, the days spent traveling the four reservoirs on the Snake, and the days traveling the four reservoirs on the Columbia. In a year with average weather (medium flows), the smolts are expected to need 12.4 days on the Snake and 8.9 days on the Columbia. Since the Snake reservoirs are all around the same size, the 12.4 days is split, with 25 percent going to each reservoir. The splits are not as even on the Columbia.

Smolt travel times are linked in a complex manner with water particle travel times. If you have ever played with a water hose, you know that water tends to travel faster when there is more flow passing through a fixed area. And you know that you can speed the flow by compressing the area. The river system water travel times are similar. We expect water travel times to be low in "wet years" with high flow, and we expect them to be high in "dry years" with low flow. Water travel times may be increased by augmenting the river flows. And they may be increased by lowering the river level in order to send the same flow through a smaller cross-sectional area.

Experts are relatively confident that they can predict changes in water travel times under different flow assumptions. But there are unanswered questions about the relationship between water travel time and smolt travel time. This model does not answer those questions. Rather, it requires you to specify the smolt travel times as inputs. The model may then be used to learn if the changes in smolt travel times are important. To put the travel time assumptions into perspective, let's compare the total time from hatchery to ocean under medium flow conditions with the estimate that the *fresh days before smoltification* is 25 days (see table 13.1). With this combination of assumptions, mortality effects from smoltification are expected under average flow conditions. With high flow conditions, the total time from hatchery to ocean is around 23 days, so the smolts would escape the high stress of smoltification. The years with low flow conditions are much different. With low flows, the total time from hatchery to ocean is around 39 days, and the smolts would be exposed to a prolonged period of high stress due to smoltification.

Table 13.1. Smolt travel time in the Snake and Columbia rivers.

Upstream sector	2.0 days
Days in Snake reservoirs	12.4 days
Days in Columbia reservoirs	8.9 days
Days in final reach	4.0 days
TOTAL DAYS	27.3 days

Base Case Results and Interface

Figure 13.5 shows the simulated migration with base case assumptions. Ten million smolts are released at the hatchery, and half of these arrive at the first reservoir in the second day of the simulation. The time graph shows the downward slant for smolts in the first reservoir. A similar pattern appears in each of the remaining reservoirs. (The seventh reservoir is the small reservoir behind the Dalles dam. The travel time through this reservoir is so short that the smolts curve appears as a spike in figure 13.5.) The down trend in the eight reservoirs is caused by the 2 percent/day mortality from starvation and predation assumed for slack water.

There is no barging in this simulation, so all of the smolts that pass through or around the Lower Granite dam arrive at the second reservoir. If you look closely, you will notice a drop between the end of the curve in the first reservoir and the beginning of the curve for the second reservoir. This is caused by the mortality in the turbines at the first dam. Similar declines appear wherever a significant fraction of the smolts pass through the turbines at the remaining dams.

Some of the smolts survive to reach the river below Bonneville dam. Their final challenge is to reach the ocean before they feel the deadly effects of smoltification. This part of the simulation is represented by *smolts in final reach*. Figure 13.5 shows that this curve does not decline in a constant, linear manner like the previous curves. It shows a steeper and steeper downward slope as the smolts spend more time in the final reach, a sign that the losses from smoltification are becoming more serious with each passing day. The simulation concludes when the remaining smolts reach the saline waters of the estuary and enter the ocean. This first test suggests that 1.16 million smolts would survive the trip to the ocean.

Figure 13.6 shows an interface to facilitate your use of the model. You'll see this interface when you download the model from the home page. It provides instructions in the scrolling

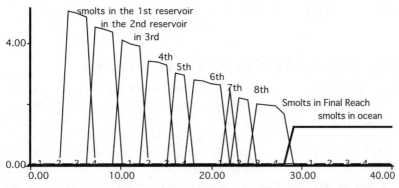

Figure 13.5. Base case simulation with average weather and no barging. (This graph is adapted from three separate Stella graphs.)

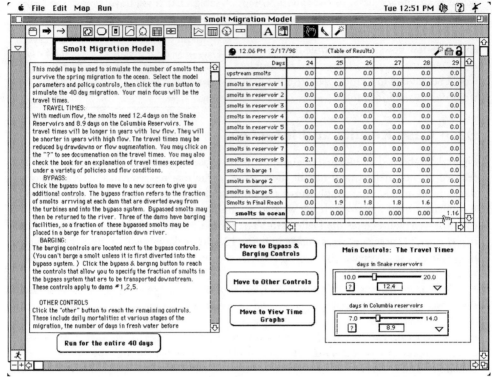

Figure 13.6. Base case results on the main screen of the interface.

field and a table of results. This "screen capture" shows the monitor of a Macintosh computer at the conclusion of the base case simulation. The cursor ("finger") is pointed at the key result in the final row of the table. The *smolts in ocean* reaches 1.16 million by the end of the simulation.

The main controls appear as "sliders" in the lower right corner of the screen. The slider positions reveal the base case assumption that 12.4 days are required for the reservoirs on the Snake and 8.9 days for the reservoirs on the Columbia. Other controls are located on additional screens, which may be reached by clicking the buttons on the main screen. The model may be used to test policies to increase the fraction that survive the trip. So far, we have 1.16 million, only 11.6 percent of the original 10 million. Perhaps barging will improve on this result.

Barging, Tagging Studies, and Latent Deaths

Limited transportation of juveniles began in the late 1960s for research purposes. The smolts were transported by tanker trucks, fish trailers, and eventually barges. Mass transportation of juveniles began in 1981 (with five tanker trucks and four barges). For evaluation purposes, some smolts are tagged with a PIT, a passive integrated transponder. (The tags are installed when the fish are held in the bypass system.) Some of the tagged fish are transported; others are returned to the river. The transported fish are called T fish. The control fish are called C fish. By measuring how many actually return as adults, tagging studies provide some perspective on the benefits of transportation. Mundy (1994, 70) describes studies over the time period from 1968 to 1989. His most important observation is that return counts tend to be quite small. The returning C fish can range from 0.01 percent to 0.3 percent. The returning T fish range from 0.02 percent to 0.6 percent. The study of yearling chinook tagged at Lower Granite in 1975 is illustrative: C fish return, 0.31 percent; T fish return, 0.64 percent; T:C ratio, 2.0.

The T:C ratio can be used to help us estimate the size of the latent deaths fraction. We use the smolt model to simulate the relative values of the T fish and the C fish surviving the trip to the ocean. To mimic the collection and tagging of fish at Lower Granite, for example, we may set the Lower Granite bypass fraction to 100 percent. Then we set the fraction of bypassed fish to barge at 1.0 to simulate the T fish. Then we conduct a second simulation with zero barging to simulate the C fish. These two simulations were performed with the bypass fractions at the downstream dams set to values said to characterize the 1970s. The simulation with barging shows 4.14 million smolts reaching the ocean. The simulation with the control fish returned to the river shows 1.01 million smolts reaching the ocean. Now, suppose there were no differences between these two groups as they carry on with their life cycle. Let's assume that 1 percent of each group returned to the counting station. Then a tagging study would show:

returning T fish: 1% * 4.14 million = 0.0414 million

returning C fish: 1% * 1.01 million = 0.0101 million

expected T:C ratio: 4.1

Now, we face a contradiction. The expected T:C ratio is 4.1, but the observed T:C ratio is 2.0. This contradiction cannot be explained, but it is sometimes interpreted as evidence that the barged smolts are less capable of finding their way back as adults. (Marmorek and Peters [1996] explain the considerable evidence of the delayed mortality from barging.) The term "latent deaths" is used to remind ourselves that the cause of the low returns is not understood. We may then estimate the size of the latent deaths fraction to reconcile the two T:C ratios. In our case, the latent deaths fraction is set at 51 percent, so 49 percent of the transported fish will survive. This allows us to reconcile the simulation results with a typical tagging study as follows:

returning T fish: 1% * 4.14 million * 49% = 0.0202 million

returning C fish: 1% * 1.01 million = 0.0101 million

expected T:C ratio: 2.0

The 51 percent latent deaths may surprise you, and you may wonder how we can proceed with this assumption without more details on how the barging disrupts the salmon life cycle. But to ignore the latent deaths is equivalent to ignoring the data that has been gathered from the tagging studies. The best approach is to proceed with a rough estimate of latent deaths and to remember that this parameter is likely to be highly uncertain. The 51 percent latent death fraction is somewhat lower than the 62 percent estimate used by Olsen (1992).

Using the Smolt Model

You've seen one example of a simulated migration without barging. To test the impact of barging at Lower Granite, set the barging fraction at 100 percent. Recall that you can't barge a smolt until it is captured in the bypass system, and the maximum feasible bypass fraction is

70 percent. So full barging means that 70 percent of the smolts arriving at Lower Granite will be transported to the release point below the Bonneville dam. You should try this test with the model. It will show that 1.73 million smolts reach the ocean. Compared with the base case, barging increases the survival from 11.6 percent to 17.3 percent.

This sounds like a promising result, but you might be wondering whether we could get better results with a drawdown. With that policy, we leave the fish in the river and look for shorter travel times to improve their prospects to survive the migration. Table 13.2 summarizes travel times for regular river operations and for two types of drawdowns. The bold entries show the base case travel times described previously. These are based on "regular" operations in which the flows are controlled primarily for hydroelectric generation. The bold entries appear in the "medium flow" column, which describes travel times in a year with average runoff.

Smolt travel times are described in great detail in the 1992 "Options" environmental impact statement (EIS) by the U.S. Army Corps of Engineers, the Bonneville Power Administration, and the Bureau of Reclamation (1992). The EIS looks at water particle travel times for a variety of "options" for managing the river. Their "medium flow" conditions correspond to 80 kcfs (thousand cubic feet per second) on the Snake and 200 kcfs on the Columbia. The EIS links smolt travel times to particle travel times following the approach by Berggren and Filardo (1991). The EIS shows 8.9 days on the Columbia and 9.3 days on the Snake. The 8.9 days appears in table 13.2, but the 9.3 day estimate has to be expanded by 133 percent to arrive at the 12.4 days to be used in the model. The expansion is needed to account for the Lower Granite reservoir (which was not included in the EIS measurement). A comparison of the columns in table 13.2 shows that the travel times are much shorter with high flow conditions and substantially longer with low flow conditions.

One of the options in the "Options" study is to draw the reservoirs down to minimum operating pools during the time of the smolts migration. With average weather, the time on the Snake would be reduced by 1.6 days; the time on the Columbia by 1 day. The 2.6 days is a "modest reduction," which could be achieved by a variety of measures studied by the Environmental Defense Fund (Diamant and Wiley 1995) as well as the Corps (1992).

One of the more ambitious policies is to draw down the reservoirs to the spillway crest during the smolts migration. This approach would be much more disruptive to normal river operations. At Lower Granite, for example, the spillway crest is 57 feet below the maximum operating elevation of the reservoir (U.S. Army Corps of Engineers 1992, 2–10). The minimum operating level, on the other hand, is only 5 feet below the maximum oper-

Table 13.2. Suggested travel times.

on the Snake:	Low flow	Medium flow	High flow
Regular operations	20 days	**12.4 days**	10 days
Modest reduction (e.g., draw down to minimum operating pool)	14.8 days	10.8 days	9.2 days
Major reduction (e.g., draw down to spillway crest)	10.3 days	8.4 days	8.0 days
on the Columbia:	Low flow	Medium flow	High flow
Regular operations	12.9 days	**8.9 days**	7.0 days
Modest reduction (i.e., draw down to minimum operating pool)	10.5 days	7.9 days	7.1 days
Major reduction (i.e., draw down to spillway crest)	12.9 days	7.9 days	7.0 days

ating elevation. The drawdown to spillway crest would cut the travel time on the Snake to 8.4 days under medium flow conditions. (The EIS did not estimate travel times for the Columbia, so table 13.2 shows the same estimate used with a modest drawdown.) The two drawdowns in table 13.2 have been selected to illustrate "modest" and "major" changes in travel times that might be achieved by a wide variety of measures. There are many ways to achieve the modest reduction of 2.6 days. The major reduction of 5 days can be viewed as an upper limit on the reductions that could be achieved (Diamant and Wiley 1995, vi).

Summary

This chapter describes a model designed for an analysis of the relative merits of barging versus drawdowns to aid the smolts' spring migration. The stock-and-flow structure of pieces of the model are explained here. You can see the entire structure by downloading the model from the home page. The parameters have been estimated from travel times reported by U.S. Army Corps of Engineers (1992) and the Environmental Defense Fund (Diamant and Wiley 1995). Many of the loss fractions have been estimated from the spreadsheet modeling by Olsen (1992). You can learn more of the detailed thinking behind each parameter by studying the documentation that accompanies the model. (Documentation is visible by clicking on the "?" button on any slider or by double clicking on any variable in the mapping mode.) If you have lived in the Northwest, you'll know that there is a lot of heat in the debate over whether smolts should be barged or left in the river. The exercises call upon you to use the smolt model to shed some light on this hotly debated topic.

Exercises

1. **Model check—zero mortality:**

    Use the slider controls to eliminate all sources of mortality in the model. Then run the model to verify that the 10 million hatchery smolts will reach the ocean within 30 days under average flow conditions.

2. **Model check—turbine mortality:**

    Using a hand calculator, estimate the number of smolts that would reach the ocean if turbines were the only source of mortality. (The mortality at each dam is 15 percent and there are eight dams on the river.) Set the turbine survival fraction at 85 percent; set the bypass fractions to zero; and run the model. You should see 2.725 million smolts reach the ocean.

3. **Barging or modest drawdown?**

    Assume that the coming hydroelectric year will experience medium flows. You are asked to recommend either a modest drawdown or 100 percent barging at Lower Granite. (But you can't recommend both.) Which policy would allow more smolts to reach the ocean?

4. **Barging or major drawdown?**

    Assume that the year will experience medium flows, and you are asked to recommend either a major drawdown or 100 percent barging at Lower Granite. (But we can't do both.) Which would you recommend to allow more smolts to reach the ocean?

5. **What about low flow conditions?**

   Repeat the analysis from the third and fourth exercises with low flow conditions. Remember you must recommend either a drawdown or barging, but not both. Which would you recommend?

6. **What about high flow conditions?**

   Repeat the analysis from the third and fourth exercises under high flow conditions. Would you recommend barging or a drawdown?

7. **Sensitivity test—latent mortality:**

   Lower the *latent deaths fraction* from 51 percent to 25 percent and repeat the analysis from the third exercise. Then raise the fraction from 51 percent to 75 percent and repeat the analysis. Would you change your recommendations from the third exercise based on the sensitivity tests?

8. **Why study drawdowns?**

   The Northwest region has long experience with barging. More recently, it has begun testing the feasibility of drawdowns. The drawdown tests are vigorously opposed by groups that advocate "regular river operations." They claim that there is no reason to experiment with drawdowns when we have barging. Do your analyses shed any light on why the region would be interested in both barging and a drawdown?

9. **Fish friendly turbines:**

   Researchers at INEEL, the Idaho National Engineering and Environmental Laboratory, are working on a new turbine design that would lower smolt mortality. Let's suppose they succeed in reducing the turbine mortality from 15 percent to 7 percent. Now let's suppose we have initial funding to install the new turbines at only one of the dams. You might install them at Lower Granite, at Bonneville, or at any of the dams in between. Which dam would you select if your goal was to install the new turbines where they would deliver the most benefit to the smolts?

10. **Friendly turbine analysis:**

    Expand the model by introducing a new turbine survival fraction at the dam to receive the friendly turbines. Then use the model to check your answer to the previous exercise. You may assume medium flow conditions, regular river operations, and no barging.

Further Readings

- A "backgrounder" from the Bonneville Power Administration (BPA 1986) entitled *The Magnificent Journey* provides a general overview of the life cycle of the Northwest salmon.
- The declining salmon runs in the Northwest are described by the Northwest Power Planning Council (NPPC 1987).
- Duncan (1994) describes the fragmentation in planning between various federal and state agencies, the province of British Columbia, and the Indian tribes.
- Olsen's (1992) spreadsheet model provides support for many of the parameter estimates in this chapter, but you should know that his model is not necessarily endorsed by a majority of planners in the region.

- Marmorek and Peters (1996) describe a "weight of evidence approach" to evaluate competing hypotheses regarding the causes of salmon decline.
- The *Return to the River* study by its Independent Scientific Group provides a review and synthesis of the science underlying the fish and wildlife program of the Northwest Power Planning Council (Williams 1996).

Chapter 14

<hr>

The Tucannon Salmon

System dynamics can be used to help policy makers and environmental managers improve their instinctive understanding of dynamic behavior. This chapter illustrates how this may be done with a simulation model of the salmon population of the Tucannon River. The model simulates the long-term trends in the population over successive generations. The model is then used to simulate the impact of land-use development, hydroelectric development, and harvesting. The Tucannon model illustrates the value of building more than one model of the same system. As a long-term model of the entire population, it serves as a natural accompaniment to the short-term model from the previous chapter.

This chapter demonstrates how simulation might be used in fishery management. Fisheries have declined in the northwest United States and around the world. You will learn how previous simulation models have been used to help managers deal with the many factors contributing to the decline. This chapter concludes with exercises to apply and improve the Tucannon model. It also includes an interactive exercise to place you in the role of fishery manager.

Background

The Tucannon rises in the Blue Mountains and flows toward the Snake River, as shown in figure 14.1. About 50 miles are suitable for chinook salmon or steelhead trout habitat, and each mile supports around sixty-five redds. (A redd is the spawning nest formed in the gravel.) Each redd contains thousands of eggs, which hatch in the spring. The hatchlings live for a month or more on nutrients stored in their yolk sacs. Once the sac is absorbed, the young fish (called fry) must find and capture food. The juveniles spend a year in the Tucannon competing for food. Those that survive undergo a biochemical change called smoltification that triggers the migration urge. The smolts migrate around 50 miles to reach the Snake River. The remainder of the trip down the Snake and Columbia is around 400 miles. You have read about the challenges in the spring migration in the previous chapter, so you know that many of the smolts will die before reaching the ocean.

The ocean provides the larger and more abundant food that the salmon require to grow to maturity. They spend two years in the ocean and return to the mouth of the Columbia in the spring of their final year. They migrate up the Columbia and Snake rivers to reach the mouth of the Tucannon. (It is believed that they find their way by distinguishing minute differences in the chemical composition of the streams along the way.) They reach the spawning grounds in the fall to build the redds for the next generation.

The Tucannon habitat has been studied by Bjornn (1987) in research for the U.S. Soil Conservation Service. He developed estimates of various population parameters and combined the parameters in a spreadsheet model to project changes in the population from one generation to the next. He used the spreadsheet to find the harvest that would be possible if the population were managed to achieve maximum sustained yield. With predevelopment assump-

Figure 14.1. Location of the Tucannon River.

tions, Bjornn calculated that around 20,000 adults could return to the mouth of the Columbia each year and that 13,000 could be harvested in a sustainable manner.

By Northwest standards, the Tucannon is a small river. (The entire basin covers only 210,000 acres.) So you might be skeptical about 20,000 fish returning to such a small river. To gain some perspective, let's amplify the Tucannon estimate based on the relative size of the watershed. The entire Columbia River Basin is around 800 times larger than the Tucannon, so let's amplify the 20,000 returning adults to obtain an estimate of adults returning for the entire basin. The result staggers the mind: around 16 million salmon would return to the mouth of the Columbia every year! Such a migration is hard to comprehend with current conditions on the river.

Bjornn used the spreadsheet model to find the maximum sustainable harvest under conditions in the 1970s. Development was represented by changes in the habitat parameters (due to land-use development) and by changes in migration parameters (due to hydroelectric development). His calculations with these changes revealed that only around 2,400 adults could return to the Columbia, and only around 600 could be harvested in a sustainable manner.

Bjornn's analysis suggests that development has reduced the overall size of the fishery by around ten- to twentyfold. You should know that a twentyfold reduction is not out of line with trends in the Columbia River Basin. The Columbia River salmon and steelhead runs have been impacted by a combination of factors including harvesting, dams, irrigation, mining, and livestock grazing. Before any of these impacts, up to 16 million wild salmon and steelhead returned to spawn in the streams where they were born. By 1938, the year when the Bonneville Dam was completed, the number of returning adults had fallen to 5 or 6 million, due to a combination of overfishing and upstream activities that blocked spawning access or degraded habitat. By the end of the 1980s, the total was "around 2.5 million, including known fish harvested in the ocean, with about 0.5 million of these as wild fish" (U.S. Army Corps of Engineers 1992, 1–6).

Purpose and Reference Mode

The purpose of the model is to simulate the long-term trends in the salmon population over several decades. We will initialize the model with a small number of fish. The initial conditions could represent a small number that found their way to the Tucannon in the era prior to development. They would discover suitable conditions for growth, and our instincts tell us that they would probably grow from one generation to the next until their numbers reached a limit on the Tucannon. Given the fundamental patterns in chapter 1, our best choice for a reference mode is s-shaped growth. Our initial objective, therefore, is to develop a model that simulates s-shaped growth in the salmon population under predevelopment conditions. We will check the equilibrium population with the corresponding estimates by Bjornn. Then we can use the model to look at the impact of land-use development, hydroelectric development, and harvesting.

Model Design

The model is designed with seven stocks to keep track of the population in various phases of the salmon move through the phases in tightly controlled patterns, so it makes good sense to use conveyors. The seven conveyors are assigned the transit times shown in table 14.1. The life cycle begins in the fall when spawners build the redds. The eggs hatch 6 months later. The juveniles need 12 months to grow into smolts; the smolts need 1 month to reach the ocean. After 2 years in the ocean, they return to the Columbia, where their upstream migration requires 4 months. The total life cycle is 4 years.

Table 14.1. Lengths of salmon life-cycle phases.

Adults about to spawn	1 month
Eggs in redds	6 months
Juveniles in Tucannon	12 months
Smolts in migration	1 month
One year olds in ocean	12 months
Two year olds in ocean	12 months
Adults in migration	4 months

The model uses seven population parameters, which are assumed to remain constant over time. These are sometimes called density-independent parameters because their values do not change with changes in the size of the population (see table 14.2). The first three parameters match Bjornn's (1987) assumptions for the Tucannon under predevelopment conditions. The 50 percent fraction female is typical of the chinook salmon. Each female would deposit around 3,900 eggs, and 50 percent of the eggs would survive with pristine conditions. The 25 percent adult migration loss fraction is taken from Bjornn's estimate of conditions prior to the

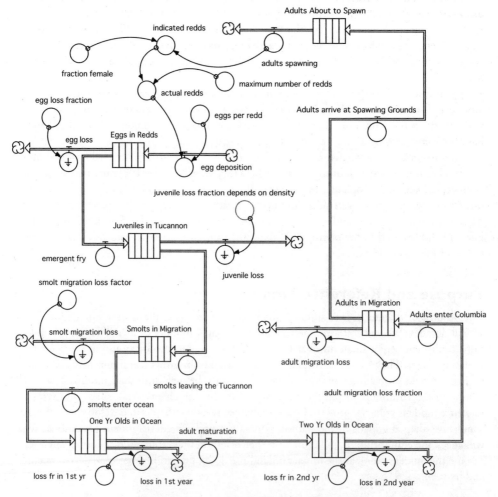

Figure 14.2. A model of the salmon life cycle.

hydroelectric development on the Snake and Columbia rivers. The loss fraction during the smolt migration and the two loss fractions in the ocean were not available from Bjornn's analysis. These parameters are based on other sources and are combined so that the combination of losses is similar to the losses expected by Bjornn.

Let's place some of the assumptions in perspective by starting at the top of the diagram with 2,000 adults about to spawn. With 50 percent female, there would be 1,000 redds formed in the

Table 14.2. Density-independent parameters in salmon life-cycle model.

Fraction female	50%
Eggs per redd	3,900
Egg loss fraction	50%
Smolt migration loss factor	90%
Loss fraction for 1st year	35%
Loss fraction for 2nd year	10%
Adult migration loss fraction	25%

Tucannon. (You would see 20 redds if you walked a mile of the river.) With 3,900 eggs per redd, there would be 3.9 million eggs in the gravel nests. Half of these would survive to emerge as fry the following spring. Now we have 1.95 million fry in the river. You'll learn shortly that only around 280,000 of these juveniles will survive the first year in the river. These are the smolts that migrate to the ocean the following spring. With 90 percent migration losses, 28,000 reach the ocean. And with 35 percent losses in the first year and 10 percent in the second year, around 16,000 adults will return to the mouth of the Columbia two years later. The adult migration loss is expected to be 25 percent, so around 12,000 adults will reach the spawning grounds. This calculation starts with 2,000 spawners. Four years later, there are 12,000 spawners. The annual growth rate is over 100 percent/yr! The conditions are certainly suitable for rapid growth in the population.

You know that no system grows forever, so it is logical to ask ourselves about the limits to the growth in the Tucannon population. One limit is the maximum number of redds that can be built in the river. At 65 redds/mile, the 50 miles of the Tucannon can support around 3,250 redds. This limit can be imposed by setting the maximum number of redds to 3,250 (which you can do in an exercise). For now, let's concentrate on a second limit, which involves the carrying capacity of the river.

The Carrying Capacity

There are limits to the number of juveniles that can survive their first year in the Tucannon. During the summer, the juveniles must compete for a limited number of feeding sites. Later in the fall, they must compete for a limited amount of cover. Bjornn believes that summer conditions will constrain the size of the juvenile population, and he argues that juvenile survival is heavily dependent on density. Figure 14.3 shows a density-dependent relationship between the number of surviving smolts and the number of emergent fry. The horizontal axis is the number of fry that emerge in the spring. The vertical axis is the number of juveniles that will still be in the river one year later ready to begin the smolt migration.

Figure 14.3 is highly nonlinear. We see a steep slope at the origin, but the curve is almost flat when the number of fry reaches 10 million. No matter how many fry emerge, there can never be more than 400,000 smolts one year later. The steep slope at the origin suggests that 1 million emergent fry would lead to over 200,000 smolts at the end of the year. We can obtain half of the river's carrying capacity with only 1 million fry. Further increases in the number of emergent fry do little to increase the number of smolts. If the fry were to increase from 5 to 10 million, for example, the surviving smolt population would increase only from around 340,000 to 370,000.

The shape of the nonlinear survival curve is based on the Beverton-Holt equation, which has been found useful in interpreting fish populations (Ricker 1975). The equation gives the number of surviving smolts as a simple function of the number of fry and two "curve-fitting" parameters:

surviving smolts = Fry/[(Fry/CC) + (1/S)]

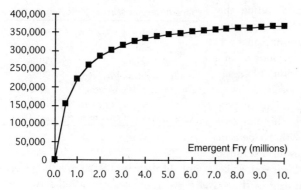

Figure 14.3. Number of juveniles expected to survive the first year of life in the Tucannon.

Bjornn recommends that CC, the carrying capacity, be set to 400,000 smolts. He recommends that S, the slope at the origin, be set to 0.5. The nonlinear relationship could be entered with a graph function (~), or we could enter the Beverton-Holt equation directly in the model. If we enter the equation, we will be in a better position to conduct sensitivity tests on parameters like CC, the carrying capacity. The relevant variable in figure 14.2 is the shadowed variable *juvenile loss fraction depends on density*:

```
juvenile_loss_fraction_depends_on_density =
    (Fe-Expected_Smolt_Survival)/Max(1,Fe)
Expected_Smolt_Survival = Fe/((Fe/X4)+(1/X5))
X4 = Smolt_Carrying_Capacity
X5 = Fraction_of_Smolts_to_Survive_at_Very_Low_Density
Fraction_of_Smolts_to_Survive_at_Very_Low_Density = .5
Smolt_Carrying_Capacity = 400000
```

The short variable names (i.e., X4 and X5) match the terminology used by Bjornn (1987), and they allow the algebra to be clear. The longer names are used to communicate the meaning of each variable.

Simulation Results

The first test of the model is shown in figure 14.4. The population is initialized at a low level and allowed to grow over time with all parameters held at predevelopment conditions. The time graph shows the simulated number of smolts migrating downstream and adults migrating upstream over a 10-year period. Since the smolt migration lasts only 1 month, we see a series of ten spikes for each year of the simulation. The *smolts in migration* begins the simulation at around 100,000. (This starting value is the result of the initial value assigned to the stock of *Juveniles in Tucannon* at the start of the simulation.) The number of migrating smolts dips in the second year but increases strongly in the third year. Eventually, the number of smolts reaches around 380,000, and this number appears year after year. To check if we are observing s-shaped growth, you might pencil in a smooth curve connecting the top of each spike in figure 14.4. Your curve will reveal a 4-year cycle in the number of smolts. These oscillations are to be expected with an animal population with a 4-year life cycle. Figure 14.4 suggests that the oscillations will dampen out over time.

    The second variable in figure 14.4 is the number of adults migrating upstream. It begins the simulation at around 1,000. (This initial value is the result of the initial value assigned to

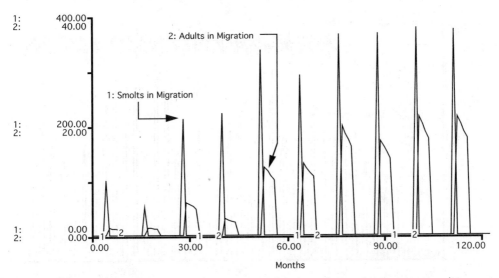

Figure 14.4. Simulated growth in the migrating populations under predevelopment conditions.

the stock of *Two Yr Olds in Ocean*.) Recall that the adult migration lasts 4 months and that 25 percent of the adults do not survive the migration. Figure 14.4 reveals these losses as a downward slope associated with each of the ten migrations. If you pencil in a smooth curve connecting the peak number of adults, your curve will reveal a cycle in the number of migrating adults. Figure 14.4 shows that this oscillation also dampens out, and the number of adults levels off at around 22,000. This equilibrium value is approximately what we should expect based on the spreadsheet calculations by Bjornn (1987).

Equilibrium and Stability

You know from chapter 5 that it's useful to check the numbers whenever a situation reaches equilibrium. This is normally done in an equilibrium diagram, but the salmon's complex life cycle makes it difficult to prepare a traditional equilibrium diagram. Nevertheless, we should be able to check the numbers to understand why the same number of adults return to the Columbia year after year. Let's start with the 22,000 adults, which appear near the end of the simulation. With 25 percent migration losses, around 16,500 will reach the spawning grounds, so there will be around 8,000 redds and a total of around 30 million eggs. With 50 percent egg loss, around 15 million fry would emerge the following spring. Their numbers would be "off the chart" in figure 14.3. The number of juveniles to survive the year in the river would be around 380,000, just slightly less than the river's total carrying capacity. About 38,000 would survive the migration to the ocean. Ocean losses are 35 percent in the first year, followed by 10 percent in the second year, so we would expect around 22,000 to return to the Columbia after 2 years at sea. We have equilibrium from one generation to the next.

You also know from chapter 5 that it's useful to check the stability of an equilibrium situation by introducing an outside disturbance. Figure 14.5 reveals the general stability of the salmon model by introducing random disturbances in the smolt migration loss factor. The normal value of 90 percent applies for the first 120 months. Then the losses vary randomly from a low of 85 percent to a high of 95 percent for the remainder of the simulation. All other parameters are maintained at the same values used in the previous simulation. The test continues for forty years to see the pattern in the number of adults.

This simple test reveals low runs of around 10,000 and high runs at over 30,000. We have

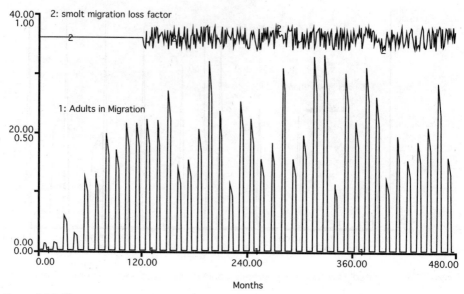

Figure 14.5. Test simulation with random variations in the smolt migration loss factor after the first 120 months.

a threefold variation in the number of returning adults due to random changes in just one of the model parameters. The test simulation also reveals a somewhat cyclical pattern to the variations. The cycles seem to match the 4-year life cycle of the salmon; you can check this match statistically as one of the exercises at the end of the chapter.

Feedback Structure

The salmon model exhibits s-shaped growth over time, so we should expect to see a feedback loop structure similar to the flowered area and sales company described in chapter 6. Specifically, we should expect to see at least one positive loop that gives the population the power to grow over time. There should be at least one decay loop that is similar to the decay of flowers. It will create constant losses in the system. And finally, there should be at least one negative feedback loop that acts to slow the rate of growth as the salmon fill up the river. Figure 14.6 shows these loops and more.

The main positive feedback loop is highlighted by the darker arrows. We can follow their course around the perimeter of the causal loop diagram. If we start at the top with an increase in egg deposition, we will expect more fry, more juveniles, more smolts in migration, more salmon in the ocean, more adults entering the Columbia, more adults spawning, and a subsequent increase in egg deposition.

Now, do you see any examples of negative feedback loops that remind you of the flower decay loop? If you start at the bottom, you will see a negative loop associated with the loss during the first year in the ocean. Moving to the right, you will see another negative loop involving losses during the second year in the ocean. And as you continue around the life cycle, you will see a total of six negative feedback loops. (Each loop involves only two variables, so the diagram doesn't include the (–) within each small loop.)

Now, turn your attention to the negative loop that is highlighted in figure 14.6. It works its way around the entire life cycle, much like the positive feedback loop. If you begin at the top with higher egg deposition, you will see more fry, a greater juvenile loss, less juveniles in the Tucannon, fewer smolts in migration, fewer salmon in the ocean, fewer adults return-

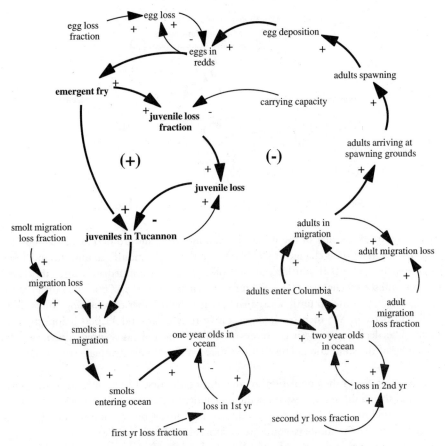

Figure 14.6. Information feedback in the salmon model.

ing to spawn, and less egg deposition in the future. This negative loop gradually applies the brakes to the growth. When would the growth eventually come to a stop? If you check the two sets of arrows leading from emergent fry to juveniles in the Tucannon, you would expect the system to slow down considerably when an increase in the emergent fry no longer leads to an increase in the number of juveniles. In other words, we would expect the system to grow until it reaches the flat portion of the nonlinear curve shown in figure 14.3. Somewhere on the flat portion of the curve, the growth forces will be exactly balanced by the losses in the system.

Harvesting

Let's expand the model to simulate harvesting of the adults as they enter the Columbia, as shown in figure 14.7. A user-specified harvest fraction is used to calculate the adult harvest and the number of adults that escape the harvest. The escaping adults then enter the conveyor for adults in migration to continue upriver, as in the previous model. By specifying a fraction, we are assuming that the harvest manager knows how to measure the number of adults entering the Columbia in the current year.

The best way to test harvesting is to allow the salmon population to grow to its equilibrium size before any changes are made in the harvest fraction. Let's keep the harvest fraction at zero for the first 10 years and then see what happens if we attempt to harvest 95 percent of the returning adults as they enter the Columbia. Figure 14.8 shows a 40-year simulation.

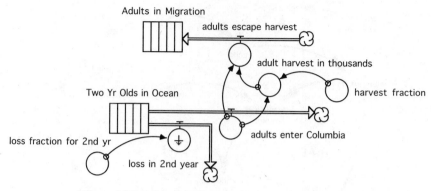

Figure 14.7. Adding the harvest fraction to the model.

The first 10 years are similar to the initial simulation—the runs grow to exceed 20,000 per year. The harvest fraction is changed to 95 percent in the 120th month, so only around 1,000 adults escape the harvest. If you look at the spikes following immediately after the 120th month, you will see no change. The next four runs remain at over 20,000. The impact of the harvesting does not show up until 4 years later, when the number of returning adults drops by almost 50 percent. We then see four successive runs of around 11,000 before the runs fall again. The declining pattern continues to follow this staircase pattern downward for the remainder of the simulation. This first test suggests that 95 percent harvesting is not sustainable.

The next test allows the population to grow during the first 120 months as before. Then 50 percent of the adults are harvested for the remainder of the simulation. If you look at figure 14.9, you will observe that there is no discernible impact on the number of adults that return each year. Their numbers continue at around 22,000 year after year even though 11,000 adults are harvested at the mouth of the Columbia. How can this possibly be?

The results in figure 14.9 arise, in part, from the nonlinear shape of the juvenile survival curve. Recall the equilibrium conditions around the 120th month—there were around 16,000 spawners, 8,000 redds, 30 million eggs, and 15 million emergent fry. With 15 million fry emerging each year, the Tucannon is at its limit—around 380,000 juveniles would survive their first year in the river. Now let's ask ourselves what would happen if 50 percent of the adults are harvested as they enter the Columbia. Half as many would escape, so we would expect to see around 7.5 million emergent fry. According to figure 14.3, the number of surviving juveniles with 7.5 million fry is almost identical to the number with 15 million fry. (The system is on the flat portion of the survival curve.) This simulation suggests that half

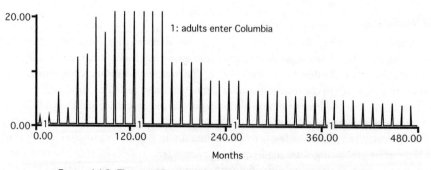

Figure 14.8. Testing 95 percent harvesting after the 120th month.

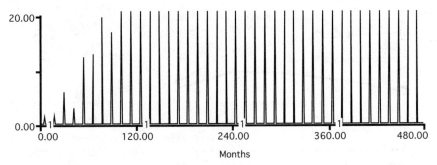

Figure 14.9. Simulated number of adults returning to the Columbia if 50 percent harvesting is begun in the 10th year.

of the adult population could be harvested without any visible impact on the number of adults that would return to the Columbia each year. This important result arises from the competition for space among the juveniles during their first year in the Tucannon. Harvesting cuts the number of escaping adults in half, but the progeny from the escaping adults will have a much greater chance of survival during their first year in the Tucannon.

Maximum Sustainable Yield

It is common practice in the study of fisheries to calculate the MSY, the maximum sustainable yield. MSY is defined by Botkin and Keller (1995, G-10) as "the maximum usable production of a biological resource that can be obtained in a specified time period." Kenneth Watt (1968, 404) explains the search for MSY starting with minimal harvesting: "If we fish too little, the fish population left in the water after fishing will build up to densities at which intraspecific competition for food stunts fish growth and diminishes the probability of survival." Then he explains that "if we fish too hard, too few adults are left behind to spawn, and the stock goes into a decline." You can infer from the previous simulation that the 50 percent harvest fraction corresponds to "too little" fishing and the 95 percent corresponds to fishing "too hard." Somewhere in between, we expect to find the maximum sustainable yield.

Figure 14.10 summarizes the results of five experiments with a constant harvest fraction imposed after the 120th month of the simulation. The 50 percent results from the previous figure are highlighted at the left edge of the diagram. The number of returning adults is just over 21,200, and the annual harvest is just over 10,600. When a similar test is conducted with 60 percent harvesting, the number of returning adults is almost 20,700 and the annual harvest is around 12,400. This result is also sustainable year after year. The experiment with 70 percent harvesting leads to a somewhat smaller number of returning adults. But since we are harvesting a larger fraction, the annual harvest turns out to be higher than in the previous experiments. The remaining two experiments allowed 80 percent and 90 percent harvesting. Both experiments revealed a sustainable situation. With 90 percent harvesting, for example, around 12,500 adults returned to the Columbia year after year. The annual harvest was around 11,240. This harvest was sustainable, but it turns out to be somewhat lower than the harvest observed in the experiment with 80 percent harvesting.

These experiments reveal an amazingly powerful system that will permit large annual harvests with a wide range of decisions on the harvest fraction. If we are asked to focus on the MSY, we would say that 80 percent would deliver an annual yield of over 14,000 salmon per year. If we were asked to recommend a policy to deliver at least 10,000 salmon per year, our job would be easy. Set the harvest fraction anywhere from 50 percent to 90 percent, and the system will allow the goal to be met year after year.

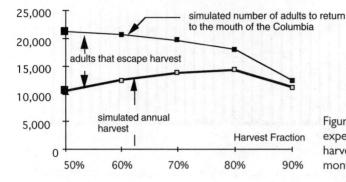

Figure 14.10. Results of five experiments with a constant harvest fraction after the 120th month of a simulation.

Graphical Analysis

Traditional fishery studies often use graphical analysis to find the MSY. We have already found the maximum yield using multiple experiments with the Tucannon model, so we don't need a graphical analysis. But since the graphical approach is common, it's useful to illustrate the approach. The illustration will serve to reinforce the previous findings, and it will provide an example of the sort of analysis that is often conducted when managers do not have a dynamic model.

The graphical approach begins with the juvenile survival curve shown in figure 14.11. Juvenile loss is the only loss in the model that depends on density. All other losses may be combined in a single line whose slope varies with changes in the harvesting fraction. (Go to the home page for a step-by-step derivation of the slope of the lines.) Figure 14.11 demonstrates with four lines corresponding to harvest fractions of 0 percent, 50 percent, 75 percent, and 90 percent. The fact that the straight lines intersect the survival curve is a sign that the harvest fraction is sustainable.

The intersection points reveal the number of fry and the number of smolts that are consistent with all the assumptions of the model and with the assumption that the harvest is sustainable. With 50 percent harvesting, for example, the intersection point shows around 8 million fry and around 360,000 smolts. These values agree with the values simulated in the model.

The point of most graphical analyses is to find the annual harvest under sustainable con-

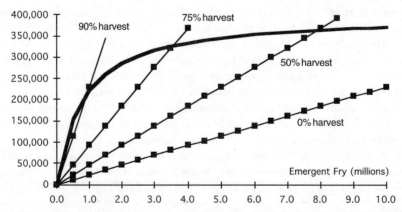

Figure 14.11. Graphical analysis of the number of smolts and fry in a sustainable system with different values of the harvest fraction.

ditions. You can go to the home page to verify that the total annual harvest turns out to be 5.85 percent of the product of the number of smolts and the harvest fraction. If we take the approximate number of smolts from three of the intersection points in figure 14.11, we obtain the following approximations of the annual harvest that are possible under sustained conditions:

Harvest fraction	Number of smolts	Annual harvest
50%	380,000	11,000
75%	330,000	14,000
90%	220,000	11,500

These values confirm the findings from the simulation experiments summarized in figure 14.10. That is, the maximum sustainable yield is around 14,000, and it is possible to obtain yields of over 10,000 with harvest fractions ranging anywhere from 50 percent to 90 percent.

Graphical Analysis, Simulation Analysis, and the MSY

The graphical approach provides a different perspective on the fishery, and it is encouraging to see the graphical results confirm the findings from the simulation model. But you might be wondering at this point why we should bother with the model. If we can find the maximum harvest graphically, why do we need computer simulation?

You should be aware of the highly restrictive assumptions that are required for the graphical approach to arrive at the intersection points. First, we must be willing to assume that the system is predominantly linear. In the case of figure 14.11, we are willing to tolerate a nonlinear relationship for the smolt survival curve, but all other relationships are linear. If some of the remaining relationships were nonlinear, you can imagine the complexities in finding the intersection points. In simulation modeling, on the other hand, we are free to consider each relationship separately. If a linear representation seems more realistic, we can simply employ a graph function (~) and repeat the simulation.

A second restriction in the graphical approach is the assumption that the system is operating in a sustainable manner. For the algebra underlying figure 14.11 to make sense, we must assume that the same number of fish appear in the system from one generation to another. This assumption is suitable in searching for the MSY, but it certainly restricts our ability to analyze a broad range of situations (such as the oscillating situation in figure 14.5).

Now, what about the MSY? The MSY is emphasized by Bjornn (1987), and it certainly appears frequently in the literature. Indeed, the idea was considered "virtually sacred to many wildlife managers until quite recently" (Botkin and Keller 1995, 232). But you should regard the MSY with great skepticism, as it is an artificially determined number. To appreciate the artificiality, think of the unusual conditions that were created in the simulation experiments to find the MSY. Each experiment held the values of all parameters constant over time at values representing predevelopment conditions. There were no random disturbances, and the harvest fraction was implemented once the population reached equilibrium. We then held the harvest fraction constant for 30 years and recorded the simulated response. This was done not once but five times. The results are reported in figure 14.10; they indicate that the MSY is around 14,000 and that it could be obtained with a harvest fraction of around 80 percent.

You shouldn't pay too much attention to these two numbers. The important conclusion from the preceding analysis is not the 80 percent or the 14,000. What we really learn from the previous simulations is that the predevelopment conditions allow for a wonderfully powerful and stable system. We have learned that the Tucannon salmon system could allow for major harvests that could be sustained year after year if we set the harvest fraction anywhere from 50 percent to 90 percent and if we maintain the rivers and the habitat in good condition.

The Impact of Development

Bjornn was primarily interested in land-use development, which has lowered the quality of the salmon habitat. An example is the heavy erosion from dry cropland and cattle grazing that dumps sediments into the Tucannon (Harrison 1992). Bjornn suggests that the impact of land use may be simulated by changing the egg loss fraction and the carrying capacity. Egg loss increases as sediment ruins the quality of the gravel beds. Bjornn suggests increasing the loss from 50 percent to 75 percent to represent the deterioration of water quality. Land use has also degraded the habitat that the juveniles will experience after hatching. Bjornn suggests that degradation in the lower sections of the river can be represented by lowering the carrying capacity from 400,000 to 170,000. Development has brought important changes in the large rivers as well. Hydroelectric development on the Snake and the Columbia has placed six dams and reservoirs between the smolts and the ocean. Bjornn suggests that the impact of hydroelectric development can be represented by increasing the smolt migration loss fraction from 90 percent to 95 percent and the adult migration loss fraction from 25 percent to 37.5 percent.

Figure 14.12 shows the simulated number of returning adults if all four of these changes are implemented after the 120th month of a simulation. The first 10 years appears as in each of the previous simulations. The population is allowed to grow to the equilibrium value of 22,000. The impact of development is abrupt and dramatic. The number of returning adults declines within a few generations to less than 20 percent of the predevelopment population. The population is simulated to find a new equilibrium and remains stable at slightly below 4,000.

At this point, you can experiment with different harvesting policies to learn if the post-development salmon population could be harvested in a sustainable manner. For example, 25 percent harvesting begun after the salmon reach the post-development equilibrium could deliver a sustainable harvest of around 900 fish per year. You can try alternative harvest fractions to find the MSY under developed conditions as an exercise at the end of the chapter. You'll learn that the harvest is nowhere close to the harvests that were possible with predevelopment conditions.

Summary

This chapter describes a system dynamics model of the salmon population in a small river in southeastern Washington. The model simulates the salmon's complex life cycle, and it has been used to test the impact of land-use development, hydroelectric development, and harvesting. The model can certainly be improved, and you will be challenged to do that in the exercises at the end of the chapter. The exercises also allow you to experiment with the

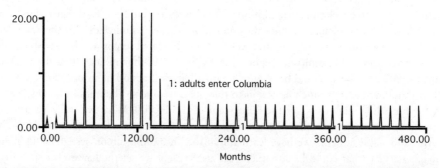

Figure 14.12. Simulated impact of land-use changes and hydroelectric system development starting in the 120th month of the simulation.

model while assuming the role of fishery manager. To appreciate the relevance of the Tucannon example to other systems, it's useful to review the state of fisheries around the world.

Post Script

The World's Fisheries

The decline in the Tucannon salmon parallels the overall decline in the salmon and steelhead populations of the Northwest. Unfortunately, the Northwest salmon fishery is not unique. Clark (1985, 5) observes that the "depletion of major fish stocks and the impoverishment of fishing fleets and processing companies have become common phenomena worldwide." Clark comments that several major fisheries have collapsed completely, largely as a result of over-fishing. For example:

- Antarctic blue whales and fin whales showed peak catches of around 30,000 in the 1930s; by 1981, the catch in both fisheries was nil.
- Peruvian anchoveta supported a peak catch of over 12 million tons in 1970; by 1981, the catch was only 0.3 million tons.
- California sardine supported a catch of over 600,000 tons in 1936; by 1981 the catch was nil.

Clark believes that fisheries biologists are well aware that many fish populations undergo large-scale natural fluctuations. But the development of a commercial fishery may be "first precipitated when a population is at a peak of abundance. If the stock subsequently declines, it may be difficult to disentangle the influences of fishing pressure and natural processes." He concludes that it has become clear "that the uncontrolled growth of a large fishing industry has the potential for hastening and exacerbating the decline, as well as preventing the recovery of such stocks" (Clark 1985, 6)

Clark's commentary raises the question of how to prevent "uncontrolled growth" of a large fishing industry. We might look to market forces to slow the growth of the industry. We could reason that lower catches will discourage new entry; existing fishermen will switch to a different vocation; and the stocks might recover over time. But the evidence from one fishery after another suggests that the markets don't provide the controls needed to prevent over-fishing:

> The fishing industry around the world enjoys fairly free and vigorous markets, and it has seen in the past few decades extraordinary technological development. . . . The result is that more and more fisheries are overshooting their sustainable limits. The technology being called forth is not that which enhances fish stocks, but that which seeks to catch every last fish. (Meadows, Meadows, and Randers 1992, 186)

As the companies succeed in catching the last few fish, they find themselves left with excessive capacity. One example is the Pacific Northwest salmon fishery studied by Paulik and Greenough (1966). It was described as heavily overinvested in the "gear" needed to catch salmon (Watt 1968). In writing about fisheries in general, Clark (1985, 7) explains that "in practice . . . it often appears that the effort capacity of fishing fleets is much larger than twice the optimum level."

Computer simulation can help us think about the many interacting forces that pose such difficult problems in fisheries. At a basic level, a model may trigger a fundamental change in thinking, as when a company decides to change its goal from catching more fish to catching fewer fish. A model may also be used to help participants in a fishery work through the challenges of survival if they commit to lowering the annual catch. The salmon gear modeling of

Paulik and Greenough (1966) is an interesting example from the 1960s. Two recent examples are the Fish Banks Ltd. and the Norwegian fjord experiments. Both examples are exemplary for their use of models within a learning exercise.

Lessons from Fish Banks, Ltd.

The first example is Meadows, Fiddaman, and Shannon's (1989) "Fish Banks, Ltd." simulation game. The model simulates the interactions of a hypothetical fishing fleet and fish populations in coastal waters and in deep waters. Teams of participants are formed to represent fishing companies. Each team is free to experiment with different policies to grow their fleets and to achieve a high, sustainable income. The game has been played by resource planners and students from around the world. The results are similar for students and planners alike: They tend to overinvest in the number of boats. Then they operate the boats to the point that the fish populations are depleted. The depletion tends to occur first in the deep sea, then in the coastal waters.

Participants in the Fish Banks exercises argue that it was not possible for them to avoid overfishing, even when they feared that their actions were depleting the stock. They faced the fundamental challenge of a "common" resource. They knew that the combined actions of all the teams were depleting the fishery, but they did not want to be the only team to cut back on fishing. Their reactions were similar to the reaction of an American fisherman working the Bristol Bay salmon fishery in Alaska. According to Howe (1979, 272), the American fisherman knew he was simply one player in a system that was headed in a tragic direction. When asked if the fishing season should be closed, he responded: "Why should they close it if the Japanese are going to be out there? I'd just as soon wreck it ourselves as have them wreck it."

This fundamental and tragic problem is called the "tragedy of the commons" (Gordon 1954; Hardin 1968). The main source of the problem is often attributed to open access to the stocks. Howe (1979, 257) explains that "where resources are unowned or the common property of a community, there are no controls over access and no means of allocating or restricting inputs of capital and labor." Under these conditions, there is simply no way to prevent "declining yields and the disappearance of net revenues to the industry."

Lessons from the Norwegian Fjord Experiment

The second exemplary example is the Norwegian fjord experiment by Erling Moxnes. He recruited eighty-three subjects from the fishery sector in Norway to conduct harvesting experiments with a simulated cod population in an isolated fjord. His subjects were granted exclusive property rights, so all participants were free to make decisions about the size and the use of their fleet without fear that a competitor would deplete the cod population. In other words, his experiment ruled out the "commons" problem that is at the heart of Fish Banks Ltd. Moxnes's findings are intriguing because the participants consistently overbuilt their fleets. For example, a typical participant would buy five boats to work the fjord when three boats would deliver the maximum sustainable yield. All of the participants had exclusive rights to the simulated fishery, so they were free to "lay-up" their boats when they discovered their overinvestment. To their credit, they managed to idle their boats and avoid decimating the fishery. Moxnes (1996, 23) observes that the experimental situation is quite similar to the Norwegian fishing situation, in which capacity has been estimated to be about twice the optimal size for the past fifteen years. He believes that quotas in Norway have probably been closer to optimal levels.

At this point, you might be wondering why the Norwegian participants overinvested in their fishing fleets. Moxnes reports that the information was available for them to determine the maximum sustainable harvest, but, somehow, they didn't see it. He describes their inability to see the situation properly as a "misperception of feedback."

Misperception of Feedback

Misperception of feedback is a general term coined by Sterman (1989) to explain poor performance by participants in complex systems in general and in carefully controlled management experiments. The term is often taken as shorthand for a combination of system features that seem to be beyond our ability to understand. One feature is nonlinearity, like the highly nonlinear juvenile survival curve discussed in this chapter. Another feature is delays, like the 4-year delay before changes in harvesting show up as possible changes in the number of returning adults. Finally, and most important, misperception of feedback refers to our apparent inability to see the feedback at work in the system. To understand what Sterman has concluded from management experiments, imagine a scene from ordinary life. Imagine that a visitor arrives at your house to find that it is terribly overheated. (You love a warm room, and you've set the thermostat at 90 degrees.) Your visitor arrives to find you gone and the house unbearably hot. What might he do if he did not appreciate the feedback control of the furnace through the thermostat? He might launch into a series of wasteful activities to correct the problem. He could open the windows to let cool air into the house. And when that didn't work, he might open the refrigerator door to let cool air out of the freezer. Of course, you recognize immediately that these actions will not succeed. But that's because you do not suffer from misperception of feedback.

System dynamics models can play the same role in fisheries management as they play in other complex systems—they help us to see the feedback at work in the system. Their main benefit is likely to be an improved understanding of dynamic behavior and better instincts for managing the system. They can be constructed for extended analysis by a team of managers and experts, or they can be designed for workshops and training as in the examples of Fish Banks, Ltd., and the Norwegian fjord experiment.

Exercises

The first exercise calls upon you to experiment with a highly interactive version of the Tucannon model. Such models are sometimes called management flight simulators. You will learn more about their purpose in chapter 20. For now, you can download the Tucannon harvest model for the first exercise. The remaining exercises are similar to exercises in the previous chapter. They call on you to verify, apply, and improve the model.

1. **Tucannon harvest exercise:**

    The harvest exercise is a game for three. You will assume the role of harvest manager. One classmate assumes control of hydroelectric development, and another assumes control of land use in the watershed. Your job is to find a strategy for setting the harvest fraction as conditions change over time. Meanwhile, your classmates will be changing the simulated conditions. Their job is to test your ability to react to conditions beyond your control.

    The "screen capture" shows the monitor of a Macintosh computer midway through a student experiment with the harvesting model. Instructions are given in the scrolling field on the left side of the screen. You are to experiment with the harvest fraction to maximize the total harvest over a 40-year period. In this screen, the classmates have raised the egg loss fraction and lowered the carrying capacity. You can imagine that their goal was to create a challenging situation for the harvest manager. Results for the first 240 months are on display in the main graph, and the "finger" is pointed at the harvest fraction, which is currently at 90 percent. The harvest manager is probably wondering whether to change the fraction before advancing through another 24 months of the simulation.

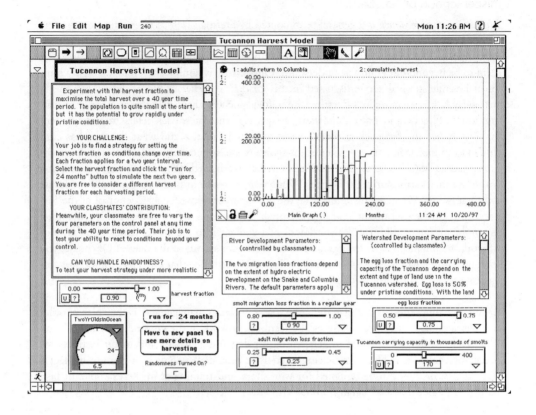

Experiment with the interactive model until you feel that you have demonstrated your ability to manage the system. Conduct a final simulation that reveals your ability to manage the system under challenging conditions. Document the results of the final simulation with the "print map" command.

2. **Verify:**

    Use the downloaded model to verify the simulation results in figure 14.4.

3. **MSY check:**

    Confirm the 50 percent harvesting result shown in figure 14.9. Then select a harvesting fraction between 50 percent and 90 percent and run the model to see if the simulated harvest matches what you would expect from figure 14.10.

4. **Relative losses:**

    The Tucannon model sets the smolt migration loss at 90 percent and the ocean losses at 35 percent in the first year and 10 percent in the second year. Based on discussion with Ted Bjornn, the smolt loss fraction could be reduced and the ocean losses increased. Conduct a test with the smolt migration loss fraction at 50 percent and the ocean losses set at 75 percent and 50 percent. How does the new simulation compare with the simulation in the second exercise?

5. **Verify stability check:**

    Use the model to verify the stability check in figure 14.5. (*Caution:* Your random variations in the smolt migration loss fraction may not match exactly the sequence used in figure 14.5, so you should not expect to match each and every variation.)

6. **Harvesting with random disturbances:**

    Introduce 90 percent harvesting midway through the previous simulation to learn if 90 percent harvesting is sustainable when the system is subjected to random disturbances.

7. **Verify developed conditions:**

    Use the model to verify the simulated impact of development shown in figure 14.12. Then conduct an additional experiment with 25 percent harvesting starting in the 240th month of the simulation. You should see annual returns of 3,490 and an annual harvest of 870. Can you do better with a higher harvest fraction?

8. **Limit on the number of redds:**

    The *indicated redds* in figure 14.2 is the product of the *adults spawning* and the *fraction female*. The *actual redds* takes the value of the *indicated redds* or the *maximum number of redds*, whichever is smaller. Set the *maximum number of redds* to 3.27 to represent Bjornn's estimate that the Tucannon could support 3,270 redds. Run the model to learn if this limit leads to any changes in the results in figure 14.4.

9. **Time series analysis:**

    If you have studied time series analysis, you will have learned about the stationary, autoregressive model to explain the variation in population numbers based on variations 1 year ago, 2 years ago, 3 years ago, etc. Repeat the simulation from the fifth exercise and ask for a table of results. You might imagine that the table of results is similar to time series data that might be collected on the returning adults. But since these results are created by a model, they might be called *synthetic data*. If you have access to a statistical analysis program, export results to the statistical program. Create a stationary, autoregressive model, and run the program to estimate the coefficients from the synthetic data. Does your analysis reveal a 4-year lag in the salmon population?

10. **Combine the salmon models?**

    The model in chapter 13 provides a detailed simulation of hatchery smolts during their spring migration. Do you think it would be useful to combine the model from chapter 13 with the life cycle model in this chapter? If the DT is set to 1 day (as in chapter 13), how many steps would be needed to run the new model to compare to figure 14.12?

Further Reading

- The Tucannon basin is home to around eight hundred people. Harrison (1992) describes their efforts to improve farming methods and salmon habitat.
- The world's imperiled fisheries are described by Safina (1995).
- More information on graphical analyses in fisheries studies is given by Bjornn (1987, 25), Paulik and Greenough (1966, 225), and Clark (1985, 4).
- Botkin and Keller (1995, 234) explain the dangers of linking harvest policy too closely to a predetermined MSY, especially if the MSY is derived from a "logistic model" of the animal population.

- Larkin (1988) discusses the relative advantages of simulation modeling versus analytical solutions in fishery management. He believes "there is virtually no limit to the variety of and complexity of simulations," and he argues that simulation models should be viewed as "tools to assist the imagination."

PART III

THE MODELING PROCESS

Chapter 15

The Steps of Modeling

Building a model is an iterative, trial-and-error process. A model is usually built up in steps of increasing complexity until it is capable of replicating the observed behavior of the system. Then it is used to learn whether the simulated behavior can be improved by changes in policy variables. You've seen the elements of good modeling in previous chapters, and you've seen the iterative approach used to build the Mono Lake model. You've also seen models used to study rather complex systems such as the flow of DDT and the harvesting of salmon.

It's useful at this point to review what you've learned and to think about a step-by-step approach that will prove useful for all environmental systems. This chapter describes an eight-step approach for building and testing a model. It describes each step in the sequence, and it explains why experienced modelers repeat the sequence in an iterative manner. The next chapter demonstrates the approach with a model of the deer herd on the Kaibab Plateau.

Step 1. Get Acquainted with the System

Table 15.1 lists the eight steps to build and test a model. The first step is to get acquainted with the system. Models should not be constructed in isolation from the people who will use them to deal with a serious problem. So your first task is to become familiar with these people and their problem. You should also learn about their institutional arrangements. For example, take the time to observe their modes of communication (e.g., memos, weekly meetings, journal publications, home pages) and think about the best way to communicate model-based findings within the organization. The organization may be a business, a public agency, a narrow community of specialists, or a broad community of concerned citizens. Learn how the organization measures system performance and why it feels the system is performing poorly. Become familiar with the policies that have been proposed to "fix" the problem and learn the pros and cons of each proposal. If the organization has a history of quantitative analysis, it may well have access to computer models. You should become acquainted with these models. Ask yourself whether a system dynamics model would provide additional insights. Finally, and most importantly, you should identify the key individuals with the power to implement the findings of a modeling exercise. These individuals are sometimes called the "client." The client may be a single individual in a position of leadership, or, more commonly, a team of individuals that has gained respect from many corners of the organization. You may be working with a broad community of concerned citizens with the power to make a difference. In this case, the citizens are your client. And, at the opposite extreme, you may build a model to expand your own understanding. In this case you are the client.

Table 15.1. The steps of modeling.

Step 1. A is for Acquainted:	Get Acquainted with the system.
Step 2. B is for Be specific:	Be specific about the dynamic problem.
Step 3. C is for Construct:	Construct the stock and flow diagram.
Step 4. D is for Draw:	Draw the causal loop diagram.
Step 5. E is for Estimate:	Estimate the parameter values.
Step 6. R is for Run:	Run the model to get the reference mode.
Step 7. S is for Sensitivity:	Conduct Sensitivity analysis.
Step 8. T is for Test:	Test the impact of policies.

Step 2. Be Specific about the Dynamic Problem

Step 2 is to be specific about the dynamic problem. This is probably the most important step in the process. It's also the easiest step to skip over in a rush to get to work on the computer. As you become acquainted with the organization, you should ask yourself if the organization really has a "dynamic problem." If it does, you should be able to draw a graph of an important variable that changes over time. The graph should summarize why the people are dissatisfied with the system's performance. The graph should not be an abstract representation that you create to make the modeling easy. Quite the contrary. The people in the organization should immediately recognize the graph as a summary of "their problem."

You know that this graph is called the reference mode and that it serves as a target pattern of behavior. Drawing the reference mode at the outset is one of the most helpful steps in the process. It forces us to be clear about the dynamic pattern we are trying to explain. Think of the graph as the focal point of your modeling effort, and think of the model as a "dynamic hypothesis" (Richardson and Pugh 1981, 55; Randers 1980, 131) for the system behavior.

The reference mode will always have time on the horizontal axis and an important system variable on the vertical axis. You have learned that the length of time is called the time horizon. You have already seen models with dramatically different time horizons:

- salmon smolts (chapter 13): 40 days
- Tucannon salmon (chapter 14): 40 years
- Mono Lake (chapter 4): 100 years

The time horizon should be sufficiently long to allow the dynamic behavior to be seen. In setting the time horizon for the Mono Lake model, for example, we allowed that 100 years would be required before the lake finds a new equilibrium size. In the smolts model, on the other hand, we needed to simulate only 40 days to learn how many smolts would survive to reach the ocean. If the reference mode shows a highly volatile oscillatory system, the time horizon would allow sufficient time to see two or three oscillations so we can observe whether the oscillations dampen out over time.

You know that the reference mode will probably correspond to one of the fundamental dynamic patterns explained in chapter 1. In more complex systems, the reference mode might be a combination of two of the fundamental patterns. In some cases, the reference mode will be known from historical performance, or it will be a relatively simple extension of the historical trend, as was the case with Mono Lake. In other cases, it may be necessary to draw the target pattern based on your intuition and inferences from the limited data available (Richardson and Pugh 1981, 49). And in some cases, your team may be concerned about a possible pattern of behavior that has not yet materialized. In this situation, think of the reference mode as a "hypothesis" about the possible pattern. Randers (1980, 124) explains how a "hypothesized reference mode" was used by the team that constructed the WORLD3 model described in *The Limits to Growth* (Meadows et al. 1972).

The reference mode is the best way to be specific about the dynamic problem. If you discover that you cannot draw this graph, you might want to reconsider why you are building a model. It's also helpful at this early stage to make a list of two or three policies that might lead to an improvement in system behavior. You should be clear about what you mean by "improved behavior." This can be done by drawing a second time graph. The second graph will show the same variable seen in the reference mode, and it will have the same time horizon. The new graph should show a qualitatively different pattern of behavior. The new pattern should be clearly recognized by people in the organization as a more desirable pattern of behavior.

Step 3. Construct the Stock-and-Flow Diagram

Step 3 calls for you to construct the flow diagram. Recall the advice from chapter 2: Start with the stocks; then add the flows; and round out the model with the converters. Also, don't forget to check your units at each step of the way. The flow diagram should contain the variable shown in the reference mode. It should also contain variables to represent the two or three policies listed previously. If you are having trouble identifying the stocks and flows in the system, you probably haven't spent enough time getting acquainted with the system.

At this point in the book, you've seen stock-and-flow diagrams for models of Mono Lake, DDT, salmon smolts, and salmon harvesting. These are all complex systems, yet we were able to show the entire flow diagram on a single page. You will do well to aim for a model of similar size when you construct the first flow diagram.

Step 4. Draw the Causal Loop Diagram

Step 4 is to draw the causal loop diagram (see box 15.1). You've learned the diagramming conventions in chapter 7, and you've seen the diagrams used to describe systems as complex as the human body and the global climate. You know that the diagrams can be constructed in a step-by-step manner by "translating" from the stock-and-flow diagram. The purpose of the diagram is to help us appreciate the key loops in the model. In some systems, we must be prepared for the loop structure to become rather complicated. When this happens, you may find it helpful to draw several diagrams. Each diagram may be used to highlight a different loop

---

Box 15.1. Which comes first, flow diagrams or causal loop diagrams?

Table 15.1 recommends that you construct the flow diagram before you turn to the causal loop diagram. This is not a hard-and-fast rule. It is simply a pragmatic recommendation based on observing that most people see the stocks and flows more easily than they "see" the feedback at work in the system. Once you have constructed the flow diagram, you may follow the "translation" procedure explained in chapter 7 to identify the feedback loops. Odum (1971, 283) notes that the feedback mechanisms are often identified after the model is constructed as the modeler observes the "emergent properties" of the interactions of the model components.

But you should feel free to reverse the order of these steps. Perhaps you will see the feedback loops immediately, but find the stocks and flows to be obscure. You might feel more comfortable with the word-and-arrow diagrams as an aid to conceptualizing the structure of the system. Several authors recommend that you use the causal loop diagrams earlier in the process. Richardson and Pugh (1981, 16) explain a seven-step process in which word-and-arrow diagrams are used in a conceptualization stage prior to formulating the stocks and flows. Similar advice is given by Meadows (1974, 5) and by House and McLeod (1977, p. 149).

There is no need to worry about which of these diagramming steps comes first. By the end of the modeling process, you will repeat these steps many times and, it won't necessarily matter which step came first during your initial pass through the modeling process.

in the system. Remember, ~~causal loop diagrams are a communication tool, not an analytical tool.~~ You don't need to show each and every reationship in the diagram. Your goal is to show the loops, not the clutter.

If the causal loop diagram does not show any feedback loops, return to the flow diagram in step 3, and ask yourself whether some of the model inputs could be changed from exogenous to endogenous variables. Also, you should take advantage of your knowledge of the combination of loops needed to generate the fundamental patterns. If your reference mode shows exponential growth, for example, the causal loop diagram must include at least one positive feedback loop. If you don't see the minimum combination of loops in the diagram, return to step 3 and expand the flow diagram.

Step 5. Estimate the Parameter Values

Step 5 is to estimate the parameters. You should estimate the parameters in a "one-at-a-time" fashion, taking advantage of every source of information at your disposal. Be prepared for a wide range of uncertainties on the estimated values. Some parameters may be known with perfect accuracy (e.g., conversion factors, or well-known physical constants). Others may be known to within 10 percent. Still others may be highly uncertain. Their range of uncertainty could be plus or minus 50 percent, or even plus or minus 100 percent.

At this point, you will face a puzzling question: How much effort should be invested to pin down the highly uncertain parameters? Should we aim to have all parameters estimated to within plus or minus 20 percent? Can we proceed if two-thirds of the parameters are known with great certainty, or do we need to pin down the values of 90 percent of the parameters? These questions are addressed in Richardson and Pugh's text on *System Dynamics Modeling with Dynamo*. They observe that the purpose of most system dynamics studies is policy analysis, the final step listed in table 15.1. They reason that, ~~if the policy implications of a model do not change when its parameters are varied, then the modeler does not need to spend more time estimating their value with greater accuracy:~~

> ~~To decide how much effort to put into estimating a given parameter value, one ought to know how sensitive the behavior of the model is to the value of that parameter.~~ Yet to know that, one must run the model, and that requires parameter values. To resolve the dilemma, the modeler picks some values rather quickly and simulates the model. Initial estimates are made carefully, to be sure, with as much concern for accuracy as can be easily mustered, but keeping in mind that one can always go back and estimate more carefully if it makes a difference. (Richardson and Pugh 1981, 230)

This is sound reasoning that you should follow whenever you encounter highly uncertain parameters. Don't let uncertain parameters derail you from the modeling process. The only way you will learn if the uncertainty is important is to move forward with a step-by-step approach like the one in table 15.1.

You should take advantage of all sources of information at your disposal. Useful information may be stored in the organization's numerical data sets and in its annual reports and memos. And don't forget the vast body of information stored in the minds of the participants. Forrester (1980) refers to these three categories of information as the numerical database, the written database, and the mental database. He emphasizes that the numerical database may be minuscule when stacked up against the written database and mental database available within an organization. We will make more progress if we draw on all three bases of information when structuring a model and estimating the parameters. For example, Khalid Saeed (1996, 61) describes a modeling project on agricultural feudalism that was stymied as long as his information sources were limited to one database. When he widened his base of informa-

physical laws	controlled physical experiments	uncontrolled physical experiments	social system data	social system cases	expert judgment	personal intuition

Figure 15.1. The information spectrum.

tion to include the writings of the economic historians, his view of land ownership patterns was solidified in a simulation model.

The range of information sources at your disposal is portrayed along the "information spectrum" in figure 15.1. The spectrum is explained by Meadows et al. (1974). It begins with "hard" sources on the left. These include physical laws and physical experiments in which measurements are made. The measurements may be made in a controlled experiment or in an uncontrolled experiment. Information from this end of the spectrum is frequently used for parameter estimates in system dynamics models of systems with a heavy engineering and technological content.

The center position of the spectrum is occupied by "social system data." The data may include time series data as well as cross-sectional data, and the data could describe biological as well as social systems. Various statistical techniques can be used to take advantage of time series and cross-sectional data. Statistical methods provide useful "tests" to help you select variables to be included in the model. Two of the more popular tests are the T-test and the partial correlation coefficient. These are "single equation statistical tests that focus on hypothesized relationships in isolation from context of feedback relationships" (Mass and Senge 1980, 206). Most statistical tests employed in econometric practice fall into this category. Mass and Senge prefer statistical tests that examine a variable's influence on overall model behavior. To serve this purpose, they recommend the statistical methods based on the Kalman filter (Kalman 1960; Schweppe 1973; Peterson 1975). Richardson and Pugh (1981, 239) give similar advice after discussing the problems with the use of ordinary correlation coefficients: "The problem is that correlations made from total system behavior do not measure ceteris paribus causal relationships. Nature tends not to hold everything else constant while we collect data for a correlation. Yet a single link assumed in a system dynamics model is a ceteris paribus assumption." They conclude that we should be "wary of correlational data in setting parameters," and they caution us that "multiple regression procedures to estimate a parameter can suffer from similar difficulties." Their advice is similar to the advice by Mass and Senge: The best approach to statistical estimation of parameters in system dynamics models will involve "full-information maximum likelihood via optimal filtering."

Social system case studies are positioned in figure 15.1 to the "soft" side of social system data. Case studies are frequently used when time series data are not available. A good case study sometimes takes the appearance of a good "story" about the institution and the problems (Wilber and Harrison 1978). A well-told story will frequently provide insights that could not be obtained by inference from the limited numerical data. In economics, for example, the preference for a well-told story may be the distinguishing feature between "institutional economists" and the more traditional economists who adhere to "neoclassical economics" (Radzicki 1988).

Expert judgment is used extensively in system dynamics projects. Frequently, the experts are part of the model building team, and their best estimates for uncertain parameters are incorporated into the model. In some cases, it may be useful to call upon a panel of outside experts. They might be polled in an iterative fashion following the popular Delphi method (Turoff 1970). A panel of experts could be surveyed to obtain their best estimates of highly uncertain parameters. Then the results from the first survey could be returned to the panel members. Each expert would be invited to submit a revised estimate and comment on why their estimate differs from the mean estimate. The end result of a Delphi survey could be better estimates of highly uncertain parameters as well as new ideas for additional variables to be included in the model.

Personal intuition is listed to the far side of figure 15.1. Intuition should be used when the other sources of information are not helpful. In his text *Systems Ecology*, Kitching explains a variety of situations

> where the measurement of real values may be difficult or even impossible. Under these circumstances the value used in the model, legitimately, may be a straight-out guess. Of course, such a value cannot be regarded and treated in the same way as other parameters in the model. It must be treated tentatively and its role can be evaluated using techniques of sensitivity analysis. (Kitching 1983, 41)

At this point, you might be wondering about the use of a "straight-out guess." Maybe it would be better to eliminate the uncertain parameter from the model. Wouldn't it be better to have a model filled with accurate parameters?

You should resist the temptation to eliminate highly uncertain parameters. Remember that excluding a parameter is equivalent to adopting an implicit estimate of the numerical value. Specifically, you would be setting the parameter value to zero. If you are confident that you can "do better than zero," take advantage of your personal intuition. Insert your best guess and proceed with the modeling process. You won't learn until later in the process whether your best guess needs to be replaced with a better estimate.

Step 6. Run the Model to Get the Reference Mode

The sixth step is to run the model and compare it to the reference mode. This is the first opportunity to test the model. Robinson describes testing as "the intellectual highpoint" of the modeling process:

> In a sense, formal models are built to allow testing. Were mathematical models not amenable to a diverse spectrum of testing procedures, they would have little advantage over verbal models. Procedurally, too, testing is a climactic activity. Suspense tends to build from the time the model is conceptualized to the time it is ready to be tested, as the modeler wonders how it will work. (Robinson 1980, 262)

The important question at this stage is whether the simulation result matches the target pattern established in step 2. If it does, you have reached a major milestone in the modelng process. You have confirmed your "dynamic hypothesis" established early in the process (Randers 1980, 131). If the simulation result does not match the target pattern, return to step 3 (flow diagram) or possibly to step 2 (draw the reference mode) or step 1 (get acquainted).

Step 7. Conduct Sensitivity Analysis

Step 7 is sensitivity analysis. Run the model several times with variations in the parameter values. Your goal is to learn if the basic pattern of results is "sensitive" to changes in the uncertain parameters. Pay particular attention to the "best guess" parameters and be sure to allow the parameters to vary across their full range of uncertainty. Check to see if you get the reference mode after each test. If you do, you have reached another important milestone in the process—you have discovered that you have a "robust" model. A model is called "robust" when it generates the same general pattern despite the great uncertainty in parameter values.

Sensitivity analysis can be conducted in an informal, one-at-a-time fashion based on our instincts about which parameters are likely to be important. The informal approach is demonstrated with the deer herd example in the next chapter. Sensitivity analysis can also be conducted in a comprehensive, thorough manner. The comprehensive approach relies on formal sampling methods, as explained in appendix J.

Experienced practitioners have learned that a well-structured model will frequently turn out to be "robust." They expect the key to the model's behavioral tendencies to be the underlying feedback loop structure, not the exact numerical values assigned to the parameters. If, on the other hand, you find that your model changes its basic pattern of behavior with changes in parameter estimates, it's time to return to step 5 (parameter estimation). As you invest more time in parameter estimation, you will do so with the knowledge that you are working on one of the truly important parameters in the model.

Step 8. Test the Impact of Policies

The final step in table 15.1 is policy testing. Run the model several times with variations in the values assigned to the "policy variables." These simulations will reveal whether the policies lead to the desired changes in the simulated behavior (see box 15.2). If you learn that the policy test is promising, you should return to step 7 (sensitivity analysis) to learn if the policy performs well under a wide range of values assigned to the uncertain parameters. Also, if you have ignored random variations up to this point in the analysis, you should introduce randomness to produce a more realistic setting for the policy analysis. If the policy results are encouraging, you will probably wish to define the policy variables in a more detailed manner. At this stage, you would return to step 3 (flow diagram) to describe the details of policy implementation.

You might be wondering about the difference between a "policy test" and a "sensitivity test." Both tests sound the same in terms of procedure: you change a parameter value, rerun the model, and compare the results. The difference is the nature of the parameters that are changed. In a policy test, you change the value of a parameter under the organization's con-

---

Box 15.2. How do we judge a simulation as good or bad?

A system dynamics model may be used to simulate changes in dynamic behavior due to a change in policy. The question of whether the simulated changes are "good" or "bad" is not amenable to system dynamics analysis.

Such questions are best addressed with evaluation tools from the field of decision analysis. Formal evaluation tools are designed to reveal tradeoffs between competing goals and the possibility that different groups may assign entirely different priorities to the goals. One of the more useful evaluation methodologies is multi-attribute utility measurement, or MAUM (Keeney and Raiffa 1976; Edwards 1977).

MAUM and system dynamics may be combined, as demonstrated by Gardiner and Ford (1980). They used a system dynamics model to simulate the population and infrastructure changes in a rapidly growing boom town. MAUM was used to reveal whether the simulated changes were viewed as good or bad by different participants in the town. (An existing home owner might view higher housing prices as good; a newcomer might view them as bad.) Their demonstration shows a formal approach to answer the question of "which policy run is best, and who says so?"

trol. In a sensitivity test, the parameter is beyond your control. Examples of policy tests in previous chapters include:

- water export from the Mono Basin (chapter 4)
- barging smolts on the Snake River (chapter 13), and
- harvest fraction at the mouth of the Columbia River (chapter 14).

Be prepared for some confusion with these labels. In the model of the Tucannon salmon, for example, testing the importance of the *egg loss fraction* might be interpreted both ways. If you feel that the estimate of 50 percent egg loss is uncertain and beyond your control, the test would be called a sensitivity test. But if your policy focus is on improvements in land-use practices in the Tucannon watershed, you would view tests of the *egg loss fraction* as a policy test. Don't be bothered by the ambiguity in these labels. The labels are not as important as what we learn from the tests.

Why We Iterate

The iterative nature of model building is illustrated in the chapter 4 description of the Mono Lake model. Four iterations were required before we were ready to test the impact of changes in water export policy. You might wonder why it is necessary to iterate. You might be asking yourself "Why don't we get it right the first time around?" If you pose this question to teams with successful projects, they will probably tell you that the iterative process was crucial to their success. They will comment that communication among the team members and with management was vastly improved by starting with a simple model and gradually building more realism over time. They are likely to add that the modeling process turned out to be more important than the actual model (De Geus 1988; Lane 1992; Morecroft 1992; Randers 1980; Vennix 1990; Verburgh 1994; Weil 1980). In other words, it's the journey that counts, not the destination!

A useful rule of thumb is to complete the initial iteration within the first 25 percent of the time interval available for the modeling project. If you have four years, make sure you complete the first iteration within a year. If you have only four months, complete all the steps in table 15.1 within the first month of the project. This will provide ample opportunity for reflection on the initial model. With the initial results completed, the team members will be in a better position to provide concrete suggestions for improvement. Also, a short time interval between model construction and simulation results will minimize the loss of client interest and understanding that occurs while the team is engaged in model construction (Robinson 1980, 262).

I try to follow the 25 percent rule in my own work, because I have seen a dramatic increase in the contributions from other members of a project team once a "demonstration model" is available. At times, the reaction of team members has resembled the reaction when a seed crystal is dropped into a supersaturated solution. Suddenly, there are useful ideas popping up everywhere! After several of these experiences, I came to realize that the useful suggestions don't rise to the surface until the team members see a concrete example of the system dynamics approach applied to their organization. Further information on the challenges of creating and sustaining client interest is given by Robinson (1980).

Exemplary examples of iterative models are reported by Jack Homer (1996) in his award-winning article "Why We Iterate: Scientific Modeling in Theory and Practice." Homer begins with a dictionary definition of iteration: "procedure in which repetition of a sequence of operations yields results successively closer to a desired result." He follows that with Meadows and Robinson's (1985, 419) definition of science: "[Real] science is, quite simply, the scientific method, the relentless iteration of induction and deduction, of precise hypothesis formation and careful experimentation."

Homer explains that scientific modeling "is distinguished from other approaches largely by the quality of evaluation and revision performed and by the insistence upon empirical evidence to support hypothesis and formulations." He provides three case studies from his consulting practice. His work for the Justice Department on the prevalence of cocaine use in the United States is particularly instructive.

The Cocaine Study

Homer began with the central hypothesis that "initiation to cocaine use was driven largely by price, with some fraction of casual users escalating to compulsive use." He modeled price as a function of supply versus consumption. Supply, in turn, was represented as a delayed response to price. The initial model was circulated to team members for review. He then altered the model structure to accommodate the reviewers' critiques and to obtain closer matches between the simulated behavior and the time series information from eight different databases.

> During a development period of three years, various causal hypotheses were translated into equations, and these equations were tested to determine whether they were capable of reproducing historical data and doing so with plausible parameter values. . . . Parameter values were estimated through a combination of expert knowledge, which established plausible ranges, and model tuning to achieve the closest possible fit to the indicator data. The tuning process consisted of some statistical regression but more often involved running multiple simulations and evaluating their fit to the data. (Homer 1993, 55, 77)

Homer faced a difficult challenge tuning the model. The historical data suggested that cocaine use was in major decline during the late 1980s. But his simulations did not show the decline as long as the parameters were restricted to the plausible ranges established in his interviews with experts. At this point, he might have "stretched" the parameter values to obtain a better match with the time series. Perhaps a closer match would be viewed as "proof" that the model is a valid representation of cocaine use. But the purpose of model testing is to improve, not to prove, a model (Robinson 1980, 264).

The discrepancy between the model projections and the downward trend in reported cocaine use was not resolved until raw data from the Drug Enforcement Agency (DEA) became available:

> The DEA provided raw data tape documenting, without summary, thousands of undercover cocaine purchases and seizures from 1977 to 1990. These data were our most reliable and complete source of information on price and purity at the retail and wholesale levels. . . . The DEA data dispelled some key assumptions of the initial model including the notion that there is a fixed relationship between wholesale and retail price and that supply is driven primarily by domestic price. (Homer 1996, 6)

Homer's final model places more importance on sociological variables. Supply and price "still play a role, but they primarily reflect and amplify trends in demand rather than reshape them." The final model treats the spread of highly addictive crack cocaine as separate from the spread of powder cocaine. It also distinguishes between the reported and the actual number of users. Homer believes there has been a growing tendency to underreport cocaine use in the 1980s. He attributes the underreporting to "fear of legal sanctions and partly the result of changing distribution of users." He concluded that the time series information on cocaine use in general and the initiation of new users during the mid 1980s is "simply not credible. . . .

Rather than 20 to 25 million lifetime users of cocaine in the US as the Household Survey estimates, there are now probably 50 to 60 million" (Homer 1997).

Homer's cocaine study is exemplary of system dynamics applied to a complex and serious
problem. Homer draws several practical lessons that are useful for all system dynamics studies. He suggests, for example, that modelers should be willing to make model revisions con-
tinually, nearly to the end of the project. He reinforces Forrester's advice that "mental, written and numerical data all have important roles to play" in support of scientific, system
dynamics modeling. But he adds that:

> Mental and written data (the latter often in the form of company reports and
> memos) are rich and plentiful, but also imprecise and often ambiguous or even
> contradictory. They are much better at describing how things work and how peo-
> ple behave than they are at specifying the magnitude and timing of historical
> trends. Such measurements are the special domain of numerical data, but even in
> the case of supposedly solid numbers one must look closely at what exactly has
> been measured and the possibility of measurement error or bias. (Homer 1996,
> 16)

Modeling Within Your Organization

You should think of the modeling process as embedded in a larger effort to help you and your
organization to be more effective. Models can be helpful in guiding research, in setting policy, and in building a learning organization:

- If your organization is focused on scientific research, models may provide the largest benefit in helping researchers to design useful experiments. Watt (1968, 349) reports that a
  common characteristic of successful application of large-scale simulation studies in biology
  is "an enormous amount of feedback between the experimental work and the computer
  activity." The role of systems modeling within the processes of scientific research is
  explained by Kitching (1983, 27) in his text titled *Systems Ecology.*
- If you are designing a model to test the impact of a policy, you should not expect that policy implementation will be automatic. The key to actual implementation is sustained
  client interest and close communication between the client and the modeling team
  throughout the process. Further details on the policy process are given by Roberts (1978),
  Greenberger, Crenson, and Crissey (1976), Robinson (1980), Weil (1980), and Sterman
  (forthcoming).
- You may see the greatest opportunity as helping your organization to overcome obstacles
  to learning. Strategies for building a learning organization are explained by Senge (1990),
  and the role of modeling within a learning organization is discussed by Morecroft and
  Sterman (1994).

My own observations about the use of models within a complex organization are given in
chapter 23.

Further Reading

- Graham (1980) explains the advantages of "using data below the level of aggregation of
  model variables." He uses a housing model as an example. If housing is a stock in the
  model, we should not confine our parameter estimates to statistical analysis of data on
  housing stocks. We should take advantage of useful information that might be available
  (e.g., city hall records, interviews with housing developers, or even personal observations).
  Richardson and Pugh (1981, 238) echo Graham's advice that "where possible it is prefer-

able to estimate parameters below the level of aggregation in the model." Kitching (1983, 217) explains the relevance of regression analysis with aggregate data. His comments on the "biological basis" for model parameters reinforces Graham's advice on aggregate data.

- Senge (1977) conducts a revealing experiment to show the accuracy of ordinary least squares (OLS) and generalized least squares (GLS) techniques in estimating parameters in a market-growth model. His experiment reveals the hazards of applying conventional econometric techniques to estimating the parameters in a system dynamics model. System dynamics practitioners are often skeptical of multiple regression analysis to aid in estimating model parameters. They often prefer the method of full-information maximum likelihood via optimal filtering (FIMLOF) described by Peterson (1980).

- Radzicki (1988, 1990) compares "institution economics" and the more traditional "neoclassical economics." Greenberger (1976) has argued that both system dynamics and economics would benefit if bridges were built between the fields. Radzicki explains that the natural approach to bridge building is to form closer links between system dynamics and institutional economics.

- Wolstenholme (1990) recommends that a system dynamics inquiry be viewed as a two-stage process. The first stage is "qualitative system dynamics," which is devoted to conceptualization. Causal loop diagrams play an important role in the conceptual stage. Stage 2 is "quantitative system dynamics." It involves flow diagrams, parameter estimation, and computer simulation. He argues that the first stage can "provide a significant level of understanding for a minimum investment of time and effort," and he recommends that teams concentrate on the qualitative approach when resources are limited.

- Richardson and Anderson (1995) describe a two-day workshop format to facilitate rapid construction and testing of system dynamics models. They have conducted workshops on child foster care, medicaid, and homelessness. Their experiences suggest that workshop participants should organize themselves with at least one participant serving as facilitator, another as coach, and a third as recorder. The roles of those three are to keep the group processes in order. A fourth person should serve as the modeler-reflector to focus on how the model is changing during the course of the workshop. This role is normally filled by a person with experience in system dynamics. Finally, the workshops seem to work best with a fifth person assigned as a "gatekeeper" to keep the group properly connected with the parent organization.

Chapter 16

The Kaibab Deer Herd

This chapter illustrates the iterative nature of the modeling process with a concrete and important example. The example is the deer population that occupied the Kaibab Plateau in northern Arizona at the turn of the century. The Kaibab deer herd warrants special attention because of its sudden and explosive growth in the early years of the century.

A sudden increase in an animal population is called an irruption. The Kaibab irruption is thought to be the first of a series of irruptions that "have since threatened the future productivity of deer ranges from Oregon to North Carolina, California to Pennsylvania, Texas to Michigan." Leopold (1943) reports finding no record of a deer irruption in North America "antequating the removal of deer predators. Those parts of the continent which still retain the native predators have reported no irruptions." Leopold interprets this as circumstantial evidence to support "the surmise that removal of predators predisposes a deer herd to irruptive behavior." The Kaibab story has become widely known as scientists interpret and reinterpret the cause and consequences of the irruption (Botkin 1990; Caughley 1970; Kormondy 1976; Lack 1954; and Odum 1971).

This chapter uses the Kaibab example to provide an opportunity for model building and testing. The main purpose is to illustrate the iterative, trial-and-error process explained in the previous chapter. This is a long chapter that does not reach its destination immediately. Along the way, you will appreciate the many decisions to be made in building a model. By the end of the chapter, you will see a model that simulates the dynamics of the deer herd irruption and the subsequent collapse of the herd due to starvation. The chapter concludes with exercises to verify, apply, and improve the model. One of the more challenging exercises is to expand the model to learn if it can accommodate alternative interpretations of the Kaibab irruption.

Get Acquainted with the System

The Kaibab Plateau is located north of the Colorado River in north-central Arizona. The plateau extends around 60 miles north and south. It is around 45 miles wide at its widest point. Rasmussen (1941) describes the area as one of the largest and best-defined "block plateaus and one of the very few that is bounded on all sides by escarpments and slopes which descend to lower lands." Russo (1970, 10) describes the "south end of the plateau as falling away precipitously to form the North Rim of the Grand Canyon" and says, "This is a setting of tremendous beauty and splendor, enjoyed by thousands of tourists each year." When traveling to the plateau, the visitor will notice pronounced changes in vegetation with changes in elevation. The vegetation types include shrubs, sagebrush, grasslands, pinon-juniper, and spruce-fir. The pinon-juniper woodlands provide the winter range for the deer. The summer range includes Ponderosa pine and spruce-fir forests as well as open mountain grasslands.

The Kaibab deer is a Rocky Mountain mule deer, known scientifically as *Odocoileus hemionus*. The deer attain reproductive maturity at about one and a half years of age. They normally mate in November and December; fawning normally occurs in June and July. Twins are very common, and occasionally triplets are seen. A typical buck grows to weigh around 150 pounds. Russo reports that there is little information available on the total size of the mule deer population prior to 1906. He cites Rasmussen's (1941) estimate of around 3,000 to 4,000 deer at the turn of the century. (He also shows Indian artifacts carbon-dated at over 3,000 years old.) Although information on the deer population is sparse, there are extensive records on livestock. Cattle and sheep were first introduced to the plateau in the 1880s; around 20,000 cattle and 200,000 sheep grazed on the plateau in the 1880s. By 1907, the domestic livestock numbers were considerably lower—around 8,000 cattle and 10,000 sheep.

The Kaibab Plateau was also home to populations of coyotes, bobcats, mountain lions, and wolves. Data on the size of these predator populations is lacking, but we do have information on predator kills (Russo 1970, 126). During the interval from 1907 to 1923, for example, predator kills were estimated at 3,000 coyotes, 674 lions, 120 bobcats, and 11 wolves. It is believed that the wolf was exterminated in those years and that the mountain lion population was greatly reduced. Russo (p. 127) explains that predators were indigenous species to the Kaibab north. Nevertheless, their removal by hunting and trapping was based on a general consensus that predator control was beneficial. He observes, "It was in reality a blanket policy that may have grown from an idea of protecting desirable wildlife by eliminating its enemies."

The deer population grew rapidly around this time. By 1918, there was recognition that the large number of deer was beginning to influence the condition of the forage. Continued bad reports in 1920 and 1922 led to the formation of a special committee to investigate the size of the deer population. In August of 1924, committee members spent ten days on the plateau. The reconnaissance party reported that it was common to see over a hundred deer in a day's drive. One member reported seeing over a thousand deer along a twenty-six-mile highway leading to the rim of the Grand Canyon. The committee was not sure of the size of the population, but "all local witnesses examined placed the number of deer in the Kaibab Forest at not less than 50,000." Rasmussen (1941) estimated the deer population in 1924 at around 100,000.

The reconnaissance party reported that the forage could "only be characterized as deplorable, in fact they were the worst that any member of the Committee had ever seen." The committee noted that forage conditions were "far from desirable in every respect. . . . No new growth of aspen was located, and all the trees were highlined." The committee observed that white fir, which is commonly eaten by deer only under stress of food shortage, showed effects of recent and heavy use. Skirted trees became a common sight, as indicated in photo 16.1. "Any spruce or fir tree within reach was nipped and fed upon," according to the committee. The reconnaissance party found the deer to be in deplorable condition as well: "In nearly every case the outline of the ribs could be easily seen through the skin."

Russo describes a major die-off during the years 1924–28. He cites one report that 75 percent of the previous year's fawns died during the winter. Total deer losses during these years were estimated at around 3,000–4,000 due to a combination of starvation, hunting, and predators. Leopold (1943) describes the deer population falling by around 60 percent during two successive winters. He adds, "By then, the girdling of so much of the vegetation through browsing precluded recovery of the food reserve."

The extraordinary conditions prompted local groups to initiate some extraordinary but futile efforts to rescue the deer. Russo (1970, 39) describes one "as an event that sounds more like fiction than fact." Over one hundred people loaded down with cowbells, tin cans, and

Photo 16.1. Skirted trees became a common sight on the Kaibab North. Any spruce or fir tree within reach was nipped and fed upon. The scars of abuse from the early twenties did not have a chance to heal before another great deer herd built up in the early fifties and added to the damage. Source: Courtesy of the Arizona Game and Fish Department.

other noisemakers formed a line on foot and horseback, determined to drive the deer to the south rim of the Grand Canyon (where they would be collected and transferred to better range). The people knew their effort was futile when they reached Saddle Canyon. By that point, "there were no deer in front of the men but thousands of deer behind them." Another extraordinary but futile effort was the removal of fawns. Organizers signed contracts to deliver over a thousand fawns to private parties, but most fawns died during the first day of capture or shortly thereafter in so-called fawn farms.

By 1928, government hunters were deployed to reduce the size of the deer population. Russo describes the hunters as "reminiscent of the buffalo hide-hunters." The deer slayers took to the field in December of 1928 and killed over 1,100 deer. The government program was highly controversial and was discontinued in the following year. During all this time, the policy of hunting and trapping predators continued. During 1927, predator "control measures" eliminated 403 coyotes, 111 "wildcats," and 11 mountain lions. Russo (1970, 46) describes all of this with a sense of incredulity: "Paradoxical situations? Here the deer are dropping dead from starvation by the hundreds and outwardly every effort is being made to reduce the population because the range is in poor condition . . . but, the predator is still controlled."

The year 1930 was a year of extra summer rainfall, and Russo reports that the deer enjoyed a good growth of "weeds, grass, and mushrooms" and "were reported in good condition throughout the year." By 1932, the deer population was estimated at around 14,000. The range was recorded as "in better condition than it has been in a great many years," and one of the Forest Service game reports declared that the number of deer appeared "to be about right for the range" (Russo 1970, 50).

Be Specific about the Problem

The next step in the modeling process is to be specific about the dynamic problem. In this case, we are looking back in time to see if modeling can clarify the dynamics of an important historical event. We might imagine that the model would lead to insights on measures to prevent the irruption. And if that were not possible, it might be used to deal with the difficult consequences of the irruption.

The best way to be specific about the nature of the "dynamic problem" is to draw a reference mode. The reference mode provides a target pattern of behavior, and it usually corresponds to one of the fundamental patterns described in chapter 1. The overshoot pattern is the one that best fits the Kaibab situation. Figure 16.1 shows the overshoot pattern drawn as a time graph of the deer population from 1900 to 1940. The initial population is shown at around 4,000, based on the estimate by Rasmussen (1941). The population is assumed to have been relatively constant in the early years of the century and to have grown rapidly during the interval from 1910 to 1924, perhaps reaching a peak of around 100,000. The subsequent die-off is thought to have occurred in the late 1920s. Perhaps 60 percent of the deer died in just two years. By the 1930s, conditions on the plateau had improved, and the population was thought to be around 14,000.

Notice that the time graph is sketched by hand, and the vertical axis is not labeled. The sketch in figure 16.1 is not a compilation of precise estimates of the deer population. Quite the contrary. It is simply a rough drawing to depict a possible pattern of behavior based on the accounts by Russo, Rasmussen, and others. We wish to use computer simulation to explain a population pattern that remains stable during the initial years and grows rapidly when predators are removed from the system. The population is expected to peak at anywhere from 50,000 to 100,000 and to die off rapidly due to starvation. The model should

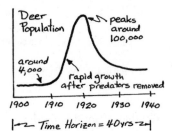

Figure 16.1. Reference mode for the Kaibab model.

help us understand how the forces at work in the Kaibab system could interact in such a way as to produce the overshoot. A relevant "policy variable" would be the number of predators on the plateau. So, to be more specific, our purpose is to develop a model that can simulate the pattern shown in figure 16.1 and be used to test how that pattern changes with changes in the number of predators on the plateau.

First Model

The next step is to construct a stock-and-flow diagram to show a minimum combination of stocks and flows that can explain the reference mode. Since our focus is the deer population, and the policy variable is the predator population, a logical combination of stocks and flows is shown in figure 16.2. One stock is assigned to the *deer population*. The number of deer is increased by *births* and decreased by *deaths from predation* and *deaths from nutrition*. The *predator population* is increased by *predator births* and decreased by *deaths from nutrition* and *deaths from trapping*. This is a reasonably simple starting point. For example, we have combined the coyotes, bobcats, and mountain lions into an aggregate category of predators in order to keep the model simple. Also, it is simpler to begin with a single stock of deer (rather than assigning separate stocks to males and females, young and old, etc.).

If we were to fill out the model in figure 16.2 with converters, we would face the challenge of modeling a predator-prey interaction. Predator births and deaths would depend on the availability of deer, and the deer deaths from predation would depend on the number of predators. Let's leave this topic for chapter 18. Also, since the hunters and trappers were an

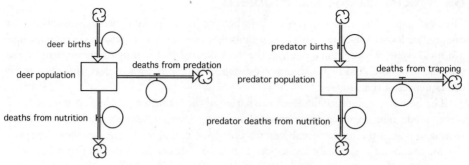

Figure 16.2. Assigning a stock to the deer population and a second stock to the predator population.

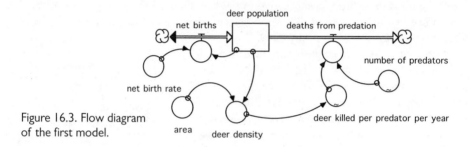

Figure 16.3. Flow diagram of the first model.

overriding factor driving the predator numbers lower and lower over time, let's simplify the model further by simply setting the *number of predators* as a converter to be specified by the user. And to save space in the diagram, let's combine the births and deaths of deer into a single biflow called *net births*, as shown in Figure 16.3.

This first model assumes that the predators' success depends on the density of deer. Higher density leads to more deer killed per predator per year. Let's measure the deer density per thousand acres and set the relevant area to 800 thousand acres. With the 4,000 deer thought to be on the plateau at the turn of the century, the *deer density* would be 5 deer per thousand acres. Figure 16.4 shows these assumptions alongside the remaining assumptions used to start the model in the year 1900. The *net birth rate* is set at 50 percent per year, which means that a population of 4,000 deer would have 2,000 net births per year. In other words, births would outnumber deaths by 2,000 deer/year.

The 50 percent/yr *net birth rate* is based on favorable range conditions. First, let's assume that the average deer lives around 15 years with ample food supply and in the absence of predators (Armstrong 1987, 180). So the death rate from old age would be around 7 percent/yr. To estimate the birth rate, assume that half of the deer population is female, that two-

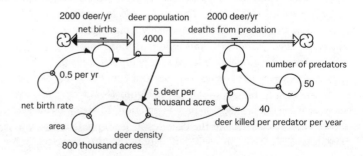

Figure 16.4. Equilibrium diagram and parameter estimates for the first model.

thirds of the females are in the fertile stage of their life cycle, and that each fertile female has a litter every year. Some litters may be twins, other litters may be only a single fawn. If we adopt Armstrong's (1987, 180) estimated litter size of 1.6 (which implies twins are born about every other year), the birth rate would then be

(0.5)*(2/3)*(1.6) or 54 percent/yr.

Subtracting the death rate from the birth rate gives a *net birth rate* of 0.47/yr. And since this estimate is not sufficiently precise to warrant two significant digits, we should round off to 50 percent/yr in the interest of simplicity.

The number of deer killed by each predator in a year is set at 40, based on the assumption that predators can be measured by the equivalent number of cougars. (A cougar is a mountain lion.) Let's assume that about 75 percent of the cougar diet is mule deer, and that the average cougar requires about one kill per week (Armstrong 1987, 165). So 75 percent of 52 kills/year is around 40 kills/year.

The final parameter in figure 16.4 is the number of predators, a combination of the populations of bobcats, coyotes, and cougars that occupied the plateau. We are treating the single number as if we knew the equivalent number of cougars. But whether we are talking cougars or a combination of several predators, there is little direct information on their numbers. In this situation, a plausible way to proceed is to assume that there are 50 predators, based on our intuition that the deer population and predator population were likely to be in approximate equilibrium at the start of the time period. With this estimate there would be around 80 prey for each predator. This ratio seems reasonable given the variety of surveys summarized by Ricklefs (1990, 436). Notice that the number of predators is represented by a graph function (~). We'll use this graph to hold the number of predators at 50 during the first decade and then reduce their number to zero during the second decade when they were hunted and trapped in great numbers.

Figure 16.5 shows a causal loop diagram for this first model. It shows a single positive feedback loop involving the size of the deer population. With a higher population we expect more net births and a still higher population in the future. We also see a negative loop that involves the deer density and the deer killed by each predator in a year. A higher population leads to higher density and a larger number of deer kills, greater deaths from predation, and a reduction in the future size of the deer population.

The simulation results from the first model are shown in figure 16.6. The deer population remains constant at 4,000 during the first 10 years of the simulation because the number of predators is held at 50, exactly the number to keep the deer herd in equilibrium. The predators are simulated to be satiated at a rate of 40 deer kills per year, but the number of predators is reduced to zero during the decade from 1910 to 1920. This allows the deer population to grow rapidly. Before the end of the decade, the deer population has grown by ten-

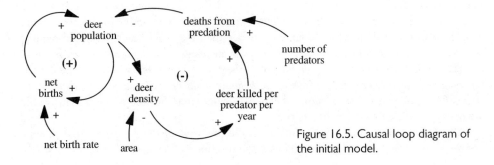

Figure 16.5. Causal loop diagram of the initial model.

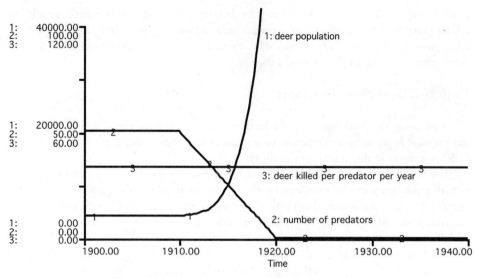

Figure 16.6. Simulation results from the first model.

fold. The population heads off the chart around the year 1920, and it never comes back. This is definitely not the reference mode.

A Second Model with Forage

The previous model does not generate the reference mode, so it is time for improvements. The next model will keep track of the forage requirements and the forage available on the plateau. According to Vallentine (1990, 224), the deer are "browsers" (as compared to cattle, which are "grazers"). The second model will proceed with the assumption that the total forage requirement is 1 metric ton (MT) of dry biomass per year. This estimate is based on Vallentine's (p. 279) suggestion that mule deer require roughly 23 percent of an "animal unit equivalent" (AUE). The AUE is the dry matter that would be consumed by a 1,000-pound nonlactating cow (about 12 kilograms of dry matter per day). You can work through the units to learn that the average mule deer would consume 2.76 kilograms per day, or 1,007 kilograms/year. Let's round this estimate off to 1,000 kilograms/yr, or one metric ton (MT) per year.

Figure 16.7 shows an equilibrium diagram for the new model at the start of a simulation with 4,000 deer on the plateau. The predation assumptions are the same as in the previous model, so the initial predator population accounts for 2,000 deaths per year. With a *forage requirement* of 1 MT/yr per deer, the total *forage required* is 4,000 MT/yr.

The model assumes that the plateau produces a huge amount of green matter each year. All plants are combined into a single category, and the *forage production* is set at 40,000 MT/yr, ten times what the deer require. This estimate is based on an instinctive assumption that the plateau is able to produce far more forage than the small deer herd would require. The *forage availability ratio* is defined as the ratio of the *forage production* to the *forage required*. As long as the *forage availability ratio* exceeds 1, the *fr forage needs met* will be 100 percent. If the *forage availability ratio* falls below 1, the *fr forage needs met* will fall as well. If the availability falls to 50 percent, for example, the model assumes that the deer are able to satisfy only 50 percent of their forage requirement.

The *fr forage needs met*, in turn, influences the deer's *net birth rate*. Figure 16.8 shows a *net birth rate* of 50 percent/yr when the deer are meeting 100 percent of their forage needs.

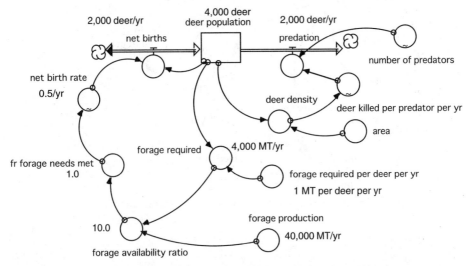

Figure 16.7. Equilibrium diagram for the second model.

But if the *fr forage needs met* falls, the *net birth rate* will decline. If the deer are meeting only half of their needs, the net birth rate is assumed to be zero. That is, births and deaths will cancel. The *net birth rate* is assumed to reach a negative 40 percent/yr if the deer are meeting 30 percent or less of their need for forage. The negative 40 percent/yr is an extreme situation. For example, it could represent a herd in which none of the females are able to give birth and the average deer lives only 2.5 years. The nonlinear relationship in figure 16.8 should be viewed as a "plausible guess," as little information is available on birth rates and death rates under difficult conditions. (Information on deer reproductive power is available for deer observed in New York State [Ricklefs 1979, 337], but the range of conditions corresponds to only a small portion of the horizontal axis in figure 16.8.)

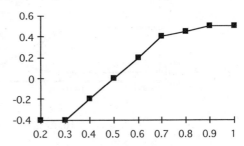

Figure 16.8. Relationship between the deer net birth rate (*y*-axis) and the fraction of forage needs met (*x*-axis).

The causal loop diagram for the second model is shown in figure 16.9. It shows that the forage calculations have introduced an additional negative feedback loop into the system. Perhaps this new loop will work to stop the runaway behavior seen in the previous model.

Figure 16.10 shows the simulation results from the third model. The deer population remains at 4,000 until the predators are reduced, starting in 1910. The deer population grows rapidly, reaching a population of around 80,000 by the year 1920. By this time, the net birth rate has declined to zero, and the population remains constant for the remainder of the simulation.

The results in figure 16.10 are certainly much closer to the target pattern. The population is shown to grow rapidly during the decade that the predators were removed. The population reaches quite a high value characteristic of the numbers reported by some of the observers from the 1920s. But the simulation does not show the die-off that is reported to have happened in the late 1920s. Let's check whether the die-off might appear if we experiment further. Figure 16.11 shows three different simulations with different values of the *forage required per deer per year*. The middle curve is the same as in the previous figure. The upper

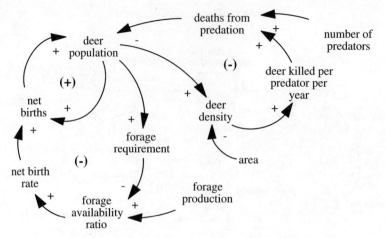

Figure 16.9. Causal loop diagram of the second model.

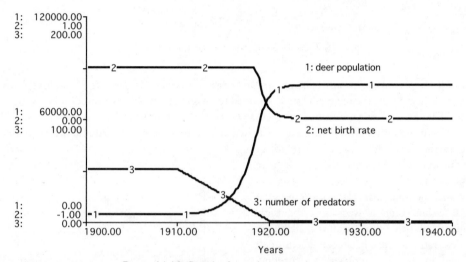

Figure 16.10. Results from the second model.

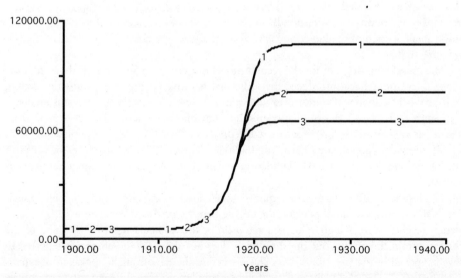

Figure 16.11. Sensitivity of the deer population in the second model to changes in the forage required per deer per year (run 1, 0.75 MT; run 2, 1 MT; run 3, 1.25 MT).

and lower curves demonstrate that the general pattern of behavior does not change with the changes in the estimate of each deer's forage requirement. The general pattern is the same— the deer population will grow rapidly after the predators are removed. But the growth comes to a controlled stop in all three cases.

The second model comes closer to the reference mode, but it fails to simulate the decline in the deer population that occurred when the deer population reached an unsustainable size. This problem may be attributed to the assumption of constant forage production. The model simply assumes that the same green matter is available, regardless of how many deer are on the plateau. One way to improve the model is to keep track of the growth, decay, and consumption of the biomass on the plateau.

Third Model: Forage Production and Consumption

To simulate the growth and decay of biomass, let's adopt the simple approach to simulating s-shaped growth from chapter 6. Figure 16.12 shows a model with a single stock variable used to accumulate the *standing biomass* on the plateau. This stock represents the combination of the grasses, pinon, juniper, pine, spruce, cliff rose, and other vegetation found on the plateau. The model was initialized with a small amount of biomass and allowed to follow its natural s-shaped path to the equilibrium conditions shown in the diagram. The diagram is based on a constant deer population of 4,000, so the *forage required* is set to 4,000 MT/yr. The *standing biomass* is 303,480 MT, which is 76 percent of the maximum value. The *bio decay rate* is constant at 10 percent/yr, so the *decay* is 30,341 MT/yr. The *bioproductivity* reaches an equilibrium value of 11 percent/yr, which means that the system generates 34,341 MT/yr of new growth. The deer consume 4,000 MT/yr of the *new growth,* leaving 30,341 MT/yr as *additions to standing biomass.*

This model retains the basic assumption that the forage requirement of a small deer herd will not impose a major stress on the biomass. In the figure 16.12 example, the *forage requirement* is less than an eighth of the *new growth* created each year. The biomass model provides a dynamic portrayal of the generation of new growth, so it is a good building block to combine with the previous model of the deer population.

Figure 16.13 shows the biomass model enclosed within the "Biomass Sector" of the third model of the deer herd. The "Animals Sector" encloses the variables used to keep track of the deer and predator populations. The numbers show the results in the year 1910, when the deer population is still held in check by the predators. The forage required is 4,000 MT/yr, which is much smaller than the 34,344 MT/yr of new growth. Let's assume that 75 percent of the

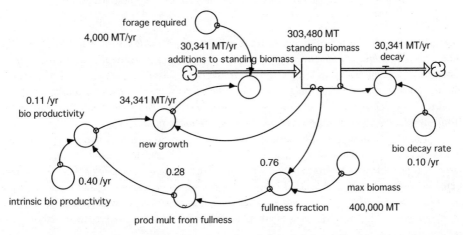

Figure 16.12. Equilibrium diagram of a model of the standing biomass.

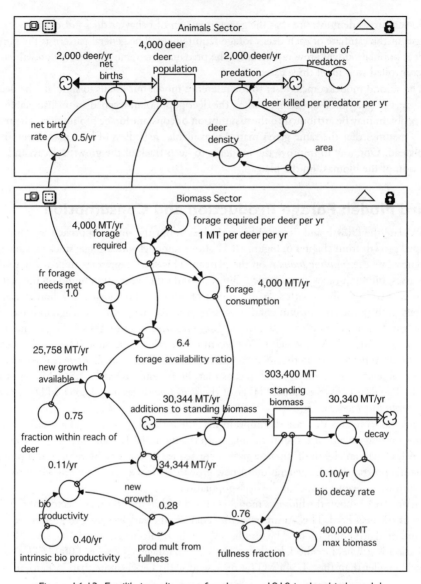

Figure 16.13. Equilibrium diagram for the year 1910 in the third model.

new growth is within reach of the deer, so the *new growth available* is shown as 25,758 MT/yr. The *forage availability ratio* shows that this is 6.4 times larger than the *forage required*. The *fr forage needs met* will be 1.0 as long as the *forage availability ratio* is larger than 1.0. If the ratio should fall below 1, the *fr of forage needs met* will fall as well. The *forage consumption* is the product of the *forage required* and the *fr forage needs met*. The *forage consumption* is subtracted from the *new growth* to find the *additions to standing biomass*.

Figure 16.13 shows no difference between the *forage required* and the *forage consumed*. This is to be expected when the deer herd is small. But if the deer population grows quite large, it is possible for the *forage required* to exceed the *new growth available*. When this happens, the *fr forage needs met* will fall below 1; the *forage consumption* will be limited; and the *net birth rate* will decline. If the *net birth rate* becomes negative, we will see a decline in the *deer population*. This new model appears to have the potential to generate the overshoot pattern of behavior.

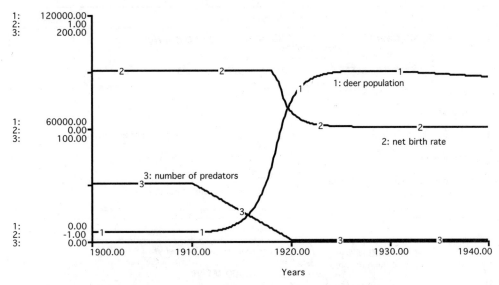

Figure 16.14. Simulation results from the third model.

Figure 16.14 shows the simulation results over the entire time interval from 1900 to 1940. The deer population grows to around 80,000 by the year 1920, and the net birth rate declines to slightly below zero. The population shows a small decline during the 1920s and 1930s, but the decline is nothing like the sharp decline we have been looking for to match the die-off that is thought to have happened in the late 1920s.

At this point, we might test the third model to learn if we would see a simulated die-off with different parameters. If you experiment with three values of the annual forage needed for each deer, for example, the test results would be similar to the previous test with the second model. All three simulations will show basically the same result: The deer population grows rapidly after the predators are removed. But the population does not appear inclined to exhibit the overshoot-and-collapse pattern we have been looking for.

Fourth Model: Deer May Consume the Older Biomass

The previous model limits the deer's forage consumption to the fraction of the new growth that they can reach. This limitation is plausible under most conditions, as the deer prefer the new growth. But under highly stressed conditions, the deer have been observed to consume some of the older biomass in desperation. The clearest evidence comes from the photograph of skirted trees shown previously.

Figure 16.15 shows an equilibrium diagram of the fourth model, which includes the possibility that the deer will consume the old biomass. The equilibrium conditions are reported for the year 1910, when the population is still at 4,000 and the forage requirements are easily accommodated with the *new growth*. Thus, 100 percent of the forage requirement is met; the *additional consumption required* is zero; and the *old biomass consumption* is zero. So far, the new model looks pretty much like the previous model. When the deer population becomes quite large, the new model will keep track of any *additional consumption* that is required when the *fr forage needs met* falls below 1. It assumes that 25 percent of the *standing biomass* is available to the deer to meet their additional needs each year. Thus, Figure 16.15 shows the *standing biomass available* at 75,850 MT/yr. But the deer do not need any additional biomass in the year 1910, so the *fr additional needs met* is 1.0.

The deer may meet their food needs from two sources, so the model must keep track of

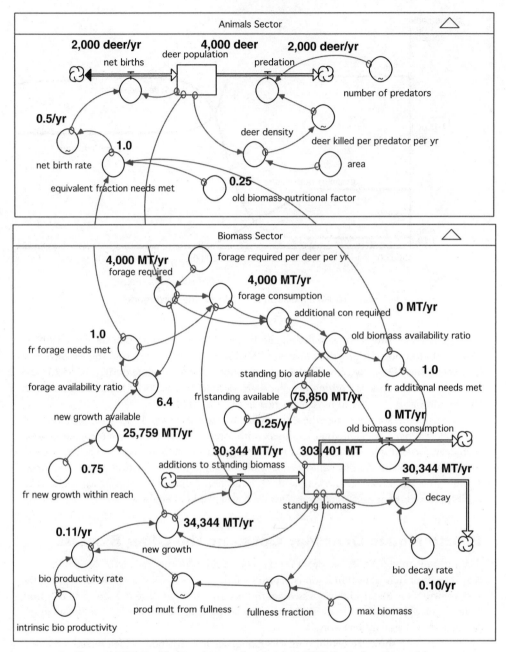

Figure 16.15. Equilibrium diagram for the year 1910 in the fourth model.

an "equivalent fraction" of their food needs met. This is done by weighting the fraction of their needs met by consuming the older, less nutritious biomass by the *old biomass nutritional factor,* which is set at 25 percent. In other words, a deer must consume 4 kilograms of older biomass to match the equivalent of 1 kilogram of new growth. In the figure 16.15 example, the deer have no problem meeting their need for food, so the *equivalent fraction of needs met* is shown at 1.0 and the *net birth rate* is 50 percent/yr.

Figure 16.16 shows the simulation results for the new model. The *deer population* grows to a peak over 100,000 in the early 1920s and then declines rapidly. The *net birth rate* falls to zero around the year 1921, and it continues to fall reaching around –25 percent/yr by the end

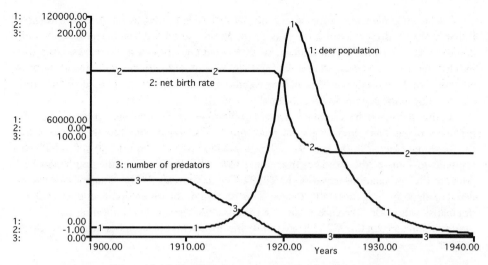

Figure 16.16. Simulated overshoot in the fourth model.

of the 1920s. (By this time, the deer's combined consumption of new growth and old biomass is sufficient to meet only 38 percent of their food needs.) The net birth rate remains at –25 percent/yr for the remainder of the simulation, and the deer population continues to decline toward zero.

Figure 16.16 shows the overshoot pattern we have been looking for, so it is useful to look at the simulated behavior of some of the other variables. Figure 16.17 shows the simulated results for the *forage required,* the *forage consumption,* and the *standing biomass. Forage required* grows to over 100,000 MT/yr during the 1920s, and the *forage consumption* keeps pace with that growth until around the year 1918, at which time it falls behind the requirement, and the deer are simulated to begin consuming older biomass.

Old biomass consumption rises steeply around the year 1920. By that time, the deer population reaches its peak and is beginning to decline due to inadequate food. If we compare the *forage consumption* and the *old biomass consumption* around this time, the two curves are approximately equal. In other words, the deer are consuming 1 kilogram of old biomass for every kilogram of new growth.

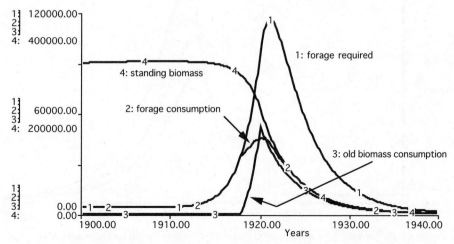

Figure 16.17. Simulation results for the forage variables in the fourth model.

The *standing biomass* is stable at around 300,000 MT as long as the deer herd is small. But it begins to decline around the year 1918. By the year 1920, there appears to be only 200,000 MT of biomass on the plateau. With the standing biomass declining year after year, the deer left on the plateau will see less and less new growth and less and less old biomass available. Their consumption of both forage and old biomass declines, and so does their population. The entire system declines inexorably to zero.

At this point, we have reached a major milestone in the modeling process. We have reached a model that generates the reference mode. The model simulates the irruption and the subsequent die-off in the late 1920s. The population peaks at around 100,000, which corresponds to some of the estimates from the 1920s. The die-off brings the population back down to the low values observed in the 1930s. The final decade of the simulation shows the deer population falling inexorably to zero. This portion of the simulation does not match the original sketch of the reference mode from the start of the chapter, indicating that further improvements are useful. We will save these improvements for exercises at the end of the chapter.

Sensitivity Analysis

Some limited sensitivity testing has been shown previously. But now that the model generates the reference mode, it is time to conduct more extensive sensitivity analysis. The purpose is to learn if the model's general pattern of behavior is strongly influenced by changes in the uncertain parameters. The mechanics of a sensitivity test are simple. Select an individual parameter that is uncertain; change the estimate; and repeat the simulation. Then compare the simulations to see if the parameter change leads to an important change in the simulated behavior. If we continue to see the same general pattern of behavior in many different simulations, the model is said to be robust. Robust models are useful in studying environmental systems, as the models are likely to be filled with highly uncertain parameters. The Kaibab draws heavily on partial information and our own intuition. It is certainly filled with uncertain parameters, and it is important to learn if the model's tendency to overshoot is robust.

Figure 16.18 shows the first sensitivity test to learn if the overshoot pattern is altered by changes in the forage requirement. The middle simulation is the base case, with a forage

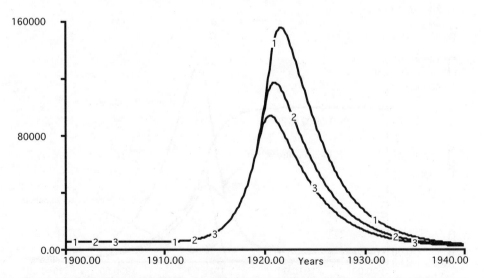

Figure 16.18. Sensitivity of the deer population to changes in the forage required per year (run 1, 0.75 MT; run 2, 1 MT; run 3, 1.25 MT).

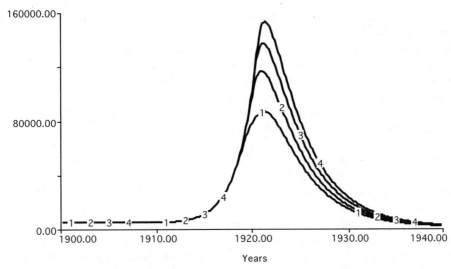

Figure 16.19. Sensitivity of the deer population to changes in the old biomass nutritional factor (run 1, 0; run 2, 0.25; run 3, 0.5; run 4, 0.75).

requirement of 1 MT per deer per year. The simulation with the peak population near 160,000 assumes the forage requirement of 0.75 MT/yr. And the lower simulation assumes that each deer needs 1.25 MT/yr. The three simulations are quite different when judged in terms of their peak populations. Indeed, the peak in the first simulation is nearly twice as high as the peak in the third simulation.

On the other hand, the three simulations are similar in many other respects. For example, they show identical behavior in the years from 1900 to 1915. Then all three simulations show the population climbing to a level that cannot be sustained. Once the peak is reached, all three simulations show the population declining inexorably to zero. In other words, all three simulations show the same tendency of the deer population to exhibit the overshoot pattern once the predators are removed from the plateau. Since our purpose is to understand the system's tendency to overshoot, we would say the model is robust with respect to changes in this first parameter.

Figure 16.19 shows a second sensitivity test to learn if the overshoot will appear with large changes in the value of the *old biomass nutritional factor*. This is a highly uncertain parameter, which was set at 0.25 in the previous simulations. Figure 16.19 shows four simulations with this parameter ranging from a low of zero to a high of 75 percent. The test results yield the same finding as in the previous test. The model shows the same general tendency to overshoot despite large variations in these uncertain parameters.

The previous tests are easily implemented with Stella because the changes are limited to one of the constants in the model. But it is also important to test the sensitivity of the model to changes in the nonlinear functions. Figures 16.20 and 16.21 illustrate how such tests are conducted. Figure 16.20 shows three possible assumptions for the nonlinear relationship between the deer *net birth rate* and the *equivalent fraction of the deer needs met*. The middle graph is the base case assumption used previously. All three graphs adopt the same assumption when the deer are able to satisfy 100 percent of their needs. And all three graphs show that the *net birth rate* will be highly negative if the fraction should fall to zero. The top graph assumes that the net birth rate responds less rapidly to a decline in the deer's ability to meet their food needs. And the lower graph assumes a more rapid response.

Figure 16.21 shows a comparison of the deer population with the three assumptions on this nonlinear relationship. The middle simulation is the same as the base case simulation

shown previously. The deer population climbs
to over 100,000 shortly after the year 1920.
The first of the three simulations adopts the
assumption that the *net birth rate* responds only
slowly to changes in the equivalent fraction of
needs met. If this were the case, the population
would climb to around 150,000. The third
simulation adopts the lower graph. This simulation assumes an earlier and stronger response
of the *net birth rate* to changes in the equivalent
fraction of needs met. With this third assumption, the deer population is simulated to hit a
peak of around 90,000.

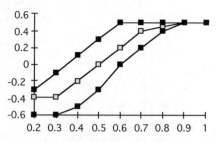

Figure 16.20. Three possible
relationships between the net birth
rate (y-axis) and the equivalent
fraction of needs met (x-axis).

The pattern of results in this test is similar to previous sensitivity tests. If we were trying
to predict the peak population, we would not be able to proceed without more confidence in
the parameter values. But our purpose is not to predict one particular number. Rather, our
goal is to obtain a general understanding of the system's tendency to overshoot. Figure 16.21
teaches us that the model shows the same general tendencies regardless of the particular relationship.

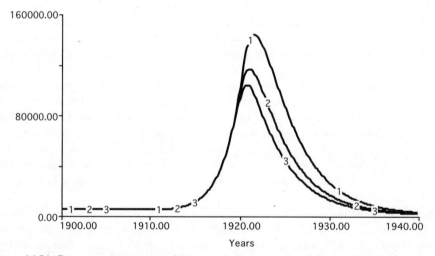

Figure 16.21. Deer population in simulations with three graphs of the net birth rate in the
previous figure (run 1, top graph; run 2, middle graph; run 3, lower graph).

The sensitivity testing concludes with a combination of changes that stretch several of the
parameters beyond what might be considered to be plausible estimates. The changes are
designed to reinforce each other by increasing the chances that the deer population could continue growing throughout the time period. This is an extreme test with the goal of learning if
the model tendency is robust over huge changes in parameters. First, three changes will be
made to effectively double the size of the plateau:

- double the area from 800 to 1,600 thousand acres;
- double the initial value of the standing biomass from 300,000 to 600,000 MT; and
- double the maximum biomass from 400,000 to 800,000 MT.

Then let's cut the deer's food requirements in half by lowering the food required from 1 to
0.5 MT per deer per year. And finally, assume that the old biomass has twice as much nutri-

tional value as in the base case. That is, increase the old biomass nutritional factor from 0.25 to 0.50. This combination of changes makes the biomass twice as large and twice as nutritious, and the deer's need for forage half as great as in the previous case. We might expect the population to soar to a peak eight times higher than in the base case. The result might be a deer population that continues to grow well into the 1930s and perhaps the 1940s.

Figure 16.22 shows the simulation results from this extreme test alongside the base case results. The base case shows a peak of around 100,000, while the extreme test shows a peak of over 500,000. If we believed all the assumptions that were adopted for this test, there could be over half a million deer on the plateau at the peak. The extreme test was created with the idea that the deer population might continue to grow for several decades before reaching an unsustainable size. But figure 16.22 shows that the higher peak is reached in the late 1920s, only around 5 years later than the peak in the base case simulation. This comparison reveals an important feature of exponentially growing systems—they can reach surprisingly high values in a short time interval. This feature is most notable when the doubling time is short compared to the time period of study.

Figure 16.22 is an extreme result that should not be taken as a plausible estimate of the peak population. Rather, the purpose is to learn if the model's general tendency is robust over a wide range of parameter values. Extreme tests are also useful tests to build confidence in a model, a point to be explained further in chapter 22. At this point, the main conclusion is that the model has a robust tendency to exhibit the overshoot pattern once the predators are removed from the plateau.

This combination of sensitivity tests confirms that the model's general tendencies are robust across wide variations in the numerical estimates of the uncertain parameters. It appears that the underlying structure of the model is far more important than the numerical estimates of the model parameters. This is another important milestone in the modeling process, for we may now proceed to the final, and most rewarding, step of all—testing the impact of policies to improve the system behavior.

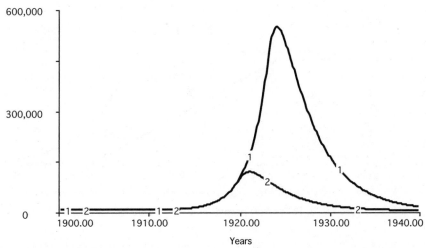

Figure 16.22. Deer population in an extreme simulation (run 1) and the base case simulation (run 2).

Test the Impact of Policies

The eighth and final step in the modeling process is usually the most interesting and the most important—to use the model to test how changes in policies might improve the simulated behavior of the system. The *number of predators* was listed as a policy variable at the outset of this chapter, so let's begin with policy tests to learn how changes in the *number of predators* might alter the tendency of the deer population to overshoot.

Figure 16.23 shows a policy test in which the predator population is exterminated less rapidly than in the base case simulation. The purpose of this test is to learn if we can avoid the overshoot if the predators are removed in a more gradual manner. The simulation shows that the *deer population* undergoes the same overshoot pattern regardless of the speed of the removal of the predators. Once the predators are removed, the *deer population* undergoes exponential growth and reaches a level that is not sustainable by the biomass on the plateau.

You might be wondering if the overshoot could be avoided if the *number of predators* were increased from twenty-five to fifty during the interval from 1915 to 1920. If you perform this simulation, it will reveal that returning the number of predators to the original value after the irruption has begun is not sufficient to prevent the overshoot. The deer population continues to grow after the year 1920 because deer are too numerous for the fixed number of predators to control.

One possible conclusion from these tests is that a good way to manage the Kaibab system was simply to leave the predators on the plateau. (And, indeed, this was the conclusion from many commentators on the Kaibab situation.) To test the ability of the predators to "control" the deer population, we would need to expand the model to allow the number of predators to rise and fall with changes in the deer population. That is, we would require a predator-prey model to keep track of the interactions between the two animal populations and to learn whether those interactions would lead to a stable system. This task will be addressed later in chapter 18.

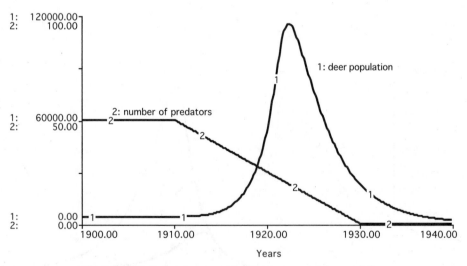

Figure 16.23. Policy test: predators are removed less rapidly.

Additional Policy Tests: Deer Hunting

To continue the example with the Kaibab model, let's turn to deer hunting as an alternative method of controlling the deer population. The rationale might be that managers wish to

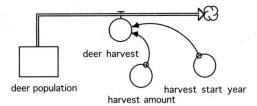

Figure 16.24. Additional variables to
test the impact of deer hunting.

control the deer population in the absence of natural predators. Controlled hunting is a common practice in Europe and North America. In 1985, for example, around 7 million deer were killed from populations totaling at least 37 million in Europe and North America. The economics of hunting are substantial. In 1976, for example, $2.6 billion was spent by hunters killing white-tail and mule deer in the United States, the equivalent of around $1,000 per animal killed (Clutton-Brock and Albon 1992.) Deer hunts on the Kaibab Plateau are described in great detail by Russo (1970).

Figure 16.24 shows the addition of a *deer harvest* flow to the model to account for a policy to "harvest" a fixed number of deer each year after a start date. We can now use the model to experiment with different values of the *harvest amount* and *start year* to learn about the timing of hunting.

First, set the *harvest start year* to 1915; then experiment with different values of the *harvest amount* to learn if a fixed level of hunting could control the deer population. For example:

> *harvest amount* of 1,000 deer/year: too small to prevent the irruption
>
> *harvest amount* of 2,000 deer/year: too small to prevent the irruption
>
> *harvest amount* of 3,000 deer/year: too small to prevent the irruption

Eventually, a *harvest amount* will be found that achieves some degree of control. A *harvest amount* of 4,700 deer/year would prevent the *deer population* from growing for about 15 years, according to simulation. But by the year 1930, the *deer population* would begin to increase in exponential fashion, and we would see the familiar overshoot pattern appear during the final decade of the simulation.

At this point, one might be tempted to experiment with a slightly higher value of the *harvest amount.* If you experiment with 4,704 deer per year, you will discover that the deer population is held in check throughout the 1920s but then begins to decline after 1930. Since the harvest amount is maintained year after year, the decline continues unabated, and the population actually falls below zero. At this point, you might be tempted to try harvesting 4,702 deer per year. But there is a fundamental problem with the search for an exact number that will control the deer population under the particular circumstances simulated in the model. This search will never be satisfactory. Even if we found the exact amount that would lead to an equilibrium under these simulated conditions, the slightest disturbance in any of the model variables would reveal that the equilibrium is not a stable one.

What we need is not a better number. We need a better policy for hunting. We need a policy that incorporates some information feedback from the size of the deer population to control the deer hunting. Figure 16.25 shows a simple change in the *deer harvest* flow that incorporates some information feedback. The new policy assumes that the deer population is known without error and without delay, and it assumes that the hunters meet the targeted amount without error. This idealized policy is tested with the *harvest fraction* set to 0.5/yr to match the deer *net birth rate.*

Figure 16.26 shows the results of this hunting policy if the *harvest start year* is set to 1915.

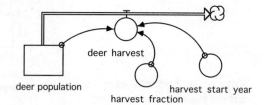

Figure 16.25. Deer harvest based
on the size of the population.

The *deer harvest* and the *predation* are shown on the same vertical scale so their relative size
can be compared. The *deer harvest* jumps to around 5,000 in 1915, which is more than twice
as great as the *predation* shown in the previous decade. Then the *deer harvest* is adjusted downward, and the system reaches equilibrium. The *deer population* remains around 10,000 for the
rest of the simulation, and there is no significant change in the *standing biomass* on the
plateau.

Figure 16.27 shows the results of this policy if the *harvest start year* is delayed to 1918.
The *deer harvest* jumps to around 20,000 in 1918 (ten times larger than the *predation* in the

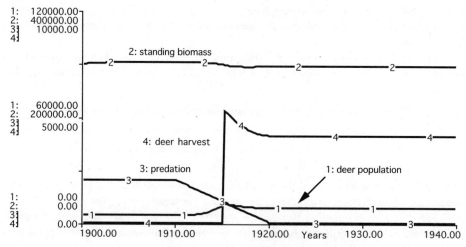

Figure 16.26. Harvest 50 percent starting in 1915.

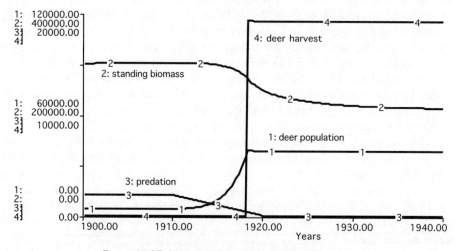

Figure 16.27. Harvest 50 percent starting in 1918.

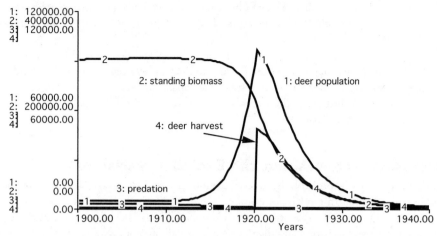

Figure 16.28. Harvest 50 percent starting in 1920.

previous decade). The *deer population* remains at around 40,000, and the *standing biomass* gradually declines to a new equilibrium. There is around 20–30 percent less biomass at the end of the simulation than at the start.

Figure 16.28 shows the results of this policy if the *harvest start year* is delayed still further to 1920. The *deer harvest* jumps to around 60,000, but the policy is too late to prevent the irruption. The deer are already on the decline due to the lack of food. The harvest policy appears to hasten their decline, but it does not allow the biomass to recover. This final test shows that the hunting must be implemented prior to the severe signs of overbrowsing if the irruption is to be prevented.

Additional Policy Tests

At this point, we have found a potentially useful result. We have an idealized policy that can control the deer population in the absence of predators. If we were encouraged by this result, the next set of policy tests should elaborate on the policy. Five examples of policy tests are listed below.

1. First, we might ask ourselves if the 50 percent harvest policy would control the deer population if we were to simulate the delays in measuring the size of the population. Also, we might wonder if the hunting policy would work given discrepancies in what the hunters harvest and the target amount.

2. A second question has to do with the size of the deer herd that we would like to see on the plateau. The previous hunting policy does not make the "target population" explicit. The result is an equilibrium population that appears to be a coincidence of when the hunting policy is started. We might expand the hunting policy so that the desired size of the deer population is an explicit policy variable.

3. A third example involves the weather. It is important to consider whether a policy would work with the changes in the many variables that would be influenced by random changes in the weather. One weather-sensitive variable is the *biomass productivity;* a second is the *biomass decay rate;* a third is the *deer net birth rate.* Random changes in the weather could introduce disturbances in these and other variables. It would be important to learn if the hunting policy that appears to work well with constant weather would work well in the presence of random changes in the weather.

4. A fourth example involves the condition of the biomass on the plateau. The 50 percent harvesting policy is "blind " to the amount of the *standing biomass* and to whether the

deer are able to meet their needs from new growth. Perhaps the hunting policy should be expanded to include some measure of whether the deer are on the verge of over-browsing.

5. A fifth example involves the policy of hunting bucks and does. The 50 percent policy makes no distinction between the bucks and does or between the young and old. An interesting area for further policy testing is to expand the model to test alternative policies on the age and sex of the animals to be harvested. (See the "Bucks-Only" exercise on the book's home page.)

Discussion: What About the Excluded Variables?

At this point, you will probably be able to compile a long list of variables that have been excluded from the fourth model. For example, the list might include the five hunting examples mentioned previously. Also, it's clear that the model ignores changes in elevation across the plateau, changes in seasons, and the impact of snowfall on biomass availability. Many variables are excluded by the high level of aggregation. For example, there are no distinctions among cougars, coyotes, and bobcats and there are no distinctions among different types of vegetation such as shrubs, grasses, pine, and spruce. Furthermore, we don't distinguish between the conditions on the summer range and the winter range. Finally, and perhaps most important, the model does not deal with the cattle and sheep that occupied portions of the plateau in considerable number during the time of the irruption.

Now suppose you were to draw a bull's-eye diagram for the Kaibab model. If you placed all of the excluded variables around the outside of the diagram, it would be immediately obvious that there are more items left out of the model than are in the model. It would be natural to react to the long list of excluded variables in an anxious manner. After all, one of the excluded variables could be more important than the variables that have been simulated to date. You might worry that the "computer could give the wrong answer." But if you try to add each and every variable to the model, the modeling process could go on and on. Will the model ever be big enough to deliver the "right answer"?

As we contemplate these questions, it's useful to remember that computer simulation is not a magic path to a right answer. Simulation modeling should be viewed as a method to gain an improved understanding of the dynamics of the system. With this limited goal in mind, we should resist the inevitable temptation to add more and more variables to a model. Indeed, we should feel proud if we arrive at a relatively simple model that can explain the reference mode of a system. Also, it's important to remember that adding more and more variables will sometimes confuse the issues rather than illuminate them. As a practical suggestion, it's good practice to limit our initial modeling effort to a model that is similar to the fourth version of the Kaibab model. The model is sufficiently complex to generate the reference mode from "inside the system." Yet it is sufficiently simple that we can see every variable and every interconnection on a single page.

Post Script

This chapter uses the Kaibab case to illustrate the steps of modeling and the iterative nature of the modeling process. Before we move on to other examples, it is important that you be aware of the considerable uncertainty about what actually happened on the Kaibab Plateau back in the 1920s. Caughley's (1970) article from *Ecology* is useful here. He begins by defining a *population irruption* as an "increase in numbers over at least two generations, followed by a marked decline." He then notes that irruptions in ungulates (e.g., mule deer) have been initiated by a change in food or habitat. The process is terminated by overgrazing. Since the Kaibab irruption is widely known, Caughley carefully reviewed the evidence accumulated by different observers. His review revealed an accumulation of "evidence" that was powered by the willingness of one author after another to accept the previous author's account of the Kaibab situation. He concluded that the "cause of the eruption is more doubtful than the literature suggests." He does not dismiss the removal of predators as the primary factor initiating the irruption. Nor does he spend much time with an alternative explanation. His only reference to an alternative is that the "increase in deer numbers was certainly concomitant with reduction of pumas and coyotes, but it also coincided with a reduction of sheep and cattle." Caughley noted that two observers writing in the 1960s "considered that the increase of deer was a consequence of habitat being altered by fire and grazing, and that the reduction of predators was of minor influence." Caughley concludes that the data on the deer herd in the period from 1906 to 1939 are unreliable and inconsistent, and he believes that the many factors that could have contributed to the upsurge in the deer population are hopelessly confounded. He concluded his review by asserting that the Kaibab case is "unlikely to teach us much about eruption of ungulate populations."

A more recent discussion of the Kaibab story appears in Botkin's (1990) *Discordant Harmonies*. Botkin describes Caughley's review and seems to agree that the Kaibab case is unlikely to teach us much about the irruption. But Botkin feels that there is a lesson to be learned about why the Kaibab story is told and retold by prominent naturalists. Botkin argues that their eagerness to retell reveals their paradigm (their way of viewing the world):

> It is surprising that such careful and observant naturalists as Leopold, Rasmussen, and the others who examined the Kaibab history and to whom the study of nature was important would have accepted one explanation among many when the facts were so ambiguous. Many interpretations are possible, only one of the possible stories was accepted, a story that painted a clear picture of highly ordered nature within which even predators had a highly essential role.

Botkin believes that the story of the mule deer on the Kaibab Plateau is only one of the many from the first half of the twentieth century regarding the removal of predators. He believes that the information on each case is sketchy, but "to proclaim that we do not have enough information to know if an irruption of mule deer was caused by the removal of the mountain lion, or even if the irruption occurred at all, is to speak against deep-seated beliefs about the necessity for the existence of predators as well as all other creatures on the Earth."

As students learning how to build and test models, you should remember that constructing and testing a model of the Kaibab story does not make the story true. It does reveal that the story "hangs together" in an internally consistent manner. That is, the model shows that the original description of the irruption can be explained through computer simulation in which the interrelationships in the model give rise to the rapid growth and subsequent collapse of the deer population. If you embrace this account of the Kaibab case, you could then use the simulation model to test policies to manage the deer herd. Alternatively, if you are skeptical of the original story, you could expand the model to learn if the irruption could be explained in an entirely different manner. For example, you might introduce livestock to the model and alter the assumptions to minimize the role of the predators. The new model could be used to learn if the removal of livestock leads to an internally consistent explanation of the irruption.

Exercises

1. **Verify the model:**

    Build the Kaibab model and verify that it works as shown in figures 16.16 and 16.17. There are three nonlinear relationships used in the model, one of which is portrayed in figure 16.8. The other two are shown in the following diagrams.

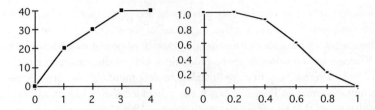

The left-hand chart shows how the *deer killed per predator per year* varies with changes in the *deer density*. With a *deer density* of 4 or more deer per thousand acres, for example, each predator is assumed to kill 40 deer per year. The deer kill will decline with a decline in the *deer density*. The right-hand chart shows the *biomass productivity multiplier from fullness*. With a *fullness* of 0, for example, the multiplier is at 1.0 (which means that the bioproductivity will be equal to the intrinsic bioproductivity). If *fullness* reaches 1, the multiplier will fall to zero.

The equations for the "Animals Sector" are as follows:

```
deer_population(t) = deer_population(t - dt) + (net_births - predation) * dt
INIT deer_population = 4000
INFLOWS:
net_births = net_birth_rate*deer_population
OUTFLOWS:
predation = number_of_predators*deer_killed_per_predator_per_yr
area = 800
deer_density = deer_population/area
equivalent_fraction_needs_met =
Min(1,fr_forage_needs_met+fr_additional_needs_met*old_biomass_nutrional_factor)
old_biomass_nutrional_factor = .25
deer_killed_per_predator_per_yr = GRAPH(deer_density)
(0.00, 0.00), (1.00, 20.0), (2.00, 30.0), (3.00, 40.0), (4.00, 40.0)
net_birth_rate = GRAPH(equivalent_fraction_needs_met)
(0.3, -0.4), (0.4, -0.2), (0.5, 0.00), (0.6, 0.2), (0.7, 0.4), (0.8, 0.45),
(0.9, 0.5)
number_of_predators = GRAPH(TIME)
(1900, 50.0), (1905, 50.0), (1910, 50.0), (1915, 25.0), (1920, 0.00)
```

The equations for the biomass sector are as follows:

```
standing_biomass(t) = standing_biomass(t - dt) + (additions_to_standing_biomass - decay
- old_biomass_consumption) * dt
INIT standing_biomass = 300000
INFLOWS:
additions_to_standing_biomass = new_growth - forage_consumption
OUTFLOWS:
decay = standing_biomass*bio_decay_rate
old_biomass_consumption = additional_con_required*fr_additional_needs_met
additional_con_required = forage_required-forage_consumption
bio_decay_rate = .1
bio_productivity_rate = intrinsic_bio_productivity*prod_mult_from_fullness
forage_availability_ratio = new_growth_available/forage_required
forage_consumption = forage_required*fr_forage_needs_met
forage_required = deer_population*forage_required_per_deer_per_yr
forage_required_per_deer_per_yr = 1
fr_additional_needs_met = min(1,old_biomass_availability_ratio)
fr_forage_needs_met = min(1,forage_availability_ratio)
fr_new_growth_within_reach = .75
fr_standing_available = .25
fullness_fraction = standing_biomass/max_biomass
```

```
intrinsic_bio_productivity = .4
max_biomass = 400000
new_growth = standing_biomass*bio_productivity_rate
new_growth_available = fr_new_growth_within_reach*new_growth
old_biomass_availability_ratio =
standing_bio_available/max(1,additional_con_required)
standing_bio_available = standing_biomass*fr_standing_available
prod_mult_from_fullness = GRAPH(fullness_fraction)
 (0.00, 1.00), (0.2, 1.00), (0.4, 0.9), (0.6, 0.6), (0.8, 0.2), (1.00, 0.00)
```

2. **DT test:**

   If you didn't think about the DT, it is most likely set at 0.25 year. Cut this value in half and repeat the simulation to learn if 0.25 year is sufficiently small to give accurate, numerical results.

3. **Time constants:**

   Review the chapter 11 description of time constants and identify the shortest time constant in the Kaibab model. Is the DT smaller than one-half of the shortest time constant?

4. **Biomass declines to zero?**

   The model's tendency for the biomass to decline inexorably to zero is not realistic, as the biomass has recovered sufficiently to support today's deer population. Explain why the standing biomass declines to zero even though the fraction of standing biomass available to the deer is set only to 25 percent/yr. Or to put the question differently, why doesn't 25 percent of the biomass escape consumption and provide a foundation for the biomass to grow back when the deer population becomes quite small?

5. **Causal loop diagrams:**

   There are many feedback loops in the fourth model, so a complete causal loop diagram would be quite complicated and perhaps more confusing than helpful. But it is useful to expand upon the diagram shown in figure 16.9 to include three new feedback loops:

   - More standing biomass means more new growth and more additions to the standing biomass.
   - More standing biomass means more new growth, more new growth available, a higher forage availability ratio, a higher fraction of forage needs met, a higher net birth rate, more net births, a higher deer population, a higher forage requirement, a higher forage consumption, and a reduction in the standing biomass.
   - Less standing biomass means less new growth and less new growth available to meet the deer need for forage. This, in turn, can mean more consumption of older biomass and a further reduction in the standing biomass.

6. **Eliminate net births:**

   The switch from *births* and *deaths* to *net births* in figure 16.3 might be convenient, but it can be confusing. Expand the model in figure 16.15 to include separate flows for *births* and *deaths*. Include a separate *birth rate* linked to the *equivalent fraction of needs met*. Include a separate *death rate* also linked to the *equivalent fraction of needs met*. Use nonlinear graphs for these two variables so that their combined impact is similar to the assumptions in the first exercise. Then run the expanded model to see if it generates an overshoot similar to the overshoot in figure 16.16.

7. **Check results against the cliff-rose study:**

Russo (1970, 71) reports the results from studies of the deer consumption of new growth on cliff-rose plants. Around one thousand twigs on the plants were tagged with plastic bird bands to allow investigators to measure both new growth and the portion of the new growth consumed by the deer. As a general rule, the deer appeared to have consumed around 40–65 percent of the new growth during the late 1950s and early 1960s. Russo (p. 96) reports that the deer population was around 10,000 to 13,000 during this time period.

Now the cliff rose is just one of many plants that serve the forage needs of the deer, and the biomass situation back in the years before the irruption is not necessarily the same as the situation in the 1950s. But just out of curiosity, run the model from the first exercise to compare the simulated new growth consumption with the cliff-rose studies. That is, run the model with a short pause interval to allow you to find a year when the population is around 10,000–13,000. Then stop the simulation and record the *forage consumption* and the *new growth*. What fraction of the new growth are the deer consuming?

8. **Hunting loops:**

Draw a causal loop diagram to reveal any new feedback loops that the hunting policy in figure 16.24 may have introduced into the system. Draw a causal loop diagram to reveal any new feedback loops that the hunting policy in figure 16.25 may have introduced into the system.

9. **Measured deer population:**

Expand the diagram in figure 16.25 to distinguish between the actual *deer population* and the *measured deer population*. Assume that Stella's smooth function (see chapter 17) is used to represent the delay in updating the census on the deer population. Set the length of the census delay to 2 years. Rerun the 1918 policy test from figure 16.27 to learn if the policy would still prevent the irruption.

10. **Random weather:**

Check the variables in figure 16.15 that you think would vary with variations in weather from one year to the next. Expand the diagram to introduce an *annual weather index* that varies in a random manner from one year to the next (see appendix H). Introduce an information link from the *annual weather index* to one of the weather-dependent variables in figure 16.15. Rerun the 1918 policy test to learn if the policy would still prevent the irruption.

PART IV

SIMULATING CYCLICAL SYSTEMS

Chapter 17

Introduction to Oscillations

Many systems exhibit intriguing oscillations over time. You will probably recall becoming intrigued the first time you felt the rhythmic beating of your heart, and perhaps you have become intrigued by the rhythmic crashing of ocean waves at the seashore. These and other oscillatory systems are fascinating to observe. But they are difficult to understand. A basic understanding of oscillations is useful for professionals in many fields. For example, cycles in the national economy challenge economic planners; cycles in animal and plant populations challenge environmental managers; and cycles in insulin secretion challenge biomedical scientists.

This chapter, and the following two chapters, demonstrate how models can be used to improve our understanding of oscillatory behavior. This chapter begins with the flower and sales models from chapter 6. The opening example shows oscillations imposed by outside forces. The remaining examples are more interesting. They describe oscillations that arise from inside the flower system and the sales system. The introductory examples set the stage for the more detailed examples. Oscillations in predator and prey populations are described in chapter 18; oscillations in aluminum production are described in chapter 19. You'll see from these concrete examples that system dynamics is a powerful tool to help us look "inside a system" for an explanation of oscillatory behavior.

First Example: Variable Rainfall

Recall the model of flower growth from chapter 6. It generates s-shaped growth in the area covered by flowers. Figure 17.1 shows a new version of that model to allow for variability in rainfall. The *intrinsic growth rate* is no longer constant at 100 percent/yr but changes with variations in *rainfall*. Let's assume that *rainfall* varies around a mean of 20 inches/year using one of the standard sinusoidal functions. The amplitude is set to 15 inches/yr and the period to 5 years:

```
rainfall = 20+SINWAVE(15,5)
```

The optimum rainfall for flower growth is assumed to be 20 inches/year. The *intrinsic growth rate* will be less if there is either too much or too little rainfall. The nonlinear graph (~) sets the *intrinsic growth rate:*

```
intrinsic_growth_rate = GRAPH(rainfall)
(0.00, 0.00), (10.0, 0.6), (20.0, 1.00), (30.0, 0.6), (40.0, 0.00)
```

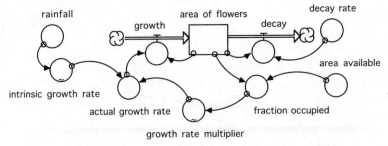

Figure 17.1. Flower-growth model with variable rainfall.

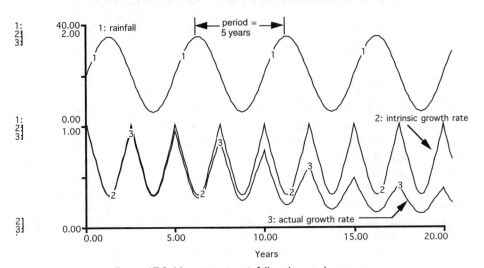

Figure 17.2. Variations in rainfall and growth rates.

Figure 17.2 shows the assumed variation in *rainfall*. It can reach 35 inches/year and fall as low as 5 inches/year. The *intrinsic growth rate* peaks at 100 percent/yr whenever the rainfall is at the optimum value of 20 inches/yr. But it falls below 100 percent/yr whenever the rainfall is too low or too high. Figure 17.2 shows a sinusoidal pattern of rainfall with a 5-year period. The intrinsic growth rate varies from a low of 30 percent/yr to a high of 100 percent/yr with a period of 2.5 years. The *actual growth rate* and the *intrinsic growth rate* are nearly identical during the first 6 years of the simulation. This is to be expected when the flowers cover only a small portion of the area. The decline in the *actual growth rate* after the 6th year is caused by an increase in the *fraction occupied* and the *growth rate multiplier*.

Figure 17.3 shows the simulated *area of flowers* along with their *growth* and *decay*. The sinusoidal changes in *rainfall* cause large swings in the *growth* but only minor swings in the area and the decay. The impact of the variable rainfall may be seen by comparing figure 17.3 with figure 6.4. The general pattern could be described as s-shaped growth, with a superimposed cycle with a period of 2.5 years. A close inspection of the two simulations reveals that the variations in rainfall do more than simply add a cyclical variation to the previous results. The *area of flowers* takes longer to reach quasi-equilibrium conditions, and the equilibrium values are somewhat lower than in the previous chapter. These changes are logical because the previous model assumes that flowers enjoy optimum growth conditions in each and every year, whereas the new model assumes that rainfall will vary around the optimum conditions.

This first example reveals some general conclusions that may apply to all systems, not just to flowers. First, we see that cycles imposed from outside a system can be transformed and

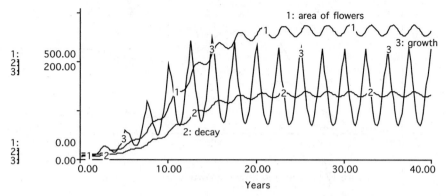

Figure 17.3. Simulated oscillations in area of flowers.

moderated as their effects "pass through" the system. In this example, a 5-year cycle in rainfall is imposed from the outside. The system then changes the pattern to a 2.5-year cycle in the intrinsic growth rate. The simulation demonstrates that a large cycle in flower growth would persist throughout the time period, but there would be only small cycles in the area covered by flowers and in the decay of flowers. It appears that the system acts to buffer (moderate) the impact of variable rainfall. The flower example is typical of most systems—the buffering takes place at the stock in the system.

Oscillations from Inside the Flower System

The previous example demonstrates how oscillations arising from outside the system are altered as they pass through a system. In the next example, the oscillations originate from inside the system itself. Figure 17.4 shows a new version of the flower model. The *intrinsic growth rate* is returned to the constant value of 100 percent/yr used in chapter 6. The new variable in figure 17.4 is the *lagged value of fraction*. The new model assumes that the impact of the spreading area on growth is not immediate. Rather, there is a lag before a change in the *fraction occupied* is translated into a change in growth rate. The *lag time* is set at 2 years, and Stella's smooth function is used as follows:

```
lagged_value_of_fraction = smth1(fraction occupied,lag_time)
```

The "smth1" stands for first-order smoothing of information flow. The first-order response is shown in figure 10.13. It assumes that some impact is felt immediately, but the total impact is spread out over a longer time interval. As a rough rule of thumb, you may expect two-thirds of the impact to have materialized after the designated *lag time*.

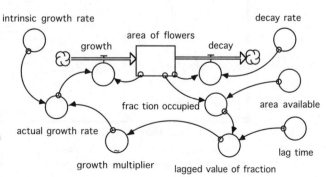

Figure 17.4. Flower model with a lag in the effect of fraction occupied on the growth rate.

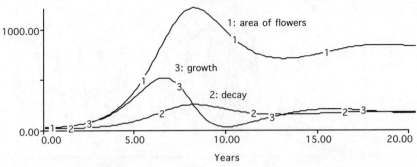

Figure 17.5. Simulated flower growth with a lagged effect.

Figure 17.5 shows the simulated *area of flowers* as well as their *growth* and *decay.* The new model shows that the area would grow past the normal limit of 1,000 acres. (It seems to shoot past the limit seen in the previous chapter.) This causes a major decline in the *growth,* and *decay* exceeds *growth* by around the 8th year of the simulation. The area declines during the next several years, "freeing up" space, and the extra space allows for an increase in the growth of new flowers. The variations in *growth* eventually fade away, and the system finds its way to dynamic equilibrium. The equilibrium in figure 17.5 turns out to be identical to the results in chapter 6: 800 acres are covered by flowers; growth and decay are in balance at 160 acres/year.

Figure 17.6 shows the impact of a change in the nature of the lagged relationship between *fraction occupied* and the *growth multiplier.* Run 1 is the same as in figure 17.5; it uses a first-order lag. Run 2 assumes that the lagged value is found with Stella's third-order smooth function via:

```
lagged_value_of_fraction = smth3(fraction occupied,lag_time)
```

Third-order smoothing is more appropriate if you feel that there would be no immediate impact of changes in the fraction occupied on the growth of new flowers. The third-order response pattern is shown in figure 10.13. It assumes that the bulk of the impact would occur 2 years after the change in area. The comparison in figure 17.6 shows that the third-order response introduces somewhat more volatility into the system. The flowers shoot farther past the normal limit of 1,000 acres and go through larger oscillations before finding their way to

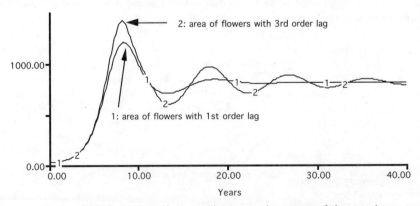

Figure 17.6. Sensitivity of the oscillations to the nature of the time lag.

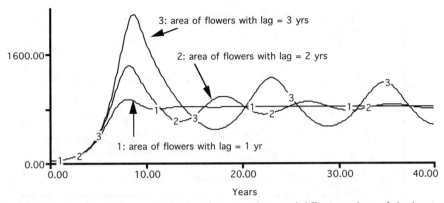

Figure 17.7. Simulated areas with third-order smoothing and different values of the lag time.

the equilibrium conditions. The added volatility comes from the somewhat longer lag implicit in a third-order smoothing of the information.

Figure 17.7 further illuminates the role of the lag by comparing the area of flowers in three simulations with different values assigned to the length of the lag time. (Each simulation uses third-order smoothing.) Figure 17.7 shows that a longer lag means greater volatility in the oscillations and a longer period in the oscillations.

The third run in figure 17.7 is particularly volatile. It shows the area of flowers shooting far past the normally suitable area of 1,000 acres. This large overshoot may seem unreasonable, but it is the logical consequence of the assumptions adopted so far. Remember that the intrinsic rate of growth is 100 percent/year, and there is a 3-year lag before the flowers "feel the effect" of their spread to an unsuitable area.

Figure 17.8 shows this volatile result more clearly. Notice the steep slope in the graph of the area of flowers at the start of the simulation. The flowers appear not to feel the effect of the space limitations at this point in the simulation. After a time lag, however, the growth drops rapidly to zero. This causes the area of flowers to decline until around the 15th year of the simulation. By this time, some space has been made available to permit new growth to occur, and we see a new spurt of growth around the 22nd year of the simulation. There is another spurt around the 32nd year, and a third spurt about to appear at the end of the simulation. Figure 17.8 shows the oscillations continuing with very little dampening over time. It appears that this system could oscillate forever. One reason for the volatility in figure 17.8 is the rapid rate of growth in the area of flowers during the first few years of the simulation when the growth rate is similar to the intrinsic growth rate.

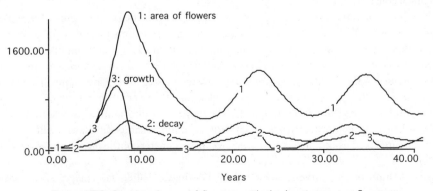

Figure 17.8. Simulated area of flowers with the lag time set at 3 years.

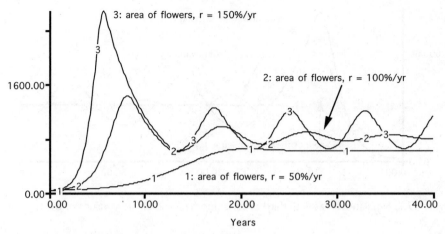

Figure 17.9. Simulated area of flowers with the lag time at 2 years and different values of the intrinsic growth rate.

Figure 17.9 shows the importance of this parameter by comparing three simulations with different values of *r*, the intrinsic growth rate. The most dramatic simulation in figure 17.9 assumes *r* is set to 150 percent/yr. It shows a major overshoot as the area shoots past the normal limit of 1,000 acres. The area then declines well below the limit and falls into a pattern of sustained oscillations. That is, there is very little dampening over time, and it appears that the system could continue oscillating forever. Run 2 has been shown previously. It assumes that *r* is 100 percent/yr, and it shows damped oscillations. That is, the oscillations become smaller and smaller over time, and it is clear that the system will eventually reach equilibrium. The first run in figure 17.9 is quite different from the other two. It shows no oscillations whatsoever. Systems that show no oscillations (even though we know they have the potential to oscillate) are said to be overdamped.

Summarizing Oscillatory Tendencies

The flower model is relatively simple, yet it gives rise to three different patterns of oscillatory behavior. We see overdamped, damped, or sustained oscillations depending on the values of the two parameters. One way to summarize these results is with a parameter space diagram like the one shown in figure 17.10. The *x*-axis corresponds to *r*, the intrinsic growth rate; the *y*-axis corresponds to the length of the lag time. These are the only two parameters in the flower model, so we should be able to summarize the model's oscillatory tendencies with a two-dimensional diagram.

The three simulations in figure 17.7 were conducted with the intrinsic growth rate fixed at 100 percent/yr. In figure 17.10 the position of each simulation is marked in parameter space with a + and is labeled. The three simulations in figure 17.9 were conducted with the lag time fixed at 2 years. Their positions are marked and labeled in a similar manner. The curve in figure 17.10 is drawn to separate the parameter space into two sections. If the parameters fall above the curve, we expect to see oscillations. If they fall below the curve, we won't see oscillations. (The system is overdamped.) The term "critically damped" is used to describe a system that is sitting on the fence between damped and overdamped behavior. Think of the curve in figure 17.10 as the "fence" that separates the parameters of the flower model into two sections.

The position of the curve is suggested by Hastings's (1997, 94) analysis of a logistic

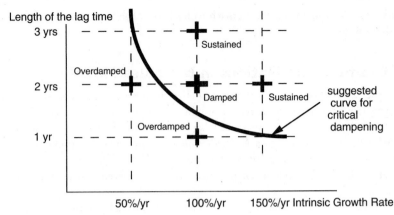

Figure 17.10. Parameter space diagram for the flower model.

growth model with lags. His model is prone to oscillations, but the oscillations do not appear unless the combination of the intrinsic growth rate and the lag time is sufficiently large. Hastings defines a dimensionless number by multiplying the lag time by r, the intrinsic growth rate. He reports that his "lagged logistic model" will not exhibit cycles unless the dimensionless number is greater than 1.57.

Now, the flower model is not identical to Hastings's model, but there is sufficient similarity that we might use his finding as a working hypothesis for the position of the curve in figure 17.10. Let's call the dimensionless number the FMVI, the flower model volatility index. The curve in figure 17.10 is drawn so that the index is at 1.5 everywhere along the curve. For example:

r = 50 percent/yr,   lag = 3.0 years,   FMVI = 1.5
r = 100 percent/yr,   lag = 1.5 years,   FMVI = 1.5
r = 150 percent/yr,   lag = 1.0 years,   FMVI = 1.5

Using the FMVI of 1.5 as similar to Hastings's 1.57, we may adopt the hypothesis that oscillations will appear whenever the parameter values land above the curve. The six simulations summarized in figure 17.10 seem to fit the hypothesis. Further tests are left for you as exercises at the end of the chapter.

The Volatility Index

You might wonder why the FMVI is a good measure of the volatility of the flower model. Hastings makes a good point about the dimensionless nature of the index. There are only two parameters in the model, and their product is the only plausible combination that yields a dimensionless number. Hastings's argument on behalf of dimensionless indicators is reported in appendix A. It boils down to the fact that a fundamental indicator should not change in value just because we happen to switch the units of measure.

The product of the intrinsic growth rate and the lag time is a plausible measure of volatility because it tells us about the tendency of the system to overshoot its limit. You may interpret the index as telling us the fractional growth of the flowers during the time interval required for information on congestion to be fed back to stop the growth. The higher the index, the greater the tendency to overshoot. Think of how the index would apply when we "overshoot" (overeat) at the dinner table. If we are consuming food at a rapid rate during the time interval for the signal from the stomach to feed back, the tendency for an uncomfortable overshoot is greater.

Third Example: Oscillations in the Sales Model

Chapter 6 uses a sales model and a flower model to demonstrate that systems with similar structure generate similar behavior. So you might expect that oscillations could arise from inside both systems if we were to introduce a lag in the flow of information. The sales company model is documented in figure 6.12. The model begins the simulation with 50 people and shows s-shaped growth eventually ending up with 750 people. The growth slows in a gradual manner as the sales personnel experience reduced effectiveness when they crowd into the same area.

Figure 17.11 shows a new version of this model to allow for a lag in the effect of the number of salespeople on their effectiveness. The new model assumes that it takes time for the congestion in salespeople to translate into a reduction in their individual effectiveness. A third-order smooth is used to simulate a delay in the flow of information. The *lag time* is set at 1 year; the *fraction to sales* is increased to 55 percent; and all other parameters retain the values from chapter 6.

The new model generates the dynamic behavior shown in figure 17.12. The company is simulated to grow from 50 to 750, but the approach to the 750 level is much more rapid. The rapid approach is made possible by the delay in the loss of effectiveness of each salesperson. (If each person continues to sell 2 widgets a day, the company will still be in a position to rapidly expand the sales force.) New hires peak in around the 8th year and fall quickly to zero. With 20 percent of the sales force departing each year, the total sales force declines to below the previous peak. This allows for an improvement in the effectiveness of each salesperson, and the company finds itself in a more favorable financial position. New hires increase around the 12th year and push the sales force back over the 750 level. The company will experience another decline in effectiveness, a decline in the sales department budget, and a subsequent drop in new hires. Figure 17.12 shows that this oscillatory pattern would continue for the remainder of the 40-year simulation with very little dampening.

Figure 17.13 reveals the importance of the time lag. The run with the 2-year lag shows the greatest overshoot. The sales force is simulated to grow past 1,200 and then declines well

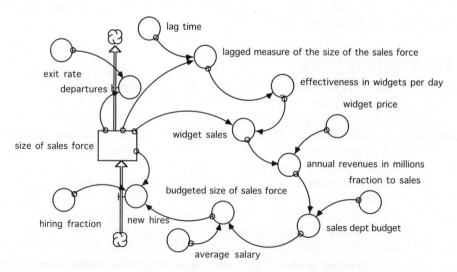

Figure 17.11. New model of the growth in a sales company.

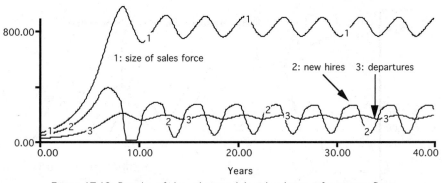

Figure 17.12. Results of the sales model with a lag in information flow.

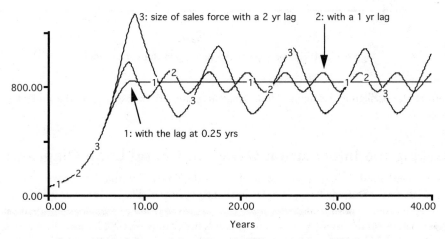

Figure 17.13. Sales model results with different values of the lag time.

below 750. This simulation shows sustained oscillations with a period of around 8 years. The run with a 1-year lag is the same as in the previous figure. It shows sustained oscillations with a period of around 4 years. The simulation with a lag time of 0.25 year is overdamped. It approaches equilibrium without any oscillations whatsoever.

The simulation with the lag time set to 2 years is particularly volatile, so let's take a closer look at those results in figure 17.14. Notice that the *lagged measure of the size of the sales force* follows the actual size, but it lags behind by around 2 years. The 2-year lag is most visible when you compare the peak values in the actual sales force and the lagged sales force. The "lagged value" does not correspond to any concrete measure of the sales force. It is simply a convenient way to implement the plausible assumption that there is some time delay before congestion in the number of salespeople translates into a reduction in their individual effectiveness. Individual effectiveness is constant at 2 widgets per day for the first 7 years of the simulation, even though there are well over 750 salespeople working the area. The decline in effectiveness does not appear until the lagged measure grows too high. The lagged measure peaks around the 10th year, and effectiveness falls to the lowest value in the same year. Notice that the low points in effectiveness coincide with the high points in the lagged measure of the size of the sales force throughout the remainder of the simulation.

The oscillations in the sales model arise for the same reasons they arise in the flower model, so it should be possible to draw a parameter space diagram to summarize the model's tendencies to oscillate. Also, you should be able to invent a sales model volatility index to help

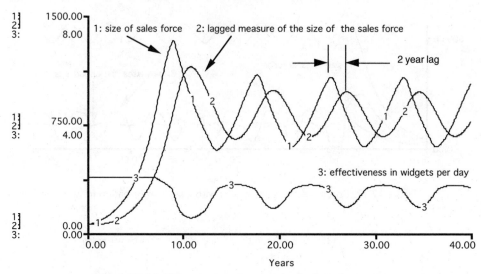

Figure 17.14. Closer look at the time lag in the sales model.

interpret the oscillatory behavior. These challenges are left as exercises at the end of the chapter.

Marking the Information Delays in Causal Loop Diagrams

These examples reveal the importance of delays in the flow of information within a system. Systems that were found to be quite stable in chapter 6 show oscillatory behavior in this chapter. In both cases, the oscillations were caused by the introduction of a single time lag into the system. Because of the importance of time lags, it is useful to mark their location in the causal loop diagrams. This is often done by adding // marks as shown in the diagrams that follow.

Figure 17.15 shows that the link from the *fraction occupied* to *growth rate* involves a time lag. The \\ marks keep the diagram simple and alert us to the particular feedback loop that operates with a time lag. Notice that the new variable in figure 17.4, the *lagged value of fraction*, does not appear in the causal loop diagram. Such new variables are often left out of the causal loop diagrams since the \\ marks tell the story. But if the lagged value corresponds directly to a well-recognized variable in the system, the lagged value would be included to improve communication.

Figure 17.16 shows the addition of the // marks to alert us to the time lag between the change in the size of the sales force and the change in the effectiveness of each salesperson. As in the previous diagram, the name of the new variable does not appear in the causal loop diagram. Comparing the two diagrams reveals that the time lags have been introduced in the

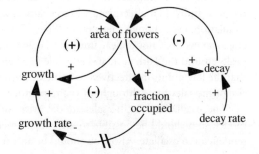

Figure 17.15. Feedback loops in the flower model with a \\ to mark the information delay.

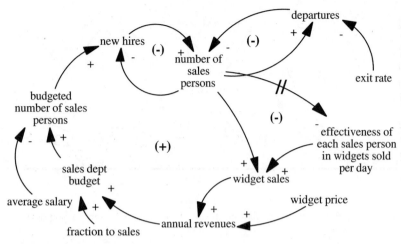

Figure 17.16. Feedback loops in the sales model with a // to mark the information delay.

same place in both systems. They appear in the negative feedback loops, which operate to bring the system into balance. In both cases, the introduction of the time lag can cause the system to shoot past the balance point and begin to oscillate.

Material Delays

The previous examples introduce a delay in the flow of information. Recall that information flows are represented by the connectors in a Stella diagram, and the material flows are represented by the flows. Figure 17.17 includes a delay in the flow of material in the sales model. In this case, the "material" is people. A new stock variable is introduced to keep track of the delay before the new employees are qualified to become part of the sales force. The diagram shows the stock of *trainees* fed by the flow of *new hires* and drained by the *complete training*

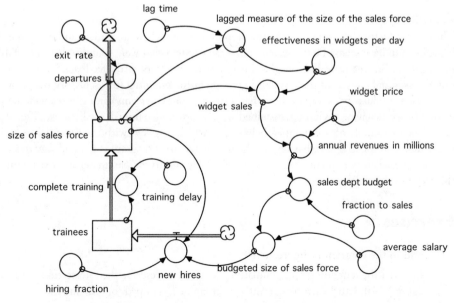

Figure 17.17. Adding a training delay to the sales model.

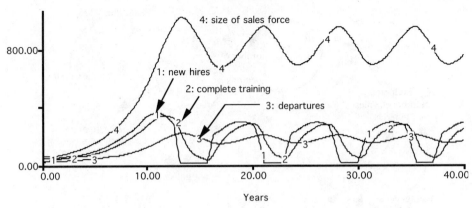

Figure 17.18. Simulated oscillations in sales force with a 1-year training delay.

flow. The *new hires* are calculated as in the previous model. The flow *complete training* is found by dividing the number of *trainees* by the *training delay*. The model is initialized with 45 people in the sales force and 5 in training.

Figure 17.18 shows the simulated behavior of the new model with the *training delay* set at 1 year. The figure shows cycles similar to the cycles shown previously in figure 17.13. A comparison of figures 17.13 and 17.18 will reveal that the new model takes longer to reach the quasi-equilibrium conditions. The slower approach is caused by the 1-year delay before new hires can begin selling widgets. Figure 17.18 shows that the period of the oscillations is longer than in the previous model. The longer period arises from the additional delay introduced by training. Notice, for example, that new hires peak around the 10th year of the simulation and fall rapidly to zero. But the number of people to complete training does not decline until after the 1-year lag for training. This causes a delay before the sales force can decline in size and "free up the space" for the next spurt in the hiring of new people. You can tell from this sales example that a combination of material delays and information delays gives rise to the oscillatory tendencies of the system

Conclusion

These introductory examples reveal the importance of delays in understanding dynamic behavior. You have seen a flower system and a sales system that were found to be quite stable in chapter 6. But the introduction of a single time lag in the negative feedback loop controlling the eventual growth of these systems gives them the potential for oscillatory behavior.

These introductory examples show that relatively simple systems can exhibit a wide range of oscillatory behavior including sustained oscillations and damped oscillations. Also, you have seen an example of overdamped behavior in which a system with the potential to oscillate exhibits no oscillations whatsoever. The parameter space diagram is a useful way to summarize the oscillatory tendencies of a system. You may add to the parameter space diagram in the exercises that follow.

Exercises

1. **Add to the diagram in figure 17.10:**

   Conduct the remaining four simulations required to describe the intersection points in figure 17.10. Label each new result as overdamped, damped, or sustained.

2. **Critical dampening curve in figure 17.10:**

Two of the tests from the previous exercise land on the curve that separates the parameter space into two sections. Do you see oscillations in these simulations? Do you need to move the curve to a new position? If so, what is the critical value of the FMVI?

3. **Parameter space for the sales model:**

The sales model in Figure 17.11 includes six parameters:

- lag time = 1 year
- initial sales effectiveness = 2 widgets/day
- widget price = $100/widget
- fraction to sales = 55 percent
- average salary = $25,000/year
- hiring fraction = 100 percent/yr

Each of these parameters could contribute to the oscillatory tendencies of the model. Suppose we wish to summarize the oscillatory tendencies of the sales model, and we know that each of the six parameters plays some role in the dynamic behavior. Now, the last thing we need is a six-dimensional parameter space diagram, so your exercise is to think of a way to combine these parameters in order to draw a two-dimensional diagram. You'll do well to place the lag time on the vertical axis, as in figure 17.10. Now what about the intrinsic growth rate for the sales company? Can you think of how to combine the model parameters to show the equivalent of the *r* in the flower model?

4. **Summarizing the sales model:**

Design a collection of nine experiments that will fill out the space in the diagram from the previous exercise. Report the results following the approach used in figure 17.10.

5. **Sales model volatility index:**

Derive an index to serve as a plausible indicator of the tendency of the sales model to oscillate. Name the index SMVI, sales model volatility index. The SMVI should be a dimensionless combination of the parameters on the *x*-axis and *y*-axis of the space diagram. Use the SMVI to derive a "critical dampening curve," which can be added to the parameter space diagram following the approach shown in figure 17.10. What is the critical value of the SMVI?

6. **Trainees earn a salary:**

The model in figure 17.17 finds the *budgeted size of sales force* from the *sales dept budget* and the *average salary. New hires* are then calculated based on the *size of the sales force* compared to the budgeted size. These assumptions imply that the trainees do not earn a salary. Change the model to allow the trainees to earn the same salary as the other employees. Introduce new variables called *total employees* and *budgeted level of employees.* Run the model to learn if you get the growth followed by oscillations as in figure 17.18.

7. **Raise the price to pay trainee salaries:**

The model in the previous exercise may not grow at the start of the simulation, so you may need to experiment with higher widget prices to generate the extra revenues needed to allow the company to grow. How high does the price have to be to allow the company to grow?

8. **New hiring policy to account for departures:**

    The flow of *new hires* in figure 17.11 is based on the difference between the *budgeted size of the sales* and the current *size of the sales force*. If the difference is zero, the *new hires* is zero. Expand the model to represent a policy to hire sufficient workers to replace *departures* when the budgeted sales force and the actual sales force are equal. Do you think the new model will be more stable than the model in figure 17.11? Build the new model and compare its base simulation with figure 17.12. Is the company more stable with the new hiring policy?

9. **Home page exercise—adding random, annual disturbances:**

    All of the previous examples ignore the effects of random disturbances, even though disturbances are always present in environmental systems. It is useful to ignore random disturbances at the outset because the simulated behavior is easier to interpret. But later in a study, you may wish to simulate the combined effect of internal cycles and outside disturbances. An exercise on the home page leads you through an example of how this can be done with the flower model. The exercise asks you to sample from a random distribution for the intrinsic growth rate, and you are to hold the sampled values for 1 year at a time. (This makes sense if the flowers experience "good years" and "bad years.") Recall from figure 17.7 that the flower model generates damped oscillations in the absence of random disturbances if the lag time is set to 2 years. The home page shows that the addition of random disturbances creates an entirely different pattern. The flowered area appears headed toward 800 acres from time to time, but the disturbances act to keep the oscillatory behavior alive for an 80-year simulation. This is an important result to remember when studying time series data on oscillatory systems. If the data reveal oscillations that persist over time, you may be able to explain the oscillations with a model that exhibits damped oscillations in the absence of random disturbances.

Chapter 18

Predator-Prey Oscillations on the Kaibab Plateau

The relationship between predators and their prey has always occupied a special place in the minds of ecologists. There has probably been more written on the subject of predator-prey interactions than on any other single topic in ecology (Matson and Berryman 1992). Ricklefs (1990, 403) observes that population biologists have used predator-prey and parasitoid-host relationships as the basis for more general models of consumer-resource interactions. He describes "predation as a *clean* demographic event that readily lends itself to modeling," and he believes that predator-prey systems (and especially parasitoid-host systems) "can be brought into the laboratory and subjected to experimentation." The experiments reveal a fascinating variety of possibilities ranging from stable oscillations to violently unstable behavior.

The great interest in predator-prey systems makes them an ideal case for system dynamics. This chapter builds upon your previous understanding of the Kaibab system. It demonstrates how system dynamics can be used to examine the interaction between the deer herd and the predators on the Kaibab Plateau. Our purpose is to learn about the possible behavior of the predator and prey populations if the predators had not been exterminated in the early years of the century. The issue of predator removal is addressed in exercises at the end of the chapter.

Background

Information on both the deer and the predators of the Kaibab Plateau is provided by Russo (1970). Further information on cougars is provided in Armstrong's (1987) book *Rocky Mountain Mammals*. You learned in chapter 16 that the accounts of the Kaibab deer irruption are somewhat unreliable. And since the predators are elusive animals, information on the predator populations is even more sketchy. We must proceed with very little data specific to the Kaibab case, so it is useful to learn what we can from other predator-prey systems.

One of the most famous predator-prey examples is the snowshoe hare–lynx system of North America. The hare-lynx system is well known because of extensive time series data from the Hudson Bay Company (Elton 1933). The data provide a long history of the ups and downs in the number of pelts sold to the company. The records show a peak in the number of lynx pelts every 9 to 10 years. If we assume that the number of pelts is a good measure of the relative size of the population, we would conclude that these two populations have oscillated in a cyclical manner for over 100 years.

Odum (1971, 191) describes the hare-lynx cycle as an example of population cycles that are "not related to seasonal or obvious annual changes, but which involve regular oscillations or cycles of abundance with peaks and depressions every few years, often occurring with such regularity that population size may be predicted in advance." Odum explains that the best studied examples among the mammals are cycles with a 9–10-year or a 3–4-year periodicity. He cites the hare-lynx as a "classic example" of a 9–10-year oscillation. The shorter 3–4-year cycle is said to be characteristic of many northern murids (lemmings, mice, voles) and their predators (such as the snowy owl).

Reference Mode

With this background, we might draw the reference mode as cyclical behavior in the deer and cougar population. We would expect the period to be around 9–10 years given the two choices from Odum's characterization. Based on the hare-lynx example, we would expect to see a peak in the deer population followed a few years later by a peak in the cougar population. But how would the cycles change over time? Should the reference mode show sustained oscillations, damped oscillations, or growing oscillations?

Your first instinct might be to draw sustained oscillations based on the long-running cycle in the hare-lynx populations. But Odum cautions us not to automatically expect predator-prey populations to interact in a stable manner. He describes experiments by Pimentel (1968) in which house flies and parasitic wasps were first placed together in a limited culture system. The intriguing results arose from newly associated populations that were brought from the wilds and inserted into the controlled laboratory experiment. These experiments showed that the populations would oscillate "violently." The population of flies increased sharply, followed by a sharp increase in the population of wasps. Their interactions were highly unstable, leading to a crash to zero. Pimentel's experiments also showed that it was possible for the flies and wasps to interact in a stable manner. Test populations derived from colonies in which the two species had been associated for 2 years could coexist in the experimental environment. In the stable experiment, wasps taken from the colonies were found to have fewer progeny per female. Apparently, their lower natality made the difference between a stable and unstable system.

Odum believes that Pimentel's experiment is instructive for natural systems in general. He believes that there are "hundreds of similar examples which show (1) that where parasites and predators have long been associated with their respective hosts and prey, the effect is moderate, neutral, or even beneficial from the long term view and (2) that newly acquired parasites or predators are the most damaging" (Odum 1971, 222).

For the purpose of the Kaibab predator-prey model, it makes sense to assume that the deer and cougars found at the turn of the century had ample opportunity to coexist with one another. Let's proceed with a reference mode that shows stable oscillations over time. From the introductory examples in chapter 17, we should look for the model to exhibit either damped or sustained oscillations in the absence of random disturbances. We might expect the oscillations to repeat themselves with a period of 9–10 years, and we would expect the peaks in the cougar population to lag behind the peaks in deer population by a few years.

An Initial Model

Figure 18.1 shows an equilibrium diagram of an initial model adapted from the deer model explained previously. The deer population is initialized at 4,000 and the predator population at 50, the same values used in chapter 16. There would be 80 prey for each predator, and the 80:1 ratio appears reasonable compared to ratios observed in systems with similar-sized animals (Ricklefs 1990, 436).

Recall from chapter 16 that each deer needs 1 MT/year of forage, and the plateau is nor-

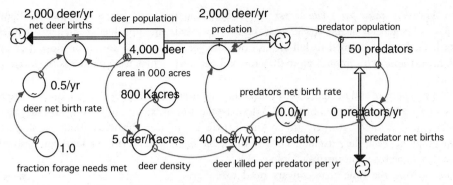

Figure 18.1. Equilibrium diagram for the initial model.

mally able to generate more than enough new growth to meet the deer needs. Since our focus is the animal populations, let's ignore the biomass portion of the model in chapter 16. We may assume that the plateau will generate ample forage and set the *net birth rate* at 50 percent/yr, the same value used in chapter 16. Figure 18.1 shows that births would outnumber deaths by 2,000 deer/yr with this assumption.

The important difference between figure 18.1 and the previous model involves the *predator population.* In chapter 16, the number of predators was specified exogenously. The number was fixed at 50 in the early years, and then reduced to zero during the years when they were exterminated. In this chapter, we treat the predators as an endogenous variable so that their numbers are simulated as a logical consequence of their success in predation. We assign a separate stock for the *predator population,* and the *predator net births* is a biflow. A positive value implies that births outnumber deaths; a negative value means that deaths outnumber births. In the equilibrium situation in figure 18.1, the *predator net birth rate* is zero, which suggests that births and deaths are balanced. The *predator population* would remain constant at 50, which turns out to be exactly the number needed to keep the *deer population* in balance.

The *predator net birth rate* is based on the number of *deer killed per predator per yr* as shown in figure 18.2. The general shape in figure 18.2 shows that higher deer kills lead to higher net birth rates. The highest values in figure 18.2 are set at 45 percent/yr. Cougars breed first at two to three years of age. They tend to breed every 2 years with an average of 3 kittens per litter. These assumptions translate into a relatively high net growth rate of 40 to 50 percent/year. Interestingly, the net growth rate for the cougars (when well fed) is similar to the deer net growth rate. So it seems that we are working with two populations with high intrinsic rates of growth, and we should expect them to rebound quickly if conditions are favorable. The downward slope means that declining success in predation leads to a lower and lower net birth rate. The extreme value is –60 percent/yr if deer kills fall to zero. To interpret the negative 60 percent/yr, you might imagine that the kittens would not survive and the average adult would live for only 1.7 years before dying from poor nutrition. (The model does not show alternative prey, but you might imagine that the 1.7 years is spent struggling to survive by searching for other prey with minimal nutritional value.)

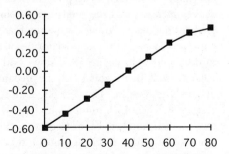

Figure 18.2. Predators' net birth rate (*y*-axis) and the deer killed per predator per year (*x*-axis).

The *deer killed per predator per year* is based on the *deer density* as shown in figure 18.3. The general shape shows that higher deer kills are possible at higher densities. Each predator is assumed to kill around 60 deer per year if there are 10 or more deer per thousand acres. This implies more than one kill per week, which we will take as the satiation limit.

The opposite end of figure 18.3 shows that the deer kill will be zero when no deer are to be found. The end points in figure 18.3 describe the extreme situations. At one extreme, there is satiation; at the other, there are no kills if there are no deer. But what about the shape of the graph between the extremes? Do you think the shape is reasonable? Could you rationalize this shape based on intrinsic biological factors such as the time that cougars need to locate and kill the deer? At this point, you should keep in mind that we are dealing with a very elusive animal, so there is little direct information to help us specify the particular shape. You should view figure 18.3 as simply one possible description of the predators' success at different densities. If you have studied predation, you will probably recognize this particular choice as a combination of "Type I and II" functional forms found useful in describing predator behavior (Pratt 1995, 75; Hastings 1997, 169; Taylor 1984, 83; Watt 1968, 136).

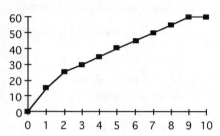

Figure 18.3. Deer killed per predator per year (*y*-axis) and the deer density in deer per thousand acres (*x*-axis).

Figure 18.4 lists the equations. The model is initialized with 4,000 deer and 50 predators. The 4,000 deer are spread over 800 thousand acres for a density of 5 deer per thousand acres. Figure 18.3 tells us that each predator would kill 40 deer per year with this value of density, so the 50 predators would kill 2,000 deer per year, exactly the amount needed to keep the deer population constant at 4,000. Figure 18.2 shows us that 40 kills per year would cause the predator *net birth rate* to be zero, so the predator population would remain constant at 50. If you simulate the equations in figure 18.4, you will find that the populations will remain at their initial values throughout the simulation. We have equilibrium, but do you think the equilibrium is stable? Suppose we simulate the model with 45 predators as the starting population?

Figure 18.5 shows a simulation starting with 45 predators and 4,000 deer in the year 1900. (The simulation begins in the year 1900 to show us what might have occurred had the predators not been exterminated.) The deer population grows initially, as the 45 predators are not numerous enough to keep the deer in check. As the deer become more numerous, their density increases and the predators are simulated to be more successful in predation. The predator population grows during the first 6–8 years, and the larger numbers cause the deer population to decline. The predator population first peaks around the year 1908 and begins to decline as well. Figure 18.5 shows both populations declining during the interval from 1908 to 1912. By the year 1912, the predator population is low enough to allow the deer population to grow again. The deer population reaches 4,000 by the year 1915 and 8,000 by the year 1918. These high numbers lead to high deer densities and higher success by the predators, so their numbers begin to grow rapidly after 1918. By the year 1924, there would be around 150 predators on the plateau, over three times as many as at the start of the simulation. The large population is simulated to drive the prey population to zero. This simulation shows that the deer population would be eliminated by around the year 1925, and the predator population would be eliminated a few years later.

```
deer_population(t) = deer_population(t - dt) + (net_deer_births - predation) * dt
INIT deer_population = 4000
net_deer_births = deer_population*deer_net_birth_rate
OUTFLOWS:
predation = predator_population*deer_killed_per_predator_per_yr
predator_population(t) = predator_population(t - dt) + (predator_net_births) * dt
INIT predator_population = 50
predator_net_births = predator_population*predators_net_birth_rate
area_in_000_acres = 800
deer_density = deer_population/area_in_000_acres
fraction_forage_needs_met = 1
deer_killed_per_predator_per_yr = GRAPH(deer_density)
(0.00, 0.00), (1.00, 15.0), (2.00, 25.0), (3.00, 30.0), (4.00, 35.0), (5.00,
40.0), (6.00, 45.0), (7.00, 50.0), (8.00, 55.0), (9.00, 60.0), (10.0, 60.0)
deer_net_birth_rate = GRAPH(fraction_forage_needs_met)
(0.3, -0.4), (0.4, -0.2), (0.5, 0.00), (0.6, 0.2), (0.7, 0.4), (0.8, 0.45), (0.9, 0.5), (1, 0.5)
predators_net_birth_rate = GRAPH(deer_killed_per_predator_per_yr)
(0.00, -0.6), (10.0, -0.45), (20.0, -0.3), (30.0, -0.15), (40.0, 0.00), (50.0, 0.15),
(60.0, 0.3), (70.0, 0.4), (80.0, 0.45)
```

Figure 18.4. Equations for the initial model.

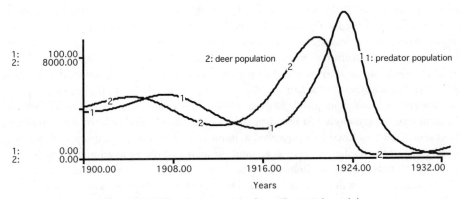

Figure 18.5. Simulation results from the initial model.

Why Don't Predators Annihilate Their Prey?

You might be wondering if the results in figure 18.5 are a coincidence of the initial values assigned to the predator population or the deer population. Or you might be wondering if the unstable behavior could be attributed to the high birth rate of the deer or to the high birth rate of the predators. These sensitivity tests are left as exercises at the end of the chapter. The tests will reveal a consistent pattern of unstable behavior. In each simulation, the deer population will eventually be driven to extremely small numbers.

These results raise an interesting question. It's the same question asked by Kenneth Watt over thirty years ago in his text *Ecology and Resource Management*:

> A natural question is "Why don't predators annihilate their prey?" The big cats and other large predators are impressively efficient machines of destruction, so one would assume that they would denude the landscape of food, and then die from starvation. (Watt 1968, 134)

Watt tells us that predators are not normally observed to hunt the prey population to zero. Rather, they have been observed to select those individuals from the prey population that have the least chance of escape and are easiest to catch (such as the young, the old, and the weak). Pratt (1995, 76) describes some predators as killing nearly all of a prey in excess of some minimum or threshold number. At prey densities below the threshold, the predators would no longer find it profitable to hunt the prey and would switch to a different prey. Pratt alerts us to the possibility that the threshold is determined by the availability of prey hiding places and the prey's social behavior.

The importance of hiding places (refuge) is confirmed in various experiments in which prey are provided with additional refuge or in which extra time requirements are imposed on the predators. Hastings (1997, 166) describes Huffaker's (1958) experiments with a predator-prey system in which predatory mites search for prey mites on 40 oranges arrayed in a grid pattern. By arranging the oranges in different patterns, Huffaker was able to obtain both stable and unstable cycles in the mite populations. These results suggest that the spatial structure of the system can improve stability of the population cycles if the prey are better able to find refuge.

Revising the Model

From the previous discussion, you might think that we should revise the model to include the effect of prey hiding places, prey social behavior, threshold levels, and distinctions between strong and weak prey. Perhaps we should add a variable to account for the number of hiding places, another variable for the threshold level, and still another variable to account for the social behavior that allows the deer to avoid predation. Also, it might make sense to expand the deer population from one stock to three stocks to simulate the deer age structure. The expanded model might show young deer maturing to mature deer and mature deer aging to older deer. It could then be used to simulate the system with the assumption that the predators concentrate on the young and old deer. Adding these many factors would greatly increase the complexity of the model. At this stage, it would be more useful to learn if the combined effect of these factors could be represented in implicit fashion. Let's experiment with a change in the shape of the predation curve to account for increased refuge in an implicit fashion.

Figure 18.6 shows one possibility. This chart shows a new assumption on predation alongside the assumption in the previous model. The two models adopt the same assumption for high values of deer density: the predators would be satiated at 60 kills per year. The chart shows the same assumption if deer density falls to zero: the predators would not kill any deer. And the two curves have another point in common in the mid-range. That is, with a deer density of 5 deer per thousand acres, both curves show that the average predator would kill 40 deer per year.

The differences between the two curves are most visible at low values of deer density. For example, if the density should fall below 2 deer per thousand acres, the new curve assumes that the predators would not kill any deer. You might think of this value as corresponding to the threshold level described by Pratt (1995, 76). Zero kills at low density might be attributed to the ability of deer to find safe refuge when their numbers fall below the threshold level. Once the density rises above 2 deer/thousand acres, the new curve in figure 18.6 shows a "steeper" response of the predators. The new graph in figure 18.6 is shaped like an "S" so it might be called a sigmoidal function. If you have studied predation, you will appreciate that the new shape corresponds to the "Type III function" for describing predator behavior (Pratt 1995, 75; Hastings 1997, 169; Taylor 1984, 83; Watt 1968, 136).

Figure 18.7 shows the simulated behavior of the new model with 4,000 deer and 100 predators at the start of the simulation. The large predator population causes a decline in the deer population during the first few years of the simulation, and the predator population declines quickly thereafter. By the year 1905, there are only about 40 predators on the plateau. Their low number allows the deer population to grow, and it reaches a peak of around 5,000 by the year 1908. The higher deer density would improve the predator situation, and the predators are simulated to grow to a peak of around 60 predators shortly after the year 1910. Figure 18.7 shows that the peak in the predator population lags behind the peak in the deer population by around 2 years. The predator population peaks first around the year 1910, again around 1920, and for a third

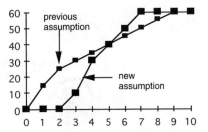

Figure 18.6. Relationships between the deer killed per predator per year (y-axis) and the deer density in deer per thousand acres (x-axis).

time around 1930. We have a damped cycle with a period of 10 years. As the cycles fade in magnitude, the populations find their way to the equilibrium values shown in figure 18.1— there would be 4,000 deer and 50 predators.

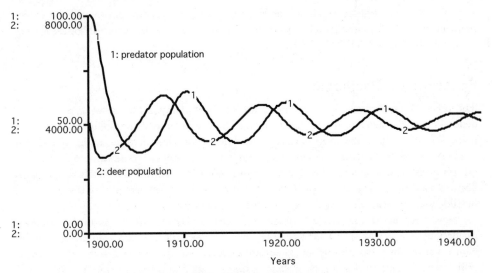

Figure 18.7. New simulation results.

Closer Look at the Stable Oscillations

Figure 18.7 shows the reference mode established at the start of the chapter. We set out with the "dynamic hypothesis" that the cougar and deer populations could interact to produce stable cycles with a period similar to the classic 9–10-year cycle observed in other predator-prey populations. A comparison of the two simulations reveals the importance of the functional form assigned to the graph describing the predator's success in killing deer. The sigmoidal shape is important to the stability of the system. You may interpret these simulations as confirming the importance of prey refuge or threshold levels if the populations are to interact in a stable manner.

Figure 18.8 provides a different perspective on the oscillations with a scatter graph. Each dot in the scatter graph corresponds to another step in the simulation. The first dot is located at the top of the graph with 4,000 deer and 100 predators. The dots are shown to move downward in the first few steps and then begin to spiral inward toward the equilibrium value of

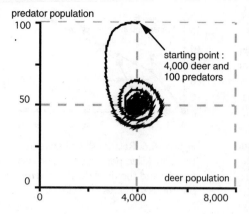

Figure 18.8. Scatter graph showing predators and prey from the previous simulation. The point in the middle of the diagram would be called a point attractor.

4,000 deer and 50 predators. Scatter graphs are often created with one stock variable on the *x*-axis and another stock on the *y*-axis. These graphs are sometimes called "state space diagrams" because the stocks are sometimes referred to as the "state variables" of the system. In this example, the state space diagram reveals the model's tendency to search out the equilibrium point in ever tighter spirals. It's as if the populations are attracted toward the center point in figure 18.8. Scientists refer to the center point as the "point attractor" of the system (Capra 1996, 132; Gleick 1988, 134).

Patterns of Oscillation

The previous simulations show the possibility for both damped and growing oscillations, depending on the shape of the predation curve. The key to the overall stability of the system is the sigmoidal shape that implies adequate refuge at low deer density. At this point, you might ask yourself if further changes in the predation assumption could cause the model to exhibit overdamped behavior. Perhaps the population could move immediately to the equilibrium conditions without any oscillations whatsoever. You can confirm that this pattern is possible with experiments with a steeper shape in the predation curve.

Now, what about the reference mode? This chapter began with the goal of simulating oscillations that persist over a long time interval, but we still have not seen an example in which oscillations persist throughout the simulation interval. You learned in the final exercise of the previous chapter that it is possible for a system with damped oscillations to exhibit persistent cycles if random disturbances are added to the system. Perhaps random disturbances are all that is needed to complete our search for persistent cycles. To check this possibility, we could introduce randomness into the deer net birth rate with the following equations:

```
net_birth_rate = .5+random_factor
random_factor = random(-.2,.2,123)
```

The additional *random factor* allows the *net birth rate* to vary in a uniform manner from a low of 30 percent/yr to a high of 70 percent/yr during each time step of the simulation. The 123 is a "seed" to guarantee that the same random sequence is repeated each time we perform the simulation.

Figure 18.9 shows the new simulation results, with all other assumptions identical to the assumptions used in figure 18.7. The populations are shown to oscillate during the first two decades, but the cycles appear to be dampening out over time, just as in figure 18.7. Indeed, there is very little oscillation evident during the third decade of the simulation. But something

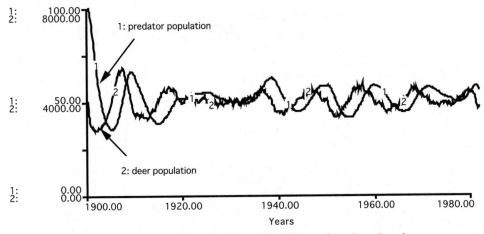

Figure 18.9. Persistent oscillations due to the addition of random disturbances.

seems to change during the late 1930s. Apparently, one of the random variations hits the system at just the right moment to trigger strong growth in the deer population. This, in turn, triggers growth in the predator population, and the predators reach a peak around the year 1940. The next four decades of the simulation show the predator and prey populations undergoing four additional oscillations. We now see persistent cycles with a period of around 10 years. This pattern is taken as confirmation that we are able to generate the reference mode adopted at the outset of the chapter.

Policy Test: Selective Removal of Predators

Figure 18.9 shows that stable predator-prey interactions would have been possible if the predators had been left on the Kaibab plateau. The predators are generally near equilibrium value of 50, but some years see more predators on the plateau. Those years might pose problems for ranchers and livestock, as the predators are then about to experience a decline due to a relative shortage of prey. In such years, it might be possible to allow hunters to kill predators to remove the potential threat to livestock. Figure 18.10 shows an expansion of the predator-prey model to simulate an idealized predator-removal program. Imagine that we were able to count the predator population and call on hunters to kill any predators in excess of a maximum acceptable number.

The new equation would be:

```
predator_kills = if (time>program_start_year) then
(predator_population-maximum_acceptable_predators) else 0
program_start_year = 1920
maximum_acceptable_predators = 55
```

Figure 18.11 shows the simulated impact of an idealized program to remove predators in excess of 55 starting in the year 1920. The first year in which the predators climb beyond the acceptable number is 1936, and around 3 predators would be killed. Figure 18.11 shows that additional predator kills would occur in subsequent years, but the annual kill is only around 1–2 predators.

The simulation in figure 18.11 shows that it might be possible to reduce the peak values of the predator population without destroying the intrinsic stability of the predator-prey sys-

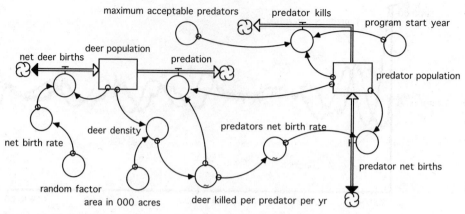

Figure 18.10. Expanding the predator-prey model to simulate an idealized predator removal program.

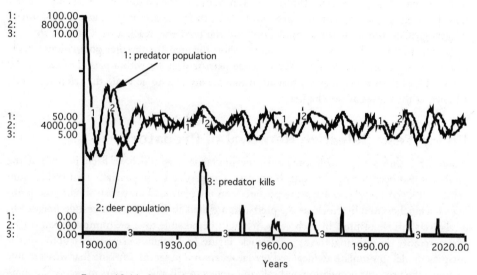

Figure 18.11. Simulated impact of a predator removal program.

tem. But you might argue that that is possible in this case only because the hunting is limited to a very few years in the entire simulation. At this point you might be wondering whether it is possible to pursue this policy in a more aggressive manner without destroying the intrinsic stability of the predator-prey system. This question is left for you to explore as one of the exercises.

Exercises

1. **Sensitivity to initial conditions:**

    Change the initial number of predators from 45 to 55 and rerun the simulation. Do you still get unstable behavior like that shown in figure 18.5? Now change the initial number of deer from 4,000 to 4,500 and rerun the model. Do you still see unstable behavior? Do you think the initial conditions are responsible for the unstable behavior?

2. **Sensitivity to the net birth rates:**

Rerun the model with the deer net birth rate changed from 50 percent/yr to 70 percent/yr. Then rerun the model with 30 percent/yr. Is this assumption responsible for the unstable behavior shown in figure 18.5? Rerun the model with the maximum value of the predator net birth rate changed from 45 percent/yr to 65 percent/yr. Then rerun the model with the maximum value set at 25 percent/yr. Is this assumption responsible for the unstable behavior shown in figure 18.5? Ricklefs (1990, 507) suggests that "higher prey production" could tend to destabilize predator-prey models. Review his graphical analysis of predator-prey isoclines. Then test whether his assertion applies to the Kaibab model in figure 18.7 by rerunning the model with the deer net birth rate changed from 50 percent/yr to 75 percent/yr. Does the higher birth rate make the system less stable or more stable?

3. **Will the model exhibit overdamped behavior?**

Figure 18.7 shows damped oscillations if the density-dependent relationship is changed to the sigmoidal shape shown in figure 18.6. With further adjustments in the predation graph, we might expect to see even more stable behavior. Change the predation graph to:

```
deer_killed_per_predator_per_yr = GRAPH(deer_density)
(0.00, 0.00), (1.00, 0.00), (2.00, 0.00), (3.00, 5.00), (4.00, 10.0),
(5.00, 40.0), (6.00, 55.0), (7.00, 60.0), (8.00, 60.0), (9.00, 60.0), (10.0, 60.0)
```

and repeat the simulation shown in figure 18.7. Does the model find its way to the equilibrium conditions without any oscillations?

4. **Distinguish between predator-births and deaths:**

Expand the model to distinguish between *predator births* and *predator deaths*. Introduce a *predator birth rate* to control the *predator births* and a *predator death rate* to control the *predator deaths*. Then link these two rates to the *deer killed per predator per year*. Select plausible parameter values that would yield similar results to the existing model. Run the new model to learn if you still get the unstable pattern in figure 18.5 and the stable pattern in figure 18.7.

5. **Build and verify the predator-removal model:**

Build the model shown in figure 18.10. Simulate the model (with DT set to 0.125 years) to verify that you get the results shown in figure 18.11.

6. **How far can you push the predator-removal program?**

Experiment with lower and lower values of the *maximum acceptable predators* in figure 18.10. How low can you set this policy parameter before the intervention by hunters destroys the intrinsic stability of the predator-prey system? Document your work with a stable simulation result (similar to that in figure 18.11) with the lowest possible value of the *maximum acceptable predators*.

7. **Causal loop diagram:**

This causal loop diagram describes the model in figure 18.1 (which generated the unstable oscillations in figure 18.5). Complete the diagram by labeling each arrow with a + or − and each loop as (+) or (−).

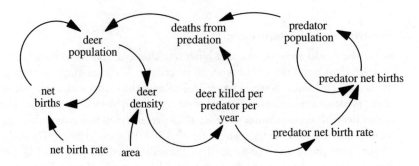

8. **New causal loop diagram?**

    Do you need to change this causal loop diagram to describe the model that generated the stable results in figure 18.7?

9. **Where are the delays in the system?**

    You learned in chapter 17 that delays in information feedback can lead to oscillatory behavior. The delays were represented by Stella's smooth function. You also learned that a stock variable could be used to represent a delay in the flow of material. Do you see similar delays in the predator-prey model?

Further Readings

- Lotka (1925) and Volterra (1926) were the first to use a mathematical model to describe cycles in predator-prey populations. Their analyses suggest that when either the predator population or the prey population is displaced from its equilibrium, the system will oscillate in a closed cycle. In his text *Ecology*, Ricklefs (1990, 416) explains that the "closed cycles greatly oversimplify nature." Johan Swart (1990) examines and extends the classic Lotka-Volterra model using system dynamics.
- For additional reading on predation, you can turn to the special feature of *Ecology* devoted to predator-prey theory (Matson and Berryman 1992) and to Taylor's (1984) book *Predation*.

Chapter 19

Volatility in Aluminum Production

Aluminum smelting is a commodity industry with highly volatile prices. This chapter uses system dynamics to look inside the industry to help us understand the volatility. Aluminum smelting is of special interest to environmental students because of its huge electricity requirement and the potential to reduce electricity consumption through recycling.

Background

For most of the nineteenth century, aluminum was an economic paradox, naturally abundant but extremely expensive. The oxide of aluminum (alumina) is found in nearly all common rocks, but aluminum was a precious metal, costing as much as $500 per pound due to the technical difficulties in separating aluminum from the oxide of aluminum (Smith 1988). The technical challenge was overcome in 1886 when Charles Hall and Paul Heroult demonstrated how to remove aluminum metal from alumina through electrolysis. The challenge was to find a stable bath of molten salts so that electrolytic reduction could proceed on a continuous basis. An electric current was established from a carbon anode inserted into the bath to the carbon-lined walls of the pot holding the bath. Alumina was fed into the bath, and metallic aluminum precipitated on the walls of the pot. The experiments of Hall and Heroult provided the basis for the Hall-Heroult process, which continues as the only commercially viable means for smelting aluminum (Smith 1988, 17). In today's industry, a large smelter might produce 200,000 metric tons/yr. If ingots were priced at $1 per pound, the annual revenues would be $440 million. The smelters spread around the world have a total capacity exceeding 16 million metric tons (mmt) per year. If ingots sell for $1 per pound, total annual revenues would exceed $35 billion.

Aluminum and Electricity

Aluminum smelting is extremely energy intensive, so electricity generation and aluminum production are tightly connected. Indeed, the connection dates to the birth of the industry. In the early years, the Pittsburgh Reduction Company held Hall's patent and used electricity from burning coal and gas to run a small smelting works in New Kensington, Pennsylvania. But the company knew that a growing industry would require cheap and massive quantities of electricity. In June of 1893, it built a new smelting works near Niagara Falls and became the first customer of the Niagara Falls Power Company. The partnership between large-scale aluminum production and power generation was established. This small company succeeded in building capacity and a market for the metal. It grew into the Aluminum Company of America, one of the most successful monopolies in American history (Smith 1988).

To appreciate the massive electricity requirements, imagine a modern smelter with 0.2 mmt/yr of capacity operating at 7 kilowatt hours (kwh) per pound. The smelter would consume around 3 billion kwh/yr. Now, imagine that the electricity comes from a dam with 100 feet of head over the turbines. Each acre-foot (AF) of water through the turbines generates 870 kwh of electricity. You can work through the unit conversions to learn that the flow through the turbines must be 3.4 million AF/yr. Contrast this flow with the annual flow of 0.6 million AF needed to serve the City of Los Angeles (see the Mono Lake segment of the home page), and you can gain a perspective on the immense power requirements in this industry.

The power requirement makes the aluminum industry an important case study for students of the environment. The aluminum in recycled products can be converted to metal ingots with only around 5 percent of the electricity required in primary production (Berk 1982, 47). Secondary and primary production are two parts of an interconnected system, so it is not immediately clear how much total energy will be saved when programs are launched to increase recycling. The challenge of simulating system-wide energy savings from recycling is left for you as an exercise.

Volatility in Aluminum Prices

Figure 19.1 shows the price of aluminum ingots during the 1970s and 1980s. Notice the major swings in the price in a relatively short time interval. Near the end of the 1980s, the price increased to over 100 cents/pound. But within the next 2 years, it had fallen to only 50 cents/lb. Another upswing in the late 1980s brought the price back to over 100 cents/pound, but it returned to around 60 cents/pound by the end of the decade.

The large price variations pose difficult problems for the smelter operators as well as their customers. Smelters are complex facilities with a highly trained work force. The owners can't simply turn the smelter on with each upswing in price or turn it off with each downswing. Consequently, the price volatility poses the risk of highly volatile profit and loss from smelter operation.

Figure 19.2 summarizes the costs of operating smelters around the world. This graph is organized with cumulative smelting capacity on the horizontal axis and the variable cost of operation on the vertical axis. This particular curve has been adapted from a confidential review in 1994. Variable costs are reported in cents/pound, using 1993 U.S. dollars. They are composed mainly of the costs of alumina, electricity, and labor. Smelting capacity is based on the 146 smelters in the "western world." (The review did not include smelters in eastern Europe or the former USSR.) This single curve shows the gradual increase in variable costs as

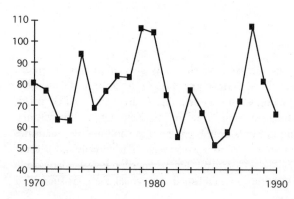

Figure 19.1. Price of aluminum ingots in cents/pound, in constant 1987 dollars (Knight-Ridder 1993, 4).

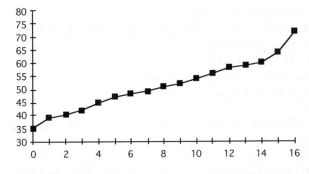

Figure 19.2. Industry cost curve with variable cost (cents/pound) on the y-axis and cumulative smelting capacity (mmt/yr) on the x-axis.

we proceed from the cheapest to the most expensive smelters. The low-cost smelters are located in regions with cheap electricity. Many of these are in the "ABC" countries: Australia, Brazil, and Canada (Peck 1988, 15). Thirty-two of the smelters are in the United States, with many located close to large-scale hydroelectric development in the Tennessee Valley and along the Columbia River. The highest-cost smelters tend to be in western Europe, where power rates and wages are higher than in the rest of the world.

To interpret the cost curve, suppose you operate a smelter with a variable cost of 60 cents/pound. There are plenty of smelters in the world with lower costs. Figure 19.2 shows their cumulative capacity at 14 mmt/yr. Some smelters have higher operating costs; their combined capacity is 2 mmt/yr. If the market were to remain constant at 61 cents/pound, you could operate your smelter and earn 1 cent/pound. You would expect the 14 mmt/yr of lower cost capacity to be in operation as well, and you would probably expect the remaining 2 mmt/yr of capacity to be idle. If the total demand were 14 mmt/yr, demand would be satisfied, and the price would remain at 61 cents/pound in the future.

But figure 19.1 shows that the price is not inclined to remain constant. Rather, we see major fluctuations by plus or minus 100 percent in just a few years. The price swings present major opportunities. If your smelter were operating near the end of the 1970s, you could sell ingots at 110 cents/pound, earning around 50 cents/pound after covering your variable costs. But what would you have done in the early 1980s when the price dipped below 60 cents/pound? Would you have closed the smelter in 1982? Would you have reopened in 1983? shut down again in 1985? These are difficult questions whose answers impact the livelihood of thousands of families across the country. The problem is particularly acute in the Northwest, as indicated by the following headlines: "Northwest Aluminum Approaches Meltdown" (*Oregonian*, February 6, 1994) and "Reynolds Rides Roller Coaster: Ex-Workers Wait" (*Oregonian*, April 27, 1995).

The roller coaster image is not limited to dramatic news headlines. It also appears on the cover of Kaufmann's (1983) detailed assessment of aluminum industry prospects. Kaufmann displays the peaks and troughs in aluminum shipments over several decades to reveal a pattern of oscillations with larger amplitude over time. This chapter uses system dynamics to explore the underlying causes of volatility in this roller coaster industry.

External versus Internal Sources of Volatility

Some experts attribute the price volatility of aluminum in the 1970s to major increases in electricity prices during the decade of the "energy crisis." This was a decade in which skyrocketing oil prices triggered major increases in all fossil fuel prices and subsequent increases in electricity prices. Smelters in areas served by higher-cost power stations experienced major increases in operating costs. Smelters in Japan were particularly vulnerable, and 75 percent of Japan's smelting capacity was closed during the 1980s (Peck 1988, 90). With a combination of permanent and temporary closures, aluminum prices soared to high levels in the 1970s.

Now, suppose we attribute the volatility in the 1970s to the energy crisis, an external factor beyond the normal range of managerial control of the aluminum industry. What about the volatility in the 1980s? Many experts point to the dissolution of the Soviet Union as the key event of the 1980s. The dissolution caused a massive reduction in the soviet military, one of the most important customers for Russian smelters. The Russians turned to western markets, and the market responded with depressed prices and a major effort to deal with the "Russian problem."

Both the energy crisis of the 1970s and the Russian problem of the 1980s might be viewed by aluminum industry leaders as external trends. These trends clearly contribute to industry volatility, but industry leaders may not be able to control or shape the trends. Industry leaders might also look to other external factors, such as volatility in the industries that use aluminum. Volatile demand could be especially important in the United States where highly cyclical industries such as automobile manufacturing and building construction account for over half the aluminum shipments (Kaufmann 1983).

External trends are certainly important to the aluminum industry, but they are not necessarily the keys to understanding the industry volatility. A physiological analogy will illustrate why this is so. Suppose we wish to understand how the human body controls its core temperature near 98.6 degrees despite many external shocks. Should we focus our attention on the outside disturbances? Or will we learn more by looking "inside the body"? You probably know instinctively (and from chapter 8) that the key to improved understanding is inside the body. We need to understand the physiological mechanisms such as sweating and shivering that allow the body to maintain a homeostatic state. The same reasoning makes sense in the aluminum industry. A fundamental understanding of this roller coaster industry will not emerge from the study of the many external shocks. The key to improved understanding is much more likely to emerge when we look inside the industry. This chapter describes an introductory model to get us started in that direction.

An Initial Model

Figure 19.3 shows an equilibrium diagram for an initial model. One stock is used to keep track of the aluminum held in inventory at the smelters and the mills around the world. A second stock represents the aluminum products in use. The model distinguishes between primary production at smelters and secondary production from the recycling of used products. Stocks are measured in millions of metric tons of metallic aluminum. Time is measured in months, and each of the flows is measured in mmt/month. Annual amounts are reported to aid in interpretation. For example, *primary production* is 14 mmt/yr; *secondary production* is 2 mmt/yr; and *annual demand* is 16 mmt/yr. Starting at the top of figure 19.3, the world *smelting capacity* is assumed to be 16 mmt/yr. (The model does not include the smelters in the former USSR). The fraction of smelting capacity in operation depends on the producer's view of the ingot price. Figure 19.3 shows both the *ingot price* and the *producers' lagged price* at 60 cents/pound.

The fraction of smelting capacity that would operate at 60 cents/pound is found by a nonlinear graph (~) shaped to match the industry cost curve in figure 19.2. At 60 cents/pound, for example, 88 percent of the world's smelting capacity would be in operation. Primary production would be 14 mmt/yr, building the stock of inventory held by the smelters and the mills around the world. The inventory is initialized at 3.4 mmt, and this amount is taken as the *regular inventory* needed to ensure efficient operation (Espinosa 1996, 123). To judge the adequacy of inventories, one might calculate the days of coverage provided by current inventory if shipments were to remain constant. With shipments of 16 mmt/yr, for example, the 3.4 mmt of *regular inventory* would provide 78 days of coverage. Industry leaders set coverage targets to deal with volatility in both production and shipments, and their

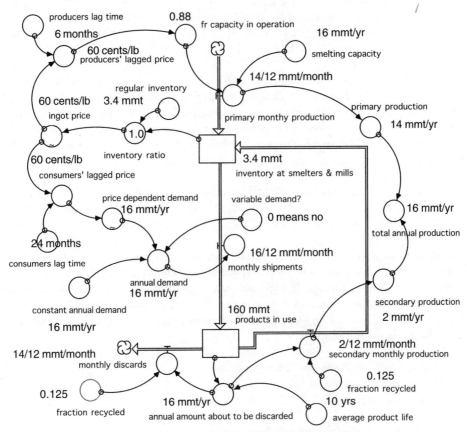

Figure 19.3. Aluminum model with equilibrium conditions.

actual targets are difficult to discern. One "guesstimate" is that producers aim for 45–50 days of coverage while fabricators aim for 35 days (Kaufmann 1983, 6). The *inventory at smelters & mills* represents the combination of producers' and fabricators' inventories, so the 78 days of coverage appears reasonable. You can see from figure 19.3 that the inventory would be maintained at 3.4 mmt because there is 14 mmt/yr of *primary production* and 2 mmt/yr of *secondary production,* exactly the amount needed to satisfy the *annual demand* of 16 mmt/yr. The annual demand is fixed at 16 mmt/yr by setting the *variable demand?* to zero. The ? reminds us that this is a binary variable, as explained in appendix H.

The *monthly shipments* move the aluminum from the mill to the ultimate consumers. The model combines the many uses of aluminum (e.g., automobiles, airplanes, housing, beverages, etc.) into a single category with an *average product life* of 10 years. The total stock of aluminum *products in use* is initialized at 160 mmt. With a 10-year product life, around 16 mmt/yr would be ready for discard in the first year. The user specifies the fraction of the potential discards that will be collected and shipped to secondary producers. The United States has a relatively well-developed system for collection, and secondary production amounts to about 16 percent of total demand (Espinosa 1996, 318). The *fraction recycled* in figure 19.3 is set at 12.5 percent on the assumption that recycling is less developed in the world as a whole. The recycled products are delivered to secondary producers who extract the aluminum and sell the metal to the mill operators.

You should be able to write the equations for most of the variables in figure 19.3 based on the names and the numbers in the equilibrium diagram. The model includes three non-linear relationships represented by graph functions. For example:

```
fr_capacity_in_operation = GRAPH(producers'_lagged_price)
(20.0, 0.00), (30.0, 0.00), (40.0, 0.19), (50.0, 0.63), (60.0, 0.88),
(70.0, 0.97), (80.0, 1.00)
```

which shows the fraction of smelting capacity that is expected to be in operation based on the *producers' lagged price*. The graph is designed to match the industry cost curve shown in figure 19.2. If producers base their decision on 80 cents/pound, for example, 100 percent of the smelters would be in operation. If the producers' price were to fall to 30 cents/pound, none of the smelters would operate. The next nonlinear relationship controls the demand for ingots:

```
price_dependent_demand = GRAPH(consumers'_lagged_price)
(20.0, 24.0), (30.0, 22.0), (40.0, 20.0), (50.0, 18.0), (60.0, 16.0),
(70.0, 14.0), (80.0, 12.0), (90.0, 10.0), (100, 10.0), (110, 10.0), (120, 10.0)
```

The demand for aluminum may change with changes in the consumers' view of price. If the price were to increase from 60 to 70 cents/pound, for example, this graph would lower the demand from 16 to 14 mmt/yr. In other words, a 17 percent increase in price would trigger a 13 percent reduction in demand. If we compare the relative changes, we would say that the "price elasticity of demand" is –0.75. The third graph represents changes in the *ingot price* with changes in the inventory ratio:

```
ingot_price = GRAPH(inventory_ratio)
(0.00, 200), (0.25, 190), (0.5, 150), (0.75, 100), (1.00, 60.0),
(1.25, 50.0), (1.50, 45.0), (1.75, 40.0), (2.00, 40.0)
```

A ratio of 1.0 means that the industry has approximately the inventory needed to allow efficient operations of the smelters and the mills. The model assumes that ingot prices would be at 60 cents/pound under these "regular" conditions. Lower values of the inventory ratio are assumed to push the price higher. If the ratio falls to 75 percent, for example, ingot prices are assumed to increase to 100 cents/pound. If inventories fall to 50 percent of the regular levels, ingot price is assumed to climb even higher, to 150 cents/pound. The shape of this graph function is generally descriptive of inventory and price changes reported over 1984 to 1994 in a survey of inventories maintained at the London Metals Exchange (Standard & Poors 1994).

The model uses two lagged relationships. The first involves the producers' reaction to a change in prices. Let's assume that smelter operators watch price changes over a time interval before committing to opening or closing a smelter. Closing costs could be several million dollars (Peck 1988, 10), so we should assume that operators will not react to each and every fluctuation in the ingot price. It makes more sense to assume that they react to a time-averaged price, which can be represented by a third-order smooth function. The length of the lag is uncertain, but let's begin with a value of 6 months.

```
producers'_lagged_price = smth3(ingot_price,producers'_lag_time,60)
producers'_lag_time = 6
```

Consumers are not likely to react instantaneously to price changes either. The initial model assumes that the delay in the consumers' reactions can be described by a third-order smoothing delay with a 2-year lag time:

```
consumers'_lagged_price = smth3(ingot_price,consumers'_lag_time,60)
consumers'_lag_time = 24
```

The third entry in the smth3 function is 60 for both the producers and the consumers. This means that the simulation begins with both producers and consumers using 60 cents/pound as the appropriate price for decision making.

Simulating a Production Cycle

The equilibrium conditions will persist from one year to another if you simulate the model over time. Every year will show a demand for 16 mmt/yr of aluminum. Total production will exactly balance the demand; ingot prices will remain constant at 60 cents/pound; and 88 percent of the world's smelting capacity will remain in operation. To learn if this equilibrium is stable, we should introduce a disturbance. One way to disturb the equilibrium is to assume that the industry begins the simulation with extra inventory.

Figure 19.4 shows the simulation results with the initial inventory set at 4.4 mmt rather than 3.4 mmt. The *annual demand* for aluminum is held constant at 16 mmt/yr to allow us to concentrate on a situation in which only the producers react to changes in prices. In other words, the initial simulation is designed to test for a "production cycle" in aluminum. The simulation runs for 96 months to allow sufficient time to see if there are volatile swings in prices. This simulation reveals a production cycle that can be attributed entirely to the operating decisions of the primary producers. *Annual demand* and *secondary production* are both constant throughout the simulation. *Primary production* is simulated to decline in the first few months of the simulation because of the low ingot prices. The decline in *primary production* causes total production to fall below demand during the first few months. This allows the inventory to decline to more regular levels, and prices are simulated to swing upward. Producers react to the upswing after a delay, and more capacity comes into operation.

Figure 19.5 shows that almost all of the smelting capacity would be in operation shortly after the peak in ingot prices. This high production causes inventories to build past the regular levels, causing the drop in prices seen around the 2nd year of the simulation. Smelters are gradually taken out of operation during this time period, and the excess inventories are reduced. Figure 19.5 shows a second upswing in prices around the 30th month of the simulation, and the smelters' response is similar to their response to the first upswing in prices.

The initial simulation reveals that the action of primary aluminum producers could be a major contributor to the volatility in the industry. The simulation shows price swings from a low of around 50 cents/pound to a high of over 90 cents/pound. These large swings are quite surprising when you consider that there are no further disturbances after starting out the simulation with extra inventory. Moreover, the price swings occur even though there are no vari-

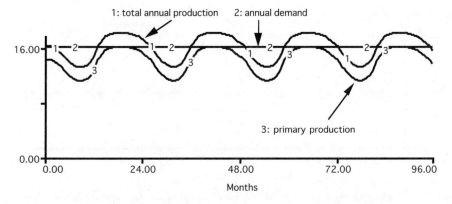

Figure 19.4. Initial simulation of aluminum production and demand.

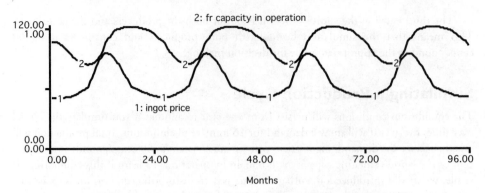

Figure 19.5. Initial simulation of ingot prices and capacity operation.

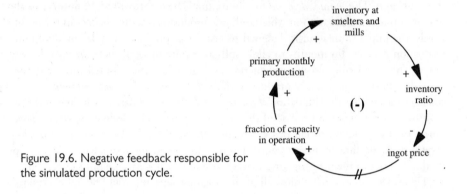

Figure 19.6. Negative feedback responsible for the simulated production cycle.

ations in the demand for aluminum, in the amount of secondary production, or in the total smelting capacity.

The primary producer's role in the system is portrayed in the causal loop diagram in figure 19.6. Primary monthly production builds the inventory at smelters and mills. This builds the inventory ratio and lowers the ingot price. After a delay to watch and evaluate the price changes, the primary producers reduce the fraction of capacity in operation. This lowers monthly production and allows monthly shipments to lower inventory levels to regular levels. The // on the arrow from the ingot price to the fraction of capacity operation draws our attention to the key delay in the loop. You learned in chapter 17 that the length of the time lag can be a crucial factor in controlling the stability of an oscillatory system. So it is important to test the sensitivity of the model to changes in the length of the producers' lag time.

Figure 19.7 shows three simulations of the aluminum production cycle. The first run

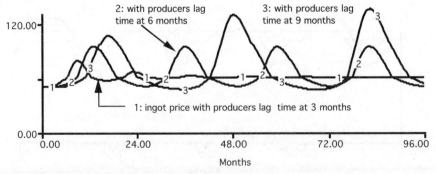

Figure 19.7. Simulated production cycle with three values of the lag in producers' reaction to ingot prices.

assumes that producers average the ingot prices for 3 months before opening or closing their smelters. With this lag time, the industry is simulated to react in a highly stable manner. The second run in figure 19.7 is the same as the simulation shown previously. It shows that a 6-month lag would create sustained oscillations with a period of around 2 years. The third run assumes that producers average the price over 9 months before committing to opening or closing their smelters. This longer lag time causes more volatile cycles, with a period of around 3 years. Clearly, the length of the producers' lag time is an important determinant of the over-all stability of the industry

Adding the Consumers' Reaction

Let's expand the picture to include the consumers' reaction to price changes, as depicted in figure 19.8. An increase in price will cause a reduction in consumption and a corresponding reduction in monthly shipments. When less aluminum is shipped, the inventory tends to build more rapidly, causing a reduction in the price.

The demand loop can be activated in the model by changing the *variable demand?* input from 0 to 1. With this change, the *annual demand* will be based on *price dependent demand* by the following equations:

```
variable_demand? = 1
annual_demand = if (variable_demand?=1) then price_dependent_demand
else constant_annual_demand
```

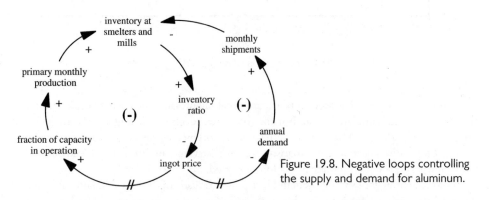

Figure 19.8. Negative loops controlling the supply and demand for aluminum.

Recall that the price-induced change in demand corresponds to a price elasticity of –0.75. Long-run price elasticities have been estimated to range from –0.78 to –1.60 (CRA 1971). The short-run and long-run elasticities in the CRA (Charles River Associates) study may be compared to gain an understanding of the time interval required for the full consumer response to materialize. (The comparison supports the 24-month consumers' lag time mentioned previously.)

Figure 19.9 shows the simulated changes in production and consumption when the consumers' price response is added to the model. The *annual demand* is no longer constant at 16 mmt/yr. Instead, we see modest fluctuations in demand as consumers react to the changes in ingot prices. *Total annual production* varies in a cyclical fashion, due to cycles in *primary production*. We now see cycles in both the demand and the production of aluminum, but the swings in aluminum production are much larger. Data from the United States confirm the relative size of these swings. For example, the Aluminum Association Statistical Review (AAI 1986) shows variations in primary production as well as per capita consumption. A comparison of the largest swings reveals that variations in primary production can be up to ten times larger than the variations in consumption.

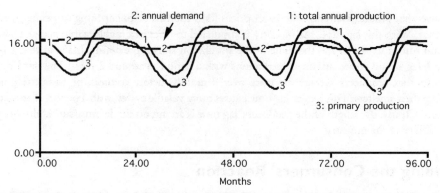

Figure 19.9. Production and demand in a simulation with both producers and consumers reacting to ingot prices.

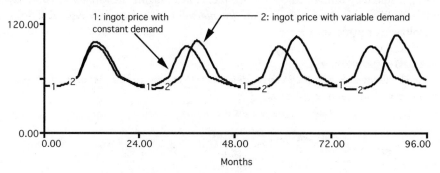

Figure 19.10. Comparison of simulated ingot prices.

Figure 19.9 suggests that producers' decision making provides the primary explanation for the volatility in the simulated cycle. But the consumers' decision making adds to the volatile mixture. Figure 19.10 demonstrates the relative importance of consumers' decision making with a comparative chart. The comparison reveals that variability in demand leads to cycles with somewhat greater amplitude and a longer period.

The simulation with variable demand is the more realistic of the two simulations. It shows cyclical behavior in ingot prices with the cycles taking on the characteristic look of a limit cycle. You have read about limit cycles in chapter 1, but this is your first opportunity to see their shape over time. You can spot limit cycles by their clipped or nonlinear appearance. Scatter graphs are often used to provide a different perspective on limit cycles. Figure 19.11 gives an example. It shows the ingot price versus the fraction of capacity in operation from each month of the simulation. The starting point is 88 percent operation and 50 cents/pound. The first few months show a drop in the fraction of capacity in operation. By the time the fraction reaches 70 percent, the ingot price is increasing, so the dots in figure 19.11 change course from a southerly to an easterly direction. The dots then circle up toward 100 percent and come back around. By the time they have completed one cycle, the system is further removed from the starting point. This outward-growing spiral is characteristic of an unstable system.

Unstable systems cannot grow forever; they will eventually encounter limits. In this example, the limits are reached after only one or two cycles. The most visible limit is on the top of the scatter graph. The fraction of capacity in operation cannot exceed 100 percent. Figure 19.11 also reveals a nonlinear limit on the left side of the diagram. This limitation corre-

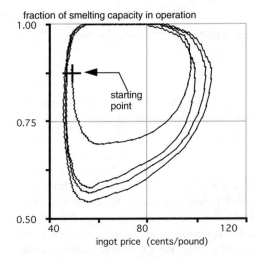

fraction of smelting capacity in operation

Figure 19.11. Scatter graph depicting the limit cycle in the simulated aluminum industry.

sponds to the assumption that aluminum prices are not likely to fall below 40 cents/pound even if inventories build to very high levels.

Conclusions

This chapter illustrates the use of system dynamics to look inside a system for an explanation of volatile behavior. The aluminum model indicates that the operating decisions of primary producers could cause substantial price volatility, especially if there are significant lags in their reaction to price changes. If we are to obtain a deeper understanding of industry volatility, it appears that we should concentrate further model improvements in the area of smelter operations. The aluminum model provides a good illustration of system dynamics to study cyclical behavior in an economic system. The example is especially relevant to environmentalists interested in the potential benefits of recycling. But you should know that the general approach could be applied to other commodities such as cotton, cocoa, coffee, etc. Commodity production cycles are particularly important in developing countries, where the export of primary commodities may account for the bulk of the foreign exchange.

Meadows (1970) used system dynamics to explain cyclical production in a hypothetical commodity. His general simulations demonstrated that the cycles arise in large part from the delays that businesses face in expanding production capacity. He expanded on the general model by replacing hypothetical parameters with parameters drawn from the U.S. hog industry. The new model generated a 4-year cycle characteristic of U.S. hog production. He then conducted similar demonstrations for the poultry and cattle industries. The overall approach is an exemplary example of the development of a "generic structure" followed by tailored applications to specific problems (Lane and Smart 1996, 105). Meadows suggested that the basic commodity model could be extended to other commodities, and Arquitt's (1995) work on shrimp farming in Thailand confirms the usefulness of Meadows's model. And in several respects, the aluminum model in this chapter builds from Meadows's original commodity model.

Exercises

The model in this chapter is a starting point to look inside the industry. Ten exercises are listed here to allow you to expand and improve the initial model. Another ten exercises are available on the home page.

1. **Build and verify:**

   Build the model shown in figure 19.3 and verify the simulation results shown in figures 19.4 and 19.9.

2. **Sensitivity to consumers' lag time:**

   Conduct a sensitivity test with the consumers' lag time at 12, 18, and 24 months. Document your results with a comparative graph like the one in figure 19.7. Does a faster consumer response make the system more stable?

3. **Expand the model with arrays:**

   To add realism in the treatment of primary producers' decision making, let's change from our view of an aggregate industry with a single cost curve. We might learn more if we viewed the industry as composed of individual smelters. There are 146 smelters in the western world with widely different operating costs. To bring the new model "closer" to the producers, it would be useful to allow for a smelter-by-smelter simulation. The diagram shows how this might be done by invoking Stella's array feature for the *variable cost* of individual smelters. This diagram concentrates on the top portion of the flow diagram shown previously.

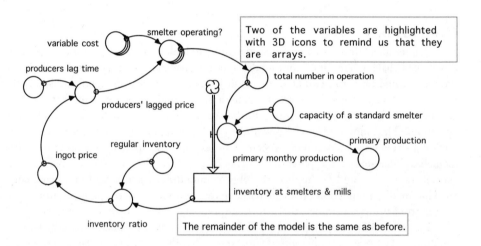

   Notice the three-dimensional icons for *smelter operating?* and for *variable cost*. The 3-D effect reminds us that these variables are defined as arrays. The model defines an array dimension called *smelter*. Build this model using a smelter index to take on the values 1, 2, 3 . . . 16 as if there were 16 "standard" smelters in the world. Assign a capacity of 1 mmt/yr and a 6-month lag time to each of the smelters. Then assign each smelter a different variable cost, based on the shape of the industry cost curve in figure 19.2. Define *smelter operating?* as a binary variable that will be set to 1 if the smelter is in operation. Use Stella's ARRAYSUM function to sum the values of the array to find the total number of smelters in operation. You should be able to build this model and compare the simulated cycles with the cycles from the previous model. Does the treatment of individual smelters change the overall volatility of the system? (You may check your work by comparing with the model on the home page.)

4. **More detail on operating costs:**

   Expand the model in the third exercise to include the additional arrays shown in the following diagram. They provide greater detail on the *total variable cost* at each smelter.

Assume that all 16 smelters pay 10 cents/pound for labor, 15 cents/pound (of aluminum) for alumina, and 5 cents/pound to transport aluminum to market. Assume that each smelter needs 7 kwh of electricity per pound of aluminum. To create some variability in operating costs, let the *cost of electricity to smelters* vary from a low of 0.7 cents/kwh for the first smelter to a high of 5.7 cents/kwh for the 16th smelter. Run the new model to learn if it generates behavior similar to that in the third exercise.

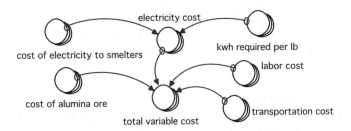

5. **Producers' lag times:**

    Expand the model in the third exercise to allow for a different lag time at each of the 16 smelters. You may assume that the 6-month lag time describes the decision making at smelters 1–8, the smelters that are likely to remain in operation for most of the simulation. Assume that the remaining smelters are more familiar with shutting down and reopening so they respond to price changes more rapidly. Set their lag time to 3 months, and run the new model to see if you get results similar to those in the third exercise. Which lag time is more important, the 6-month lag at smelters 1–8 or the 3-month lag at smelters 9–16?

6. **Keep one pot line open:**

    Expand the model in the third exercise to allow each smelter to have a different number of pot lines. (The number might range from 4 to 12.) Change the model to keep 1 pot line in operation. For example, an unprofitable smelter with 10 pot lines will close down 9 out of 10 pot lines, so 10 percent of the capacity will remain in operation. Run the new model to learn if the pot line constraint changes the simulated volatility in prices.

7. **Shut-down costs:**

    Expand the model in the third exercise to allow the user to specify the shut-down costs (in millions of $) at each smelter. Compare the variable cost and ingot prices to determine the monthly losses at each smelter. Alter the model to simulate closures based on the monthly losses. Assume that smelters with higher shut-down costs will be willing to absorb longer periods of losses before shutting down their smelters. Run the new model to see if it delivers different insights on the volatility of aluminum prices.

8. **Electricity consumption and recycling:**

    Expand the model from the fourth exercise to keep track of the electricity consumption by smelters. There are 2.2046 pounds in a kilogram, and a metric ton is 1,000 kilograms. The model should keep track of kwh requirements per month and the cumulative kwh for the entire simulation. Then expand the model to keep track of the electricity consumption by secondary producers that extract aluminum from recycled products. Each pound of secondary aluminum requires only 5 percent of the electricity needed for primary production. Keep track of the total electricity consumption per month and the cumulative consumption over the entire simulation.

Now, before running the model, use a hand calculator to estimate the reduction in electricity consumption if we could double the amount of recycling in the model. Calculate expected savings in billions of kwh/month and total savings over an entire simulation.

9. **Simulate the energy savings:**

Now, change the fraction recycled from 12.5 percent to 25 percent at the start of the simulation and run the model to obtain a "systems perspective" on the amount of electricity to be saved by increased recycling. Does the simulated savings match your previous estimate? If not, what is the model doing that you didn't do on the hand calculator?

10. **Causal loop diagram:**

Expand the causal loop diagram in figure 19.8 to show any feedback loops created by the recycling of aluminum. Then expand the diagram further to show any additional feedback loops if the recycling fraction were to increase with higher ingot prices.

PART V

MANAGEMENT FLIGHT SIMULATORS

Chapter 20

Air Pollution, Cleaner Vehicles, and Feebates

This chapter presents the first of two models to be used by students in interactive experimentation. This chapter deals with urban air pollution; the next chapter deals with global climate control. Both make use of a special type of model called a management flight simulator.

A management flight simulator is a model designed to promote learning through interactive experimentation. You've heard of a pilot flight simulator, an electromechanical model of an airplane. The model is a simplified representation of the airplane equipped with a sophisticated interface to resemble the cockpit. Pilots experiment with the simulated airplane to improve their flying instincts. A management flight simulator has a similar purpose. It's designed to help managers improve their business instincts.

Flight Simulators

Management flight simulators have proven useful in several business systems including health care, airlines, insurance, real estate, and project management (Morecroft 1988; Sterman 1992; Senge 1990; Morecroft and Sterman 1994; Senge et al. 1994). Peter Senge describes flight simulators as the "technology of the learning organization." He emphasizes the role of rapid feedback to help us learn about systems in our everyday lives:

> We learn to walk, ride a bicycle, drive an automobile, and play the piano by trial and error; we act, observe the consequences of our action and adjust. But "learning by doing" only works so long as the feedback from our actions is rapid and unambiguous. (Senge 1990, 313)

But complex organizations do not necessarily provide the same opportunity for learning. "When we act in a complex system the consequences of our actions are neither immediate nor unambiguous. Often, they are far removed from us in time and space." Senge argues that organizations face a "dilemma of learning from experience," as the consequences of our most important decisions often land in a distant part of the system or far into the future. He explains that flight simulators enable managers and management teams to improve the prospects for "learning through doing" when they "compress time and space." Time is compressed in the sense that impacts that may land far in the future appear rapidly in a computer simulation. Space is "compressed" when a team of managers from many parts of an organization gather together to experiment with a model of the entire system.

Previous Interfaces

The first thing that we normally notice when using a management flight simulator is the interface. The interface makes it easy to experiment with a model by selecting the most interesting inputs and putting them under our control with interactive icons. You have seen two interfaces previously: the Smolt Migration Model in figure 13.6, and the Tucannon Harvest Model in the first exercise of chapter 14. At first glance, these interfaces appear similar. They both make it easier for a wide group of people to experiment with the models. But the interfaces are quite different in their intended use. The smolt interface was designed to speed up a number of separate calculations. You will probably recall that there was no opportunity to "change your mind" or to adjust to changing conditions midway through the 40-day migration period. Once you committed to a certain barging policy or a certain flow scenario, you simply hit the "run" command and waited to see the results. After recording the results of a dozen simulations, you acquired a general feeling for the relative merits of barging. We might view the smolt interface as similar to the buttons and LCD panel on your electronic calculator. They make it possible to conduct a number of useful calculations, even though we may not understand the internal workings of the model or the calculator.

Now, what about the Tucannon Harvest Model? Recall that the harvest exercise was designed as a "game for three." You probably experimented with different strategies for setting the harvest fraction (while your classmates made changes in the habitat parameters and the river parameters). There was plenty of opportunity for you to reflect on the past behavior and to adjust the harvest fraction during the course of a 40-year simulation. You could see the simulated response of the fishery to your changes, and you experienced what it might be like to be responsible for the harvest fraction. Your experiences were much more comparable to the pilots' experiences in a regular flight simulator. The goal was not simply to "punch out" a series of calculations about the salmon. The goal was to learn what it might be like to take the controls of a complex system.

New Interfaces: Download or Build

The Tucannon flight simulator was presented at the end of chapter 14 after you learned how to build and simulate the model. The simulators in this chapter and the next chapter are presented differently. Each chapter begins with an introduction to a complex system and a management challenge. You may then download the simulator from the book's home page. The opening screen provides instructions, and you can immediately take up the challenge of managing the simulated system. You will discover that there is much to learn about each system even though you have not constructed the underlying model.

Now, it is also instructive to build the model "inside" the simulator. The exercises at the end of this chapter lead you through the model construction in a step-by-step manner. You can then expand the model to deal with a wider range of policies to improve urban air pollution.

The Persistence of Urban Air Pollution

Air pollution in America's urban areas became a highly publicized issue in the 1960s. The first emission standards were established in 1965; five years later, the Clean Air Act of 1970 established stricter standards to become effective in 1975. The standards were designed to protect human health. Unfortunately, the air in many of our urban areas remains unhealthy over two decades after the original 1975 target date. The most visible sign of our continuing failure is the smog that hangs over our dirtiest cities. Smog is tropospheric ozone. It is formed by a photochemical reaction between hydrocarbons (HC) and the oxides of nitrogen (NOx) in the presence of heat and sunlight. Short-term exposure to ozone can cause shortness of breath;

long-term exposure can cause permanent damage to the lungs. Gordon (1991, 62) reports that "more than 100 of the cities in the US are choking on smog, and roughly half of all Americans live in areas that exceed the ozone standard at least once a year."

One of the most polluted areas is the Southern California airshed known officially as the South Coast Air Quality Management District (SCAQMD). The SCAQMD has some of the strictest controls in the nation, but HC and NOx emissions still exceed 2,000 tons per day. These pollutants react in the presence of Southern California's ample sunshine to produce ozone concentrations roughly three times larger than the federal health standard (Ford 1995, 207). In some Southern California cities, the ozone concentrations violate health standards 125 days/year (SCAQMD 1991). The air pollution problems in America's urban areas have persisted for many decades even though the pollutants themselves are quickly dissipated in the atmosphere. The persistent problem does not stem from long lag times in the environment (as was the case with DDT in chapter 12). Rather, it stems from our continued use of polluting technologies on the ground.

One of the biggest polluters is the automobile. Gordon reports that there were 187 million cars and light trucks or vans on the road in 1989, roughly 1.5 vehicles for every working American. She reports that the transportation sector is responsible for two-thirds of the nation's carbon monoxide (CO) emissions and around 40 percent of the nation's HC and NOx emissions. Transportation is also responsible for 30 percent of the CO_2 emissions, the main pollutant contributing to global warming.

Emissions from a Conventional Vehicle

The tailpipe emissions from a conventional gasoline or diesel vehicle include HC, NOx, and CO. HC and NOx are the precursors to ozone. CO is a heavier pollutant, which becomes highly concentrated in transportation corridors and causes headaches and stress on the heart. These three pollutants are each subject to emissions standards set by the state agencies. Based on standards in California in the late 1990s, a typical conventional vehicle (CV) releases 115 pounds of HC, 133 pounds of NOx, and 1,346 pounds of CO over its lifetime (Ford 1995). These estimates may leave you with the impression that vehicle emissions are not a serious problem. After all, why should we worry about 115 pounds of HC, when total HC emissions in the SCAQMD during the 1980s were over 1,600 tons/day? (Ford 1992, 134).

One way to place a single vehicle's emissions in perspective is to review the plan to control the emissions in the airshed. The SCAQMD is a particularly interesting airshed because the district faces the most serious air pollution challenge in the nation, and it has published an ambitious plan designed to reach ambient air quality goals by the year 2010 (SCAQMD 1991). By looking to the marginal control measures in the plan, we obtain a rough indication of cost of pollution control. Since the SCAQMD is a public agency, the cost of the marginal measure serves as a general indicator of our collective "willingness to pay" for cleaner air. The marginal measures in the plan reveal a willingness to pay $8 to avoid a pound of HC emissions, $12 per pound of NOx, and $5 per pound of CO (Ford 1992, 131). Now, let's combine these cost estimates with the estimated emissions over the life of a CV:

- 115 pounds of HC @ $8 plus
- 133 pounds of NOx @ $12 plus
- 1,346 pounds of CO @ $5

to obtain a total cost of over $9,000. In other words, a conventional vehicle's lifetime emissions would force the industries and residents to spend over $9,000 to achieve compensating reductions elsewhere in the airshed. The $9,000 probably strikes you as surprisingly high, especially since the median sale price of a new car in 1990 was under $14,000. If you dig into the details (Ford 1992, 1995), you'll learn that the high cost stems, in part, from the high cost of the measures needed if Southern California is ever to achieve the air quality called for in the Clean Air Act. The cost estimates for other airsheds are considerably lower (e.g., around $2,000 in the San Francisco airshed).

Alternative Vehicles

Sperling (1988, 1995) and Gordon (1991) describe the prospects for improving urban air pollution by changing the mix of vehicles. Rather than continued reliance on conventional vehicles that burn gasoline or diesel fuel, they envision a future with a wide array of choices. The vehicles of the future might be fueled by methanol, compressed natural gas, electricity, or even a combination of these energy sources. Each of the alternative vehicles has intriguing advantages. Methanol vehicles, for example, have the advantages of minimizing the engine modifications and having a high power rating. Vehicles using compressed natural gas (CNG) offer low fuel costs, lower engine maintenance, and lower CO and HC emissions. Gordon (1991, 108) argues that CNG vehicle technology "is available today for most motor vehicle applications, and further advances could move this fuel into widespread use." She emphasizes that CNG is attractive because of its "competitive cost, low toxicity, low emissions, relative safety and secure supply."

Electric vehicles (EVs) are one of the more intriguing technologies because they offer the prospect of zero emissions. Indeed, EVs are sometimes called ZEVs or zero emission vehicles, and a major debate is underway about the role of government regulations and incentives to promote their use. In California, for example, the Air Resources Board has proposed that 10 percent of vehicles produced and delivered for sale by each of the seven largest auto manufacturers be zero emission vehicles. California is not alone. Other states have considered adopting similar programs, and other countries have debated taking action to promote the sale of EVs. In 1992, for example, the Stockholm conference "The Urban Electric Vehicle" opened with the declaration that "industrialized countries and cities throughout the world are embarking on policies which will encourage the use of tens or hundreds of thousands of electric vehicles within the next decade" (OECD 1992). Speakers at Stockholm envisioned a future with 500,000 EVs in Europe and 200,000 EVs in Japan. An executive from General Motors spoke of production requirements of 300,000–400,000 EVs/yr if states like California retained the 10 percent ZEVs requirement (Ford 1994a, 555). General Motors' "EV-1" model is shown in photo 20.1. According to the American Council for an Energy Efficient Economy's *Green Guide to Cars & Trucks* (DeCicco and Thomas 1998), "A superbly designed advanced body structure and an energy-efficient electric drive train give GM's EV-1 excellent performance along with the highest Green Score for the model year 1998."

California regulators have stepped back from the strict production requirement (Ford 1996a), but interest in EVs remains high because of the chronic need for methods to reduce urban air pollution. You can appreciate the strong interest in EVs when you recall the $9,000 associated with the air pollution from a conventional vehicle. If regulators could find a way to help the marketplace replace a CV with an EV, the airshed would be $9,000 further toward the goal of healthy air.

What about the Power Plants?

At this point, you are probably wondering whether the $9,000 exaggerates the benefits of an EV. After all, you haven't read a word about where the electricity will come from to charge the EV batteries. You might be worried that electricity generation could make air pollution worse rather than better. This is a legitimate concern, especially in the midwestern states, where much of the electricity is generated in coal-fired power stations. EVs would be a poor choice

Photo 20.1. The General Motors EV-1 represents the first generation of commercially produced electronic vehicles in the United States. Source: Courtesy of General Motors.

in those areas, so regulators there tend to focus on alternative fuels like natural gas, methanol, or ethanol.

Most of the interest in EVs is in California and on the East Coast, where utilities rely on a mix of hydro, nuclear energy, coal, and natural gas for electric generation. The mix of generating resources that would serve EVs under multiple scenarios has been analyzed for the Southern California Edison system (Ford 1994a, 1995). The analysis revealed that approximately 90 percent of the electricity generation would come from power stations burning natural gas. Compared to coal, natural gas is a relatively clean fuel for power generation, and it is becoming a popular fuel for new power stations planned for the future. Electricity generation from natural gas has negligible HC and CO emissions, but it does produce NOx emissions. The Southern California Edison study revealed that the overall impact of counting the power plant emissions turned out to be a 20 percent reduction in the net benefits to be expected in terms of NOx reduction. Now, how might we change our overall view of EVs in light of this new information about the power plants? One approach is to revisit the $9,000 calculation using 20 percent less reduction in NOx emissions. The revised value of an EV would be around $8,700.

Now that we've thought about the emissions upstream from an EV, have you asked yourself about the delivery system for a conventional gasoline vehicle? Have you thought about the emissions that arise from refueling a CV at the gas station or from a refinery within the airshed? Refueling and refining are major sources of HC emissions, and they effectively double the HC associated with a CV tailpipe. These activities also increase the total NOx emissions by around 10 percent (Ford 1992, 74). If we revisit the calculated value of an EV, the overall benefit of the electric vehicle now turns out to be approximately $10,000.

There is considerable judgment and uncertainty in arriving at the $10,000 value of a EV, however. Other investigators have obtained widely different estimates. For example, a team from the Argonne National Laboratory arrived at an estimate of $18,200 for an EV in a similar airshed (Ford 1995, 215). If you have not read about the ambitious plan required to help Southern California achieve clean air, the $10,000 value may sound extremely high. But if

Box 20.1. Should power companies provide purchase price incentives?

The provision of incentives from the power company to encourage the sale of EVs is an intriguing idea. It was first proposed by Thomas Edison, who encouraged the power companies of his day to build garages for EV owners. Modern-day utilities have proposed financial incentives to cut the purchase price of an EV, with the idea that their incentives might spur the market. Higher EV sales could lead to higher electricity demand, but if the demand were shaped to fall in the nighttime hours (when power companies have idle generating capacity), the utility might bring in more cash from electricity sales than it spends on running the power plants at night. It might then use the extra cash to finance the customer incentive program. One might envision a scenario in which both EV owners and the rest of the rate payers benefit from a utility-financed incentive program.

This intriguing idea was the subject of much debate in the mid-1990s, but it draws less attention today. Utility companies would have an extremely difficult time financing a purchase-price incentive program without raising rates to the average rate payer (Ford 1996a).

you look at some of the specific measures that homes and businesses are expected to implement, you can appreciate how valuable an EV might be. (As an example, one of the rules to be imposed on glass furnaces would cost around $24,000 to avoid a ton of NOx emissions. This measure cost leads to the value of $12 per pound of NOx that could be eliminated by an EV.) Be assured that the $10,000 is a reasonable estimate of monetary value. It is highly uncertain, but you should know that the range of uncertainty can extend well above and well below $10,000. Finally, it will help you to place the $10,000 value into proper perspective to learn about the apparent desire of California citizens to work for cleaner air. For example, a survey of stated preferences for vehicle buyers has revealed a willingness to pay an extra $10,000 for a vehicle with zero emissions (Ford 1995, 215). For the purpose of this chapter, let's proceed with the assumption that $10,000 is a reasonable estimate of the value of a zero emissions vehicle in a highly polluted airshed. Now, what policies might be implemented to encourage the sale of such a valuable vehicle?

Policies to Promote Cleaner Vehicles

A variety of policies are under debate around the world to promote the sale of alternative vehicles. They include increased government R&D to speed the development of new technologies, government purchase programs to create an early market in fleets, and federally required market shares for cleaner vehicles in privately owned fleets. State agencies responsible for air quality have implemented a variety of emissions standards targeted at both individual vehicles and the entire population of new cars sold each year. States have also proposed changes in registration fees, and they have encouraged cities to increase driving and parking privileges for cleaner vehicles. The gas and electric utilities have contributed their own policy proposals. They include vehicle demonstration programs and extra investment in refueling and recharging infrastructure. Electric utilities have proposed low, off-peak rates for nighttime electricity, and some electric utilities have suggested that they be allowed to provide financial incentives to reduce the purchase price of an EV (see box 20.1). The range of policy proposals is almost as diverse as the range of vehicles that will emerge in the coming decades.

This chapter focuses on feebates, one of the most intriguing policy proposals. The "fee" in feebates stands for a fee imposed on the purchase price of a dirty vehicle. The "bate" stands for a rebate to the person who purchases a clean vehicle. The idea is to finance the rebates for the clean vehicles with the fees imposed on the dirty vehicles. Feebate proposals have been considered at both state and federal levels (DeCicco, Geller, and Morrill 1993), and they have been endorsed by some of the nation's best energy experts. Perhaps the most resounding endorsement comes from Amory Lovins, the director of research at the Rocky Mountain Institute in Snowmass, Colorado. Lovins (1991) believes that feebates hold the ultimate promise of replacing prescriptive regulations, and he labeled a California proposal to use feebates to improve automobile fuel efficiency as the "single most important energy policy initiative now being considered at any level of government anywhere in the United States."

The Appeal of Feebates

Feebates are appealing because they would work to supplement the market forces that create the supply and demand for vehicles. The size of the feebates may be adjusted to represent the value of each vehicle within the airshed. Consider the example mentioned previously—an EV is worth $10,000 relative to a CV in a heavily polluted airshed like the SCAQMD. With current market forces, this extra cost is largely ignored by consumers. With feebates, however, this cost could be brought to the consumer's immediate attention by setting a feebate to total $10,000. For example, the fee might be set at $2,000 and the rebate at $8,000. Consumers would be free to choose whichever vehicle best meets their needs, and manufacturers would be free to produce the most profitable mix of vehicles. The marketplace would operate with proper feedback to the participants on the environmental impacts of their decisions. Lovins (1991) suggests that the market response could be revolutionary, in terms of both the new vehicles and the new companies that enter the marketplace.

Feebates are also appealing because they would promote new technologies without requiring the program administrator to play favorites. Feebate programs could be implemented in a "fuel-neutral" and a "technology-neutral" manner. Each vehicle could be evaluated solely in terms of its emissions in the airshed, and the feebates could be adjusted accordingly. Any clean vehicle would qualify for a rebate; any dirty vehicle would be subject to a fee.

Could You Manage a Feebate Program?

Feebates are an appealing idea, but could they be managed in a pragmatic manner? Do you think this is one of those ideas that sounds good in theory but isn't likely to work in practice? Let's consider some simple examples to reveal the pragmatic problems that might arise. Suppose we are running a program in a heavily polluted airshed where the EV is worth $10,000 relative to a CV. Furthermore, suppose that CVs and EVs are the only vehicle choices, and we elect to set the CV fee at $2,000 and the EV rebate at $8,000. We hope that the fees collected from the sale of CVs will provide the financing for the EV rebates. We announce the feebate for a given model year and wait to watch the market response. Suppose the market responds with 80 percent CVs and 20 percent EVs.

- If 80 out of 100 buyers purchase the CV despite the $2,000 fee, we would collect $160,000 from their fees.
- The other 20 buyers are expecting an $8,000 rebate, so total rebates would be $160,000.

This example shows the ideal situation—the program is self-financing because the cash flow from fees is exactly the amount needed for rebates. Self-financing is another reason for the popularity of feebates—they could be operated in a "revenue neutral" manner so as to avoid the unpopular "tax label" (Sperling 1995, 128).

Now, consider a somewhat different situation. Suppose the market responds with a 70–30 percent mix of CVs and EVs. For every 100 new car purchasers, we would collect $140,000 in fees, but we would be obligated for $240,000 in rebates. The program would be $100,000 out of balance for every 100 people buying a new vehicle. Think of the consequences for a major airshed where new car sales total 1 million vehicles/year. The feebate program would be out of balance by $1 billion per year!

At this point, you are probably thinking that you could avoid this problem by setting the feebate to account for the 70–30 percent market shares. You might keep the fee at $2,000 but lower the rebate to $4,667. Or you might set the fee to $1,000 and the rebate at $2,333. Both of these examples set the rebate at 2.33 times the fee because the CV market share is expected to be 2.33 times larger than the EV market share. But these examples presuppose that you can accurately forecast the 70–30 percent market shares.

Unfortunately, there is little reason to believe that state officials could develop a reliable method of forecasting market shares. Their efforts would be hampered by major uncertainties in describing consumer behavior and equally important uncertainties in describing the attributes of the vehicles to be offered for sale. If we are to seriously consider a feebate program, we must face the fact that the administrator will not have a crystal ball to forecast future market shares. But it is certainly realistic to expect that the administrator will have full information on market shares in the past. Maybe it would be possible to run the program by watching past market shares and past cash flows and adjust feebates accordingly.

Feebate Program Manager

This chapter asks you to place yourself in the position of manager of a feebate program. You are responsible for promoting the sale of alternative-fueled vehicles with the goal of reducing emission of air pollutants in the airshed over the next 16 years. You recruit an excellent staff, and they advise you that there will be 10 million CVs in the airshed when you take office in the year 2000. Vehicles operate for 10 years before retirement. Annual sales will be 1.6 million in the year 2000 and are expected to grow at 4.7 percent/yr during your tenure as manager. Although CVs dominate the existing population of vehicles, alternative-fueled vehicles will become available for sale in the year 2000. Your staff advises you that the marketplace will be dominated by five vehicles:

- the conventional vehicle (CV), fueled by gasoline or diesel;
- the alcohol vehicle (AL), fueled by methanol;
- the electric vehicle (EV), running totally on batteries;
- the hybrid electric vehicle (HEV), running on batteries and gasoline; and
- vehicles burning compressed natural gas (CNG).

You are advised that the EV is the only technology to meet the zero emissions goal, and its value in meeting your clean air goal is estimated at $10,000. Each of the other vehicles have been ranked relative to a standard emissions fraction of 100 percent for the conventional vehicle as a point of reference. The relative values are summarized in table 20.1.

Staff informs you that your job will be made easy by the fact that the emission fractions will remain constant over your tenure as program manager. Staff advises that the initial market shares for the five vehicles are uncertain, but your job is simplified by the fact that both the vehicle attributes and the consumer preferences will not change during your tenure as program manager. Because the emissions will persist throughout your tenure, you decide to organize the feebate program with fees on CV and AL vehicles. Rebates will be allowed on EVs,

Table 20.1. Vehicle choices.

Vehicle type		Emissions	Value
Conventional gasoline	CV	100%	zero
Electric	EV	0%	$10,000
Alcohol or methanol	AL	81%	$1,900
Hybrid electric	HEV	37%	$6,300
Compressed natural gas	CNG	42%	$5,800

HEVs, and CNGs. You aren't sure about the size of the fees and rebates, and you aren't sure whether the program could be operated in a prudent manner. You ask for a financial cushion, and the state responds by establishing a fund with an initial balance of $100 million. You are told that you can draw down the fund if rebates exceed fees during any particular year, but you must strive to rebuild the fund in future years. Your operating instructions are to maintain the fund reasonably close to zero so that the feebate program remains revenue-neutral over your time period as program manager.

The Feebate Control Model

Now, imagine that staff has developed a simulation model to illuminate the possible problems you might encounter during your tenure as program manager. The model is designed as a management flight simulator to allow ample opportunity for experimentation. Figure 20.1 shows the first screen to appear when you open the flight simulator. The instructions appear in the scrolling field, and the buttons allow you to move to new screens for more information. The first two sliders allow you to set the fees for the dirtier vehicles; the other three sliders control the rebates for the cleaner vehicles. Staff has selected HC emissions as an indicator of the overall success of the program, and the time graph in figure 20.1 shows total annual HC emissions from all vehicles. It grows from 25 thousand metric tons (MT) in the year 2000 toward 50 thousand MT by the end of the simulation period. The "finger" in figure 20.1 is pointed at the *Run for 1 year button*. Click on this button to complete the "do nothing" simulation in figure 20.1, and you will see that total HC emissions reach 50 thousand MT/yr if you take no action.

Table 20.2 shows the new vehicle market shares in the "do nothing" simulation. CVs are still the most popular vehicle; they capture 52 percent of new vehicle sales. CNGs are also quite popular, capturing 22 percent of the market. The methanol vehicle has slightly more than 10 percent of the market, while the two classes of electric vehicles get less than 10 percent of the market. Staff cannot explain why the market shares turned out as shown in the bottom row of table 20.2, but they can assure you that the vehicle attributes will remain constant during your tenure as program manager. Also, they assure you that consumer preferences will remain constant over time. These assurances simplify your job considerably. With these assumptions, the only reason the market shares will change is if you decide to intervene with fees and rebates. If you offer a rebate on EVs, for example, the market will respond with some increase in EV market share. Unfortunately, staff cannot tell you in advance how responsive the market will be.

Table 20.2. Attributes and market shares in the "do nothing" simulation.

Attribute	CV (conventional)	AL (alcohol)	EV (electric)	HEV (hybrid)	CNG (natural gas)
Emission fraction	1.00	0.81	0.00	0.37	0.42
Fees	$0	$0	—	—	—
Rebates	—	—	$0	$0	$0
Base price	$15,000	$18,000	$25,000	$27,000	$20,000
Purchase price	$15,000	$18,000	$25,000	$27,000	$20,000
Fuel cost (cents/mile)	4.7	7.2	5.3	6.4	2.6
Horse power	121	134	65	85	115
Range (miles)	450	250	100	200	200
Fuel availability	100%	20%	50%	100%	25%
Simulated market share	52%	12%	6%	8%	22%

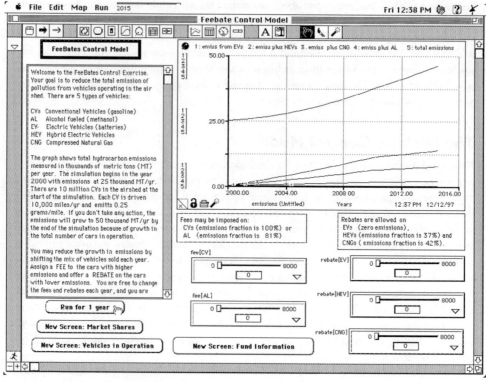

Figure 20.1. Results from the first 15 years of a "do nothing" experiment with the feebate control model. (You can download the flight simulator from the home page. It uses Stella, ver. 5.0.)

Illustrative Simulation: Focus on CVs and EVs

Figure 20.2 shows the flight simulator part way through a simple experiment with the feebates limited to CVs and EVs. Imagine that you are practicing with a two-vehicle program before considering feebates for all five vehicles. In this experiment, you do not intervene until the year 2004. Then you set the CV fee at $2,000 and the EV rebate at $8,000. The total feebate reflects the relative value of an EV discussed previously. Figure 20.2 shows the financial information screen in the year 2006, only two years after the beginning of feebates. You might be worried by the downward trend in the state fund. The finger is pointed at the *CV vs. EV bar chart* button. You could click this button to view a bar chart of the cash flowing into the state fund from CV fees and the cash flowing out to pay for EV rebates. The chart highlights the cash flow discrepancy in the numerical reports at the bottom of figure 20.2. If you were trying to correct the negative cash flow, you would probably increase the fee on the CVs or reduce the rebate on the EVs. You are free to do either or both, but your feebates must be held constant for at least one year. Also, you may not impose a fee or allow a rebate higher than $8,000 per vehicle. You may impose any additional restrictions for reasons of your own. For example, you may strive to maintain feebates that reflect environmental values, or you may strive for relatively constant fees and/or rebates over time.

The Feebate Assignment

Practice with the flight simulator to learn about the dynamics of managing a feebate program. Your main goal is to lower the HC emissions below the trend toward 50,000 MT/yr shown in figure 20.1. You have sixteen years to make the program work, and your performance will be evaluated principally on the basis of total HC emissions in the year 2016. The lower the total emissions at the end of the simulation, the better.

You are given wide latitude in setting fees and rebates. Feebates may be adjusted annually, and you have the freedom to adjust the feebates anywhere between zero and $8,000 per vehicle each and every year of the simulation. You are advised that your performance will be tarnished if you end up changing the feebates in a volatile and "unpredictable manner." Some will argue that a relatively constant, "predictable" pattern of feebates is needed to aid consumers' and manufacturers' decision making. You are also advised that it would be desirable for your feebates to reflect the environmental values of each vehicle. Otherwise, some will argue that you are "playing favorites" with your program.

You are required to operate the feebate program in a financially responsible manner. Specifically, you must not let the balance stray too far from zero. Staff advises that you will be dealing with immense cash flows, so you have asked the state to allow the balance in the state fund to vary within plus or minus $4 billion from zero. You are granted this wide latitude, but the program will be immediately terminated if you fail to control the fund within these limits. If the balance ever builds above $4 billion, for example, the program will be terminated on the basis that you are operating a taxation program (not a revenue-neutral feebate program). The program will also be terminated if you allow the program to fall more than $4 billion into debt. The final requirement is a "sunset" requirement. You are asked to close the program down in the year 2016 and leave the state with a small balance in the fund. The fund is opened with $100 million in the year 2000, and you are asked to close the fund in the year 2016 with a balance between zero and $200 million.

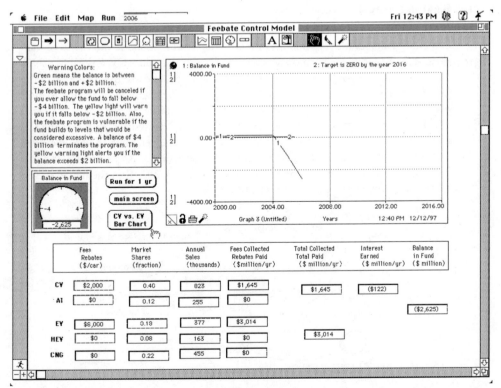

Figure 20.2. Financial information screen in the year 2006 in a simulation with a $2K fee on CVs and a $8K rebate on EVs.

The Feebate Report

Describe your findings in a feebate report. Explain whether it is possible to manage a feebate program in a controlled manner and meet the "sunset" requirement. Also, explain whether you can operate the program in a relatively constant manner that consumers and manufacturers find "predictable" and whether you can set feebates to reflect the environmental value of each vehicle. Finally, and most important, can you lower the total HC emissions by the end of your tenure?

You might reach the conclusion that feebates cannot be managed in a successful manner, even under the relatively constant conditions built into the flight simulator. If you take this position, use the feebate report to explain the fundamental obstacles to success. The report should also explain whether the obstacles could be erased, perhaps by removing some of the limitations on the program manager.

On the other hand, you might reach the conclusion that feebates can be managed in a prudent manner. In this case, your report should explain the strategy that you would follow as feebate manager. Use the report to explain why your strategy works well in the conditions built into the flight simulator. Then expand the report to explain whether your strategy is sufficiently flexible to work under more variable conditions.

Exercises

The best way to learn about flight simulators is to experiment with the feebate control model. To learn more about the underlying model, try the following exercises. They lead you through the construction of the entire model. Along the way, you will gain practice in the use of arrays. You'll also learn about a statistical model of market shares in a "discrete-choice" situation.

1. **Build and verify the vehicles sector:**

    Build the model shown below. *Cars* are measured in millions; *sales* and *retired* in million cars/yr; *annual travel* in billions of miles/yr; *annual emissions* in thousands of metric tons (MT) per yr. Define a dimension *V* to take on the values CV, EV, HEV, CNG, AL. Assign array variables as indicated by the 3-D icons, and use the ARRAYSUM to find the *total cars in use* and the *total emissions*. Set the standard emissions to 0.25 grams/mile, and the emission fractions as described previously. Set the *total sales* to start at 1.6 million cars/yr and to grow exponentially at 4.7 percent/yr. Initialize the CV stock for 10 million CVs evenly distributed across the ten slats of the conveyor. Initialize the other four stocks at zero. Set the market shares at 52 percent CV, 12 percent AL, 6 percent EV, 8 percent HEV, and 22 percent CNG. Run the model to verify that it generates the results shown in figure 20.1.

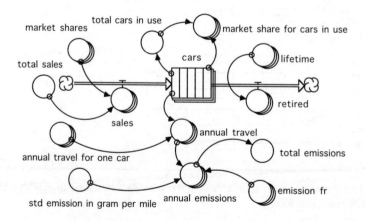

2. **Build and verify discrete choice market shares:**

Build the market shares model shown below. The base price, fuel cost, and other vehicle attributes may be specified as shown in table 20.2. The market share equations are adapted from a discrete-choice model published by researchers from the University of California (Bunch 1992). The array variable, U, stands for the utility of each vehicle. Market shares are found by:

```
market_shares[V] = numerator[V]/denominator
numerator[V] = exp(U[V])
denominator = ARRAYSUM(numerator[*])
```

which is the equivalent of the multinomial logit equation commonly expressed as:

$$MS_v = \frac{e^{U_v}}{\sum_{i=1}^{n} e^{U_i}}$$

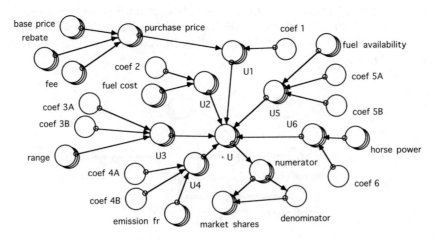

The utility of each vehicle is expressed as a sum of separate utilities based on the six attributes:

```
U[V]  = U1[V]+U2[V]+U3[V]+U4[V]+U5[V]+U6[V]
U1[V] = coef_1*purchase_price[V]/1000
U2[V] = coef_2*fuel_cost[V]
U3[V] = coef_3A*(range[V]/100) + coef_3B*((range[V]/100)^2)
U4[V] = coef_4A*emission_fr[V]+coef_4B*emission_fr[V]^2
U5[V] = coef_5A*fuel_availability[V]+coef_5B*fuel_availability[V]^2
U6[V] = coef_6*horse_power[V]
```

A single coefficient means that utility is a linear function of the attribute. For example, U1[V] is a linear function of the purchase price. Two coefficients indicate that utility is a nonlinear function of the attribute, as is the case for U3, U4, and U5. The researchers received approximately seven hundred responses to a mail-back survey. The respondents described their preferences for vehicles with different prices, fuel costs, ranges, etc. The researchers structured the statistical model to provide the best explanation of the stated preferences. The best fit was found with the following coefficients:

```
coef_1 = -.143
coef_2 = -.175
coef_3A = 2.06
coef_3B = -.303
coef_4A = -3.08
coef_4B = 1.53
coef_5A = 2.24
coef_5B = -.956
coef_6 = .00796
```

Build the discrete-choice model and verify that it gives the market shares shown in table 20.2.

3. **Build and verify the feebate control sector:**

    The final piece of the feebate control model is shown below. The *Balance in Fund* is measured in millions of dollars. The *fees collected, rebates paid,* and *interest earnings* are in millions of dollars per year. The *sales, fee,* and *rebate* are all array variables "ghosted" from other parts of the model. Set the *interest rate* at 6.5 percent/yr and the initial balance at $100 million. Build this model and link it to the models constructed in the previous two exercises. Run the combined model to verify that it gives the results shown in figure 20.2.

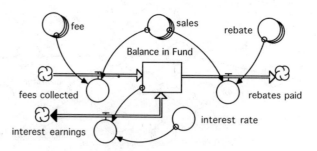

4. **Expand the model to include fuel efficiencies:**

    Expand the model from the previous exercise to represent fuel costs for CVs and EVs as a combination of the cost of fuel at a retail station and the vehicle's efficiency. Assume that the CV gets 27.5 miles/gallon and gasoline costs $1.29 per gallon at retail. The EV gets 1 mile/kwh, and a kwh costs 5.3 cents if purchased at a retail charging station. Run the model to verify that you get the same market shares as in the previous exercise.

5. **Impact of lower electric rates:**

    Use the model from the previous exercise to simulate the change in market shares if the electricity price is cut from 5.3 cents/kwh to 2 cents/kwh. (This low price might apply if the EV owner confines the battery charging to nighttime hours to qualify for "off peak" electric rates.) How many more EVs are in use in the year 2016 with the lower rates?

6. **Impact of a gasoline tax:**

    Use the model from exercise 4 to simulate the change in market shares if the state imposes a $1/gallon tax on gasoline. How many fewer CVs are in use in the year 2016 with the tax?

7. **Gas tax feeds the fund:**

   Suppose the tax revenues generated in the previous exercise were fed into the state fund. This would build the balance in the fund, allowing for larger rebates for cleaner vehicles. Expand the model from exercise 4 to allow for gasoline tax revenues to contribute to the state fund.

8. **Taxbates:**

   We might coin the term "taxbates" to stand for a program to promote the sale of cleaner vehicles through rebates financed by a tax on the fuels used by the dirtier vehicles. Experiment with the model from the previous exercise to find an appropriate combination of a gasoline tax and EV rebates to lower the emissions in the airshed. How do the financial challenges of operating a taxbate program compare with the challenges of a feebate program?

9. **Interface for a taxbates control model:**

   Expand the interface shown in figure 20.1 by adding a new slider to control the size of the gasoline tax to be used in a taxbate program. (You might make room for the new slider by shrinking the scrolling field of instructions.) Be sure to expand the financial information screen (figure 20.2) to report the contributions from the gasoline tax. Add any new screens and buttons that will help others to use your model to explore the dynamics of a taxbate program.

Further Reading

- Several successful flight simulators are described in *The Fifth Discipline* (Senge 1990) and in *The Fifth Discipline Fieldbook* (Senge et al. 1994, 529–560).
- The interfaces in this book have been designed in the "top layer" of the Stella software, but you should know that equally useful interfaces could be constructed with the other stock-and-flow programs or with the Microworlds software explained by Diehl (1994). A review of the software options along with several "off-the-shelf" flight simulators is provided by David Kreutzer in *The Fifth Discipline Fieldbook* (Senge et al. 1994, 536).
- Further reading on alternative vehicles is provided by Sperling (1988, 1995), Gordon (1991), Ford (1996a), and Lovins and Lovins (1995).
- Interesting reading on the early years of electric vehicles is given by Volti (1990). To learn about alternative vehicles available today, you might turn to the ACEEE's *Green Guide to Cars & Trucks* (DeCicco and Thomas 1998).

Chapter 21

Climate Control on Daisyworld

Imagine a planet inhabited by only two plants—white daisies and black daisies. The white daisies have a high albedo. The planet surface covered by white daisies tends to reflect much of the incoming solar luminosity. The black daisies have a low albedo. The surface covered by the black daisies tends to absorb much of the incoming luminosity. Consequently, the mix of daisies on the planet influences the absorbed luminosity and the planet's temperature. Now imagine that the planet's temperature influences the rate of growth of the daisies. If the temperature is close to the optimum value for flower growth, the flowered areas will spread across the planet. But if the temperature is too high or too low, the flowered areas will recede over time.

This imaginary world is called Daisyworld. It was created by Andrew Watson and James Lovelock to illustrate a world with close-coupling between the biota and the global environment. Lovelock used Daisyworld to counter criticism of his Gaia Hypothesis.

The Gaia Hypothesis

Lovelock, an atmospheric chemist, conceived the Gaia Hypothesis in the 1960s while working for NASA on the Viking mission to Mars. He joined a team of scientists designing experiments to detect life on Mars. Some experiments were designed to collect samples from the planet's surface, but Lovelock believed that the key insights were to be found in the Martian atmosphere. He reasoned that the atmosphere of a planet without life would be at equilibrium with the rocks (Levine 1993). He compared the gas composition of the Martian atmosphere with his own calculations for the earth's atmosphere under the assumption that the earth was devoid of life. He found a close correspondence and concluded "that there was no life on Mars. It was as dead as a cinder and no one had to spend huge sums of money to go there to find out" (Levine 1993).

Lovelock continued questioning the conditions necessary to sustain life after his NASA assignment. For example, he wondered how the earth's surface temperature has remained relatively constant over a 3.6-billion-year period in which the heat of the sun has increased by 25 percent (Capra 1996, 102). He also asked himself how the earth manages to maintain atmospheric oxygen concentration at 21 percent, a value that he feels is at that safe upper limit for life (Lovelock 1995, 65). These questions were intriguing to Lovelock, but they did not capture the attention of the scientific community. "Before the advent of the Gaia hypothesis, such questions were rarely asked, and would have been as pointless as asking an anatomist or a biochemist how human temperature is regulated"

(Lovelock 1990, 102). Lovelock believed that these questions would challenge the scientific community to adopt a systems perspective because "such questions about systems cannot be answered from the separated disciplines of biochemistry or biogeochemistry, nor from neo-Darwinist biology. The answer comes from physiology or control theory" (Lovelock 1990, 102).

You can appreciate why Lovelock would be drawn to physiology from the description of homeostasis in chapter 8. Lovelock (1990, 52) was particularly impressed with Walter Cannon's description of the coordinated physiological processes that create homeostasis. Levine reports (1993, 89) that Lovelock's conclusions on the living planet question followed from his thoughts about earth's regulatory features. "They reminded him of Cannon's central principle of physiology: that the living body strives to maintain the constancy of its internal environment." Lovelock believed that "Earth behaves in the same way: its living and non-living parts collaborate to hold temperature and other conditions at reasonably constant levels:

> In effect, the whole Earth follows Cannon's principle—rocks, grass, birds, oceans and atmosphere all pull together, act like a huge organism to regulate conditions. Lovelock thus construed these observations to mean that Earth itself must also live. (Levine 1993, 89)

The idea of a "living organism" needed a name, and Lovelock was reluctant to invent a "barbarous acronym such as Biocybernetic Universal Systems Tendency/Homeostasis." He turned to his neighbor, William Golding, who "recommended that this creature be called Gaia, after the Greek Earth goddess." Lovelock added the term *hypothesis* to emphasize the need for a different way of thinking if proper experiments are to be designed. He argued that Gaia has already proven her worth in scientific circles:

> The Gaia of this book is a hypothesis but, like other useful hypotheses, she has already proved her theoretical value, if not her existence, by giving rise to exper-imental questions and answers which were profitable in themselves. (Lovelock 1995, 10)

But Lovelock views Gaia as more than a scientific paradigm. He looks to Gaia to provide spiritual support as well: "The Gaia hypothesis is for those who like to walk or simply stand and stare, to wonder about the Earth and the life it bears, and to speculate about the consequences of our own presence here" (Levine 1993, 11).

Views of Gaia

Levine (1993) reviews Lovelock's ideas, their reception within the scientific community, and their development into a "spiritual elixir." His review closes with a resounding endorsement:

> [Gaia] is an idea with broad powerful appeal. For scientists, Gaia is a launching platform into discovery and cross-disciplinary thinking. For the disenchanted it is a perch, and for those who have strayed from the fold, a source of renewed spiritual energy. Even secular humanists may feel her draw as a metaphor for transcendence without God. To be sure, few of us who have seriously dealt with the Gaia hypothesis will ever see Earth and life in the same way again. (Levine 1993, 92)

Further readings on this fascinating topic are listed at the close of the chapter. If you read further, you'll learn that one of the main criticisms stems from Lovelock's early view that Gaia sought to create an optimal physical and chemical environment for life. This sounded too much like teleology to mainstream biologists like Dawkins (1986) and Doolittle (1981).

(Teleology is from the Greek word *telos,* or "purpose.") They argued "that nature does not think ahead or behave in any kind of purposeful manner" (Levine 1993, 90). Capra labels these critics as "representatives of mechanistic biology." He believes they "attacked the Gaia hypothesis as teleological because they could not imagine how life on Earth could create and regulate the conditions for its own existence without being conscious and purposeful" (Capra 1996, 107).

Lovelock responded to the teleological criticism with Daisyworld. His assumptions for this simple world were spelled out one by one and converted to a set of differential equations in a paper with Andrew Watson (Watson and Lovelock 1983). The solution to the differential equations revealed the imaginary world to posses homeostatic properties without an explicit, teleological assumption. Watson and Lovelock warned that they were not trying to model the earth, but rather a fictional world that displays a property that they believe is important for the earth. They believed that the sheer complexity of the earth's biota and environment argued for a hypothetical world because "the earth's biota and environment are vastly complex and there is hardly a single aspect of their interaction which can as yet be described with any confidence by a mathematical equation" (Watson and Lovelock 1983, 284). They believed their message would be better understood if they invented "an artificial world, having a very simple biota which is specifically designed to display the characteristic in which we are interested, namely, close coupling of the biota and the global environment."

Purpose of This Chapter

One way to study Daisyworld is to review the differential equations and to verify the equilibrium conditions as reported by Watson and Lovelock (1983). This chapter provides a different perspective. It asks you to "take the controls" of a Daisyworld flight simulator. You will experiment with the simulated world to learn its dynamic response to changes in solar luminosity. You will be asked to design a world that can sustain life in the presence of major changes in solar luminosity. You will also be given the chance to intervene on Daisyworld to see if you can improve the sustainability of life. But first, you need to know the details of Daisyworld.

The Flowered Areas

The planet surface is composed of white daisies, black daisies, and bare ground. The flowers are subject to a constant rate of decay of 30 percent/yr, so you might envision that they live, on average, for 3.3 years. The flowers' growth rate depends on temperature, as shown in figure 21.1. The optimum temperature for growth is 22.5 degrees C. If the local temperature were 22.5 degrees, the growth rate would be 100 percent/yr, so we would expect the flowered area to spread at 70 percent/yr after accounting for decay. Figure 21.1 shows a symmetric relationship. Should the local temperature fall to 5 degrees (or climb to 40 degrees), for example, the growth rate would decline to zero, and we would expect the flowered area to recede at the rate of 30 percent/yr.

The growth rate assumptions in figure 21.1 apply when the flowered areas are close to zero and there is plenty of bare ground available to accommodate new growth. But as the bare ground is used up, the flower growth rate will be reduced to zero. The limitation of bare ground is imposed in a linear manner. For example, with 50 percent of the bare ground available, flower growth rates would be 50 percent below the values shown in figure 21.1. If only 10 percent of the planet is bare ground, the growth rates would be only 10 percent of the values in figure 21.1.

Watson and Lovelock (1983) focus almost exclusively on the equilibrium properties of the world, so it is useful to check the equilibrium conditions. Figure 21.2 uses an equilibrium diagram (see chapter 5) to portray the dynamic equilibrium for a 1,000-acre area. Let's start at the bottom of the diagram, which shows the local temperatures. The temperature near the white daisies is 17.46 degrees; the temperature near the blacks is 27.46 degrees. The indicated growth rates can be found in figure 21.1. The white temperature is located to the cool side of the peak; the indicated growth rate is 92 percent/yr. The black temperature

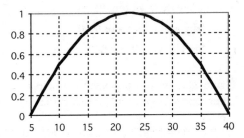

Figure 21.1. Daisy growth rate (fraction/yr) as a function of the temperature (degrees C) near the daisies.

is located to the hot side of the peak, and the indicated growth rate is also 92 percent/yr. The actual growth rates depend on the amount of empty area available to accommodate growth. Figure 21.2 shows that 32.6 percent of the area is available to accommodate new growth, and the growth reduction multiplier is at 0.326. The actual growth rates turn out to be (0.92)*(0.326), or 30 percent/yr. The decay rates are fixed at 30 percent/yr for both black and white daisies, so the flowered areas are in equilibrium. The white flowers occupy 403 acres, and the black flowers occupy 271 acres.

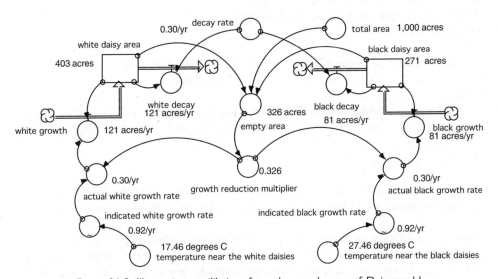

Figure 21.2. Illustrative equilibrium for a thousand acres of Daisyworld.

Temperatures

Now, let's consider Watson and Lovelock's assumptions that lead to the temperatures shown at the bottom of figure 21.2. They begin by assuming that Daisyworld's average temperature depends on the solar luminosity and the fraction of the luminosity that is absorbed. The figure 21.2 results are taken from a simulation with the solar luminosity constant at 1.0. The fraction absorbed depends on the planet's average albedo, which is a weighted average of the albedos from the three surfaces.

white daisy albedo: 0.75

bare ground albedo: 0.50

black daisy albedo: 0.25

Figure 21.2 shows 40 percent of the planet covered by whites daisies, 33 percent by bare ground, and 27 percent by black daisies. The planet's average albedo would be

$$(0.40)*(0.75) + (0.33)*(0.50) + (0.27)*(0.25) = 0.533$$

and we would expect 46.7 percent of the solar luminosity to be absorbed. The absorbed luminosity in this case is 0.467. Watson and Lovelock (1983, 285) set the planet's average temperature as a nonlinear function of the absorbed luminosity. Their fourth equation corresponds to the shape shown in figure 21.3. If absorbed luminosity is 0.467, the planet's average temperature would be 21.8 degrees.

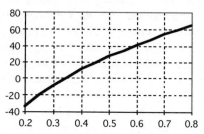

Figure 21.3. Daisyworld average planet temperature (degrees C) as a function of absorbed luminosity.

An important part of Daisyworld is local cooling in the vicinity of the white daisies and local heating in the vicinity of the black daisies. Their seventh equation leads to the following local adjustments:

local heating = 20 degrees * (planet's average albedo – black albedo), or
local heating = 20 degrees * (0.533 – 0.25) = 5.66 degrees

local cooling = 20 degrees * (white albedo – planet's average albedo), or
local cooling = 20 degrees * (0.75 – 0.533) = 4.34 degrees,

and we arrive at the temperatures shown in figure 21.2:

temp near blacks = 21.80 (average) + 5.66 (local heating) = 27.46 degrees
temp near whites = 21.80 (average) – 4.34 (local cooling) = 17.46 degrees.

Notice that the local temperatures differ by 10 degrees. This is no coincidence; the 10-degree difference will appear year after year because of the 20-degree proportionality constant and the fact that the white albedo is 0.5 larger than the black albedo. The 10-degree separation is worth noticing because it helps ensure the relative positions of the local temperatures on the growth curve in figure 21.1. For example, the 17.46-degree white temperature is located on the "cool side" of the optimum, while the 27.46-degree black temperature is located on the "hot side" of the optimum. These locations will prove important when we study the feedback in the system.

Daisyworld as a Feedback System

Causal loop diagrams proved useful in describing the global warming system in chapter 8, and they can help us visualize the keep loops in the Daisyworld system. Let's start with figure 21.4, which shows four loops that influence the spread of white daisies. You'll recognize three of the

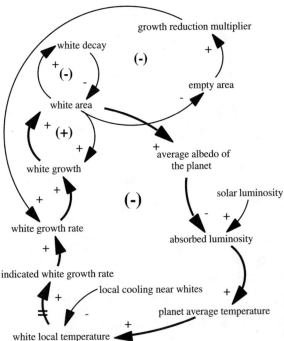

Figure 21.4. Negative feedback controlling temperature and the spread of white daisies.

loops from the simple model of flower growth in chapters 6 and 7 (see figure 7.18). Notice, for example, that the white area is controlled by a positive loop (which gives the flowers the power to grow) and by a negative loop (which drives the area toward zero through decay). You will also recognize the negative loop that acts to slow the rate of growth as the white flowers fill up the space available. And finally, you will recall from chapter 6 that this combination of loops acts to create s-shaped growth in the area of flowers.

You have read in chapter 18 that the appearance of time lags can change a system with s-shaped growth into an oscillatory system. Since lags are part of many natural systems, I have taken the liberty of expanding Watson and Lovelock's original model by introducing a time lag in the link from the local temperature to the indicated growth rate. The // marks the causal arrow at the bottom of figure 21.4 to highlight the location of this time lag in the system. The time lag means that a change in local temperature does not lead instantaneously to growth rate changes. Rather, changes will appear gradually over time as the flowers become accustomed to the new temperatures.

Figure 21.4 uses darker arrows to highlight a fourth loop acting through the average albedo and average planet temperature. Let's trace the highlighted loop starting with a possible increase in the area covered by white daisies. An increase in the white area would increase the average albedo, reduce the absorbed luminosity, and reduce the planet's average temperature. A reduction in the average temperature lowers the temperature near the white daisies, moving the local temperature further to the cool side of the optimum. This lowers the indicated growth rate, thereby reducing the growth of white daisies. The highlighted loop provides negative feedback, but notice that Watson and Lovelock do not impose an explicit goal. For example, they do not include an input variable similar to the target temperature in a thermostat-controlled cooling system.

Figure 21.5 expands the causal loop diagram by adding the black daisies to the system. The black daisies are controlled by the same combination of four feedback loops. There is a

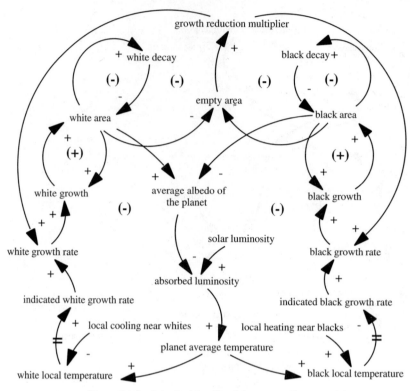

Figure 21.5. Principal feedback loops on Daisyworld.

positive feedback loop involving the growth of the area and a negative loop involving the decay of the area. The black flowers are also influenced by a negative feedback loop involving the amount of empty area remaining. This loop couples the black and white flowers, as they must compete for space on the planet. Growth in either flowered area reduces the empty space that both flowers require for growth in the future.

The fourth loop on the black side of the diagram provides additional negative feedback working through the planet's average temperature. Let's trace this loop by starting with a possible increase in the black area. An increase in the black area would reduce the average albedo, increase the absorbed luminosity, and increase the planet's average temperature. An increase in the average temperature increases the temperature near the black daisies, moving the local temperature further to the hot side of the optimum. This lowers the indicated growth rate, thereby reducing the growth of black daisies. This loop is similar to the loop highlighted in figure 21.4. It adds negative feedback, but it does not impose an explicit goal on the system.

The Daisyworld Flight Simulator

Figure 21.6 shows the first screen to appear when you download and open the flight simulator. The instructions appear in the scrolling field. They set the context for your experiments with the model. You are to learn if Daisyworld can be designed to sustain life in the face of massive uncertainties in solar luminosity. You may imagine that scientists expect major changes in the Daisyworld sun, and they have described four scenarios for the future:

1. No Crisis Scenario: luminosity remains constant at 1.0
2. Heat Shock Scenario: luminosity jumps to 1.25 in the year 2010

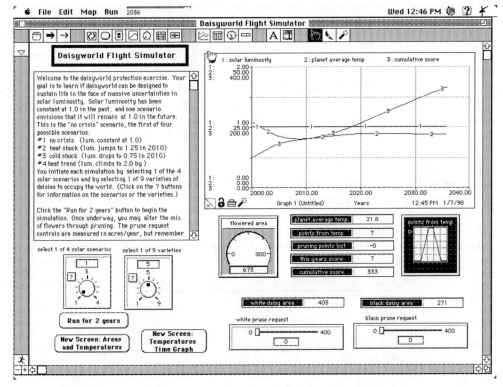

Figure 21.6. Flight simulator results near the end of a simulation with the first solar scenario and the fifth variety of flowers. (You can download the flight simulator from the home page. It uses Stella, ver. 5.0.)

3. Cold Shock Scenario: luminosity drops to 0.75 in the year 2010
4. Heat Trend Scenario: luminosity climbs from 1 to 2 by the year 2030

   The scientists cannot predict the sun's behavior in advance, but they feel that these four scenarios encompass the range of uncertainty. Now they turn to you to answer a difficult question: Does the solar uncertainty preclude the possibility of sustained life on Daisyworld? This is the question that you can study through experiments with the flight simulator. You begin by selecting one of the four scenarios. (Notice in figure 21.6 that the "no crisis" scenario has been selected, so the solar luminosity remains constant at 1.0 in the time graph.)

   Watson and Lovelock's Daisyworld has only one variety of daisies, but you will be given the opportunity to experiment with nine varieties. Your choices are listed in table 21.1 in groups of three:

1. White and Black: The first three varieties have distinctive colors, causing large differences in albedos. The white daisies are extremely white; they reflect 90 percent of the incoming luminosity. The black daisies are extremely dark; they reflect only 10 percent.

2. Light and Dark: The next three varieties possess the albedos used by Watson and Lovelock. The lights reflect 75 percent of the luminosity, while the darks reflect 25 percent.

3. Salt and Pepper: You may think of the final three varieties as gray daisies whose albedos are close to 50 percent, the value assigned to bare ground. Imagine the salts as "salted"

with white coloring, enough to increase their albedo to 0.60. The peppered daisies are peppered with black coloring, enough to reduce their albedo to 40 percent.

Each group is available with three different values of the optimum temperature. The first grows best at 20 degrees, so the optimum temperature is 2.5 degrees to the left of the peak in figure 21.1. The entire growth curve is shifted 2.5 degrees to the left. The second choice grows best at 22.5 degrees, so the growth rates are portrayed in figure 21.1. The third choice grows best at 25 degrees; the entire growth curve is shifted 2.5 degrees to the right.

The labels in table 21.1 help us remember the coloring of the flowers, but the flight simulator will adhere to the "black and white" terminology used by Watson and Lovelock (1983, 285). In figure 21.6, for example, the fifth variety of daisies has been selected. These are the daisies used by Watson and Lovelock; they are "light and dark" in color, but the simulated results will be reported as if they are white and black. Notice that the figure 21.6 simulation has reached equilibrium by the 36th year, so we should expect to see the flight simulator deliver the equilibrium results discussed previously. The numeric displays in figure 21.6 confirm our expectation: the whites occupy 403 acres and the blacks occupy 271 acres.

Table 21.1. Nine varieties of flowers for Daisyworld.

Labels	Variety	Black albedo	White albedo	Optimum temperature
	1	0.10	0.90	20.0
White & Black	2	0.10	0.90	22.5
	3	0.10	0.90	25.0
	4	0.25	0.75	20.0
Light & Dark	5	0.25	0.75	22.5
	6	0.25	0.75	25.0
	7	0.40	0.60	20.0
Salt & Pepper	8	0.40	0.60	22.5
	9	0.40	0.60	25.0

Keeping Score on Daisyworld

With nine different varieties and four different solar scenarios, it won't take long before your experiments with the flight simulator become overwhelming. It will be important to stay focused on the original question: Can Daisyworld be designed to sustain life? One way to maintain focus is to rely on the "scorekeeper." For purposes of keeping score, we will assume that Daisyworld is under consideration for human habitation, and that humans prefer to see the planet's average temperature remain close to 25 degrees C. The scorekeeper assigns 10 points/yr if the average temperature is controlled to within plus or minus 2 degrees from the 25-degree target, as shown in figure 21.7.

If you find a way to control the temperature close to 25 degrees for the entire simulation, you would earn 10 points/yr. If the temperature falls below 15 degrees or climbs above 35 degrees, you lose 10 points/yr. Your score is arbitrarily initialized at 100 points at the start of the simulation. If you manage to earn 10 points/yr for the entire simulation, your cumulative score would climb to 500 points, the maximum possible score.

The scorekeeper information is visible in the screen capture shown in the previous figure. Notice that the graph in figure 21.7 appears as an active icon (points from temp) on the right side of the main screen. When the scores change over time, you will notice the pointer moving along the vertical scale to remind you of the relative position. The planet's average temperature is 21.8 degrees in figure 21.6, so the scorekeeper grants 7 points/yr. The cumulative score is shown at 333 points by the year 2036. Since the system is in equilibrium, you would expect the temperature to remain at 21.8 degrees for the final 4 years. This means that you will earn 7 points/yr for another 4 years, so the final score will turn out to be 361 points. This is a good score (since the most you can earn is 500 points). Of course, you know that the "no crisis" scenario is not likely to be the most challenging of the four scenarios.

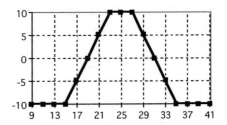

Figure 21.7. Annual points earned based on Daisyworld's average temperature (degrees C).

The Heat Shock Scenario

Figure 21.8 shows the flight simulator part way through a simulation with the heat shock scenario. As before, the fifth variety has been selected so that the results are comparable to Watson and Lovelock's Daisyworld. The screen capture shows the year 2012, just 2 years after the solar luminosity has jumped from 1.0 to 1.25. The planet's average temperature has jumped to 36.2 degrees, and the "points from temperature" has dropped to −10 points/year. The scorekeeper is recording negative annual scores, and the cumulative score has peaked and turned downward.

At this point, you might decide to ride out the heat shock scenario and hope that the situation will improve. Or you might intervene by pruning some of the flowers. The temperatures in figure 21.8 are uncomfortably hot, so you might consider reducing the black daisies, which are responsible for much of the absorbed luminosity. This may be done by submitting a black pruning request with the control in the lower right corner of the main screen. But pruning is not considered a free activity, and the scorekeeper deducts 10 points/year for any pruning request of 200 acres/yr. Higher pruning requests cost proportionately more; lower pruning requests cost proportionately less.

The Daisyworld Assignment

Practice with the flight simulator to learn about the dynamics of Daisyworld. Your goal is to develop a strategy that will provide the greatest prospects for sustaining life on the planet. Part of your strategy is to choose the best variety. Once a variety has been selected, there is no looking back—you are stuck with that variety no matter what happens later in the simulation. Don't forget that we cannot predict the future of the Daisyworld sun, so any of the four scenarios is possible. Your assignment is to learn if a particular variety offers the best prospects for life in the face of multiple scenarios.

Once the simulation is underway, you are given wide latitude to intervene through pruning. You may submit a pruning request for either the blacks or the whites (or both). The only constraint is that your request applies for 2 years, and there is a cost associated with pruning. Experiment to learn if pruning can improve the prospects for life (as measured by the cumulative score).

Describe your strategy in a Daisyworld report. (The strategy will be a combination of a recommended variety at the start of the simulation and a set of decision rules for pruning once the simulation begins.) Explain whether your strategy makes it possible to sustain com-

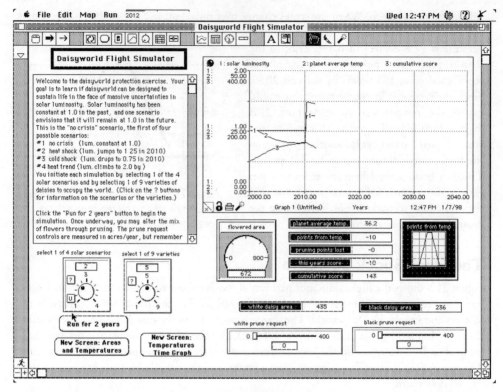

Figure 21.8. Results from 12 years of a simulation with the second solar scenario and the fifth variety of flowers.

fortable temperatures in the face of the massive uncertainly in solar luminosity. We know from figure 21.6 that sustained life is possible in the first scenario; your report should explain whether life is possible in each of the other scenarios. Explain whether one particular variety offers the best prospects for sustaining life. If one variety stands out from the rest, explain the fundamental mechanisms that allow it to outperform the other varieties. (A "fundamental" explanation goes beyond a recitation of your highest scores.) Finally, explain whether pruning is useful to enhance the simulated performance.

Exercises

The best way to "experience" the dynamics of Daisyworld is to experiment with the flight simulator, as described previously. The following exercises lead you in a different direction. You begin by downloading the model and checking the equation-by-equation documentation to satisfy yourself that the model is faithful to Watson and Lovelock (1983), hereafter called W&L. Then turn to the eight exercises to test and expand the model. Additional exercises can be found on the home page.

1. **Span of control:**

   Use the model to verify that the span of control matches the original Daisyworld (W&L, 287) by selecting variety #5 and scenario #2. Then experiment with heat shocks of higher and higher luminosities. How high can the solar luminosity become before the planet loses its ability to maintain a comfortable temperature?

Then use the model to verify the span of control for lower luminosity (W&L, 287) by selecting variety #5 and scenario #3. Experiment with cold shocks of lower and lower luminosities. How low can the solar luminosity become before the planet loses its ability to maintain a comfortable temperature?

2. **Sensitivity to the initial areas:**

Perform a sensitivity test with three simulations similar to exercise #1 to learn the importance of the initial conditions:

1st run: white area = 250, black area = 250

2nd run: white area = 500, black area = 100

3rd run: white area = 100, black area = 500

Does the temperature response to the solar heat shock depend on the initial areas? Does the planet's temperature at the end of the simulation depend on the initial areas?

3. **Sensitivity to the lag time:**

Recall that the model includes a first-order lag between the change in the local temperatures and the subsequent change in the flower growth rates. The length of the lag time is set at 4 years, somewhat longer than the 3.3-year life of a daisy. These relative values suggest that a little more than one generation of flowers must experience the new temperatures before the majority of change in their growth rate appears. Now, to match the original model by W&L, you would eliminate this lag. This may be done by setting the binary variable (*lag time?*) to zero. Also, you may leave *lag time?* at 1 and experiment with changes in the length of the lag time.

Test the importance of the lag time by simulating the planet's average temperature in three simulations with solar scenario #2 and variety #5. Set the lag time to 2 years in one simulation and 4 years in the second; eliminate the lag in the third simulation. Do your simulations show important differences in the model's response to the heat shock scenario?

4. **Additional loops from local cooling and heating:**

The local cooling and local heating are shown in figure 21.5, as if these variables are exogenous inputs to Daisyworld, but these local effects depend on the planet's average albedo. Expand the causal loop diagram to represent the local effects as endogenous variables. Do you see any new loops? Do you think they act to stabilize the system?

5. **Test the importance of the "local effects" loops:**

To test the importance of the loops identified in the previous exercise, change the model to eliminate the link between the planet's average albedo and the local heating and cooling. Simply set the local heating effect to +5 degrees and the local cooling effect to –5 degrees. Run the new model with variety #5 and scenario #2 and compare the response to the original model. Did the removal of the local effects loops make the system more stable or less stable?

6. **Additional loops from your pruning policy:**

Think about your pruning decisions when you used the simulator. Can you describe "decision rules" that you followed to control the timing and magnitude of pruning? These rules are sometimes called a "policy." Expand the causal loop diagram in figure

21.5 to include your pruning policy. (Be sure to mark any delays in the diagram with a //.) Does your policy introduce new feedback into the system?

7. **Kirchner's pathological daisies:**

Kirchner (1989) provides a detailed and informative critique of the Gaia Hypothesis in general and the Daisyworld model in particular. Review his example of a "pathological daisyworld" in which the optimum temperature for the black daisies is 15 degrees higher than the optimum temperature for the white daisies. Alter the Daisyworld model to replace the original daisies with Kirchner's daisies. Simulate the new model to test its performance over time. Does this "pathological" world behave as Kirchner suggests?

8. **Competition between Kirchner's daisies and Lovelock's daisies:**

Expand Daisyworld to be home for two groups of daisies. The first group is Lovelock's daisies; the second group is Kirchner's "pathological" daisies. You will now have four stocks, which you may initialize as follows:

Kirchner's whites: 200 acres

Kirchner's blacks: 200 acres

Lovelock's whites: 200 acres

Lovelock's blacks: 200 acres

Simulate the model over time with solar luminosity constant at 1.0. What kind of world emerges at the end of the simulation? Do you see a world with homeostatic temperature control dominated by Lovelock's daisies? Or do you see a barren, lifeless planet with temperatures that vary entirely with the amount of incoming solar luminosity? Now repeat the test with changes in the solar luminosity in the year 2010.

Further Readings

- To form your own view of Gaia, read Lovelock's work (1988, 1990, 1991, 1995) and his work with Lynn Margulis (Lovelock and Margulis 1974; Margulis and Lovelock 1989).
- It is also useful to read his critics (Dawkins 1986; Doolittle 1981; Kirchner 1989) and the various interpretations of the Gaia controversy (Capra 1996; Joseph 1990; Levine 1993).

PART VI

CONCLUSIONS

Chapter 22

Validation

You have studied dozens of models in this book, and you have probably wondered what can be done to validate one of the models. Also, you might have asked yourself if you can prove one of the models to be valid. This chapter discusses the question of model validation in a pragmatic manner. It summarizes different points of view on validation, and it concludes with concrete tests to build confidence in a model.

A Validation Scene

Imagine that you and your colleagues have just constructed a computer model to improve your understanding of a dynamic problem within your organization. You have followed the steps of modeling in chapter 15, and you are pleased that the model generates the dynamic behavior specified as the reference mode at the start of your project. You feel that the stock-and-flow structure is reasonable, and that the parameter values are reasonable as well. You have drawn causal loop diagrams, and the combination of feedback loops helps you appreciate the reasons for the dynamic behavior. Finally, and most important, you have used the model to simulate policies that might be implemented by your organization. The simulations suggest that the policies could lead to improved behavior, so you are eager to spread this encouraging news within the organization.

Fortunately, your timing couldn't be better. The organization has just convened an executive committee to examine the very dynamic problem you have been studying. The committee is composed of top leaders from all corners of the organization, and it has recruited an excellent staff with expertise in computers and modeling. The committee is open to ideas from throughout the organization, so they give you an opportunity to present your results. You and your colleagues show them everything—stocks and flows, equations, simulation results, causal loop diagrams. You conclude the presentation with the policy simulations that you feel deserve further investigation.

The committee members are impressed by your use of computers and models. They assure you that the bits and pieces of your model agree with their own views. They are especially impressed by the way the bits and pieces are assembled to provide a holistic perspective on the organization. They congratulate you for an illuminating presentation. Then they turn the next stage of the meeting over to the chief of staff.

The chief of staff is an expert in computers with a long history of success implementing computerized systems within the organization. He opens his portion of the meeting with a question: *Can you prove the model is valid?*

You are not sure how to respond because you told the committee everything in your opening presentation. But you muster a response that highlights the reasonableness of the stock-and-flow structure and the relative accuracy of the parameter values. You conclude by emphasizing the close correspondence between the simulation results and the organization's dynamic problem. As you sit down, you are left with the unsettled feeling that your description does not constitute "proof" that the model is valid.

The chief of staff agrees. He tells the committee that your work is certainly interesting, but that you have failed to prove the model is valid. He advises the committee that it would be dangerous to base important policy changes on an unproven model. The committee is inclined to agree with the chief of staff, given his expertise in computers. They adjourn the meeting by repeating their interest in your approach, and they invite you to return for another meeting once you are able to prove the model is valid.

Asking the Right Question

The preceding scene is all too common in the real world of computer modeling. The use of formal mathematical methods, sophisticated software, and high-powered computers seems to leave an impression that computer models will be constructed as perfect replicas of the system under study. But computer models are the same as any model. By design, models are simplifications of the system under study. To better understand how the system works, we build a simplified picture of the system. The key to the model's usefulness is leaving out the unimportant factors and capturing the interactions among the important factors. Once a factor is left out, the model is automatically subject to the criticism that it is invalid.

Such criticism is pointless. It reveals that the critic does not understand the nature of modeling. The important question is not "Is the model valid?" but "Is the model useful?" This is a much more pragmatic question, which may be addressed in a concrete manner. We would begin by specifying the purpose of the model and the alternative methods of achieving that purpose. Then we ask ourselves about procedures for building confidence in the model.

Greenberger, Crenson, and Crissey's (1976) description of the use of *Models in the Policy Process* is particularly instructive here. They reviewed several modeling methodologies that have been used to influence public policy making. (The methodologies include system dynamics, econometrics, and linear programming, and the examples range from highly visible budget battles between Congress and the White House to decisions on fire station locations in New York City.) The review led them to conclude:

> There is no uniform procedure for validation. No model has ever been or ever will be thoroughly validated. Since, by design, models are all simplifications of the reference system, they are never entirely valid in the sense of being fully supported by objective truth. "Useful," "illuminating," "convincing," or "inspiring confidence" are more apt descriptors applying to models than "valid." (p. 70)

Greenberger et al. argue that one can bolster confidence in a model by having it reproduce past behavior of the reference system, exploring its response to perturbations, critically examining the premises and theories on which it is based, and finally, putting it to use. Along the way, we should remember that "such tests are aimed more at invalidating than validating the model." Each new test may "only reveal the presence (not the total absence) of errors. However convincing a model, there is always a chance that its next test or use will turn up a serious shortcoming." Greenberger et al.'s review focused on public sector models, but their line of reasoning applies to models of biological systems as well. Levins outlines a general strategy for model building in population biology and concludes with the observation that:

all models leave out a lot and are in that sense false, incomplete, inadequate. The validation of a model is not that it is "true" but that it generates good testable hypotheses relevant to important problems. A model may be discarded in favor of a more powerful one, but it usually is simply outgrown when the live issues are not any longer those for which it was designed. (Levins 1966, 430)

Although Greenberger et al. and Levins may agree on the meaning of the term *validation,* there is plenty of room for confusion. Webster's defines *valid* as "sound, just, well founded," and the verb *validate* means to "substantiate." These definitions are well aligned with Greenberger et al.'s and Levins's views. But Webster's also lists definitions with a legal or procedural meaning, as in whether one has a "valid contract" or a "valid passport." With these definitions, "validate" refers to the act of proving a contract is legally binding or verifying that a passport was issued properly. These legal definitions may be what some people have in mind when they ask if a model has been validated.

Greenberger et al. encourage us to think of validation differently. They argue that "validation is not a general seal of approval" but a more general "indication of a level of confidence in the model's behavior under limited conditions and for a specific purpose." They suggest that "data provide a tangible link between a model and its reference system, and a means for gaining confidence in the model and its results." They believe that a "model that closely reproduces data on observed past behavior of the reference system gains credibility and wins the acceptance and trust of potential users."

Concrete Tests to Build Confidence

Matching historical behavior is only one of several tests that can be used to build confidence in a model. Researchers have described a wide assortment of useful tests (Forrester and Senge 1980; Richardson and Pugh 1981; Kitching 1983). From my own experiences, five tests stand out as deserving special attention:

- verification
- face validity
- historical behavior
- extreme behavior
- detailed model check

Verification

A model may be "verified" when it is run in an independent manner (typically by a different group on a different computer) to learn if the results match the published results. The goal is simply to learn if the computer model "runs as intended" (House and McLeod 1977, p. 66). Greenberger, Crenson, and Crissey (1976, 70) describe verification as a "test of whether the model has been synthesized exactly as intended. Verification of a model indicates that it has been faithful to its conception, irrespective of whether or not it and its conception are valid." Kitching (1983, 42) warns that verification may sound tautological but is "nevertheless a necessary check that the mechanisms of the model are in fact doing what the modeler thinks they are doing."

You have verified many of the models in this book as part of the student exercises. In each case, your goal was to demonstrate that the model behaves as published, regardless of whether you agreed with the model. Verification is essential if the field of modeling is to build from past models. Think of model verification in the same way a scientist thinks of experimental verification. The first step in a serious scientific endeavor is to verify the previously published results.

Although verification seems like an obvious test, you should realize that verifying models in the "real world" can often turn out to be exceedingly difficult. The problem may arise from the sheer size of the model. In some models, for example, the challenge of checking the model may increase "in relation to some power of the number of computer instructions" (House and McLeod 1977, 66). But size is not the only obstacle. You may have trouble verifying a model because of inadequate documentation or the commercial or proprietary interests of the developers. If you encounter such problems, you may be better off discarding the model from further consideration.

Face Validity

The "face validity" test is a common sense test. You simply ask yourself if the model structure and parameters make sense. This test relies on your understanding of the system to judge the structure (the combination of stocks and flows). You would also rely on your common sense to check the parameter values. If you see flows pointed in the wrong direction, or if you see negative values of a parameter that must be positive, you know there is a fundamental problem with the model. You have performed the face validity test with most of the models in the book. It was the natural thing to do, so you might be wondering why we need to invent a title for something that happened automatically in each new chapter.

A face validity test is important to remember as you move from the classroom into a large organization. An unfortunate aspect of models used in large organizations is the difficulty in checking their face validity. Many models grow to become so complex that one cannot "see inside" to perform this simple test. Such models are sometimes called black boxes. If you encounter a black box model, you may be better off discarding the model from further consideration.

Historical Behavior

One of the most common and important tests is to set the inputs to the model at their historical values and see if the outputs match history. Indeed, this test is usually what people automatically think of when discussing model validation. Kitching (1983, 43) describes several variations in the historical behavior test for ecological systems. Model parameters might be based on data from one ecological site, and the model could be simulated to learn if the population projections match data from a different site. Or a model might be estimated from data over one time period and the simulated population compared with data from a later time period.

You have seen several examples of the historical behavior test in this book. For example, the Mono Lake model was checked to learn if it showed the gradual decline in lake elevation if exports were maintained at the historical values. In the Kaibab example, you saw that the model reproduced the rapid growth and overshoot that is believed to have occurred on the Kaibab plateau in the 1920s. And in chapter 15, you read about the value of repeated comparison of model results with historical information on cocaine use.

The historical behavior test is especially informative if the model is designed with a large number of endogenous variables and only a limited number of exogenous inputs. (In other words, the bull's-eye diagram would show most of the variables in the inner circle.) Most of the models in this book fall into this category because they have been constructed from a system dynamics perspective, which encourages us to simulate the feedback loops in the system. These models tend to produce a dynamic pattern "on their own." (Examples include the overshoot in chapter 15 and the oscillations in chapters 18 and 19.) An internally generated pattern that matches history is one of the more important tests of any model.

You should be aware that not all models adopt the system dynamics emphasis on feedback. Many models are constructed with little attention to the feedback loop structure of the system, and, in some cases, the models may not contain a single feedback loop. In this extreme situation, each and every variable is exogenous, and there are no variables at the center of the bull's-eye diagram. For this category of models, the historical behavior test is meaningless. If you arrange for all the inputs to follow historical trends, it should be obvious that the "outputs" will match history as well.

Extreme Behavior

~~One of the most revealing tests is to make a major change in model parameters and see if the model's response is plausible.~~ In chapter 16, for example, we subjected the Kaibab model to an extreme combination of parameter changes just to see if the model's response was plausible. Extreme behavior testing may be facilitated by the software, as in the use of "reality checks" in the Vensim software (see appendix E). Also, a model is automatically placed under "extreme" conditions if you subject it to the comprehensive sensitivity analysis described in appendix J. When two or three parameters take on unusually low values, for example, the model may be placed in an unexpected situation. If the model is structurally flawed, the flaws will probably be revealed by a simulation with clearly spurious behavior.

You should not be surprised if this particular test is not conducted by modeling teams in large organizations. Their reluctance may seem reasonable—why subject a model to extreme conditions when it was probably designed to simulate "most likely conditions"? Their reluctance might also stem from the fact that many models are likely to exhibit spurious behavior when subjected to major changes. (For example, water in a lake may go negative or the sum of market shares might exceed 100 percent.) These problems typically arise from a variety of features that improve the cosmetic appearance of the model under "most likely conditions." If the cosmetic features are not structurally sound, the model is likely to exhibit spurious behavior under extreme conditions.

Detailed Model Check

If you are working on an important topic within a large organization, it is quite possible that there are several models describing different aspects of the system. In some cases, the other models may provide a more detailed and accurate representation of some aspect of the system. If this is true, you should take advantage of these models to provide benchmark simulations that may be used to check your own model. An illustrative example is given in the model of nitrogen accumulation in a catchment in appendix I. The simple model is checked against a detailed model that accounts for the spread of nitrogen through the spatial dimensions. You will also read in appendix I that the benchmarking approach proved useful in a system dynamics model of the Snake River. Finally, you will read in the next chapter that detailed model checks have been useful in bolstering confidence in system dynamics models of the electric power industry.

The Ultimate Test of Model Usefulness

Most models are designed to be used by their developer, and the model is discarded after the findings have been reported. They are like paper plates; use them once and throw them away. But some models are constructed to serve a longer-lasting need within an organization. This situation often occurs when the organization faces similar questions year after year. In those circumstances, a large-scale modeling effort may be justified to address the reoccurring questions in a sustained manner.

When organizing a sustained effort, validation is best viewed as a continuous, sometimes arduous process of building confidence in the model. Richardson and Pugh's (1981, 311) observations are particularly relevant to large-scale efforts. They advise us not to think of validation as a "one time process that takes place after a model is built and before it is used for policy analysis," and they warn us that "there is a tendency to think of validation as a process similar to warding off measles: a model, susceptible to contagious criticism, gets validated and becomes immune to further attack."

The ultimate test of model usefulness is whether the model is actually put to use to help your organization improve. Forrester (1961, 115) explains that "the ultimate test is whether or not better systems result from investigations based on model experimentation," and Richardson and Pugh (1981, 313) argue that "the ultimate test of a policy-oriented model would be whether policies implemented in the real system consistently produce the results predicted by the model." The next chapter describes system dynamics models that have met this ultimate test.

Further Reading

- Excellent descriptions of model testing are given in Forrester's (1961) original text, *Industrial Dynamics;* in Richardson and Pugh's (1985) *Introduction to System Dynamics Modeling with Dynamo;* in Forrester and Senge's (1980) article on confidence building; and in Barlas's (1996) article on formalizing the process of model testing.
- The previous readings focus on system dynamics models, but you will discover that similar tests are useful for a wide variety of models. For example, many of the same tests appear in the fields of physiology (Riggs 1963) and ecology (Kitching 1983).
- If you have studied the philosophy of science, you'll appreciate Barlas and Carpenter's (1990) description of two opposing views on model validity. The first school is composed of the "traditional reductionist/logical positivist" philosophies, which hold that a model can be either "correct," or "incorrect." "Once the model confronts the empirical facts, its truth or falsehood would be automatically revealed" (Barlas 1996, 187). The opposing school is composed of the "relativist, functional, holistic" philosophies of science, which hold that models "are not true or false, but lie on a continuum of usefulness."
- And if you've studied economics, you'll appreciate Radzicki's (1990) description of neoclassical and institutional economics and the accounts of system dynamics and econometrics by Greenberger, Crenson, and Crissey (1976) and by Meadows and Robinson (1985). You'll discover that practitioners in econometric modeling and system dynamics modeling do not necessarily agree on the best tests for building confidence in a model.

Chapter 23

•••

Lessons from the
Electric Power Industry

You have reached the final chapter of the book, and you see the world differently than when you began. You can now visualize the stocks, flows, and feedbacks in the systems that are important to you and your organization. You can now visualize how the system structure causes its dynamic behavior. And, finally, you have learned how to build computer models to test and communicate your new theories of how systems change over time. At this point, you are probably wondering how to make the best use of this new knowledge within your organization.

This chapter tells a story of how system dynamics practitioners put their knowledge to work in the electric power industry. Electric power is a massive industry with major impacts on the environment; it is also a capital intensive industry with a rich tradition of long-range planning. System dynamics has been applied extensively in this industry, and there is an impressive record of implementation. This chapter interprets the large body of work to reveal how system dynamics practitioners contributed a unique perspective on the power industry. You will learn that their contribution stems from an ability to "see the feedback" in the system. Their story will help you plan the best use of your new knowledge in your own organization.

Background on Electric Power in the United States

Figure 23.1 shows a historical time line starting with the birth of the industry in 1882 and concluding with the growing interest in deregulation in the 1990s (Ford 1997). This chapter provides a short review, culminating with the shift to small scale in the 1980s.

The power industry was "born" with great publicity at 3 P.M. on September 4, 1882. This is the moment when the "jumbo generator" at the Pearl Street Station in New York City began to spin. The electricity was transmitted to the Wall Street office of J.P. Morgan and to the editorial room of the *New York Times*. Within the decade, the industry was embroiled in a debate over electric transmission. The debate is sometimes called the AC/DC debate. In technical terms it was a debate over AC (alternating current) transmission versus DC (direct current) transmission. In personal terms, it was a debate between the giants of the industry. George Westinghouse favored AC; Thomas Edison favored DC. And in organizational terms, it was a debate over the fundamental shape of the industry. DC transmission relied on low-voltage power lines running short distances from the generating station to the consumer. AC transmission required transformers to "step up" the voltage for transmission over longer-

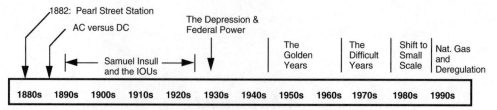

Figure 23.1. History of electric power in the United States.

distance lines. The DC proponents envisioned an industry with many small power generators that could be mass-produced and sold at a substantial profit to factories and office buildings. The AC proponents saw an industry with larger, more efficient power plants interconnected with a large number of customers. Bigger power stations could be designed to convert fuel into electricity in a more efficient manner, especially if they served a larger number of customers (with diversity in their hour-by-hour demands for power). The vision of larger power stations won out, and Edison's role in the power industry began to fade.

The most important individual to shape the American power industry is Samuel Insull, an Englishman who immigrated to America in 1881 to serve as Edison's personal secretary. Insull struck out on his own in 1892. He took the controls of the Chicago Electric Company, convinced that the path to large profits was through the sale of electricity (not necessarily the sale of electrical equipment). By 1907, Insull was a millionaire and the ruler of Chicago's electricity monopoly. By 1911, his engineers had created the world's largest power station; and by 1912, his "empire" encompassed four hundred communities throughout thirteen states.

One threat to Insull's expansion was public power. Some towns and cities believed that electric power is a basic, public service. They took over the electric power facilities and financed their subsequent expansion through the sale of public bonds. Fearing the encroachment of public power, Insull devised a plan to give the public limited control over private power. Each state would form a public utility commission to be staffed by professionals with knowledge of the industry. He argued that privately owned utility companies should continue to enjoy monopoly privilege in their service territories so that the company engineers could pursue economies of scale. Possible abuses of monopoly privilege would be controlled by the state commissions. Electricity prices were to be fixed by the state commissions to allow the power company to recover its costs and to earn a reasonable profit. Utilities, for their part, would commit themselves to building the power stations needed to serve the customers within their service territory.

The Golden Years

Insull's plan allowed privately owned power companies to grow and flourish. The private companies became known as IOUs, or investor-owned utilities. Today, the IOUs account for roughly 80 percent of electric power in the United States, a business with close to $1 trillion in assets (EPRI 1996). Their biggest challenge was to build the new power plants needed in a rapidly growing industry. The demand for electric energy grew at around 7 percent/year, doubling the need for electricity every decade. To keep pace, the IOUs turned to larger and larger power stations. Company engineers were successful in designing bigger and better power stations during the "golden years" of the 1940s, 1950s, and 1960s. Each new wave of power stations allowed the retirement of older, less efficient power stations. Regulatory commissions found themselves in an enviable position because electric rates were always sufficient. That is, the current rates, multiplied by current electricity sales, always generated the necessary revenues to pay this year's bills and finance next year's construction. Electric rates

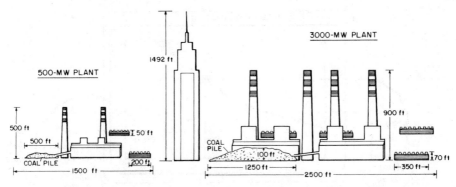

Figure 23.2. Drawing of large and small power plants (Ford 1980).

remained relatively constant (in nominal dollars) over many decades as company engineers succeeded with bigger and better power plants. By the end of the golden years, power plants were coming on line at the immense size of 3,000 MW shown in figure 23.2.

The Difficult Years

The golden years came to an end in the 1970s. Industry engineers could no longer deliver important reductions in capital with larger scale, and the larger stations were turning out to be less reliable (Ford 1980). The Arab oil embargo of 1973 signaled the beginning of the energy crisis, and the 1970s witnessed two major increases in oil prices. Higher oil prices translated into higher prices for coal and natural gas, so utility fuel payments rose dramatically. But the biggest problem was the "double-digit" inflation, and utilities faced even higher escalation in construction labor costs. Power plants were taking much longer to build, and their costs were much higher than in the golden years. Utilities found themselves with declining internal funds to help pay for construction. When they turned to Wall Street, they were confronted by unusually high costs of capital. The financial problems were painfully evident from the following headlines in the business press:

Utilities: Weak Point in the Energy Future

Utilities Need Help—Now!

Con Edison: Archetype of the Ailing Utility

Electric Industry Cutback Could Result in Blackouts

Faced with serious financial problems, some utility companies cut back on the construction of new power stations thought to be needed to serve future demand. Industry experts feared that the long, successful history of "keeping the lights on" was about to be broken.

Figures 23.3 and 23.4 use stock-and-flow diagrams to show the change in the financial situation during the 1970s. Let's begin with figure 23.3. It shows numerical values representative of the golden years. The input variable is the *capacity needed now*, which is set at 10 GW to begin the illustration. The utility has 10 GW of *installed capacity* and another 4 GW of *capacity under construction*. When the construction lead time was 5 years, the utility planners looked 5 years into the future to obtain the *forecast of future need*. Figure 23.3 shows this forecast at 14 GW based on the 7 percent annual growth that was common in the golden years. Utilities were able to maintain sufficient *capacity under construction* during the golden years, so figure 23.3 shows 4 GW under construction. One indicator of the financial challenge is to compare the *construction work in progress* with the book *assets* of the company. In the figure 23.3 example, the utility would face the challenge of financing $3 billion worth of construc-

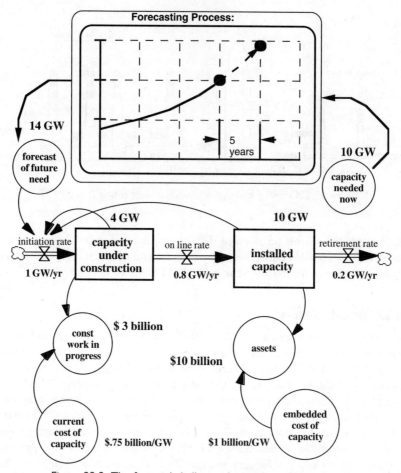

Figure 23.3. The financial challenge during the golden years.

tion from a $10 billion base. This is a substantial challenge, but utilities were able to meet this challenge throughout the golden years.

Figure 23.4 shows the same stock-and-flow structure but a different set of numbers. The starting point is the same as before: a $10 billion company has 10 GW of capacity, which is exactly the amount needed to meet current needs. But the projection for the future is quite different. First, the lead time is much longer. By the 1970s, lead times for new coal and nuclear power plants could stretch out to 10 or 15 years. Figure 23.4 shows a 10-year lead time. If utility planners expected power demands to continue growing at the historical rate of 7 percent/year, the *forecast of future need* is shown at 20 GW. Figure 23.4 shows 8 GW of *capacity under construction* to reflect a situation in which the utility is not doing enough to keep pace with forecasted demand. With new power plants costing more than the older plants, the *construction work in progress* is now shown at $10 billion. The power company now faces the challenge of financing $10 billion in expansion with an asset base of only $10 billion.

The threefold increase in the financial challenge sheds light on the dire news headlines listed previously. These headlines were not necessarily exaggerating the problem. Indeed, the financing requirements of the electric utility industry were so staggering that one expert estimated that IOUs could require one-third of all new equity available each year to the U.S. business sector (Hass, Mitchell, and Stone 1974, 85).

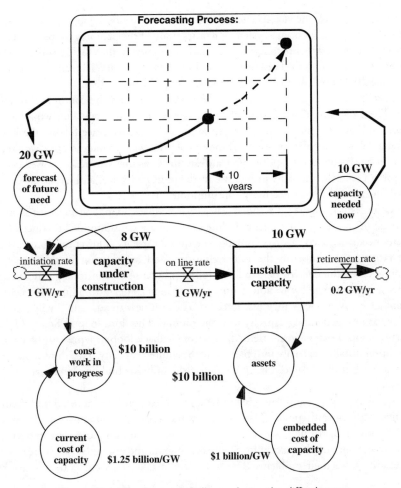

Figure 23.4. The financial challenge during the difficult years.

The IOUs, the Regulators, and the Death Spiral

Faced with this financial challenge, the IOU executives turned to the regulators for help. They believed they had kept their part of the "regulatory bargain" by expanding capacity decade after decade to serve the growing demand for power. They asked the regulators to "do their part" by permitting them to increase the electric rates. The IOUs argued that higher rates were needed to cover increased operating costs and to help the companies build their financial ratios to a sufficiently attractive level to regain the confidence of the financial community.

The regulators responded by implementing several regulatory changes to raise the electric rates, but they weren't sure that meeting all the IOUs' requests for rate increases would solve the problem. They worried about the likely consequence of large rate increases: wouldn't higher rates depress the sale of electricity and possibly reduce utility revenues? If this were to happen, the utility might return to the regulator for yet another rate increase. This vicious circle appeared in headlines as follows:

> The Vicious Circle That Utilities Can't Seem to Break: New Plants Are Forcing Rate Increases—Further Cutting the Growth in Demand

> The Electricity Curve Ball: Declining Demand and Increasing Rates

Figure 23.5 portrays the vicious circle along with other feedback loops at work in the system. This diagram is taken from a system dynamics study of the planning problems of a hypothetical IOU. The study used computer simulation to portray the IOU's problems under a wide variety of circumstances (Ford and Youngblood 1983). The model contained dozens and dozens of feedback loops, but you can see the key loops in figure 23.5.

The death spiral in figure 23.5 involves the electric rates and the consumers' reaction to the rates. The indicated price stands for the price of electricity that regulators would normally allow to let the utility generate the allowed revenues. The actual price follows the indicated price after a delay for regulatory review. If the actual price were to increase, one would expect a decline in electricity consumption after a delay for consumers to react. Lower electricity consumption could then lead to an increase in the indicated price, an increase in the actual price and further declines in electricity consumption.

The outer loop in figure 23.5 shows a negative feedback loop. Starting with an increase in the actual price, we would expect a decline in electricity consumption, a reduced forecast of capacity needs, reduced capacity initiations, reduced capacity, a lower rate base, a reduced revenue target, a reduction in the indicated price, and a reduction in the actual price. This loop is called the delayed demand control loop because its controlling influence is felt only after a regulator's delay to adjust prices, a consumer's delay to adjust electricity consumption, a forecaster's delay to adjust forecasts based on new trends, and finally a construction delay for new generating capacity to come on line. The third loop in figure 23.5 is the construction loop. This is a goal-oriented, negative feedback loop to represent the company's desire to bring installed capacity into balance with required capacity. This third loop includes only one delay, but the delay can be quite long if the utility is building large coal or nuclear power plants.

The spiral study (Ford and Youngblood 1983) revealed that utilities could find themselves in a difficult "downward spiral." Their situation was especially difficult if their customers reacted quickly and strongly while they were stuck with long-lead-time power plants under construction. Simply waiting for regulators to grant the requested rate increases would not necessarily solve their problems. The utility could take steps on its own to soften the

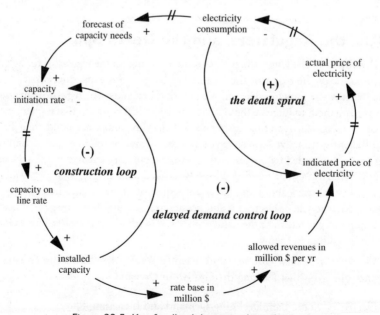

Figure 23.5. Key feedback loops in the utility system.

impact of the "death spiral." The best way to improve their situation was to shorten the length of the construction delay. This could be done by shifting investments from long-lead-time generation technologies (e.g., nuclear plants or large coal plants) to short-lead-time technologies (e.g., small coal plants, geothermal stations, or wind machines). The study revealed that the debilitating effects of the death spiral would be greatly reduced if the IOU were expanding its system to keep pace with slow growth (e.g., 1–2 percent/year) rather than the rapid growth of the golden years. Slower growth rates could be achieved by utility conservation programs that would actively encourage customers to invest in more efficient energy equipment.

The Shift to Small Scale

The 1980s was a decade in which utilities shifted emphasis from large power stations with long lead times to smaller, shorter-lead-time resources. The move to smaller scale was evident in:

- the cancellation of nuclear plants,
- a shift to smaller coal plants,
- an increase in cogeneration, and
- an increase in utility conservation programs.

Nuclear power stations were ordered in great number in the 1960s and early 1970s. They were especially popular with coastal utilities far removed from the nation's coal fields. These utilities invested in light water reactor stations because of a perceived advantage in total life-cycle cost. But the high capital cost and long lead times made nuclear reactors one of the least attractive choices for the 1980s. Orders for new reactors fell to zero, and many plants were canceled part way through construction.

Large coal-fired power plants also fell out of favor in the 1980s. The trend toward extremely large coal plants led to the 3,000 MW example shown in figure 23.2, but the long lead time and high capital costs made the super-large power stations a poor choice for the 1980s. The 500 MW variety shown in figure 23.2 became much more attractive for utilities facing major uncertainties in demand growth (Ford 1980).

Cogeneration resources were also popular in the 1980s. Encouraged by the passage of the Public Utility Regulatory Policy Act (PURPA) of 1978, private companies invested in small-scale machinery to produce both steam and electric energy. These companies were able to sell their "extra electricity" back to the power utility at a guaranteed rate. Cogeneration is attractive because the combined generation of steam and electricity makes more efficient use of fossil fuels. And cogeneration purchases were viewed as especially attractive to IOUs (and their regulators) facing the problems of the death spiral.

The fourth and most dramatic shift in the 1980s took the form of increased emphasis on conservation. Utilities no longer viewed a rapid growth in demand as desirable for the company. They began to pay attention to how their customers used electric energy, and they discovered that electric energy was being consumed in a highly inefficient manner. If their customers could be encouraged to use electricity more efficiently, the pace of demand growth could be slowed and utilities could reduce the risks of carrying long-lead-time construction projects to completion.

Figure 23.6 symbolizes the shift to conservation by showing the Northwest region wrapped in a blanket of insulation. Northwest utilities went from home to home to encourage their customers to take advantage of cost-effective measures like insulation. Utilities provided audits, loans, and direct financial incentives to encourage their customers to use energy more efficiently. These programs would have been inconceivable during the golden years. Indeed, it is probably hard for many business leaders to appreciate why a private company

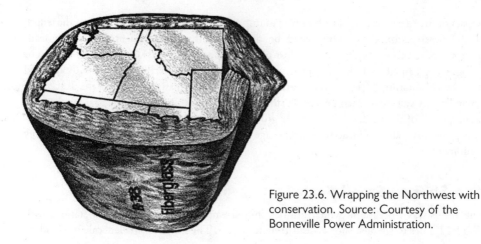

Figure 23.6. Wrapping the Northwest with conservation. Source: Courtesy of the Bonneville Power Administration.

would encourage its customers to use less of its product. But, to their credit, utility leaders saw the wisdom in encouraging efficiency. They had learned that it made good business sense to help the customer plug the leaks in their houses. Helping customers plug the leaks was much less risky than investing in long-lead-time power plants.

System Dynamics Applications

System dynamics models have been used extensively in the energy industry. One of the earliest models was Roger Naill's model of the exploration and production of natural gas (Naill 1973). (This model is available as one of the exercises on this book's home page.) It was the starting point for a series of models for policy support within the U.S. Department of Energy (Naill 1992). Another model deals with electric cars and their impact on the electric utility company (Ford 1994a, 1995). A third example is the work at the London Business School to simulate the implications of proposals for the privatization of government-owned generating facilities in the United Kingdom (Bunn, Dyner, and Larsen 1997). These and other applications are cataloged and summarized in my recent article in the *System Dynamics Review* (Ford 1997). The *Review* article provides a gateway to over thirty publications describing work in the public and private sectors in this country and abroad. The publications also describe models with a long history of use within power companies and government agencies.

To help us interpret this large body of work, it's useful to take a closer look at the CPAM project. CPAM stands for the conservation policy analysis model, a system dynamics model developed to aid resource planning at the Bonneville Power Administraion (Ford and Bull 1989). The CPAM project illustrates the key differences between the system dynamics approach and the more common approach used by utility companies. I have selected the Bonneville model for discussion because of the project's longevity and the several publications that can fill in details missing from this chapter (Ford, Bull, and Naill 1987; Ford and Bull 1989; Ford 1990). But you should know that the observations from the Bonneville project apply to utilities in general, not just to the Bonneville Power Administration.

Bonneville and the Conservation Policy Analysis Model

The Bonneville Power Administration was created in the 1930s, when the federal government invested in hydroelectric development on the Columbia River. Bonneville's job is to market the electric power from federal resources in the Northwest. Like many utilities, Bonneville encountered some serious difficulties in the 1970s, and its leaders saw the wisdom of shifting

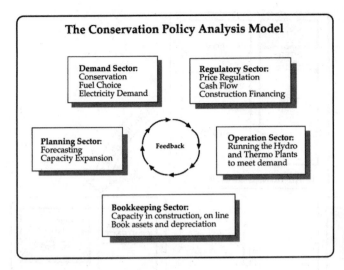

Figure 23.7. Design of the CPAM.

to small-scale resources. Bonneville became a national leader in conservation programs with the creation of a separate Office of Conservation in 1983. This office turned to system dynamics to provide analytical support for policy issues regarding the magnitude, mix, and timing of conservation programs.

Figure 23.7 depicts five separate "sectors" to keep track of electricity demand, capacity expansion planning, bookkeeping, system operations, and the setting of electricity rates. The model was originally constructed in Dynamo, and you will appreciate that each sector is simply a group of Dynamo equations devoted to a different part of the system. You will also appreciate that the information feedback loops will be automatically closed when the entire collection of equations is simulated on the computer.

The system operation sector is shown in figure 23.8 to give you a taste of some of the details. Figure 23.8 shows a four-step procedure to calculate the annual operating costs for the three groups of utilities in the Northwest. Starting at the top, the model compares loads and resources in the entire region. This comparison reveals the best way to balance the supply and demand for electric energy. (In this illustration, the system would be balanced by the sale of secondary energy to utilities outside the region, as noted by the shaded box at the top of the stack of loads.) The regional comparison yields "operating rules" that all utilities will follow. In this example, utilities will run nuclear and coal plants at full availability, but oil- and gas-fired plants will remain idle. The separate balancing of loads and resources reveals that neither the IOUs nor the public utilities can satisfy their demands unless they place loads on Bonneville. Bonneville's operations are portrayed at the bottom of figure 23.8. Bonneville meets the loads from the direct service industries and the loads from retail utilities and has some extra energy left over to sell on the secondary market.

You should know that the approach in figure 23.8 was implemented in a highly aggregated manner. For example, all of the IOUs' coal-burning units, were combined into a single category. The calculations were also aggregated over the twelve months in a year. The highly aggregated calculations were then checked against the more detailed results available from Bonneville's existing models of system operations. (The detailed models operated on a month-by-month basis and included each and every generating unit in the Northwest.) After benchmarking, the figure 23.8 approach provided a unique portrayal of system operations. The unique feature was not the accuracy of the estimated operating costs. Rather, the unique and important feature was the inclusion of the operating costs within a larger model that automatically closes the feedback loops in the system. This approach may seem natural to you at

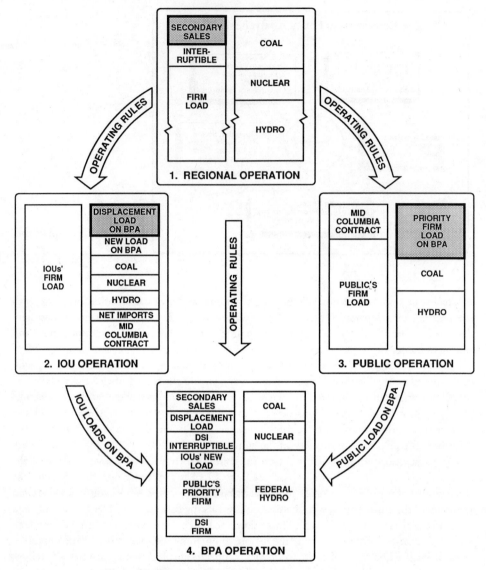

Figure 23.8. Simulating hydrothermal system operations.

this stage of the book. But it was neither natural nor customary to utility planners and analysts.

The Common Utility Approach

The common utility approach is to link a series of departmental models, as shown in figure 23.9. This diagram is limited to three models for pedagogical purposes, but you should realize that a large, well-staffed utility might develop a system with thirty models. Figure 23.9 begins with a set of electric rates needed as input to a demand model. The output of the demand model takes the form of electric load for each of 20 years in the future. These results could be fed to a capacity expansion model. The output of the expansion model is shown as a plan for new power plant construction during the 20-year planning period. This plan would form the input for a third model to calculate the utility revenue requirements and electric

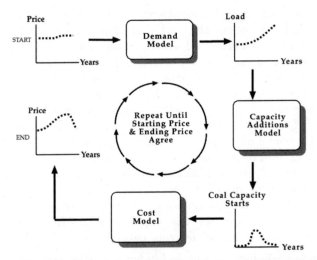

Figure 23.9. The iterative modeling approach often used by utility companies.

rates. The electric rates at the end of the process are then compared with the rates used to start the modeling. If the two sets of rates are significantly different, the utility analysts might adjust the input rates and repeat the entire sequence of calculations. Through artful manipulation of the starting rates, the modeling team might obtain a consistent set of projections with a small number of iterations.

The iterative approach in figure 23.9 was popular with utilities because it allowed them to take advantage of existing models. The existing models were often developed in separate departments and had grown to be quite complex in order to serve each department's need for detail. They were sometimes implemented in different programming languages, and they sometimes resided on different computers, depending on the needs of each department. The principal drawback of the iterative approach was the long time interval required to prepare and complete an internally consistent set of projections. In practical terms, the iterative approach seldom resulted in a consistent set of projections. The more common approach was to simply ignore the inconsistencies that arose from the lack of information feedback within the system. When the analysts took this approach, they found themselves arguing that they could ignore key feedback loops like the death spiral shown in figure 23.5. But their arguments sounded hollow, as industry leaders, both within the IOUs and at the regulatory commissions, were well aware of the potential problems with the death spiral.

Faced with the problems in figure 23.9, some utilities developed a single computer model to cover all aspects of the company. The models were frequently developed by outside consultants who had established their credibility with one of the departmental models. The single models were designed with a single programming language and to reside on a single computer. They were successful in reducing the time interval required to obtain a comprehensive projection. But the common utility models were not successful in simulating the information feedback at work in the system. In a forum with twelve corporate models convened by the Electric Power Research Institute, for example, all but one of the models ignored the price feedback loop shown in figure 23.5 (EPRI 1981). And in a workshop with thirteen models of utility regulatory-financial problems, all but two of the models ignored the price feedback loop shown in figure 23.5 (Ford and Mann 1982). In both of these workshops, the exceptional models used system dynamics.

The first workshop was conducted in 1981 to compare "corporate models." The forum members agreed that the top-priority issue needing modeling support was utility conservation

programs. Each modeling team agreed to a common collection of assumptions about inflation, economic growth, fuel prices, etc. Then each team adopted a common description of a
conservation program. Each team performed a variety of computer studies to show the simulated impact of the conservation programs. The modeling results were arranged side by side
to allow a broad comparison. Each model's results were labeled by letters (e.g., A, B, C) to
preserve anonymity, but you should know that "Model D" was the system dynamics model.
The forum team compared the simulations with an eye toward general conclusions about
modeling approaches. They were not out to label one result as "right" and another as "wrong."
Rather, they wanted to learn if the differences in underlying approach would lead to qualitatively different findings. Their findings are especially noteworthy because of the prominence
of Model D, the only system dynamics model at the forum. (Remember that the forum members were especially well informed on corporate planning issues and computer simulation
models. Also remember that many of the modeling teams had committed company resources
to approaches other than system dynamics.) Given the unusual qualifications and position of
the members, their observations are worth repeating in detail:

> Model D consistently displayed startlingly different and counterintuitive patterns
> of behavior—so much so that it quickly became the focal point of the Working
> Group's efforts to compare model capabilities. . . . Model D was found to be less
> detailed, contain fewer equations (by far), and cost less to develop and run than
> the detailed models. . . . From this information alone, it might have been con-
> cluded that Model D was likely to be "inferior" to the larger models. . . . By the
> time the group had completed a very probing assessment of Model D, a number
> of important changes in the thinking of the group had occurred. . . . The under-
> lying bases for the dynamic features were highly intuitive, but were also likely to
> cause more rapid response and a greater degree of instability (i.e., large price elas-
> ticities reduced demand which lowered revenues and led to a spiraling decline in
> financial performance). . . . Overall, what initially could have been dismissed as
> an interesting but unsuccessful experiment in small model building came to be
> viewed as a potentially useful and powerful corporate modeling tool. (EPRI
> 1981, II-10)

The forum report turns out to be a resounding endorsement of system dynamics in general and for the team of managers and consultants that developed Model D for the Florida
Power and Light Company in particular.

The Florida team joined a dozen other utility modeling groups in a workshop conducted
at the Los Alamos National Laboratory in 1982. The modelers assembled to review different
approaches to simulating the financial problems that plagued IOUs at the end of the 1970s.
The number one issue was "regulatory reform," a general term for a variety of proposals to
improve utilities' cash flow through higher rates or lower taxes. Thirteen models were represented, but only two of the models closed the feedback loops shown in figure 23.5. One was
the Florida model; the second was the death spiral model (Ford and Youngblood 1983). The
workshop provided an opportunity to compare model designs and the modeling environ-
ments. The conventional view (by the eleven models without feedback) was that price feedback could be distracting to top management. Several of the most experienced modelers
argued that utility companies invested considerable time and expense arriving at their best
demand forecast. The conventional view was that price feedback could confuse top management because each new simulation might show a different pattern of demand growth. The
conventional modelers also argued that closing the price feedback loop required them to specify the price elasticity of demand. With uncertainties in the price elasticity, they suggested that
closing the loop would be speculative rather than informative. The Florida Power and Light
team responded to this criticism by acknowledging the importance of delivering a credible

forecast to various commissions. But they argued that they could turn to conventional forecasting techniques to meet this need. They argued that they had an entirely different goal in mind for the system dynamics model—their goal was to generate insights, not numbers.

Personal Reflections

The extensive use of system dynamics in the electric power industry leads many to ask about the ultimate impact of modeling on the "real world." For example, my colleagues and I are often asked if any of us made a difference in the energy industry. That question is often followed by a closely related question: Did the system dynamics approach give us the power to make a difference? Perhaps system dynamics is simply a convenient tool in the hands of a lot of bright people who would have made their impact regardless.

My experiences have convinced me that system dynamics is much more than a convenient modeling tool. I'm convinced that system dynamics has led practitioners to focus on the key feedback loops in the system. Our training leads us to first "see the feedback" in our mind's eye. But equally important, our ability to translate mental models into computer models allows us to test our ideas through computer simulation. My experiences with energy industry models convince me that the ability to simulate the information feedback in the energy system is a truly unique feature of the system dynamics approach. In the case of the electric power industry, for example, the ability to simulate the interplay of the feedback loops in figure 23.5 proved to be an important and distinctive feature of system dynamics.

But did we make a difference in the world? I've posed this question to many of the investigators who have worked in the energy field, and I've asked myself if my own studies have contributed to useful change in the industry. I believe that our work has helped shift industry opinions in a useful direction. When the collective work of system dynamics practitioners is judged in light of industry trends, I believe we can all take some credit for contributing to useful change. A fundamental contribution of system dynamics has been to add a unique voice to the many voices calling for a shift to small-scale resources in the 1980s. The industry shift to smaller coal plants, cogeneration, and conservation was extremely beneficial to the power companies, both to their stock holders and to their customers. The shift was good for the environment as well.

Summary

System dynamics practitioners have accumulated an impressive record of applications in the electric power industry. System dynamics has given us a unique capability to see the feedback at work in the power system, and our work has contributed to useful changes in the power industry. As you think about the problems in your own industry, your study of system dynamics will give you the ability to see the feedback in your mind's eye. And your ability to build and test computer simulation models will give you the power to contribute to your own industry in this unique manner. May your contributions lead to better understanding and to a better world.

REVIEW

Appendix A

Units of Measurement

We must pay attention to the units of measurement if we expect to build useful models. We should start by selecting units that will make the variables' meaning clear to the people who will use the model. Then we should check the equations to make sure that the variables are combined in an internally consistent manner. This appendix provides an opportunity to refresh your understanding of units. It concludes with practical advice on the use of units in system dynamics models.

Review

You have probably already learned that there are simple rules for combining units and manipulating units. One of the first rules to recall from your previous schooling is that variables to be added or subtracted must be expressed in the same units. If we were to add the weights of all the students in the classroom to get their total weight, for example, each student's weight would have to be expressed in the same units. And when you add or subtract variables, the answer will be expressed in the same units.

Addition or subtraction leaves the units of measurement unchanged. But that is not the case with multiplication and division. To illustrate, consider the rectangular solid in figure A.1. It has a length of 10, a width of 5, and a height of 4. Let's suppose the dimensions are measured in centimeters (cm), and you wish to find the volume. You would multiply 10*4*5, to obtain a volume of 200. You have probably learned that we would "multiply the units" as well. That is, the units for volume would be cm*cm*cm, or cubic centimeters (cc). If we were asked for the area of the front face of the solid, we would multiply 4 cm by 10 cm to get a surface area of 40 square cm. Once again, you multiply the units as well as the numbers.

If you use division to find some attribute of the solid, you would divide the units as well as the numbers. For example, we might define the "relative length" of the solid object as the ratio of the length to the height. In that case the relative length would be 10 cm divided by 4 cm, or 2.5. In other words, the front face is two and a half times longer than it is tall. When dividing cm by cm, the units cancel out, and you are left with a number that does not have any units. This number might be called a pure number, a nondimensional number, or a normalized number. This book uses the term *dimensionless*.

Dimensionless variables are frequently formed by taking the ratio of two numbers measured in the same units. One of the best-known dimensionless numbers is π, the Greek letter pi. Pi is the ratio of the circumference of a circle to its diameter; it is a dimensionless number

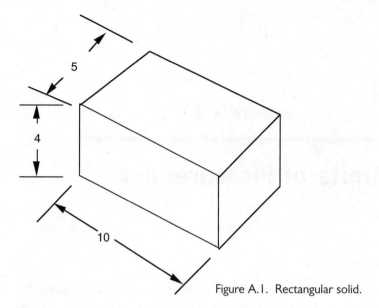

Figure A.1. Rectangular solid.

whose value is approximately 3.14. That is, the circumference of any circle is around 3.14 times longer than the diameter.

We've covered addition, subtraction, multiplication, and division. You should also recall what you've learned about exponents. For example, any number appearing as an exponent will be a dimensionless number. Take the expression

$$Y = 10^2$$

as an example. You know that 10 squared is 100 and that the "2" in the exponent stands for ten times ten. The "2" does not have any units. A similar rule applies to logarithms. If you calculate $Y = \log (100)$, for example, Y is 2 and is dimensionless.

Importance of Units

The importance of units was appreciated at the outset of the field of system dynamics. Forrester (1961) observed that dimensional analysis plays an important part in guiding equation writing in engineering and in the physical sciences, and he argued that the same standards should apply in the emerging field of industrial dynamics. The units of all variables and constants should be precisely stated and checked for consistency. Forrester warned that "carelessness on this point can lead to much needless confusion" (p. 64). This good advice applies to all models, not just models of industrial systems. When modeling biological or ecological systems, Nisbet and Gurney (1982, 21) advise that any equations representing a real biological system should be valid irrespective of the units. Like Forrester's advice, their advice is simple and practical—"regularly checking the dimensions in the course of a long calculation provides a rapid check on algebraic accuracy." They note that a dimensionally correct equation need not be correct, but "a dimensionally incorrect equation is invariably nonsense!"

Pragmatic Advice

The first piece of practical advice in modeling is to take the time to get the units right from the beginning. If you develop a regular habit of checking the units, you will find that it improves your progress toward a clear and consistent model. The advice in chapter 2 regarding stocks and flows is particularly useful. Each flow must be measured in the units of the stock divided by the units that you have selected for time. If the stock is measured in tons, and time is measured in years, all flows in and out of the stock will be measured in tons/year. If you find yourself connecting a flow that is not measured in the correct units, take the opportunity to rethink the model structure. Chances are, you will come up with a better combination of stocks and flows.

Another simple, but important piece of advice is to select units that are familiar within your organization. You will read in chapter 15 that the first step in the modeling process is to get acquainted with the system. Getting acquainted with the units is a good place to start. Pay particular attention to the units commonly used in the principal "figures of merit" within your organization. If you are a newcomer, you may discover that the units are unusual and unfamiliar. You should take the time to understand the new units. If your model is to be understood by the people who manage the system, you should learn their units and their common terms for describing their system performance. It may take extra time to "speak the language" of the people managing the system. But your model is not likely to be a good communication tool if you don't invest the time.

After learning the common units of measure, notice whether managers talk in terms of simple units, or in hundreds, thousands, millions, billions, etc. If water flows in a river system range from 1,000 to 900,000 acre-feet per year, the common units might be thousands of acre-feet rather than just acre-feet. And in a larger river system, with flows ranging from 1,000,000 to 900,000,000 acre-feet per year, the common unit might be millions of acre-feet per year. Measuring the variables in thousands or millions will help in communication. It will also help us avoid the tedious task of checking all the zeros (as in 55,700,000 acre-feet when we might have said 55.7 million acre-feet). Common terms and abbreviations (used in this book) to help us avoid strings of zeros are listed in table A.1.

Table A.1. Metric system prefixes.

Number	Prefixes	Examples
1,000	kilo (k)	1 kw = 1 kilowatt = 1,000 watts
1,000,000	mega (M)	1 MW = 1 megawatt = 1 million watts
1,000,000,000	giga (g)	1 GW = 1 gigawatt = 1 billion watts
0.001	milli (m)	1 mm = 1 millimeter = 0.001 meters
0.000,001	micro (µ)	1 µg = 1 microgram = 0.000,001 grams

Dimensionless Variables

Dimensionless variables deserve special attention because they often reveal the essential features of a system. Think of pi as an example. Pi is a special number that tells us that the circumference of any circle is around 3.14 times longer than its diameter. This fundamental feature is true for any size circle, and it is true regardless of whether we measure lengths in inches, yards, meters, or kilometers.

This observation about pi is illustrative of systems in general. We should expect the fundamental properties of a system to reveal themselves to us in dimensionless form. Chapter 17 gives an example involving cyclical behavior. It describes a system that grows past its carrying capacity because of a delay in the limiting effect of the carrying capacity. The system then declines below the capacity and exhibits oscillatory behavior. The oscillatory tendencies can be summarized by a dimensionless parameter that combines the intrinsic rate of growth (measured in fraction/year) and the length of the delay time (measured in years). The product of these two factors is a dimensionless indicator of the stability of the system. This example is

based on Hastings's text *Population Biology.* He argues that it is ~~no coincidence that the key~~
~~indicator turns out to be dimensionless because "the stability of the model and of the popu-~~
~~lation obviously cannot change as we change the units,~~ . . . Our conclusion is that stability
can only depend on nondimensional groups of parameters, combinations for which all the
units cancel" (Hastings 1997, 95).

   Another example of a dimensionless variable that reveals a fundamental property of
nature is the "Reynolds number." Reynolds was interested in the conditions that would cause
the flow of a fluid to change from laminar flow to turbulent flow. He conducted experiments
with fluids of different velocities flowing down pipes with different diameters. And he studied fluids with different densities and viscosities. He summarized his experiments by report-
ing whether laminar or turbulent flow was observed depending on a dimensionless term, *R,*
which combined the velocity, diameter, density, and viscosity to create a number with no
dimensions. His experiments were published in 1883, and they are still useful today to indicate the possible onset of turbulence (Vennard and Street 1976, 301).

Conclusion

The purpose of this appendix is to refresh your memory on units and to offer practical
suggestions for using units in a model. Further suggestions appear in the chapter 2 discussion
of stocks and flows and in the chapter 5 discussion of equilibrium diagrams. You will also read
that the stock-and-flow software programs provide various ways to document and check your
units.

Exercises

1. **What are the units?**

    $Y = A + B$ What are the units for Y if A and B are measured in tons?

    $Z = A^*B/C$ What are the units for Z if A and B are measured in feet
                        and C is measured in square feet?

    $Y = X/L^3$ What are the units for Y if X is measured in pounds and L
                        is measured in feet?

    $Y = Ae^{rt}$ What are the units for r and for Y? A is measured in per-
                        sons and t in seconds.

    $Y = A \ln(x)$ What are the units for x and for Y? A is measured in tons
                        and $\ln(x)$ stands for the natural log of x.

    $C = P^* W^* D$ What are the units for C if P is the population measured in
                        millions of persons, W is waste created in tons/year per
                        million persons, and D is the unit disposal cost measured
                        in dollars per ton?

2. **Leaf area index:**

    The leaf area index (LAI) is useful for explaining how plants obtain their energy from
    photosynthesis (Pratt 1995, 8). It describes the relationship between leaves and the
    amount of sunlight they intercept as light passes through the various layers of leaves on

a plant. The LAI is defined as the ratio of the leaf area per unit of ground area. What are the units for LAI?

3. **Reynolds number:**

   $R = Vdp/u$ is the number used by Reynolds to summarize experiments with fluid flow. Prove that R is dimensionless if

   V = mean velocity of the fluid in the pipe (meters/sec)

   d = diameter of the pipe (meters)

   p = density of the fluid (kilograms per cubic meter), and

   u = viscosity of the fluid (kilograms per meter-second).

4. **River flow:**

   The stock of water in a reservoir is measured in millions of acre-feet (MAF). Time is measured in years, so each of the flows is measured in MAF/year. An extra converter called *river flow below dam* is used to show the river flow in thousands of cubic feet per second (a unit that is more familiar to many groups using the river). The equation is:

   ```
   river_flow_below_dam = outflow_in_MAF_per_year*conversion_factor
   ```

   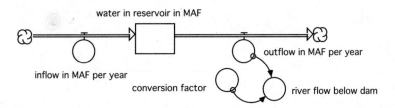

   There are 43,560 cubic feet in an acre-foot, and there are 8,760 hours in a year. What is the value of the *conversion factor*?

5. **Oil consumption using English units:**

   The stock and flows are taken from figure 2.8 and the eighth exercise in chapter 2. They show oil consumption measured in BL/month, the proper units if time is measured in months and *Personal Stocks* are in barrels. The converters allow us to find *oil consumption* using English units that would be familiar to planners in the United States and the United Kingdom. The equations are:

   ```
   oil_consumption = fuel_use*conversion_factor
   fuel_use = cars*annual_travel/fuel_efficiency
   ```

   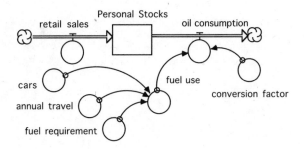

What is the value of the *conversion factor* if

    cars is measured in millions

    annual travel is measured in miles per car per year

    fuel efficiency is measured in miles per gallon

and there are 42 gallons in a barrel?

Further Readings

- Harte (1988) provides an extensive list of "useful numbers" and their units for the environmental scientist.
- Riggs's (1963) "critical primer," *The Mathematical Approach to Physiological Problems,* includes a chapter and numerous exercises on units.
- Jacobsen and Bronson (1987) describe the challenges of selecting variables (and their units) for system dynamics models of sociological systems.

Appendix B

Math Review

This book assumes that you have learned introductory algebra. You have probably studied geometry and have learned how to interpret charts and tables. These are the basic prerequisites. The book does not rely on any prior knowledge of calculus or differential equations. You will read in chapter 3 that these mathematical tools provide the foundation for "classical physics" and have been used to help environmental scientists study ecological systems. But chapter 3 also explains that these classical methods suffer from major limitations due to nonlinear relationships. You'll read that system dynamics models use numerical methods to deal with the nonlinearities in real systems. The computer performs the tedious calculations; we are free to think about the best way to design the model to represent our system.

If you've had a course in calculus, you'll find that your knowledge of differentiation and integration will come in handy as you read the book. You'll recognize, for example, that stocks act to integrate the effects of the flows over time. And if you've had a course in differential equations, you'll recognize that a system dynamics model may be viewed as a coupled set of first-order differential equations. These insights will be helpful, but they are certainly not essential to build and test useful models. Indeed, many students are learning system dynamics in K–12 classrooms with the same stock-and-flow software used in this book (Draper and Swanson 1990; Kreith 1997; Zaraza and Fisher 1997).

You've learned algebra, and you've probably been exposed to the "algebra of units." The previous appendix will help refresh your memory on units. This appendix will help refresh your memory of exponential growth and exponential decay, arguably the two most important topics covered in your previous study of mathematics. Naturally growing systems often grow in an exponential manner. And when they are in decline, their pattern of decline is often exponential decay. A review of these fundamental patterns of nature is one of the best ways to prepare for the study of modeling. For example, if we can work through the implications of exponential growth in our heads, we will be in a much stronger position to judge the plausibility of model simulations of naturally growing systems.

Exponential Growth

Figure B.1 shows a graph of the exponential function:

$$Y(x) = e^x$$

When expressed to three significant digits, the number e is 2.718. When we raise e to the 0th power, we get 1. (Any number to the 0th power is 1.) The graph in figure B.1 begins at 1 and grows to 2.718 by the time x reaches 1. You can use your hand calculator to check that e squared is 7.389, so the exponential curve is heading off the chart by the end of figure B.1.

Figure B.1 shows that Y(x) grows with x, and that the slope grows as well. Indeed, the slope of this curve turns out to be identical to the height of the curve at every point in figure B.1. This is a unique feature of the exponential function. If you've studied calculus, you'll know that this property is expressed by writing

$$\frac{dY}{dx} = e^x = Y(x)$$

Figure B.1 reveals another important property of the exponential curve—it doubles in size each time x increases by 0.69. As x moves from 0 to 0.69, Y grows from 1 to 2. Y grows from 2 to 4 by the time x reaches 1.39.

Figure B.2 shows how the exponential function appears when describing systems that grow exponentially over time. In this example

$$Y(T) = e^{rT}$$

where T is time (measured in years) and r is the growth rate (measured as a fraction per year). When time is zero, we have Y(T) = 1 as in the previous example. By the time T reaches 10 years, the product of r and T is 0.69, so Y(T) has grown to 2. When t reaches 20 years, the product of r and T is 1.39, and Y(T) has grown to 4. This illustration shows that an exponentially growing function will double in size in a fixed time interval. This time interval is called the *doubling time* of the exponential growth. For the case of exponential growth at the rate of 6.9 percent/yr, the doubling time turns out to be 10 years. The connection between the growth rate and the doubling time is based on the simple requirement that:

(growth rate) * (doubling time) = 0.69

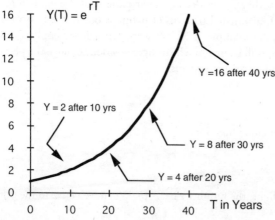

Figure B.2. Exponential growth over time at the rate of 6.9 percent/yr.

If we were to increase the growth rate from 6.9 percent/yr to 10 percent/yr, for example, the doubling time would shrink from 10 years to 6.9 years. And if we were to lower the growth rate to 1 percent/yr, the doubling time would turn out to be 69 years.

Exponential Decline

Exponential decline is represented by the expression

$$Y(x) = e^{-x} = \frac{1}{e^x}$$

You may use your hand calculator to find how $Y(x)$ changes with changes in x. The graph would start at 1 when x is zero and gradually decline with an increase in x. Y will reach 0.368 by the time x reaches 1 and 0.135 by the time x reaches 2. The downward slope of the graph would become flatter and flatter over time. Finally, your graph would reveal that $Y(x)$ declines by 50 percent each time x increases by 0.69. For example, as x moves from 0 to 0.69, Y will fall to 0.5; when x reaches 1.39, Y will fall to 0.25.

When describing systems that decline over time, the exponential decay function normally takes the form

$$Y(T) = e^{-rT}$$

where T is time (measured in years) and r is the rate of decline (measured as a fraction per year). When time is zero, we have $Y(T) = 1$ as in the previous example. By the time T reaches 10 years, the product of r and T is 0.69, so $Y(T)$ has fallen to 0.5. When T reaches 20 years, the product of r and T is 1.39, and $Y(T)$ has fallen to 0.25. This illustration shows that an exponentially declining function will fall by 50 percent in a fixed time interval. This time interval is called the half-life of the exponential decline. For the case of exponential decay at the rate of 6.9 percent/yr, the half-life turns out to be 10 years. The connection between the decay rate and the half-life is based on the simple requirement that:

(decay rate) * (half-life) = 0.69

If we were to increase the decay rate from 6.9 percent/yr to 10 percent/yr, for example, the half-life would shrink from 10 years to 6.9 years. And if we were to lower the decay rate to 1 percent/yr, the half-life would turn out to be 69 years.

Discussion

When building a model of any system in nature, it is useful to keep the rules for doubling times and half-lives in mind. If you know the rate of exponential growth, for example, you can quickly apply the doubling time to estimate how long it will take for a population to increase by twofold, by fourfold, by eightfold, etc. These simple estimates can be quite useful when it comes time to interpret model behavior. A familiarity with doubling times and half-lives can be as useful as the multiplication tables we all learned in elementary school.

Exercises

1. The first row of the following table gives the doubling time for a system growing at 7 percent/month. What are the other doubling times in the table?

Rate of exponential growth	Doubling time
7%/month	about 10 months
3.5%/month	
14%/yr	
21%/yr	
2%/yr	
1%/century	
28%/sec	

2. The first row gives the half-life for a system decaying at 7 percent/day. What are the other half-lives in the table?

Rate of exponential decline	Half-life
7%/day	about 10 days
3.5%/sec	
14%/yr	
21%/yr	
2%/yr	
1%/century	

3. The book *Land of 500 Million: A Geography of China* was published in 1955. Suppose you read in the opening paragraph that China's population has been growing in an exponential fashion at 3.5 percent/yr. And suppose that rate of growth had continued to the year 1995. How large would you guess the 1995 population to be?

4. A train wreck in 1997 led to a spill of 480 tons of the chemical XYZ, which was absorbed in the soil. Experts were called to the scene. They announced that the chemical would degrade over time with a half-life of 20 years, and they said there would be no danger once the amount of chemical in the soil falls below 30 tons. In what year will the soil be safe again?

5. Pratt (1995, 58) summarizes the range of biotic potentials for four broad classes of animals. The biotic potential is defined as the rate of exponential growth expected when the animal is free to grow without constraints from the environment. For large mammals, the biotic potential can range from a low of 2 percent/yr to a high of 50 percent/yr. What is the corresponding range of doubling times?

6. Pratt reports that biotic potentials for small mammals can range from 30 percent/yr to 800 percent/yr. The 800 percent/yr growth rate suggests that years is not the appropriate time unit for tracking the population growth. What is the doubling time in days for a small mammal with the 800 percent/yr biotic potential?

7. You open a savings account for your child on the day she is born. The bank guarantees that the balance in the account will grow exponentially at 10 percent/yr forever. Your goal is to have $1 million in the account by the time she reaches 70 years of age. How much do you deposit in the account?

8. Meadows et al. (1972, 29) describe a Persian legend about a clever courtier who presented a beautiful chessboard to his king. The courtier asked the king to show his favor

by simply giving him 1 grain of rice for the first square on the board, 2 grains for the second square, 4 grains for the third, and so on. Let's suppose the king turns to you for advice. He tells you that the kingdom's entire storage of one million tons of rice is available. Does the king have enough to accept the chessboard? (There are 64 squares on a chessboard. Assume that there are 5,760 grains in a pound, and there are 2,000 pounds in a ton.)

9. Odum (1971, 182) describes the doubling time for the rice weevil at just under 1 week if the temperature is near the optimum value. If the temperature is held at the optimum, how long will it take for a population of weevils to increase by a millionfold if they encounter no limits? Odum reports a doubling time of 5.78 weeks if the temperature is 4.5 degrees C hotter than the optimum. How long will it take for the weevils to increase by a millionfold under those conditions?

10. Odum (1971, 182) notes a doubling time of around 35 years for the worldwide human population during the 1960s. What is the corresponding rate of exponential growth?

11. Suppose someone from the 1960s looked at population trends over previous decades. They might remark that the population "has increased as much in the last 35 years as in all previously recorded time." Is this statement consistent with Odum's observation in the previous exercise?

12. Chapter 16 describes a herd of 4,000 deer whose biotic potential is around 50 percent/yr. The deer herd begins to grow when predators are removed from the region. If the herd continues to grow at 50 percent/yr, how long will it take for the deer population to exceed 120,000?

13. The home page describes a model of the Tsembaga people in the New Guinea Highlands. The Tsembaga maintain a pig herd that grows exponentially at the rate of 14 percent/yr (when there is plenty of food). But when the pigs become too numerous to care for, the Tsembaga launch a "pig festival," which could result in the slaughter of 75 percent of the pig population. The remaining pig population begins to grow again at the same rate as before. How long will it take before the pigs once again become too numerous to care for?

14. There is a French children's riddle (Meadows et al. 1972, 29) about a pond with a water lily in it. The lily doubles in size every day. In 30 days, it will cover the entire pond, killing the other creatures in the pond. The owner wants to avoid that, but he sees no hurry. He will wait till the lily plant covers half the pond before taking action. On what day will he take action?

SOFTWARE

Appendix C

$\overline{}$

Stella

The best place to learn Stella is at the computer. You will discover that the software is easy to learn and easy to use. This appendix provides some simple examples, which you should try to reproduce on your computer. Stella is well documented in technical documentation available from High Performance Systems, Inc. (HPS 1993). The Stella software is also nicely described by Hannon and Ruth (1994), Few (1996), and Soltzberg (1996). The software design philosophy is explained by Peterson (1994).

Population Example

Figure C.1 shows a Stella flow diagram of a simple model of a population that grows due to the accumulated effect of births. The stock is the *Human Population;* the flow is *Births;* and the *Birth Rate* is a converter.

You can use the up and down arrows to move between Stella's three "layers." The top layer is reserved for "high-level mapping" and the creation of user interfaces (like the interface in figure 20.1). Figure C.1 shows the middle layer, the "model construction" layer. This is where you will spend most of your time. The cursor in figure C.1 is pointed at the globe, a toggle switch that allows you to change back and forth between two modes of construction. When the globe is visible, you're in the "mapping mode." This mode is useful when you are beginning to put the stocks, flows, and converters together to form a "map" or flow diagram of the model. When you are happy with the map of the model, click on the globe to switch to the modeling mode. You'll recognize this mode when question marks appear, as shown in figure C.2. Click on any ? to open the dialog box, which has been designed to make equation writing as easy as possible. When you click on the stock variable, for example, Stella needs to know only the initial value of the stock. In this example, the initial value is 500, which stands for 500 million people. And when you click on *Births*, the dialog box will remind you that you should use the *Birth Rate* and the *Human Population* in the equation. Actually, it does more than remind you. It won't let you proceed unless you make use of those two variables. This equation is the product of the *Human Population* and the *Birth Rate*. (You will find the * for multiplication on the numeric pad, or you can type in the * from the keyboard.)

Equations are written in a "one-at-a-time" fashion within the dialog box for each variable. To see the entire list of equations, click on the down arrow to reach the equations layer. Figure C.3 shows what you will see. The *Human Population* appears as Human_Population(t). This stock is expressed as a function of time by the syntax (t) and (t – dt), where (t) stands for the

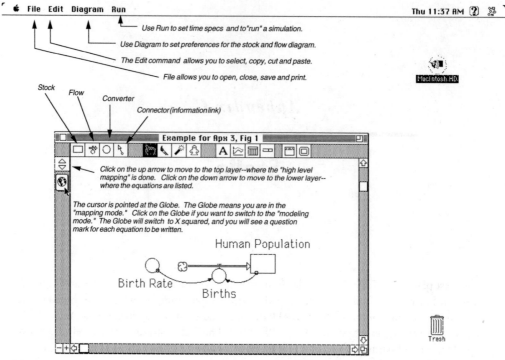

Figure C.1. Stella flow diagram of a population model in a "screen capture" of the monitor of a Macintosh computer with comments added in italics.

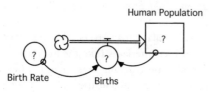

Figure C.2. Stella flow diagram in the modeling mode.

current point in time during a Stella simulation and (t − dt) stands for the previous step in time. The dt stands for "delta time," the time interval between calculations (see chapter 3). The dt is also called the "step size" for the simulation. Stella writes the equation for the *Human Population* automatically once it sees the flows that influence this stock. Your only job is to specify the initial value of the stock.

The next equation gives *Births* as the product of *Human Population* and *Birth Rate*. Stella does not bother with a (t) or (t − dt) in the equation for the flow, as it is understood that all variables in the equation are evaluated at the current point in time. The final equation shows the birth rate set at .07, which means that the population will grow at 7 percent/year.

Figure C.4 shows a screen capture with a "graph pad" and a "table pad" used to display the simulation results over time. The graph is located immediately below the flow diagram. It

```
Human_Population(t) = Human_Population(t - dt) + (Births) * dt
INIT Human_Population = 500

INFLOWS:
Births = Human_Population*Birth_Rate
Birth_Rate = .07
```

Figure C.3. Stella equations.

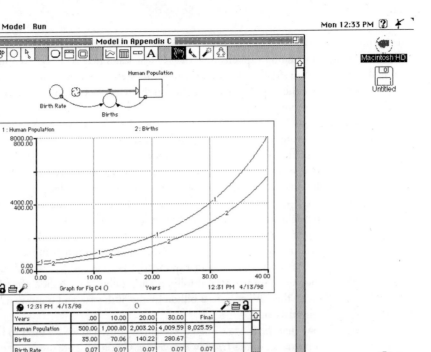

Figure C.4. Screen capture showing simulation results in a graph pad and a table pad.

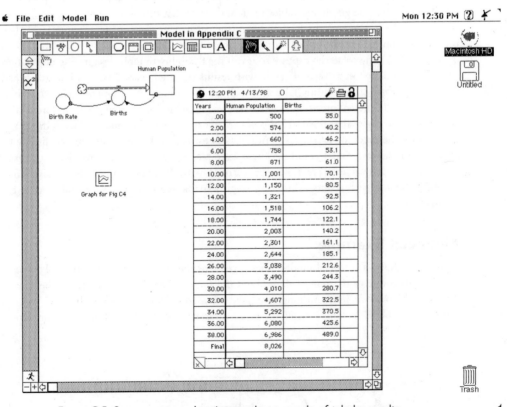

Figure C.5. Screen capture showing another example of tabular results.

shows the *Human Population* scaled from 0 to 8,000 and the *Births* scaled from 0 to 800. The HPS (1993) documentation explains how the vertical scales may be designed, either by you or by the software. You should take the time to set the vertical scales to display the results in a clear manner. Since there are four crosshatches on the vertical axis, most of the vertical scales in this book are set to an even multiple of four.

The results in figure C.4 were obtained by setting the "time specs" under the "run" command to range from 0 to 40 years; the dt was left at the default value of 0.25; and the integration method was left at Euler's method. The units for time were set at "years" and the run command was issued with the graph pad open. The 40 years of simulated results will appear "live" in the graph window. Change the pause interval if you would like to stop the simulation every few years. If you set the pause interval to 10, for example, the live display will stop after 10 years. You might use the pause time to think about what will happen in the next 10 years, or you may intervene in the simulation to change model inputs while the simulation is pausing. To continue the simulation, click "resume" under the run command. Figure C.4 shows the *Human Population* growing in exponential fashion, as you would expect from appendix B. The population starts at 500 million and doubles to 1 billion after 10 years. It doubles to 2 billion by the 20th year, to 4 billion by the 30th year, and it grows past 8 billion by the end of the simulation.

Figure C.4 shows that *Births* grow in an exponential fashion as well. This is to be expected since *Births* are proportional to the *Human Population*. Graph pads are used to show the general trends over the entire simulation. Table pads are used to show the precise numerical results from each time period of the simulation. Figure C.4 shows a table pad at the bottom. It is organized as a horizontal table with a report interval of 10 years. You'll find the "report interval" in the table dialog box. It is normally set to report results for each and every dt. A 10-year interval was selected for figure C.4. If you reproduce the results shown in figure C.4, you'll notice that the graph and tables open and close each time you switch to a new active window. To "pin" these results to the screen (for permanent viewing, as in figure C.4) click on the pushpin icon in the upper left corner of the pad.

Figure C.5 shows a screen capture to reveal the flexibility in table design. The population results are tabulated in a "vertical" table with results reported every 2 years. (The graph pad is closed in this screen capture.) Look closely at the column for *Human Population;* it is reported with a different precision than in the previous table. Population is now reported with zero significant digits after the decimal point. *Births* are tabulated to one significant digit. You can control the precision of the numerical results for each column of the tabular display by clicking on the individual column. These examples of table pads are relatively compact because only a few variables are shown every 2 or 10 years. If it suits your needs, massive tables can be generated with results from every single variable reported for every time step of the simulation.

Financial Example

Figure C.6 shows a financial model to keep track of the *Bank Balance* over time. The *Bank Balance* grows due to the *Interest Added,* and the *Interest Added* is the product of the *Interest Rate* and the *Bank Balance*. Although we have switched from population to finance, you can tell that the model is composed of the same combination of stocks, flows, and converters.

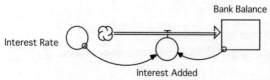

Figure C.6. Stella flow diagram of a bank balance model.

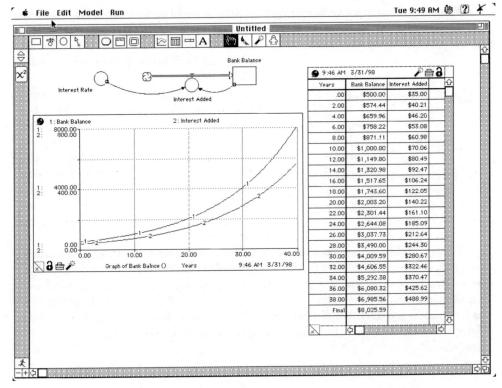

Figure C.7. Screen capture showing results from the bank balance model.

When this happens, we say the model has the "same structure." Let's adopt similar numbers as well: the initial value of the *Bank Balance* is set to 500, and the *Interest Rate* is 0.07, to stand for 7 percent/year.

The screen capture in figure C.7 shows the bank balance model along with a graph pad and a table pad that have been "pinned" to the screen. The graph pad shows that the *Bank Balance* follows the same exponential trend as the population in the previous example. The table pad in figure C.7 is arranged as a vertical table with the *Bank Balance* and the *Interest Added* displayed in "$" format. You'll find the formatting options by clicking on each column in the table. The tabular results confirm what you would expect—the *Bank Balance* grows from $500 to over $8,000 by the end of the 40-year simulation.

Adding Nonlinear Relationships

Suppose we wish to expand the bank balance model to represent the variable interest rate policy shown in figure C.8. This diagram represents a bank policy to pay higher interest for a higher balance. You might be wondering how to write an equation for the *Interest Rate* as a function of the *Bank Balance*. Perhaps one of the special functions (see appendix H) will help you explain the shape shown in figure C.8. Don't worry if a simple function does not spring immediately to mind. You can always take advantage of Stella's "graph function."

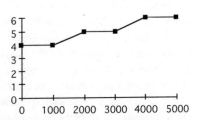

Figure C.8. Assume the interest rate (%/yr) depends on the bank balance.

Figure C.9 shows a new version of the bank balance model with the *Interest Rate* depending on the size of the *Bank Balance*. The tilde (~) signifies that Stella's graph function is used to calculate the *Interest Rate*. To reproduce these results, click on the *Interest Rate* when the ?

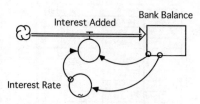

is visible. Stella will bring up the equation dialog box. Click on *Bank Balance* to bring it into the equation box. Then click on the "Become Graph" button, and you will see the graphical dialog box appear with *Bank Balance* on the x-axis and *Interest Rate* on the y-axis. To reproduce these results, ask for six "data points" with the x-axis scaled from 0 to 5,000. Then enter the values of the *Interest Rate* shown in figure C.8. If you set the vertical scales to match figure C.8, Stella's drawing of the graph will provide a visual check that you have created the correct graph.

Figure C.9. New bank model with the interest rate calculated from a "graph function" (~) based on the size of the bank balance.

Figure C.10 lists the equations for the new model. The model is initialized with a balance of $500, so the initial value of the *Interest Rate* will be 4 percent/yr. As interest is added over time, the *Bank Balance* will grow. And with a growth in the *Bank Balance*, we should see an increase in the *Interest Rate* and a faster growth in the *Bank Balance*. The graph function appears as two lines. The first line tells us that the *Bank Balance* is on the x-axis and the *Interest Rate* is on the y-axis. The second line gives the six data points as $(x1, y1), (x2, y2) \ldots (x6, y6)$.

```
Bank_Balance(t) = Bank_Balance(t - dt) + (Interest_Added) * dt
INIT Bank_Balance = 500

INFLOWS:
Interest_Added = Bank_Balance*Interest_Rate
Interest_Rate = GRAPH(Bank_Balance)
(0.00, 0.04), (1000, 0.04), (2000, 0.05), (3000, 0.05), (4000, 0.06), (5000, 0.06)
```

Figure C.10. Equations for the new bank model.

Figure C.11 shows the simulation results over an 80-year time period. The *Bank Balance* is scaled from 0 to $16,000 and the *Interest Rate* from 0 to 8 percent/yr. The graph shows that the *Interest Rate* remains at the 4 percent/yr, the lowest value for the first 20 years. The rate of interest increases when the balance climbs past $1,000 and reaches the 5 percent/yr plateau around the 30th year. By this time, the balance is growing more rapidly, so it does not take as long to leave the middle plateau and arrive at the high rate of 6 percent/yr.

Figure C.12 illustrates Stella's scatter graph, sometimes called an x–y graph. The scatter graph does not show time on the horizontal axis. Rather, it asks you to select a model variable for the x-axis. You then select a second variable for the y-axis. In figure C.12, the *Bank Balance* has been selected for the x-axis, and the *Interest Rate* for the y-axis. The dots in figure C.12 show the simulation results for each time step of the simulation. The dots are bunched tightly together when there is not much change in the x or y direction over time. This pattern of dots traces out the relationship shown previously, so the scatter graph provides a check that the bank policy is properly implemented in the model.

Scatter graphs are used occasionally in this book to provide a different perspective

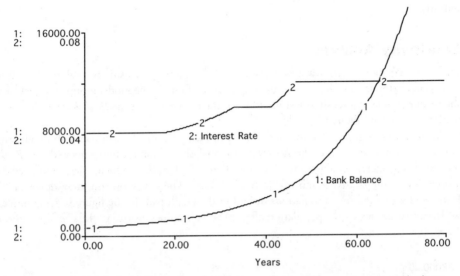

Figure C.11. Simulation results with the variable interest rate. (You won't see exactly these results on your monitor. The labels for the two curves will appear at the top of the graph pad, and you'll see the time and date at the bottom. This image was obtained by "edit copying" the graphic image to a drawing program. The extra information was deleted and the labels were moved closer to each curve for easier interpretation.)

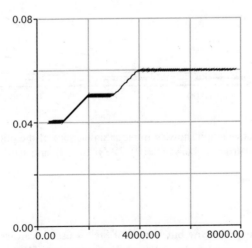

Figure C.12. Scatter graph with interest rate on the y-axis and bank balance on the x-axis.

on the system behavior. For example, you will sometimes gain a new perspective from a scatter graph with one stock variable on the *x*-axis and another stock on the *y*-axis. In chapter 18, for example, such graphs helped us see the "point attractor" in a predator-prey system. In chapter 19, a scatter graph helped us visualize the "limit cycle" in the aluminum industry.

Sensitivity Analysis

One of Stella's most useful features is the ease of conducting a sensitivity analysis. This is a collection of simulations that reveals the importance of one of the model inputs. Figure C.13 shows an example of a sensitivity study to learn the importance of the *Birth Rate* in the population model from figure C.1.

To reproduce figure C.13 on your own computer, click on the run command and drag down to "Sensi Specs." Select the *Birth Rate* for analysis and ask for four runs with the *Birth Rate* to change incrementally from a low of 0.01 to a high of 0.10. Open a new graph pad as a time series, comparative graph of the *Bank Balance*. Then click on run, drag down to "S Run," and watch the four simulations unfold in the graph pad. In the figure C.13 example, we learn that the size of the population after 40 years is quite sensitive to the size of the *Birth Rate*.

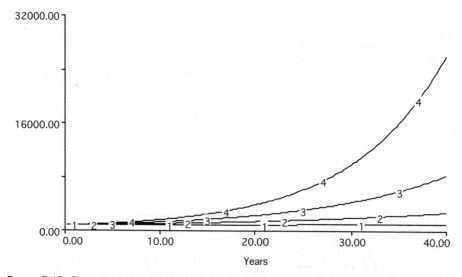

Figure C.13. Comparative graph showing the four simulations of the population model with the birth rate at 1%/yr (run 1), 4%/yr (run 2), 7%/yr (run 3), and at 10%/yr (run 4).

More to Learn

This appendix has covered many but not all of Stella's useful features. You can learn more about the remaining features in the technical documentation (HPS 1993) or by turning to examples scattered throughout the book. Table C.1 lists some of the remaining features along with the location of examples of their application. As you browse these examples, you will see that the software has been designed to make model building and model testing as convenient as possible. You'll discover a similar design philosophy for each of the stock-and-flow programs in appendices D, E, and F. Each of these programs makes the mechanics of modeling

Table C.1. Examples of other features of the Stella software.

Feature	Purpose	Examples
Animation	Shading the stocks to help one visualize the changes in an "animated" flow diagram.	Exercises C.9 and I.8
Arrays	Equations can be written once and apply for many entries in an "array."	Exercise 19.3; Figure I.3
Bar Charts	Dramatize the relative size of model variables.	Exercise 12.4
Conveyors	Used to simulate material that flows in a tightly controlled pattern.	Chapter 10
Data Import	Makes it easy to import parameter values from another program.	Exercise I.3
Data Export	Makes it easy to export simulation results to another program.	Exercise I.5
Loop Identification	Makes it easy to identify and display the feedback loops in a model.	Figure 7.17
Special Functions	Over seventy special purpose functions are available to help write equations.	Appendix H

easy. Our job is to put these convenient tools to work to gain a better understanding of environmental systems.

Exercises

1. **Population model:**
   Build the population model in figure C.1 and verify the results in figures C.4 and C.5.

2. **Bank balance model:**
   Build the bank balance model in figure C.9 and verify the results in figures C.11 and C.12.

3. **Discontinuous graph function:**
   Repeat the bank policy analysis from the previous exercise with the assumption that the interest rate changes abruptly from 4 percent/yr to 5 percent/yr when the balance reaches $2,000. Similarly, the interest rate changes abruptly from 5 percent/yr to 6 percent/yr when the balance reaches $4,000. (Hint: Experiment with the button in the lower left corner of the graphical function dialog box.) Turn in a new version of figure C.11 to document your results.

4. **Poor structure is not allowed:**
   Attempt to build a stock-and-flow diagram to match any of the erroneous examples in the first exercise of chapter 2.

5. **Two bottles—pencil forecast:**
   Imagine you have been asked to forecast the volumes and flows in the "two-bottles" system depicted in the following diagram. The volume of fluid in each bottle is measured

in cubic centimeters (cc); fluid flows are measured in cc per second (cc/sec); heights are measured in centimeters (cm); and the surface areas are measured in square centimeters. The fluid enters the first bottle at a constant rate of 5 cc/sec. The first bottle is a cylinder with a surface area of 5 square cm and an overflow tube that carries fluid to the second bottle. The overflow is zero until the height reaches 14 cm. Then it increases with further increases in height (as shown in the chart below). If the height should exceed 16 cm, the overflow will reach a maximum of 10 cc/sec.

The second bottle is a cylinder with a 10-square-cm surface area and an overflow tube located at 9 cm. The rate of overflow from the second bottle is shown on the second chart. In the illustration below, the fluid levels are at the overflow positions. At these positions, there would be 75 cc in the first bottle and 100 cc in the second bottle.

Now, with a simple pencil and paper, draw a graph of what you expect to happen over time if we start the system with empty bottles and the inflow remains constant at 5 cc/sec. Draw a graph of how you expect the volumes to change over time.

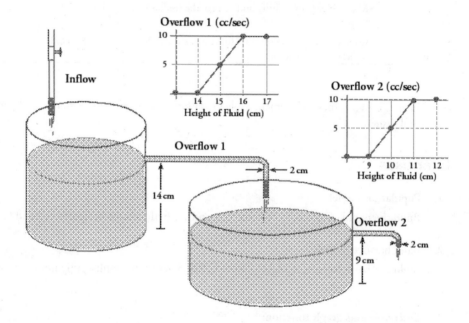

6. **Build and test the two-bottles model:**

    Build a model of the two-bottles system. Initialize the stocks at zero and set the inflow to remain constant at 5 cc/sec. Simulate the model for 80 seconds with DT at 0.25 seconds. Does the simulation match your pencil forecast from the previous exercise? Document your work with a copy of the flow diagram and equations and the following time graphs:

    - graph of the two volumes (scaled from 0 to 100 cc)
    - graph of the three flows (scaled from 0 to 10 cc/sec)
    - graph of the two heights (scaled from 0 to 20 cm)

7. **DT test:**

    Repeat the simulation from the previous exercise with DT at 0.125 seconds. Do you get the same results?

8. **Two-bottles sensitivity:**

Conduct a sensitivity test to reveal the importance the inflow rate to the height of water in the second bottle. The "S-Run" should include a test with four values of the inflow rate (2, 4, 6, 8 cc/sec). Document the test with a comparative time graph showing the height of the fluid in the second bottle from all four runs.

9. **Animate the two-bottles model:**

Read about Stella's animation feature and apply this feature to the two-bottles example. From the Diagram command, click on Diagram Preferences and select the stocks, flows, and converters to be animated. Use the Range Specs option (under the Run command) to set following ranges:

- Volume of water in the two bottles: from 0 to 150 cc
- Inflow and the two overflows: from 0 to 10 cc/sec
- Height of fluid in the two bottles: from 0 to 20 cm
- Surface area of the two bottles: from 0 to 20 square cm

Run the model with the Stella diagram visible during the simulation to see the effect of animation. To document your work, turn in a copy of the animated Stella diagram at the end of an 80-second simulation.

10. **Structural similarity—two-dams model:**

Alter the two-bottles flow diagram to represent the water flow through two reservoirs. The inflow to the first reservoir is constant, and the outflow from the first reservoir feeds immediately into the water stored in the second reservoir. You may assume that the outflow at each dam depends on the height of water at the dam. The height of water at each dam is dependent on the volume of water in each reservoir. (You may ignore evaporation from each reservoir, and don't bother to write equations.) Turn in a copy of the flow diagram to document your work.

Appendix D

Dynamo

This book uses the Stella software to implement system dynamics models, but you can build and test your own models using any of the stock-and-flow programs. This appendix introduces Dynamo, the software originally developed in the 1960s. Jim Lyneis (1994, 350) explains that the purpose of Dynamo, from its inception, has been to

> support the development and use of system dynamics models for solving real-world business and social problems. Emphasis has been on responding to the consulting and research needs of Pugh-Roberts Associates and the MIT System Dynamics Group. This has led to very powerful software for the creation and analysis of (often) large models.

Dynamo is described in Forrester's (1961) *Industrial Dynamics* and in Richardson and Pugh's (1981) *System Dynamics Modeling with Dynamo.* Concise summaries are appended to books describing major applications of system dynamics, such as Meadows et al.'s (1974) book on the "WORLD3" model and Lyneis's (1982) book *Corporate Planning and Policy Design.* Finally, you can read about Dynamo directly in the user's manuals provided by Pugh Roberts Associates, 41 William Linskey Way, Cambridge, MA 02142.

This appendix illustrates Dynamo with simple examples chosen to demonstrate the basic similarity between Dynamo and Stella. The examples reveal some differences in terminology and syntax. It is useful to learn the new terms even if you choose to implement your own models in Stella because of the large body of published work in Dynamo.

Bank Balance Example

Figure D.1 shows two flow diagrams for a model to simulate growth in a bank balance over time. The diagram on the right was created with Stella. With Stella terminology, the *Bank Balance* is a stock and the *Interest Earned* is a flow. The diagram on the left was drawn by hand and uses Dynamo terminology—the *Bank Balance* is a "level," and the *Interest Earned* is a "rate."

Richardson and Pugh (1981, 31) explain that

> accumulations in feedback systems are variously called stocks, state variables or levels. The term "level" is intended to invoke the image of the level of a liquid accumulating in a container. The system dynamicist takes the simplifying view that feedback systems involve continuous, fluid-like processes, and our terminology reinforces that interpretation. The flows increasing and decreasing a level are called "rates."

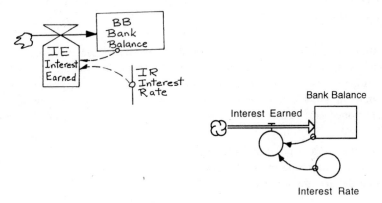

Figure D.1. Bank balance flow diagrams.

Don't worry about the choice of names. Whether you call them stocks and flows or levels and rates, they are the basic building blocks of models explained in chapter 2. The guidelines from chapter 2 will serve you well whether you are drawing a Dynamo diagram with pencil and paper or building a Stella diagram on the computer screen.

The *Interest Rate* in figure D.1 is a "converter" in Stella, a "constant" in Dynamo. Dynamo reserves the term *constant* for inputs that remain constant over the simulation. The solid line in the Dynamo diagram represents the flow of money from a cloud to the level. Solid lines are sometimes called material flows in Dynamo, and the valve symbol is used to depict the magnitude of the flow. The dotted line is called an information flow.

Dynamo does not require a flow diagram because it works directly with equations, but experienced practitioners know that a good diagram is a prerequisite to a well-structured model. The diagram normally includes short variable names (e.g., BB for bank balance) that appear directly in the equations.

The equations for the bank balance model are arranged for comparison in figure D.2. You will notice immediately that the Dynamo equations are more compact because of short names. (Dynamo accepts longer names, but it uses only the first seven characters in each name.)

Each Dynamo equation begins with a letter to designate the type of equation:

- L for a level
- N for an initial value of the level

```
Bank_Balance(t) = Bank_Balance(t - dt) + (Interest_Earned) * dt
INIT Bank_Balance = 500
Interest_Earned = Bank_Balance*Interest_Rate
Interest_Rate = .07


L  BB.K=BB.J+DT*(IE.JK)
N  BB=500
R  IE.KL=BB.K*IR
C  IR=.07
```

Figure D.2. Stella and Dynamo equations for the bank balance model.

- R for a rate
- C for a constant

Two of the equations in figure D.2 do not involve time, so their syntax is simple. The "N" equation sets the initial value of *BB* to 500, and the "C" equation sets the *IR* to 0.07. The other three variables may change over time, so their syntax is more complicated. A period is used to separate the variable name on the left from the letters J, K, or L on the right. These letters are positioned next to each other in the alphabet, and you are to think of them positioned next to each other in time.

- J stands for the previous point in time,
- K stands for the current point in time, and
- L stands for the next point in time.

Dynamo generates numerical simulations that proceed through time "one DT at a time" exactly as explained in chapter 3. So the points in time are separated by a time interval of width DT. The combination of JK is used in level equations to denote that the rate is applied over the previous time step. The combination of KL is used in rate equations to denote the estimate of the rate to be used in the next time step. The equations may be written in a word processor or within Dynamo's *editor*. The equations are then submitted to Dynamo's *compiler*, which checks that the entire collection follows the correct syntax. The compiled equations are then submitted to a *simulator* to generate the numerical results. (The simulation follows the same procedure explained in chapter 3.) Results may be viewed in graphical form or tabular form in dynamo's *viewer*.

Sales Force Example

The sales force model from chapter 6 is shown in a Stella diagram in figure D.3 and a Dynamo flow diagram in figure D.4. Using Dynamo terminology, the model is composed of one level, two rates, five constants, and five remaining variables. The remaining variables are called "auxiliaries." Webster's defines *auxiliary* as "offering or providing help" or "functioning in a subsidiary capacity." Think of the auxiliaries as helping to calculate the rates (or helping to communicate the steps in the calculation).

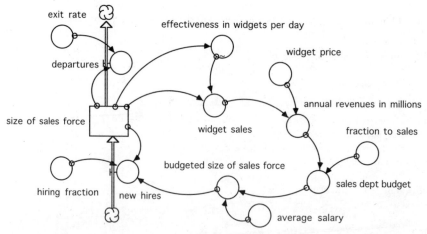

Figure D.3. Stella flow diagram of the sales model from chapter 6.

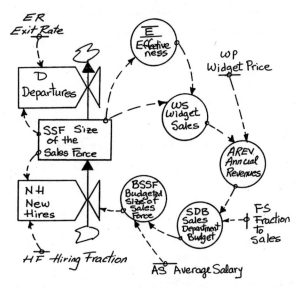

Figure D.4. Dynamo flow diagram of the sales model.

The Dynamo equations for the sales force model are listed in figure D.5. The "A" is used for each of the five auxiliaries, and the name of each auxiliary variable is followed by ".K" since the variable may change over time. Four of the auxiliaries are formed by simple multiplication or division, but "E," the effectiveness of the sales force, is different. It uses a "table function" to allow a functional shape to be entered by hand. The normal custom is to enter the name of the table within the circle enclosing the auxiliary. The table's name is often highlighted by lines above and below. These lines serve the same function in the Dynamo flow diagram as the tilde (~) in the Stella flow diagram—they remind us that a nonlinear graph is used to calculate the variable. In this example, the nonlinear graph is organized to run from a low of zero to a high of 1,200 in steps of 200. The Stella equation would appear as:

```
effectiveness_in_widgets_per_day = GRAPH(size_of_sales_force)
(0.00, 2.00), (200, 2.00), (400, 2.00), (600, 1.80), (800, 1.60),
(1000, 0.8), (1200, 0.4)
```

The corresponding Dynamo information also requires two lines. First, the "A" equation defines the auxiliary as a table with the size of the sales force on the horizontal axis. The axis is organized from 0 to 1,200 in steps of 200, just as in the Stella model. The second line is a "T," or tabular equation. It lists the seven values along the vertical axis of the table.

The final lines at the bottom of figure D.5 control the Dynamo simulation. The simulation begins in year 0; ends in year 20; and proceeds with a step size of 0.25 year. Results for the five saved variables are stored for viewing with a save period of 1 year.

Discussion

Dynamo can be used to build and test system dynamics models of environmental systems. Indeed, several of the models shown in this book were first developed in Dynamo. Richardson and Pugh's (1981) text *System Dynamics Modeling with Dynamo* is probably the best starting point to learn more. Dynamo is a powerful tool for building and simulating dynamic mod-

```
* Dynamo version of the Sales Model in Chpt. 6
note
note   start with SSF, the Size of the Sales Fore
note   this is the only "Level" variable
note
L  SSF.K=SSF.J+DT*(NH.JK-D.JK)
N  SSF=50
note
note   D is Departures, the rate that drains the level
note
R  D.KL=SSF.K*ER
C  ER=.2
note
note   NH is New Hires, the rate that builds the level
note
R  NH.KL=(BSSF.K-SSF.K)*HF
C  HF=1
note
note the rest are auxiliaries and constants
note
A   BSSF.K=SDB.K*1E6/AS        budgeted size of sales force
C   AS=25000                   average salary
A   SDB.K=AREV.K*FS            sales department budget
C   FS=.5                      fraction of revenues to sales
A   AREV.K=WS.K*WP/1E6         annual revenues
C   WP=100                     widget price
A   WS.K=SSF.K*E.K*365         widget sales
note
note effectiveness, E, is the final auxiliary.
note it uses a nonlinear table function which sets
note E as a function of SSF, the size of the sales force
note
A   E.K=TABHL(ET,SSF.K,0,1200,200)
T   ET=2/2/2/1.8/1.6/.8/.4
note
note the simulation will begin in year 0; end in year 20
note DT, the step size, is 0.25 years;
note SAVPER is 1 year, so results are saved every year
note
N      TIME=0
SPEC   DT=.25,LENGTH=20,SAVPER=1
SAVE   SSF,NH,D,AREV,E,SDB
```

Figure D.5. Dynamo equations for the sales force model.

els. But you will discover that it lacks the icon-based tools to help us visualize the stock-and-flow structure along the way. For this capability, you may turn to Stella, Vensim, or Powersim.

If you choose to implement your models with one of the icon-based programs like Stella, you may well find it useful to "translate" a previously published model from Dynamo to Stella. The translation process is relatively straightforward (if the author's intent was to provide a well-documented model). As a first step, you should adopt the short variable names used in Dynamo. (This will make it easier to ensure that each Stella equation matches the corresponding Dynamo equation.) Then simulate the model to verify that the Stella model generates the same results. At this point, you may lengthen the names to expand the communicative power of the Stella flow diagram. You should expect clear sailing in translating 90 percent of the model equations. The troublesome 10 percent will probably involve special functions. Stella comes with hundreds of special functions to expand the software beyond the normal stock-and-flow building blocks (see appendix H). Dynamo provides a similar, but not necessarily identical collection of functions.

Appendix E

Vensim

Vensim is a visual software to help conceptualize, build, and test system dynamics models. It was created by Ventana Systems, Inc. (149 Waverly Street, Belmont, MA 02178) as a "high-end tool" to support the company's consulting projects for governments and businesses:

> In order to do this work well, we needed tools that would support the efficient development of high quality models. Because we were not able to find these tools, we developed our own. Vensim was born as a high-end tool to speed the thorough analysis of models. (Ventana 1996, p. viii)

Vensim's collection of high-end features is impressive. They include optimization, Kalman filtering, macro programming, flight simulators, and risk analysis.

But you don't have to be an experienced consultant to appreciate Vensim. The developers discovered that many of the features that made their consulting projects easier are useful to students as well. So they designed Vensim PLE, the Personal Learning Edition of the software. The PLE retains the analytical capabilities of Vensim "but greatly simplifies the interface by removing all functionality that is not essential to creating high quality basic system dynamics models." Vensim is available on both PC and Macintosh platforms, and the PLE version is provided free for educational and personal use. Documentation is provided in user's guides by Ventana (1995, 1996) and in a tutorial by Kirkwood (1995).

The purpose of this appendix is to introduce the PLE version of the software using the sales force model shown previously in Stella and Dynamo. The example will reveal the fundamental similarity between the "visual stock-and-flow" programs. It will also reveal some of the useful features that the Ventana consultants developed "to speed the thorough analysis of models."

Sales Force Example

The Vensim version of the sales force model is shown in figure E.1. The stock is highlighted in bold print and enclosed within a rectangle. The flows are represented by double lines with a "bow tie" icon to depict the magnitude of the flow. The stocks and flows are assembled with the sketch tools located prominently at the top of Vensim's build window. The remaining variables in figure E.1 appear simply as names on the screen. Although Vensim provides several options to adorn the names (e.g., circles, diamonds, hexagons, etc.), this diagram uses simple names to provide the essential information without using up space on the screen. (This seems to be the custom followed by Ventana [1996] and Kirkwood [1995].)

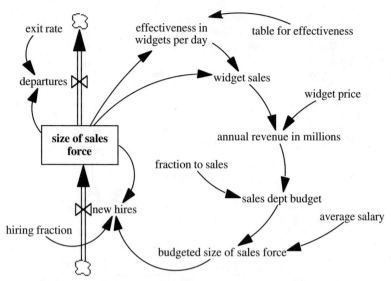

Figure E.1. Vensim stock-and-flow diagram for the sales model.

Vensim equations are entered one variable at a time in a fashion similar to that of Stella. To enter equations, click on the equation sub tool (Y=Xsquared). Vensim responds by highlighting all variables whose equations have not been written. Click on any variable to bring up a dialog window to assist in equation writing. The dialog window prompts you with a list of the variables that should appear in the equation (based on the interconnections in the flow diagram). It also provides access to Vensim's many functions and room to enter the units of measurement. You may skip the units if you wish. But if you take the time to enter the units, Vensim will keep track of the units of each and every variable. You can then click on the "$+Yen=?" tool to learn if the equations are dimensionally consistent.

Vensim's equation format is slightly different from the format you have become accustomed to with Stella. Vensim does not bother to show time, and it uses INTEG in the stock equation. In the sales model, for example, the stock and flows are written as:

```
size of sales force = INTEG(new hires – departures,50)
new hires = hiring fraction*(budgeted size of sales force – size of sales force)
departures = size of sales force*exit rate
```

The INTEG reminds us that the stock's value is found by integrating the effects of the flows over time. Vensim writes the stock equation automatically based on the flows in figure E.1. All you need to do is enter 50, the initial value of the sales force.

Vensim provides for the use of nonlinear graphs, and figure E.1 shows the custom of naming the graph in the flow diagram. In this case, the *table for effectiveness* is used to calculate the *effectiveness in widgets per day*. You might think of this procedure as Vensim's equivalent of the tilde (~) in Stella. It simply reminds us that a nonlinear graph is used to calculate the variable. Vensim provides a "graph lookup" editor to make it easy to organize the graph and enter the values.

Causal Loop Diagramming

Vensim provides several diagramming tools, and the causal loop tools are especially helpful for system dynamics applications. You can probably visualize the four feedback loops in figure

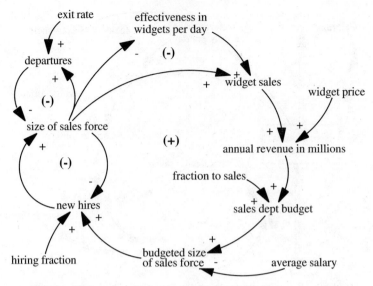

Figure E.2. Vensim sketch of the feedback loops in the sales model.

E.1 from the clarity of the stock-and-flow diagram. Vensim's sketch tools make it easy to draw the causal loop diagram so that the curvature of each arrow leads our eye around the loop. This feature was especially useful in sketching all the diagrams in this book. Figure E.2 shows the four feedback loops shown previously in chapter 7.

Vensim's causal loop diagramming support goes further than a convenient sketching tool. The software also helps you identify the loops. For example, imagine that you are unsure whether figure E.2 shows all the loops in the model. Recall from chapter 7 that all loops must include at least one stock variable. There is only one stock in this model, so we know that the *size of sales force* will appear somewhere in every loop of the model. To check that figure E.2 is complete, we would place the stock variable on the workbench and click on the "loops tool." Vensim responds that there are only four loops in the model. Each loop is reported in simple format. For example, the negative loop involving a change in the effectiveness of the workforce is reported as the fourth of the four loops:

```
Loop Number 4 of length 6
size of sales force
effectiveness in widgets per day
widget sales
annual revenue in millions
sales dept budget
budgeted size of sales force
new hires
```

This simple report will allow you to check that you have spotted all the loops in the model.

Trees and Strips

Vensim's "tree tools" provide a different way to visualize the cause-and-effect relationships in a model. Figure E.3 shows an example of a "causes tree" for the *size of sales force*. This is a screen capture showing how the monitor would appear with the flow diagram in the upper

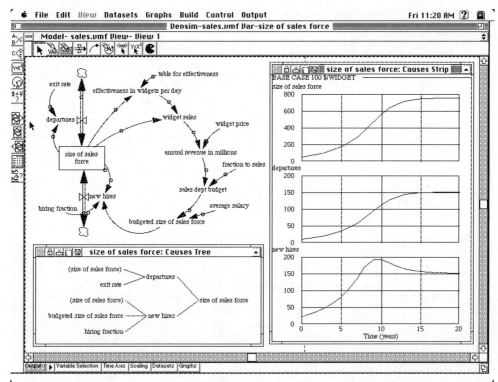

Figure E.3. Screen capture showing the flow diagram along with a causes tree and strip graph.

left corner. The tree appears below the flow diagram. A causes tree looks backward in a model from the starting variable placed in the "workbench." The example in figure E.3 shows the causal variables that directly influence the *size of sales force.* This tree was generated by first selecting the *size of the sales force* for the workbench by clicking on the Control command and dragging down to "Variable Selection." When you select the *size of sales force,* Vensim responds by placing the workbench variable in the top panel. You would then click on the "Causes Tree" tool. Vensim responds by opening the window shown at the bottom of the monitor. The tree reminds us that the *size of sales force* is immediately affected by *departures* and *new hires. Departures,* in turn, are affected by the *exit rate* and *the size of sales force.* The parenthetical entries alert us to the variables elsewhere in the tree.

Figure E.3 shows a combination of a causes tree and a causes strip graph to help us study the sales company growth. Imagine that we have simulated the sales model and stored the results as a "data set" with the name "base case $100/widget." If we are curious about why the sales force grows so rapidly at the beginning of the simulation, we could click on the causes strip graph tool (see cursor). Vensim responds with the combination of three graphs arranged in a "strip." The workbench variable appears at the top of the strip. The remaining variables are those appearing in the next leg of the tree. In this example, the strip graph makes it clear that the sales force grows rapidly because new hires far exceed departures at the beginning of the simulation.

"Uses trees" and "uses strips" support model analysis in a similar manner. The uses tree shows how the workbench variable is used elsewhere in the model. To illustrate, suppose we wish to know variables that will be influenced by the rapid growth in the sales force. To learn where the *size of sales force* is used, we select this variable for the workbench and click on the "uses tree tool." Vensim responds with the tree in figure E.4. It shows four variables that are immediately affected by a change in the *size of sales force.* The uses strip graph helps us see how the change in the workbench variables might lead to changes elsewhere in the model.

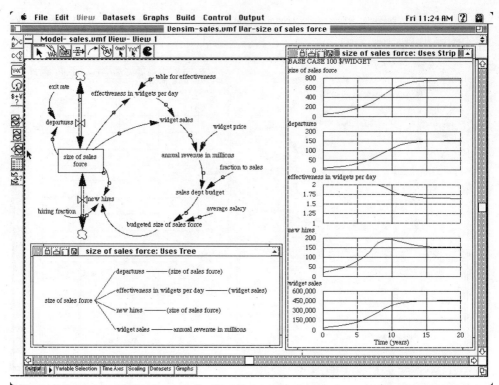

Figure E.4. Screen capture showing the flow diagram along with a uses tree and strip graph.

There are four variables in the next leg of the tree; these are arranged for easy comparison in the vertical strip in figure E.4. The strip makes it clear, for example, that departures are proportional to the size of the sales force, and the effectiveness starts out at 2 widgets/day and declines to an equilibrium value of around 1.7 widgets/day. Widget sales grow rapidly at first, but begin to slow down after the 5th year and level off at 450,000 widgets/year by the 15th year.

Comparing Multiple Simulations

Vensim asks you to name each simulation result as a "data set," and you may load the data sets for easy comparison. Figure E.5 shows an example. The flow diagram is the same as before except the *widget price* has been highlighted by a different font. Three simulations have been conducted, and the data sets have been assigned names to remind us of the value assigned to the *widget price*. The graph on the right side of the screen is a strip graph showing the *size of sales force* from three simulations. This strip is created in a manner similar to that of the causes strip and the uses strip shown previously. You begin by selecting the *size of sales force* as the workbench variable. Then click on the strip graph tool (see cursor). Vensim responds with the comparative graph shown in figure E.5. The comparison teaches us that the price of a widget determines both the initial rate of growth and the eventual size of the company.

Software Support for Thorough Analysis

The Vensim developers were looking for ways to support their consulting projects. They wanted their software to make it easier to conduct "thorough" analysis. The strip graphs are one of the innovative features to speed the analysis of models. These graphs are especially use-

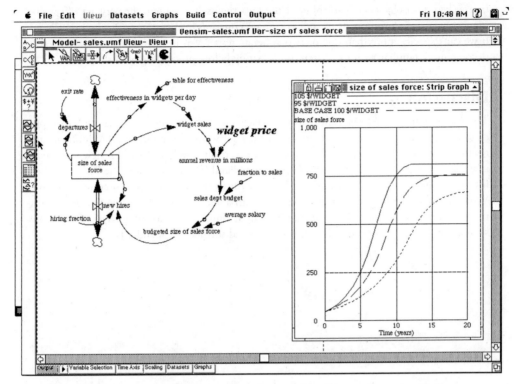

Figure E.5. Screen capture showing a flow diagram alongside a strip graph with three simulations.

ful if you find unusual behavior in one of the variables. By asking for a causes strip graph, you can quickly see the dynamic behavior of all the variables that are immediately connected to the problematical variable. If one of the variables stands out from the rest, you would select it for the workbench and ask for a new causes strip. You would then see the next collection of variables that might be responsible for the problematical behavior. This innovative feature is remarkably useful in speeding the search for erroneous model formulations in large models. The search relies on one's ability to detect unusual results in a time graph and trace the results to their source. One would hope that the search would lead quickly to errors in the model formulation. But in some cases, you might be surprised to find that the "model is right" and your preconceptions are wrong. Sometimes the search for possible errors can lead to insights in system behavior (Mass 1991).

The strip graphs are just one of several useful tools that encourage thorough model testing. The "units check" ($+Yen=?) is another tool to encourage us to improve the quality of our modeling. Vensim also provides a "reality check" feature, which encourages the model user to write down concrete tests using Vensim's reality check language (Peterson and Eberlein 1994). When checking the sales model, we might write

```
THE CONDITION: size of sales force = 0: IMPLIES: widget sales = 0
```

Vensim responds to this statement by creating a simulated condition with the size of the sales force temporarily set to zero. If it finds that widget sales are not zero, it reports an error. Peterson and Eberlein (1994) explain the many advantages of investing in reality checking, and they provide useful suggestions (e.g., the number of checks outnumber the number of equations). Their special language makes it easy to translate concrete tests into a form that can be checked. Our challenge is to think of the tests themselves. Often, the very act of specifying a concrete test prompts us to spot erroneous equation formulations. On the other hand, if we can't specify more than one or two concrete tests (even in plain language), we need to become more familiar with the system under study before proceeding with the model.

Discussion

There is certainly more to Vensim than you have seen here. But you've seen enough to appreciate that it is a visually oriented stock-and-flow software to support the development and testing of system dynamics models. Vensim's PLE version is well designed for new learners. It is available for both Macintosh and PC computers, and Ventana provides the PLE at no cost for your educational and personal use. If you wish to put your models to commercial use, Ventana provides more sophisticated versions with a wide variety of high-end analytical features such as optimization, Kalman filtering, flight simulators, and risk analysis. Risk analysis is an important and powerful tool; it is discussed further in appendix J.

Appendix F

Powersim

Like Vensim and Stella, Powersim is visual software to help you conceptualize, build, and test system dynamics models. Powersim is provided by the Powersim Corporation (1175 Herndon Parkway, Herndon, VA 20170) and is documented in the corporation's promotional and tutorial materials and its *Reference Manual* (Powersim Corp. 1996). The software is available at low cost for student use. If you wish to put your models to commercial use, Powersim Corporation provides a professional version with a wide array of supporting tools. You may also purchase the "Solver," a companion product to provide the high-end analytical features of optimization and risk analysis. And Powersim provides "Metro Server," the application that allows simulation models to run remotely via the Internet or an intranet.

Unlike Vensim or Stella, Powersim does not provide "platform independence." If you want your models to be used on both Macintosh and IBM-compatible computers, Stella or Vensim would be more suitable. Powersim is designed for IBM-compatible computers and is normally used with the Windows operating system. For Windows users, Powersim is an excellent software for model building and testing. It is especially valued by Windows users in large organizations because of its connectivity tools:

- DDE—Dynamic Data Exchange for both server and client exchange of data using standard Windows protocol;
- OLE—Object Linking and Embedding to link objects (such as flow diagrams) across applications;
- API—Application Programmers Interface to allow programmers to connect Powersim simulations to Visual Basic and other applications.

The purpose of this appendix is to introduce Powersim using the sales force model shown previously. The example will reveal the fundamental similarity between Powersim and the previous visual stock-and-flow programs.

Sales Force Example

The flow diagram for the Powersim version of the sales model is shown in figure F.1. Powersim documentation and menus refer to stocks and flows as levels and rates, so the terminology is similar to that of Dynamo. Using Dynamo terms, figure F.1 includes one level, two rates, five auxiliaries, and five constants. Powersim assigns a diamond to the constants and circles to the auxiliaries. It marks the effectiveness auxiliary with a graph icon to

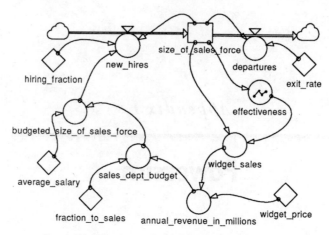

Figure F.1. Powersim flow diagram for the sales model.

remind us that a nonlinear graph is used to find the effectiveness based on the size of the sales force.

Powersim equations are written in a one-at-a-time fashion similar to that in Stella and Vensim. Clicking on any "?" variable brings up a useful window to define the equation. The window prompts you with a list of the variables that should appear in the equation (based on the interconnections in the flow diagram). It also provides access to Powersim's many functions and room to enter the units of measurement. A graph editor is also available to help you organize graphs and enter their values. Equations are normally viewed "one at a time," but you can use the View command to see the entire list of equations:

```
init   size_of_sales_force = 50
flow   size_of_sales_force = -dt*departures
       +dt*new_hires
aux    departures = size_of_sales_force*exit_rate
aux    new_hires = hiring_fraction*(budgeted_size_of_sales_force
       - size_of_sales_force
aux    annual_revenue_in_millions = widget_sales*widget_price/1e6
aux    budgeted_size_of_sales_force = sales_dept_budget*
       1e6/average_salary
aux    effectiveness = GRAPH(size_of_sales_force,0,200,
       [2,2,2,1.8,1.6,0.8,0.4"Min:0;Max:4"])
aux    sales_dept_budget = annual_revenue_in_millions*
       fraction_to_sales
aux    widget_sales = size_of_sales_force*effectiveness*365
const  average_salary = 25000
const  exit_rate = .2
const  fraction_to_sales = 0.5
const  hiring_fraction = 1
const  widget_price = 100
```

Notice that Powersim dispenses with any reference to time. We don't see (t) or (t–dt) as in Stella or a "JKL" as in Dynamo. Time is left out of the equations for simplicity. But you

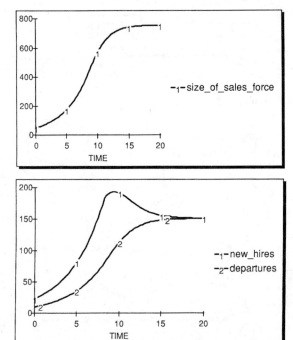

Figure F.2. Time graphs of the
Powersim results.

should know that the time dimension is treated in the same manner as in Stella, Dynamo, and Vensim. All three programs use the numerical approach explained in chapter 3. They advance through the simulation "one DT at a time."

Powersim provides several options for the display of simulation results, including time graphs, cross plots, and tables. Figure F.2 shows time graphs of the base case simulation of the sales model. The top graph shows the s-shaped growth in the size of the sales force over the 20-year simulation period. The lower graph shows the two rates that control the change in the level of the sales force over time. Figure F.2 confirms that the Powersim version of the sales model generates the same behavior seen in each of the other programs.

Powersim provides many additional symbols to enhance the communicative power of the flow diagram. Three examples appear in figure F.3. First, notice that the size of the sales force is reported in a numerical box located just above the stock. The stock's value is also animated in a miniature graph located inside the rectangle. This extra information was obtained with Powersim's animation feature. Now turn your attention to the widget price. The model has been changed to allow the widget price to vary over time. The price icon has changed from a constant (triangle) to an auxiliary (circle), and a clock has been inserted inside the auxiliary to remind us that the price may change over time.

The sales model in figure F.3 makes a final change to illustrate the extra symbols to high-light the position of information delays. The new model distinguishes between an indicated budget and the actual budget. Annual revenues multiplied by the fraction to sales gives the indicated budget. A time lag is required before the actual budget responds to changes in current revenues. Powersim's delayed link tool is useful here. It reminds us of the time lag using the // symbol explained in chapter 17. The time lag is implemented by using DELAYINF (the information delay function) when writing the equation for the actual sales department budget. Notice that a new symbol appears inside the auxiliary for the actual sales department bud-

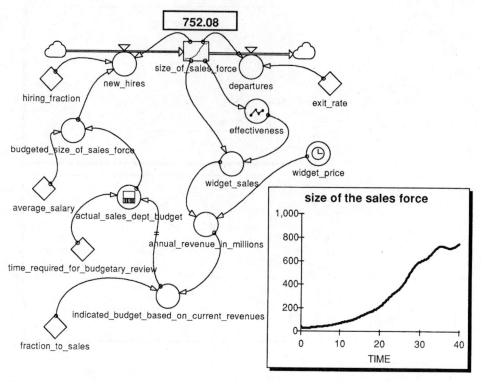

Figure F.3. New version of the sales model with time-varying prices and a lag in adjusting the sales department budget.

get. This is Powersim's additional reminder of the delay in the flow of information. The time graph in the lower right corner shows the simulated growth in the sales force with these new assumptions.

Causal Loop Diagramming

Like Stella and Vensim, Powersim supports the portrayal of the feedback loop structure of the system. Figure F.4 illustrates with a causal loop diagram of the sales company model. This drawing was constructed with Powersim's "text" and "line" tools. The curvature of the lines is controlled by four "handles." Two handles allow you to specify the starting and ending points of each line; the other two give you control over the curvature of each line. Figure F.4 follows the custom established in chapter 7 in which each causal arrow is assigned a + or − polarity. Powersim places the polarity symbols within an oval located near the arrowhead.

Discussion

There is much more to Powersim than you have seen here. But you've seen enough to appreciate that it is a visually oriented stock-and-flow software to support the development and testing of system dynamics models. Powersim operates on IBM-compatible computers and is normally used with the Windows operating system. It is especially valued by Windows users in large organizations because of its connectivity tools.

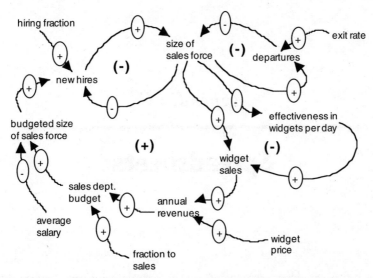

Figure F.4. Powersim sketch of the feedback loops in the sales model.

Appendix G

Spreadsheets

In the days before computers, accountants spread large sheets of paper out on their desks when it came time to update the financial status of their companies. This was a task ideally suited for microcomputers and "electronic spreadsheets." Today, spreadsheet programs like Lotus 1-2-3 and Microsoft Excel are in wide use. Their prevalence raises important questions for system dynamics: *Can we build system dynamics models in spreadsheets?* And if we can, *Shouldn't we do so?*

Using spreadsheets would certainly eliminate the need to explain the stock-and-flow concepts. Perhaps it would be better to build our models in spreadsheets to improve the prospects for communication?

This appendix demonstrates that it is, indeed, possible to build a system dynamics models within a spreadsheet. The demonstration assumes that you have acquired an introductory knowledge of spreadsheets, so you know about rows, columns, cells, etc. But most spreadsheets focus one point in time, so you may not have thought of spreadsheets for calculating changes over time. The demonstration builds from the sales force model used in the previous appendices. The appendix concludes with examples of where a spreadsheet model would be more useful than a stock-and-flow model.

Sales Force Example

Spreadsheets are composed of rows and columns. Numbers are laid out in a row-and-column grid pattern to make their interconnections plain to see. The spreadsheet in table G.1 begins with the constants. Their names appear in cells A4 through A8; their values appear in cells B4 through B8. Constants may be located at the top of the sheet because their values will not change with time. When thinking about a dynamic model, we must first ask ourselves whether we want time arranged in a row or column. For our purposes, it will be easier to visualize the model operations if time is specified to grow from column to column. Table G.1 follows this approach for the sales force model. Time occupies row 13, with the starting value set to zero in cell B13. Time is advanced one DT at a time as we move from column to column. In this example, DT is set to 0.25 year. Table G.1 shows time growing from 0.00 to 1.00 year by column F. The model will run for 20 years, so we need another 76 columns to reach the end of the calculation. But there is no need to show the remaining columns, because the approach will be clear by the time we reach column F. The starting time is entered in cell B13; the remaining entries in row 13 are found by adding 0.25 year, the value of DT.

After taking care of the time dimension, you should define a new row for each of the

Table G.1. Introductory columns in a spreadsheet model of the sales force.

This is column A:	B	C	D	E	F
1 Sales1—the sales model from fig. 6.10 in a spreadsheet					
2 Use column A for names & commentary:					
3 Constants can be placed at top:					
4 Average salary in $/yr	25,000				
5 Exit rate in fraction leaving per yr	0.20				
6 Fraction of revenues allocated to sales	0.50				
7 Hiring fraction in fraction/yr	1.00				
8 Price of a widget in $	100				
9 Next: set the time to run from 0 to 20 years in steps of 0.25 years.					
10 Column B will be Time = 0; time = 20 will not appear until column CD.					
11 The next row is for the stock; the first entry will be the initial value (i.e., 50).					
12 Each subsequent entry is calculated from the flows in the previous column.					
13 Time:	0.00	0.25	0.50	0.75	1.00
14 One stock: the size of the sales force	50.00	53.25	56.71	60.40	64.32
15 Now the five converters:					
16 Effectiveness in widgets/day per person	2.00	2.00	2.00	2.00	2.00
17 Widget sales (per year)	36,500	38,873	41,399	44,090	46,956
18 Annual revenues in $ million	3.65	3.89	4.14	4.41	4.70
19 Sales dept. budget in $million/yr	1.83	1.94	2.07	2.20	2.35
20 Budgeted number of persons in sales force	73.00	77.75	82.80	88.18	93.91
21 The final two rows calculate the flows:					
22 New hires (persons per year)	23.00	24.50	26.09	27.78	29.59
23 Departures (persons per year)	10.00	10.65	11.34	12.08	12.86
24 Now use the flows to update the stock:					

stocks. In the sales model, we have only one stock — the size of the sales force. This name is entered in cell A14, and the initial value of 50 is entered in cell B14.

The next step is to assign a separate row to each of the converters or auxiliaries. Their names are entered in cells A16 through A20. Most of the converters are calculated using simple algebra. The annual revenues in cell B18, for example, is calculated by multiplying the contents of cell B17 by the contents of cell B8 and dividing by one million to get the units right. The sales department budget in cell B19 is found by multiplying the contents of cells B18 and B6. The effectiveness in cell B16 is represented by a "vertical lookup" table, which is located off the screen in table G.1.

Once the five converters have been calculated for time = 0.00, we are ready to calculate the flows. A new row is assigned to each flow. Their names appear in cells A22 and A23; their values are found by simple algebra. The departures in cell B23, for example, are calculated by multiplying the contents of cells B14 and B5.

This brings us to the bottom of the spreadsheet and the end of one iteration through the model calculations. The next step is to update the stocks in the next column. In this example, there is only one stock variable, and its value is 50 in cell B14. With 23 new hires per year and 10 departures per year, you would expect a net growth of 13 persons/year. We are advancing time by 0.25 year, so the net growth would be 0.25*13 or 3.25 persons in the first quarter of a year. The formula in cell C14 performs this calculation to arrive at 53.25 persons.

From this point forward, the remaining cells are a repetition of previous cells. The hard work is to set up the initial values and formulas. The formulas may then be "edit copied" to the remaining columns in the spreadsheet. The calculations for the entire model will appear once the copying is complete. You can now turn to one of the graphs to portray the calcula-

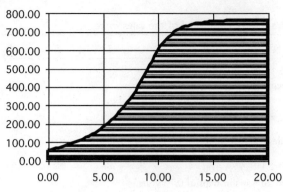

Figure G.1. Spreadsheet chart showing the calculated size of the sales force over a 20-year period.

tions as shown in figure G.1. This time graph confirms the pattern of s-shaped growth that you have seen in chapter 6 and in the previous appendices.

The Appeal of Spreadsheets

Spreadsheets draw our attention to the numbers. We see each and every number, and we can confirm the algebraic manipulations to arrive at each number. This is their main appeal. If you want to display the numbers in a clear and orderly fashion, spreadsheets are hard to beat. Spreadsheets are also popular because of their widespread use. If your colleagues think in terms of spreadsheets, you may find that the best chance to contribute within your organization is through spreadsheets.

The widespread popularity of spreadsheets has spawned a market for supplemental software to aid in the analysis of uncertainty (e.g., @Risk) or to organize the search for an optimum solution (e.g., What's Best?). Other specialized software support decision analysis, project management, and the use of expert systems. According to Sam Bodily (1986, 34), the combination of the simple row-and-column format and sophisticated supplements now gives analysts "the power to analyze their own decisions quickly and easily. These new 'modelers' aspiring to extend their spreadsheet experience will find further possibilities in decision tree analysis, expert systems, optimization, risk analysis simulation and statistical analysis and forecasting."

Clearly, spreadsheets are appealing, and they are certainly in widespread use. And with supplemental tools like @Risk, one might be drawn to the conclusion that spreadsheets are a better approach than the stock-and-flow approach explained in this book.

Discussion

Spreadsheets are the preferred approach if you are asked to perform a complex calculation for a single point in time. But this book is about dynamic systems, so we are interested in calculations that change over time. In such cases, spreadsheets can become more cumbersome, as you have seen in table G.1. Nevertheless, if you are asked to focus on a single calculation of how the system might change over time, a spreadsheet model may deliver the calculation you need.

Each of the stock-and-flow software programs can deliver the numbers shown in table G.1, but that is not their purpose. System dynamics models are seldom constructed as "fancy calculators" to arrive at a single number or a single projection over time. Rather, they are constructed to help build a shared understanding of the system's behavior. By focusing on the stocks and flows, they encourage us to think of the fundamental structure. You have learned that the dynamic behavior will follow from the fundamental structure of the system. Once you understand the stocks, flows, and feedbacks in the system, you will be in a better position to anticipate the system's dynamic behavior.

So, if you face a situation in which a spreadsheet model seems preferable to a stock-and-flow model, ask yourself whether your organization wants a number or an insight. If your team is looking for insight into the system's behavior, use Stella or one of the other stock-and-flow programs described in this book. If you are looking for a number, use whichever software delivers the number in a format that is easily recognized by your team. (This may well turn out to be a spreadsheet.) And if you are wondering about the supplemental software for risk analysis and optimization, you should know that similar high-end tools are becoming available with the growth of system dynamics software. (Vensim, for example, provides risk analysis and optimization tools to work in conjunction with stock-and-flow models.)

If you decide to build a dynamic model using one of the stock-and-flow programs, you should remember that you can still use spreadsheets for what they do best. Spreadsheets are excellent tools for the storage, manipulation, and display of numbers. They can serve as an excellent place to organize inputs for a system dynamics model. They can also be used to store and display results from a system dynamics model. You'll see an example of this approach in appendix I.

Appendix H

Special Functions

All of the system dynamics programs provide an extensive library of special functions to expand the power of the software beyond the normal stock-and-flow building blocks. This appendix highlights some of Stella's functions that are likely to be useful to a student of the environment. You will learn that each function comes with its own syntax. Once you master the syntax, it will be clear that the functions allow you to write more powerful equations. (By calling on a specialized function, you can condense rather complex equations into a single converter.) This appendix concludes with advice on when to exercise this new power.

Stella contains over seventy special-purpose functions, which are stored alphabetically in the "Builtins" window in the right side of the equations dialog box, and they are well documented in the technical documentation available from High Performance Systems (HPS 1993). The best way to learn about the many functions is to browse through the technical documentation. Many of the mathematical and trigonometric functions will be familiar to you. They include logs, exponentials, maximums, minimums, sinewaves, and coswaves. And if you have completed an introductory course in statistics, you will recognize the random, normal, and Poisson functions.

Logical Functions

The logical functions are quite useful, but their syntax may be unfamiliar to you. Logical functions work with expressions that can be evaluated as true or false. The numerical value 1 is assigned to any expression that is true; the value 0 is assigned to any expression that is false. Since there are only two numerical values, logical variables are sometimes called "binary" variables.

Logical expressions can be combined using AND or OR. When using AND, each of the expressions must be true for the combined expression to be true. With the OR statement, only one of the expressions has to be true for the combination to be true. To illustrate how these expressions might be used in a model, suppose you are simulating the temperature in a house, and suppose the furnace is controlled by three thermostats so that the furnace operates only if it is too cold in all three rooms. You could define a logical variable *Furnace On?* where the ? is added at the end of the name to make it clear that you are asking a question that must be answered as true or false. This binary variable takes on the value 1 if the furnace is on and the value 0 if it is off. You could then use this dimensionless variable to calculate the output from the furnace if you know the furnace capacity. Some of the equations would be:

```
Furnace Heat Production = Furnace Capacity * Furnace On?
Furnace Capacity = 4000
Furnace On? = (T1<70) AND (T2<70) AND (T3<70)
```

where $T1$, $T2$, and $T3$ are the temperatures in the three rooms; 70 degrees is the target temperature; and the furnace has a capacity of 4,000 BTU/hour. If the furnace were designed to turn on if only one of the rooms were too cold, the binary variable would be defined with the OR statement:

```
Furnace On? = (T1<70) OR (T2<70) OR (T3<70)
```

The IF THEN ELSE statement is one of the most useful logical statements. The syntax is simple:

```
Y = IF (expression) THEN (1st value) ELSE (2nd value)
```

where Y takes on the first value if the expression is true and the second value if the expression is false. If the furnace heat production were 4,000 BTU/hour whenever the temperature fell below 70 degrees, for example, we could write

```
Furnace Heat Production = IF (temperature < 70) THEN (4000) ELSE (0)
```

Sometimes the IF THEN ELSE will be used to change a parameter value at a certain point in time. Stella reserves the word TIME to stand for the current point of time in a simulation. To illustrate, suppose the interest rate will increase from 5 to 8 percent/yr when a promotional program is launched in the year 1998. The interest rate could be written as:

```
interest rate = IF (TIME>program start year) THEN (0.08) ELSE (0.05)
program start year = 1998
```

These examples are relatively simple, as there is only one logical expression inside each set of parentheses. But, if your situation warrants, you could string together a combination of logical expressions to create a rather complex expression within a single converter. If you find yourself losing track of the combination of logical statements, heed the advice from High Performance Systems (HPS 1993, 7–13) to divide your complex statements into logical groups using extra converters. You'll end up with more converters but less confusion.

Keeping Track of the Calendar

The MOD function turns out to be quite useful in this book because it provides a convenient way to keep track of the calendar. For example, it provides an easy way to keep track of the hour of the day, the day of the week, or the month of the year. MOD stands for modulo, the remainder left over when you divide two numbers. The syntax is MOD(first entry, second entry). The following examples, with the second entry set to 12, will help you anticipate how the function may be applied:

```
MOD(24,12) = 0
MOD(25,12) = 1
MOD(26,12) = 2
MOD(27,12) = 3
```

Now, suppose we are simulating a system with time expressed in months, and we need to keep track of the month of the year. We could define a *Monthly Counter* as:

```
Monthly Counter = MOD(TIME,12)
```

The software divides time by 12, and the remainder tells us the month of the current year. Figure H.1 illustrates how a monthly counter may be used to introduce seasonal variations into a population model.

Let's assume that the *annual birth rate* is 10 percent/yr and the *annual death rate* is 3 percent/yr. So we would expect a net growth rate of 7 percent/yr. And from the review of exponential growth in appendix B, we expect that this population would double in size in approximately 10 years. The equations would be written as follows:

```
population(t) = population(t - dt) + (births - deaths) * dt
INIT population = 500
INFLOWS:
births = population*annual_birth_rate*births_multiplier_in_spring/12
OUTFLOWS:
deaths = population*annual_death_rate*deaths_multiplier_in_winter/12
annual_birth_rate = .10
annual_death_rate = .03
monthly_counter = mod (time,12)
births_multiplier_in_spring = GRAPH(monthly_counter)
(0.00, 0.00), (1.00, 0.00), (2.00, 0.00), (3.00, 0.00), (4.00, 4.00), (5.00, 4.00), (6.00, 4.00),
(7.00, 0.00), (8.00, 0.00), (9.00, 0.00), (10.0, 0.00), (11.0, 0.00), (12.0, 0.00)
deaths_multiplier_in_winter = GRAPH(monthly_counter)
(0.00, 0.00), (1.00, 4.00), (2.00, 4.00), (3.00, 4.00), (4.00, 0.00), (5.00, 0.00), (6.00, 0.00),
(7.00, 0.00), (8.00, 0.00), (9.00, 0.00), (10.0, 0.00), (11.0, 0.00), (12.0, 0.00)
```

To keep track of monthly variations in births and deaths, time must be measured in months rather than years. With time in months, the equations for *births* and *deaths* must divide the annual variables by 12 to make sure we have births in animals/month rather than animals/year. The *monthly counter* is defined with the MOD function, so it will revert to 1 when we reach the 1st month of each new calendar year. Let's assume *deaths* are concentrated in the winter, which we might take to be the 1st, 2nd, and 3rd months of the year. *Births* are assumed to be concentrated in the spring, which is the 4th, 5th, and 6th months of the year. The *births multiplier in spring* uses a discontinuous graph function to concentrate the *births* in the 3-month interval. (Since these months comprise only 1/4 of the year, the multiplier is set to 4.) The *deaths multiplier in winter* uses a similar approach to concentrate the deaths in the first 3 months of the year.

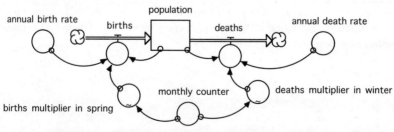

Figure H.1. A population model with monthly variations.

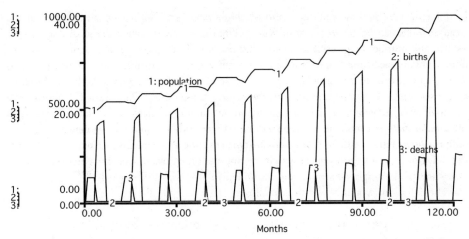

Figure H.2. Simulated population growth with births concentrated in the spring and deaths concentrated in the winter.

Figure H.2 shows the simulated behavior of the population model over a 120-month time span. *Deaths* appear at the start of each year; *births* appear in the spring of each year. The *population* shows some monthly ups and downs, but the general trend is to double in size over the 10-year period

Introducing Random Disturbances into a System

Stella's statistical functions are quite useful when it comes time to study the importance of random disturbances in the system. Figure H.3 shows an example with the population model. This illustration does not focus on the variations from one month to another due to seasonal variations within a calendar year. Rather, we are concerned with variations in the annual weather pattern from one year to another. For example, the animals may experience extremely harsh conditions in one particular year but quite beneficial conditions in the following year.

A *weather index* is defined as a model input, and the Random function is used to let the index vary between 0 and 2. Stella will select a new value of the index during each time step of the simulation. (You would set DT to 1 year so that each time step corresponds to another year in the simulation. The final exercise of chapter 17 provides advice on setting DT to smaller values while allowing random variations from year to year.) The Random function shows three entries with the following syntax:

```
RANDOM(low value, high value, arbitrary seed).
```

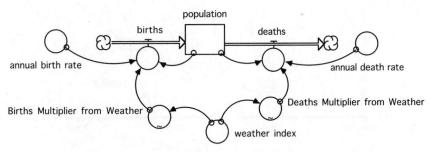

Figure H.3. A population model with random variations in weather.

In this example, the low value is 0, and the high value is 2. So it is equally likely that the weather index can be anywhere from 0 to 2. The third entry is called the seed. Let's set the seed to any number (e.g., 888) to ensure that Stella will replicate the same sequence of random numbers each time a new simulation is performed. (A replicable sequence will be useful if we plan to compare two simulations, and we don't want the comparison to be confused by a new sequence of random numbers in the second simulation.) The value of 1 stands for a "normal" weather year in which the *births* and *deaths* are identical to the values found with the *annual birth rate* and the *annual death rate*. If the index should fall to the extreme value of 0, the *births* fall to zero, and the *deaths* are twice as large as normal. At the opposite extreme, the index of 2 stands for a year in which the population enjoys unusually beneficial weather, *births* are twice as high as normal, and *deaths* fall to 10 percent of normal.

The equations would be written as follows:

```
population(t) = population(t - dt) + (births - deaths) * dt
INIT population = 500
INFLOWS:
births = population*annual_birth_rate*Births_Multiplier_from_Weather
OUTFLOWS:
deaths = population*annual_death_rate*Deaths_Multiplier_from_Weather
annual_birth_rate = .10
annual_death_rate = .03
weather_index = random (0,2,888)
Births_Multiplier_from_Weather = GRAPH(weather_index)
(0.00, 0.00), (1.00, 1.00), (2.00, 2.00)
Deaths_Multiplier_from_Weather = GRAPH(weather_index)
(0.00, 2.00), (1.00, 1.00), (2.00, 0.1)
```

and the simulation results are shown in figure H.4. The weather index is scaled from 0 to 4, so it should remain in the lower half of the graph. Population begins the simulation at 500. The time graph shows that the population will grow over time, reaching almost 8,000 at the end of the 40-year simulation. The population falls in some years with unusually harsh con-

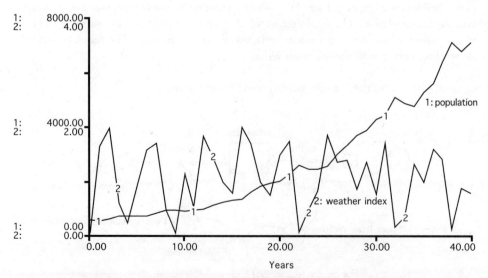

Figure H.4. Population growth with the annual weather index varying in a random manner from extremely harsh to extremely beneficial conditions.

ditions (such as the 32nd year), but the general trajectory follows the exponential path found in models without random variations in the weather.

Smoothing Out the Impact of Random Disturbances

The final function to be mentioned here is the Smooth function. The Smooth is used to smooth out the random variations in information. It is useful whenever there is a time lag before the system responds to changes in the information (see chapter 17). Figure H.5 shows an example in which the *temperature* is assumed to vary in a random manner from a low of 20 to a high of 40 degrees C from one day to another. The *growth rate* of biomass is assumed to vary with changes in the temperature, but the impact of temperate change is not immediate. Rather, the impact is felt only after a time lag. Let's set the *time interval* to 5 days. Since the *average life* of the biomass is also 5 days, we are essentially assuming that the biomass must experience the changed temperatures for around one generation before the effect is visible in the *growth rate.*

The SMTH1 function appearing in the equation for the *effective temperature* stands for 1st-order, exponential smoothing. The syntax is:

```
SMTH1(variable to be smoothed, length of time, initial value)
```

where the third entry for the initial value is optional. In this example, the *effective temperature* is a smoothed value of the actual *temperature;* the time interval is set to 5 days, and the initial value of the effective temperature has been set to 30 degrees C. The *effective temperature* is then used to find the *growth rate.* If the *effective temperature* is 30 degrees C, for example, the *growth rate* will be 25 percent/yr. The equations would be written as follows:

```
biomass(t) = biomass(t - dt) + (growth - decay) * dt
INIT biomass = 500
INFLOWS:
growth = biomass*growth_rate
OUTFLOWS:
decay = biomass/average_life
average_life = 5
effective_temperatue = SMTH1(temperature,time_interval,30)
temperature = random(20,40,888)
time_interval = 5
growth_rate = GRAPH(effective_temperatue)
(20.0, 0.00), (25.0, 0.2), (30.0, 0.25), (35.0, 0.2), (40.0, 0.00)
```

Figure H.6 shows the simulated behavior of the actual *temperature,* the *effective temperature,* and the *growth rate.* The *temperature* varies randomly from one day to the next from a low of 20 to a high of 40 degrees C. But the *effective temperature* does not vary so abruptly

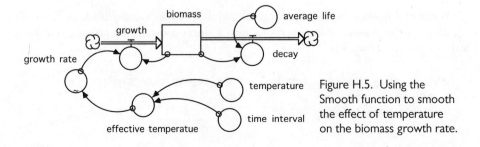

Figure H.5. Using the Smooth function to smooth the effect of temperature on the biomass growth rate.

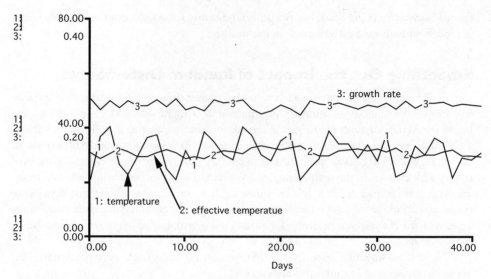

Figure H.6. Simulated changes in temperatures and growth rate with first-order exponential smoothing.

nor so rapidly. The *effective temperature* is the average value of the temperature over the past 5 days. You may think of the SMTH1 function as calculating a 5-day, moving average of the *temperature*. This averaging process "smooths out" the fluctuations in the temperature and the subsequent changes in the *growth rate*.

Concluding Advice

So far, you've seen only a few of Stella's many functions. As you browse through the technical documentation, it will be clear that the software offers a powerful library of functions. This capability raises an important question about their use: When should you use the special functions and when should you stick to stocks and flows? Let's address this question with two models of a population. Figure H.7 shows a stock-and-flow structure for a *population* expected to grow at 7 percent/yr due to the combined impact of *births* and *deaths*.

The equations would be written as:

```
population(t) = population(t - dt) + (births - deaths) * dt
INIT population = 500
INFLOWS:
births = population*birth_rate
OUTFLOWS:
deaths = population*death_rate
birth_rate = .10
death_rate = .03
```

Figure H.8 shows a more compact model that does not require any stocks or flows. The equation for the *population* is compressed into a single converter by taking advantage of Stella's exponential function:

```
population = Starting_Population*EXP(growth_rate*time)
growth_rate = .07
Starting_Population = 500
```

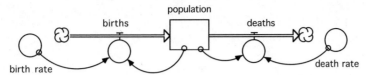

Figure H.7. Population model using stocks and flows.

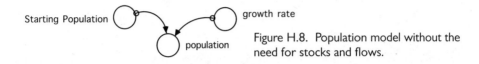

Figure H.8. Population model without the need for stocks and flows.

If you build both of these models, you will find that they both show the population growing in exponential fashion with a doubling time of approximately 10 years. The models give identical results, but which is better?

The appeal of the compact model in figure H.8 is that you "don't waste time" getting the population to grow exponentially. You simply invoke the exponential function, and you are ready to move on to other variables. The compact approach is useful if the population is an input to a larger model and your real focus is elsewhere. But what if the population is the focus of your effort? In that case, the stock-and-flow approach is better. It gives you more than the correct simulation results; it also gives a structural explanation for the results.

This simple population example is indicative of a bit of practical advice about model building. As a general rule, you should avoid the use of the special functions whenever you are writing equations close to the "heart" of your model. Indeed, you might avoid using special functions for any endogenous variable that appears in the inner ring of the bull's-eye diagram (see chapter 9). This is not a hard-and-fast rule; it's simply a piece of practical advice that comes from years of watching talented people build useful models. The best way to follow this advice is to take it as a challenge. Whenever you find yourself applying a special function (like MAX or MIN or EXP, etc.) to a key variable in the center of the bull's-eye diagram, take the opportunity to rethink your approach. Ask yourself about the combination of stocks and flows that act in the real system to produce the dynamic behavior. Based on previous experiences, the extra time will pay off in an improved approach that provides a better explanation of the dynamic behavior.

SPECIAL TOPICS

Appendix I

Spatial Dynamics

You have seen several models in this book with important spatial considerations, but the spatial dimensions are not represented in an explicit manner. Up to now, the approach has been to summarize the spatially important features of the system with one or two aggregate relationships. The Mono Lake and predator-prey models illustrate the general approach:

- The complex shape of the Mono basin influences the water flows, but there are no spatial dimensions in chapter 4. Rather, the spatially important details are summarized by nonlinear functions linking the surface area and elevation to the volume of water in the lake.
- Predators and prey interact in a spatially complicated manner on the Kaibab Plateau, but there are no spatial dimensions in chapter 18. Rather, the interactions are summarized by a nonlinear function linking predation to deer density.

Our understanding of some systems may be improved by introducing the spatial dimensions in an explicit manner, especially if the fundamental principles operate at a cellular level. The region is typically subdivided into a cellular grid pattern, and the flows between adjacent cells are simulated based on the fundamental principles. The result may be a spatially organized model that teaches us more than what we would learn from a model of a single cell. For example, Sancar and Allenstein (1989) argue that an explicit spatial dimension would enhance the usefulness of system dynamics to environmental and city planners. They implemented a dynamic model using a general programming language to permit variable resolution in cell size. Their pedagogic example reveals the power to communicate with graphic displays, but it also revealed a substantial programming challenge, given the software available in the late 1980s. More recently, Hannon and Ruth (1997) provided a pedagogic example dealing with predator-prey populations. They used Stella to simulate births, deaths, and predation within each cell of a 2x2 grid pattern. The insights from the spatial model emerge when the animals are given the opportunity to migrate between cells. This freedom may change the stability of the spatial system from what one would expect from a conventional predator-prey model.

System Dynamics and GIS

Cell-by-cell modeling can be implemented with any of the stock-and-flow software. The information in the dynamic model can be exchanged with a spreadsheet or with a geographic information system (GIS) to improve communication and interpretation. By combining system dynamics and GIS, researchers can enhance the two approaches. Dynamic models can now deal with spatially explicit information while allowing fundamental laws to be expressed at the cellular level. This can build confidence in the model, especially if the fundamental laws are well understood and the spatial simulations can be checked against a GIS. The power of GIS is enhanced as well. When linked to a system dynamics model, a GIS provides a dynamic perspective as well as a spatial perspective. These benefits have prompted several groups to combine the methods. For example:

- Costanza, Sklar, and White (1990) describe a model of coastal landscape dynamics in which Stella is used to describe the interactions of one cell of a spatial grid with links to a GIS for spatial calculations.
- Ruth and Pieper (1994) describe a model of a coastal marsh on Cape Cod. Stella is used to simulate ground cover, erosion, and elevation of a typical cell with links to the Geographical Resources Analysis Support System (GRASS), a raster-based GIS developed by the Army Corps of Engineers.
- The natural resource group at Colorado State University is combining dynamic modeling with very large data sets stored in Arc/Info, the predominant GIS system for land-use planning. Theobald and Gross (1994) report their ideas for combining the best features of dynamic modeling with GIS.
- Jordao et al. (1997) describe a project at the New University of Lisbon to link GIS with a dynamic model for watershed management. The model will be constructed in Powersim with links to *Idrisi for Windows,* a raster-based GIS.

Purpose

The purpose of this appendix is to illustrate how the spatial dimensions can be simulated within the system dynamics framework using the Stella software. Huggett's (1993) model of nitrogen flows in a catchment has been selected for the illustrative example. His model is well documented and easy to visualize. His work also provides a point of comparison in case you wish to compare the relative effort required (with and without Stella). The appendix concludes by demonstrating that the key finding from the nitrogen model can be approximated by a model without spatial detail. Such approximations can be useful as part of a larger modeling system that would be unduly encumbered by a spatial model.

Nitrogen Accumulation in a Catchment

The catchment is divided into an 4x4 grid with each cell occupying 1 hectare. Nitrogen is transferred from one cell to another by water movement. Huggett (1993) calculates the movement between adjacent cells as a function of slope. The inputs to his model are the nitrogen raining down upon the area, the initial nitrogen stored in each cell, and the elevation of each cell. The model shows the spatial patterns of nitrogen accumulation and the long time interval before nitrogen becomes concentrated at the low points in the catchment.

Figure I.1 shows elevations in a 4x4 grid to represent a 16-hectare catchment. Each bar corresponds to the average elevation of a hectare. The high spot is 100 meters above sea level, located at the (1,1) position in the western edge of the catchment. The low spot is 20 meters above sea level in the (4,4) position in the eastern edge of the catchment. We will assume that nitrogen "rains down" upon the catchment with an equal amount landing in each of the 16 cells. The nitrogen then moves in a west-to-east direction following the downward slopes in the catchment.

Figure I.2 shows a model that could be used to simulate nitrogen flows in the catchment. Each of the 16 stocks stands for nitrogen in the soil of each cell. The "Fx" flows represent

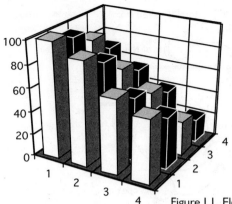

Figure I.1. Elevations in a catchment described as a 4x4 grid.

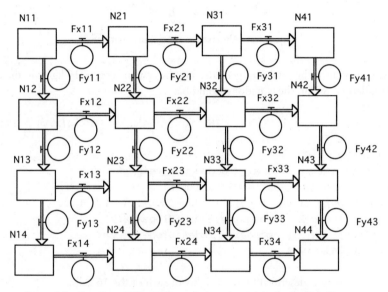

Figure I.2. Stocks and flows for a 4x4 grid model of nitrogen flows.

nitrogen flows in the x direction; the "Fy" flows represent nitrogen flows in the y direction. We could add 16 new flows to represent nitrogen entering each cell from rainfall, and we would be on the way to a useful model. This task is reserved for you as an exercise.

Arrays

Figure I.3 shows a different model that uses Stella's array features to provide a more compact diagram and a more compact set of equations. The 3D icon reminds us that N is an array variable. To build this model, use Stella's array editor to define x as a dimension with the names $x1$, $x2$, $x3$, and $x4$. Then define y as a second dimension with the names $y1$, $y2$, $y3$, and $y4$. Designate N as a two-dimensional array and set all initial values to zero. Let's assume that each cell captures 1/16th of the *total N added per year* due to rainfall. Following Huggett (1993, 67), the flow of nitrogen out of each cell is the product of the nitrogen stored in the cell and the downward slope. (A *porosity index,* which is set to 100 percent/yr, has been added to make

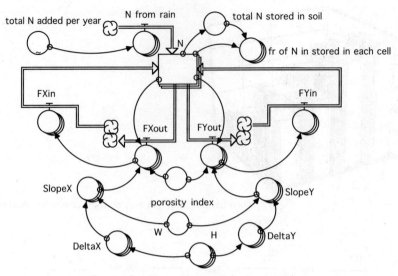

Figure I.3. Alternative model using arrays.

the units consistent.) The total nitrogen entering the system is set to 16 kg/yr in the 2nd year of the simulation. So far, the equations would be:

```
N[x,y](t) = N[x,y](t - dt) + (N_from_rain[x,y] + FXin[x,y] + FYin[x,y]
    - FXout[x,y] - FYout[x,y]) * dt
INIT N[x,y] = 0
N_from_rain[x,y] = total_N_added_per_year/16
total_N_added_per_year = GRAPH(time)
(0.00, 0.00), (1.00, 0.00), (2.00, 16.0), (3.00, 0.00), (4.00, 0.00)
FXout[x,y] = N[x,y]*porosity_index*SlopeX[x,y]
FYout[x,y] = N[x,y]*porosity_index*SlopeY[x,y]
porosity_index = 1
```

And the topography is described by the heights of each of the 16 cells:

```
H[x1,y1] = 100     H[x2,y1] = 95     H[x3,y1] = 85     H[x4,y1] = 70
H[x1,y2] = 90      H[x2,y2] = 80     H[x3,y2] = 65     H[x4,y2] = 55
H[x1,y3] = 65      H[x2,y3] = 55     H[x3,y3] = 50     H[x4,y3] = 40
H[x1,y4] = 55      H[x2,y4] = 45     H[x3,y4] = 30     H[x4,y4] = 20
```

DeltaX and *DeltaY* stand for changes in height in the two spatial directions, and the slopes are based on a cell width of 100 meters:

```
SlopeX[x,y] = DeltaX[x,y]/W
SlopeY[x,y] = DeltaY[x,y]/W
W = 100
```

DeltaX and *DeltaY* are calculated by comparing adjacent values of the entries in the two-dimensional array for *H* as shown in the equations for the cell (2,2) below:

```
DeltaX[x2,y2] = H[x2,y2] - H[x3,y2]
DeltaY[x2,y2] = H[x2,y2] - H[x2,y3]
```

Let's focus on the high spot at the (1,1) location to think through the implications of the equations explained so far. This cell is 10 meters higher than its southerly neighbor and 5 meters higher than its northerly neighbor. The downward slope is 10 percent in the y direction and 5 percent in the x direction. Huggett's model suggests that nitrogen will leave this cell at 10 percent/yr in one direction and 5 percent/yr in the other direction. If there is no nitrogen influx from rainfall, the nitrogen content will decline exponentially at 15 percent/yr.

The flow out of cell (1,1) enters the neighboring cells, as represented by *Fx11* and *Fy11* in Figure I.2. In the more compact model in figure I.3, the flows into neighboring cells are represented by *FXin* and *FYin*. The flows are arranged so that their clouds appear close to the corresponding clouds of the outflows. (This visual trick reminds us that the outflows do not leave the system.) Illustrative equations for the flows leaving cell (2,2) would be:

```
FXin[x3,y2] = FXout[x2,y2]
FYin[x2,y3] = Fyout[x2,y2]
```

The flow out of the (2,2) cell in x direction deposits nitrogen into the (3,2) cell, while the flow out of the (2,2) cell in the y direction deposits nitrogen into the (2,3) cell. Similar equations apply to the remaining cells, but you must be careful when you reach the boundary. Cells located on the boundary of the catchment cannot receive any inflows from outside the region. (Envision the boundary as marking an abrupt change in porosity.) Examples of "zero flow" equations for the (1,1) cell would be:

```
FXin[x1,y1] = FXout[x1,y1]*0
FYin[x1,y1] = FYout[x1,y1]*0
```

The remaining equations in the model keep track of the total nitrogen stored in the soil and the fraction to be found in each of the 16 cells:

```
total_N_stored_in_soil = ARRAYSUM(N[*,*])
fr_of_N_in_stored_in_each_cell[x,y] =
    N[x,y]/Max(.1,total_N_stored_in_soil)
```

(Stella's Max function is used to avoid dividing by zero during the first year when there is no nitrogen in the soil.) These final equations are not needed to match Huggett's model, but they will be useful in checking the plausibility of the model results.

Bookkeeping Chores

You have probably noticed that the preceding model description is somewhat more tedious than previous models. Equation writing has been relatively straightforward in previous models because the form of the equation is usually evident from the flow diagram and the variable names. But spatial models are somewhat more complicated because much of the information is loaded in the arrays, and the equations must be written in an internally consistent manner. The complexity of the spatial models imposes added "bookkeeping" requirements. Don't be surprised if you find your work on a spatial model proceeding slowly at this point in the model building process. The extra time to attend to the bookkeeping chores is the inevitable price of adding spatial details to a dynamic model. For example, if you examine the computer code in Huggett's model, you will discover that over 90 percent of the code is devoted to various bookkeeping chores like data entry, data display, boundary conditions, etc. Less than 10 percent of the code is devoted to calculating the slope between cells and to calculating nitrogen movement and nitrogen storage.

Simulation Results

We expect the nitrogen to accumulate in cell (4,4), the low point in the catchment. Let's focus on this cell, because it is the spot in the grid where we are most likely to see a problem with excessive nitrogen. Figure I.4 shows the simulated nitrogen in cell (4,4) over an 80-year period. It reveals that the system reaches equilibrium in 60 years with all the nitrogen stored in the lowest cell.

Figure I.5 provides a different perspective by combining four bar charts into a side-by-side comparison of nitrogen concentrations. The bar charts show that clear differences in nitrogen concentrations will appear only 4 years after the influx of 1 kg/hectare. For example, it is clear that the concentration in the (1,1) cell is well below 1 kg/hectare, and cell (4,4) already shows the highest nitrogen concentration.

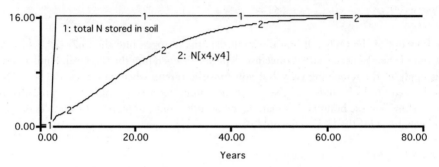

Figure I.4. Test results of the nitrogen model.

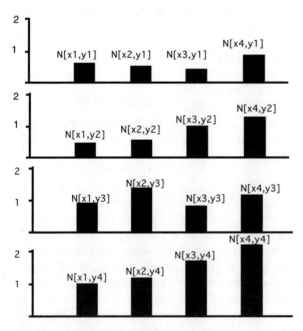

Figure I.5. Nitrogen concentrations (kg/hectare) in the 6th year of the test simulation.

Equivalent Dynamics without the Spatial Dimensions

Imagine that you have joined a research team that is primarily interested in the delay between nitrogen entering the catchment and nitrogen accumulating in cell (4,4). The team has developed a complex model to explain *total N added per year*, and they ask you to come up with a simplified model to explain the dynamics in figure I.4. Finally, imagine that you are free to use the spatial model, but the team would like you to design a simple model that would operate within their larger modeling system unencumbered by arrays and complex topography. Your challenge, therefore, is to design a simple model to produce dynamic results equivalent to those in figure I.4 without simulating the spatial dimensions in an explicit manner.

Figure I.4 shows a "step increase" in the total nitrogen alongside the simulated response of nitrogen in cell (4,4). Although the topography is complicated, the simulated response in figure I.4 turns out to be rather simple. Nitrogen in cell (4,4) responds immediately to the step increase and follows a trajectory that gradually approaches 16 kg/hectare after 60 years. The trajectory turns out to be quite similar to the response of a 1st-order exponential delay to a step increase. (The 1st-order delay is explained in chapter 10.) Examples of the 1st-order response to a step input appear in textbooks (Forrester 1961, 90; Richardson and Pugh 1981, 109) and in the Stella technical documentation (HPS 1993, 7-45). Figure I.6 shows how one could take advantage of Stella's 1st-order SMOOTH function to estimate the nitrogen in the lowest cell in the catchment.

This model operates with the *total N added per year* as an input, just as in the previous model. The stock is used to keep track of the total nitrogen that has accumulated in the soil. The equation for the nitrogen accumulated in the lowest cell would be:

```
N_in_lowest_cell = SMTH1(total_N_in_soil,lag_time)
```

We are now free to experiment with the length of the *lag time* to obtain a close approximation to the previous model. Figure I.7 shows that the previous results can be closely approximated by setting the *lag time* at 20 years. The simple estimate is slightly higher during the first 25 years of the simulation and slightly lower for the remainder. Overall, the fit is surprisingly good considering that the simple model has only one degree of freedom for matching the spatial model.

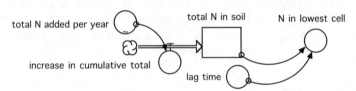

Figure I.6. Simple model to simulate equivalent dynamics without the need for spatial dimensions.

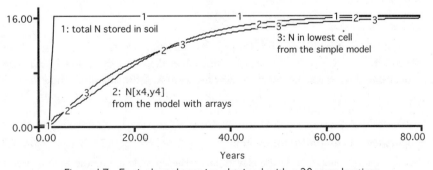

Figure I.7. Equivalent dynamics obtained with a 20-year lag time.

Discussion

This simple demonstration shows that a spatially complex model can be used to provide benchmarks for a simple model. The simple model can then be used as a small piece of a larger modeling system. I believe this two-step approach should be considered whenever you face the need to account for spatial details but want to avoid the tedious bookkeeping chores that may accompany the spatial model. This two-step approach proved particularly useful in a recent model of the Snake River (Ford 1996b).

The Snake River model was designed as a management flight simulator, so speed of operation was important. It was also important to combine surface-water flows with groundwater flows within a single model. Aquifer discharge to the Snake was crucial to the model results, but aquifer discharge is customarily simulated by hydrologic models operating in the spatial dimensions as well as the time dimension. Consequently, we were faced with the daunting task of simulating the groundwater flows through a spatial grid within a dynamic model designed for highly interactive operation. Our approach was similar to that shown in figures I.6 and I.7. We obtained a detailed spatial model of the Snake River Plain aquifer, which provided benchmark patterns over time. We then designed a simplified Stella model to generate equivalent dynamics without the need for spatial detail. The result was a highly interactive flight simulator with credible projections of aquifer discharge.

Summary

This appendix demonstrates that system dynamics models can be used to simulate flows through spatial dimensions as well as the time dimension. You can see from this simple illustration, however, that the spatial dimensions increase the bookkeeping chores of the simulation. Some of these chores can be automated (as explained in the exercises). Nevertheless, it is important to remember that adding the spatial dimensions will dramatically increase the overall complexity of the model. Consequently, you should think about the purpose of the spatial details before launching into a more complicated model. If you decide that spatial details are important, the stock-and-flow software programs are well suited for the simulation as long as the stocks and flows are clearly recognizable. The appendix concludes by demonstrating that a spatially complicated model can be approximated by a simple model that lacks spatial dimensions. Such approximations can be useful as part of a larger modeling system that would be unduly encumbered by a spatial model.

Exercises

1. **Build and verify:**

   Build the model shown in figure I.3 and verify that it generates the behavior shown in figures I.4 and I.5.

2. **Flatter catchment:**

   Change the heights of each cell to create a flatter catchment. Retain the (4,4) cell as the low point, but set its elevation at 60 meters rather than 20 meters. Retain the general assumption that the catchment slopes downward toward the east and toward the south. How long do you think it will take for 95 percent of the nitrogen to end up in the (4,4) cell? Run the new model to check your intuition.

3. **Import the topographic information:**

   Build a spreadsheet to store the elevations of the 16 cells in the catchment. Use the spreadsheet's 3D bar chart to verify the topography shown in figure I.1. Review Stella's technical documentation (HPS 1993, 8-4) for "pasting data into arrayed variables" and practice importing the data for $H(x, y)$ from the spreadsheet.

4. **8x8 grid pattern:**

Expand the precision of the topographical information by expanding the 4x4 grid into an 8x8 grid to cover the same area. Use the spreadsheet from the previous exercise to enter heights that match the heights in the current model. Be sure to expand the x and y dimensions in Stella's array editor, and don't forget to cut the width from 100 meters to 50 meters. Run the new model and compare the results with figure I.4. Does the added precision of the 8x8 grid change the dynamics in a significant manner?

5. **Export results to a spreadsheet:**

Review Stella's technical documentation (HPS 1993, 8-1) for exporting results of the model to a spreadsheet and practice by exporting the results for $N(x, y)$. Then use the spreadsheet to prepare a bar chart of the nitrogen concentrations. Verify the exported results by checking against figure I.5.

6. **Dynamic data exchange:**

Review Stella's technical documentation (HPS 1993, 8-5) for importing and exporting data using Dynamic Data Exchange (DDE). Then link the Stella model to the spreadsheet as in the previous two exercises. But now the links do not use "edit/copy/paste." Rather, they are established with DDE on Windows computers or with Publish and Subscribe on Macintosh computers.

7. **Build the original model:**

Complete the model started in figure I.2. Adopt the same assumptions used in figure I.3 and run the new model to verify that it generates the behavior shown in figures I.4 and I.5. Compare your flow diagram to the diagram in figure I.3. Which would be clearer to someone who is not familiar with Stella?

8. **Animated checkerboard:**

Hannon and Ruth (1997, 336) demonstrate an interesting application of Stella's animation feature to portray changes in cells in a two-dimensional grid. They place ghosted versions of each stock next to one another in a checkerboard pattern. Review their method of displaying spatial patterns and experiment with a similar checkerboard pattern for the nitrogen model in the previous exercise.

9. **Robustness of the simplified model:**

The model in figure I.6 provides a good match to the figure I.4 results. Do you think this close match is a coincidence of the topography? Experiment with different values of the *lag time* to see if the simple model also matches your results from the second exercise. Is there any reason to suspect that this simple model will not provide a good approximation to the spatial model as long as we are free to set the value of the *lag time*?

10. **Topography test:**

The topography in figure I.1 is relatively simple, with the high spot at one corner and the low point at the opposite corner. Change the $H[x,y]$ values to represent a catchment with the low spot at the (3,3) position. Does the model simulate the nitrogen flows correctly?

11. **Model expansion:**

Expand the model as needed to deal with the more complex topography in the previous exercise. Check the plausibility of the expanded model with a test similar to figure I.4.

Appendix J

Comprehensive Sensitivity Analysis

Chapter 15 explains a step-by-step process for building and testing a model. In step 5, we estimate the parameters in a one-at-a-time fashion, based on all the information sources at our disposal. We expect that many of the parameters will be highly uncertain. But we know that it is often useful to include uncertain parameters, especially if they are needed to close the key feedback loops in the system. Chapter 15 encourages us to make our best estimate and move on to simulating the model. In step 6, we simulate the model to see if it generates the reference mode. In step 7, we test the sensitivity of the model to changes in the uncertain parameters. Chapter 16 illustrates a typical approach to sensitivity testing with the Kaibab deer model. It shows a collection of ten simulations to reveal the importance of three parameters. The ten runs show that the Kaibab model is inclined to generate the overshoot pattern regardless of the particular parameter values adopted in the tests.

The Kaibab chapter illustrates an informal style of sensitivity analysis that is appropriate in your first few iterations through the model-building process. This appendix describes a more systematic and comprehensive approach that is useful when you've invested more time and effort in a model. Perhaps the model is gaining credibility within your organization, and you don't want any "unexpected surprises" to pop up when one of the simulations calls for an unusual (and untested) combination of parameter values. Perhaps the model has grown to include hundreds of parameters and you're wondering about the combined effect of their uncertainties. At this stage, we need to move beyond the informal approach described in chapter 16.

Is Comprehensive Analysis Possible?

Suppose we were to test the Kaibab model in a comprehensive fashion. The model has 13 uncertain parameters. They include 2 initial values, 8 constants, and 3 nonlinear graphs. How many tests do you think we should conduct to make sure we understand the combined impact of uncertainties in all 13 parameters? Suppose we select low, medium, and high "values for each of the 13 parameters, and suppose we wish to test each and every possible combination of the parameters:

(3 values for the 1st)*(3 values for the 2nd)* . . . (3 values for the 13th).

The total number of simulations would be 3 to the 13th power, which turns out to be over 1 million simulations. At this point, we might decide to eliminate the two initial values from the analysis, so there would be 11 uncertain parameters. If we wanted every combination of low, medium, and high values, there would now be over 177,000 simulations.

The idea of conducting thousands of simulations leads some researchers to conclude that comprehensive testing is simply not possible. In describing a model of fluid loss in a burn patient, for example, Bush et al. (1985, 22) argue that "minimum tests for sensitivity include a high and low value for each important factor around a baseline case. The possible combinations of parameter values grow exponentially with the number of variables being studied as well as with the number of levels taken of each variable." Bush and his colleagues concluded that "a comprehensive analysis quickly becomes intractable."

The Kaibab and burn patient examples illustrate a common misperception. Many practitioners seem to believe that comprehensive sensitivity analysis is simply not feasible in models that have grown to include more than a few parameters. This is an unfortunate misperception, which is based on an extremely inefficient sampling method.

Sampling Methods

The "sampling method" refers to the procedure for selecting a collection of experiments with the model. Suppose we were limited to only two simulations with the Kaibab model. Our "sample size" would be 2. Under these restrictive conditions, we might decide to conduct:

- one simulation with consistently "optimistic" parameter values for all 13 variables, and
- a second simulation with consistently "pessimistic" parameter values for all 13 parameters.

The sample design relies on our instinctive understanding of the system and our interpretation of "optimistic" and "pessimistic." Now, what if we could conduct 100 simulations of the Kaibab model? How would we design a collection of 100 simulations to learn as much as possible about the model's behavior?

At this point, an understanding of formal sampling methods would be useful. McKay, Buckman, and Conover (1979) describe sampling methods "with considerable intuitive appeal" such as random sampling, stratified sampling, and Latin hypercube sampling. Their experiments revealed that Latin hypercube sampling (LHS) yields the best estimates of model outputs with a given number of simulations. Reilly et al. (1987) describe the practical advantage of LHS as a tenfold reduction in the sample size relative to simple random sampling. To learn if LHS sampling could be useful with a system dynamics model, we conducted a comprehensive sensitivity analysis of a system dynamics model of an electric utility company (Ford and McKay 1985). The study considered uncertainty in 45 parameters. Our purpose was to discover any "surprises" in model behavior and to assign tolerance intervals to the projections of electricity demand and electricity price. The power of LHS was convincingly demonstrated when we learned that a sample size of 20 was sufficient. That is, we calculated the tolerance intervals with an LHS collection of 20 simulations and another LHS sample with 100 simulations. When the two tests revealed the same results, we knew 20 simulations was sufficient.

Software

Several software packages became available in the 1980s to facilitate sensitivity analysis based on LHS. Perhaps the most widely known is @Risk sold by the Palisade Corporation (1988). It supports LHS and tolerance interval estimates for models implemented in a spreadsheet (see appendix G). For system dynamics models, the best approach in the 1980s was HYPERSENS, a customized package developed by Backus and Amlin (1985). The most extensive and well-documented application of HYPERSENS was the study of uncertainty in the north-western electric system (Ford 1990). It showed how uncertainty in electric loads and prices could spread through the different utilities in the Northwest. The study was conducted for the Bonneville Power Administration to learn if Bonneville's conservation programs could help planners deal with the challenges of highly uncertain loads. The power of LHS sampling was once more confirmed when a complex and valuable analysis was completed with only 40 simulations.

It is now possible to conduct comprehensive sensitivity analysis using Latin hypercube sampling with the Vensim software. Appendix E illustrates Vensim with the PLE, the Personal Learning Edition, which is free for educational and personal use. The remainder of this appendix uses an advanced version of Vensim to demonstrate some of the insights that may emerge if we undertake a comprehensive sensitivity analysis.

First Example: Exponential Growth

Figure J.1 shows a simple population model. The population is initialized at 100 million, and the growth is governed by the values of the birth rate and the death rate. Let's assume that the birth rate is 12 percent/yr and the death rate is 5 percent/yr. The net growth rate would be 7 percent/yr, so the population will double in size every decade. The graph of the animal population shows that the population doubles to 200 million in the first decade and to just below 400 million by the end of the second decade.

Now let's consider the uncertainty in the simulated population due to the combined effect of uncertainty in both parameters. Suppose the birth rate is not necessarily 12 percent/yr but could range from a low of 8 percent/yr to a high of 16 percent/yr. And suppose the death rate is not necessarily 5 percent/yr but could range from a low of 2 percent/yr to a high of 8 percent/yr. The sensitivity graph on the right side of the screen shows the results of a sensitivity study with a sample of 100 simulations using LHS. The uncertainties in both the birth rate and the death rate are described as uniformly uncertain. Vensim designs a collection of 100 simulations, executes the simulations, and conducts a statistical analysis of the simulations. The "sensitivity graph" shows the base case run as a solid line. It climbs to just below 400 million by the end of the simulation. The inner area is shaded with dots. It shows the 75 percent confidence bound estimated from the 100 simulations. The outer areas are shaded with lines. These show the additional width needed to form the 95 percent confidence bound on the simulated population.

Figure J.1 reveals an extremely wide band of uncertainty on the simulated animal population. Given our uncertainties in the birth rate and the death rate, the 95 percent interval suggests that the animal population could range from around 100 million to over 1,000 million after two decades. The sensitivity graph also reveals how the uncertainty changes over time. For example, there is very little uncertainty in the size of the animal population in the first few years. By the 13th year, however, the range of uncertainty extends from around 100 million to 500 million. By the 20th year, it extends from around 100 million to over 1 billion.

The growing range of uncertainty in this first example is typical of systems that exhibit exponential growth and systems that are dominated by positive feedback. Small differences in the parameters can lead to large changes in the width of the uncertainty interval. And the farther we look into the future, the larger the uncertainty becomes.

You should expect to see this pattern for any system whose growth is dominated by positive feedback. Perhaps you've asked an investment advisor for a range of projections in an investment account at different rates of return. The advisor will respond with graphs similar to those in figure J.1. They will show that small changes in the rate of return will translate into huge changes in the size of your account as you look farther and farther into the future.

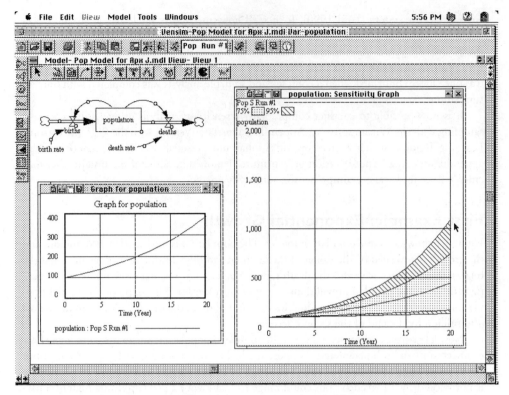

Figure J.1. Screen capture showing a sensitivity graph with 75 percent and 95 percent confidence bounds on the simulated size of the animal population.

Second Example: S-Shaped Growth

Now, let's consider a system with more complex behavior. Figure J.2 shows a sensitivity analysis of the flower model from chapter 6. There are 10 acres of flowers at the start of the simulation, and the base case simulation shows the flowered area growing to around 150 acres after 4 years. The sensitivity study assumes that the intrinsic growth rate is uniformly uncertain from a low of 80 percent/yr to a high of 120 percent/yr. The decay rate could be as low as 15 percent/yr or as high as 25 percent/yr. One hundred simulations were conducted using LHS sampling. The confidence bounds show the same pattern as in the animal population. There is a narrow band of uncertainty in early years, but the width of the uncertain intervals grow larger and larger over time. By the 4th year, the 95 percent confidence bounds suggest that the flowered area could range from a low of 80 acres to as high as 280 acres.

Now, what would you expect the confidence bounds to look like if we continue the simulation for another few years? Will the uncertainty continue to grow larger with time? Recall from chapter 6 that the flower model exhibits s-shaped growth over time. Growth is eventually slowed when there is less and less empty space to accommodate the spread of flowers. Perhaps this limit on the eventual area of flowers will act to limit the growth in uncertainty?

Figure J.3 confirms this expectation. This graph shows Vensim's analysis of 100 simulations over a 16-year interval, enough time to see the full pattern of s-shaped growth materialize in all of the simulations. The analysis reveals that the width of the simulation interval continues to grow until around the 6th year of the simulation. Then the width of the confidence bounds begins to shrink over time. Eventually, we arrive at a situation with relatively constant uncertainty. By the 14th year, for example, it appears that the 95 percent confidence

Sensitivity for 4 Years
75% ▨ 95% ■

area of flowers

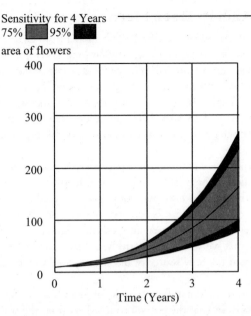

Figure J.2. Sensitivity graph for the first few years of the flower model.

bound is from around 700 to 900 acres. The width of the uncertainty interval is around 200 acres, and it appears inclined to remain at 200 acres over time.

The narrowing in the range of uncertainty during the middle years in figure J.3 is typical of systems that are dominated by negative feedback. Differences in the input parameters are eventually overridden by the actions of the negative feedback, and the uncertainty intervals may shrink over time. In the case of the flower model, the eventual equilibrium is found when the positive and negative loops come into balance. In systems where negative feedback continues to dominate, however, the uncertainty intervals will continue to shrink over time.

Sensitivity for 16 Years
75% ▨ 95% ■

area of flowers

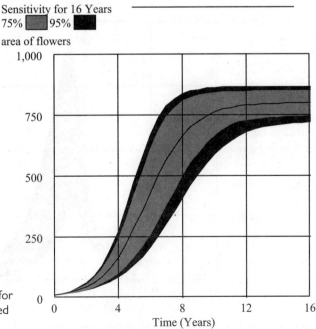

Figure J.3. Sensitivity graph for the entire pattern of s-shaped growth in flowered area.

Concluding Example: The Kaibab Deer Herd

Figure J.4 concludes the demonstration with an example of the Kaibab model from chapter 16. Recall that this model showed a constant deer population of 4,000 as long as the predator population was maintained at exactly the number needed to keep the deer population in check. The initial value of the deer population and the size of the predator population are assumed to remain at the values shown in chapter 16. But 5 of the model parameters are assumed to be highly uncertain. A sensitivity analysis with 100 runs using LHS was conducted to learn how uncertainty in the parameter estimates translates into uncertainty in the simulated deer population.

Figure J.4 shows the results. The combined uncertainty in the 5 parameters translates into a huge uncertainty in the size of the population at the peak of the irruption. Judging from the width of the 95 percent interval in the year 1922, for example, the population could range from just over 50,000 to around 175,000. Once the peak is reached, however, the Kaibab shows an inexorable decline toward zero, regardless of the particular values assigned to the 5 parameters. This sensitivity study suggests that we would be relatively certain that the deer population would eventually decline to zero if the only source of uncertainty was associated with the 5 parameters.

The Kaibab example reinforces the value of the informal style of sensitivity testing demonstrated in chapter 16. Notice, for example, that the general conclusions from the pattern in figure J.4 are the same as the conclusions drawn in chapter 16. For example, we observed in chapter 16 that the model was inclined to show a declining deer population during the second half of the simulation. An inexorable decline to zero is not necessarily plausible, and the fourth exercise of chapter 6 challenges us to improve the model. You can tell from figure J.4 that the improvement will not involve improved estimates of any of the 5 parameters. It will more likely require an improvement in the basic structure of the model.

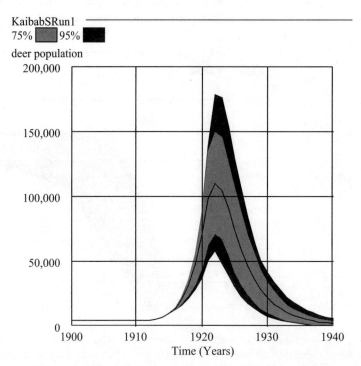

Figure J.4. Sensitivity graph for the simulated size of the Kaibab deer herd based on uncertainty in five model parameters.

Summary

It is now possible for system dynamics practitioners to conduct formal, comprehensive sensitivity analysis aided by convenient software like the sensitivity tools in the advanced version of Vensim. Comprehensive analysis is especially important when a model grows to be important within an organization. We can build confidence in the model's performance by subjecting the model to comprehensive testing. For example, a poorly structured model might not reveal structural flaws in the base case simulation or in the few simulations that may be conducted on an informal basis. But structural flaws will almost certainly be revealed if we conduct 100 simulations with the parameters allowed to vary throughout their ranges of uncertainty.

Comprehensive sensitivity analysis can teach us how uncertainty grows or shrinks over time. A common perception is that uncertainty intervals inevitably become larger and larger with time. This may certainly be true for systems that are dominated by positive feedback. But the examples in this appendix demonstrate that it is also possible for uncertainty intervals to remain constant or to shrink over time. Comprehensive sensitivity analysis can also teach us how uncertainty spreads through a system. We may learn which parts of the system are "immune" to the spread of uncertainty and which parts seem to attract more than their "fair share" of the uncertainty. A concrete example of this benefit is given in Bonneville's study of the spread of uncertainty in electric loads in the Northwest power system (Ford 1990).

Pragmatic Advice

If you undertake a comprehensive analysis, you might begin with a sample of 100 simulations using LHS sampling. It's easy to check whether your sample size is sufficiently large. Simply repeat the analysis with 200 simulations to see if you obtain the same results. (This pragmatic rule is similar to the rule for testing the size of DT in chapter 3.) If you find that the confidence bounds are essentially the same with 200 runs, you know your sample size is sufficient.

A second word of advice is to distinguish between parameter uncertainty and stochastic variations. The uncertainty examples explained in this appendix are associated with our lack of information to estimate the parameters accurately. We make our best estimate, and we acknowledge that there is a range of uncertainty associated with the estimate. Stochastic uncertainty is fundamentally different. It is associated with variations in the parameter due to variations in external factors such as the weather. The variations are normally treated as random variations, perhaps around a mean value that might be well known. You've seen examples of stochastic variations in model inputs represented in the salmon model (figure 14.5), the flower model (final exercise in chapter 17), and the predator-prey model (figure 18.9). These simulations reveal that the models' responses can be quite complex. We can probably make more productive use of models to unravel the complexity if we study the stochastic uncertainty separately from the parameter uncertainty.

Be prepared for surprise results the first time you subject a reasonably complex model to comprehensive sensitivity analysis. If one combination of inputs puts the model into an unanticipated condition, you may get spurious results. This provides an opportunity to improve the structure of the model. To do that, you might ask Vensim for a "trace" of all simulations in the sample to help diagnose the cause of the spurious behavior.

A concluding suggestion is to be prepared to study the confidence bounds in an iterative manner. The confidence bounds are estimated statistically based on the assumption that the uncertain inputs can be varied independently from one another. The independence assumption is often violated, so a natural question is whether codependency among the inputs changes the estimate of the confidence bounds in an important manner. For example, suppose the birth rate and the death rate in figure J.1 are codependent because each is influenced by the food supply per animal. To learn if this codependency is important to the confidence bounds, we could expand the model to add the food supply and the influence of food on the birth rate and the death rate. The new model would include new parameters with their own ranges of uncertainty. We could then ask for an LHS sample of 100 simulations and a new estimate of the confidence bounds. The iterative approach is explained further in the study of uncertainty in the Northwest power system (Ford 1990).

Exercises

1. **Verify:**

    Build the flower model in the advanced version of Vensim and verify the confidence bounds shown in figure J.3.

2. **Sample size test:**

    Repeat the analysis in figure J.3 with an LHS sample with 200 runs. Do you get the same results?

3. **@Risk:**

    If you have access to a spreadsheet program with @Risk, build the flower growth model following the spreadsheet approach from appendix G. Then use @Risk to find the confidence bounds. Do you get the same results as in the previous two exercises?

Appendix K

The Idagon

The Idagon is a computer simulation model of a hypothetical river. It was invented to allow you to experience the challenges of managing a complex river system. You'll have the opportunity to manage the river from month to month over a 4-year time span. This will allow you to become familiar with seasonal changes in water flows and the use of reservoirs to store the water and shape the flows. Then you'll have the opportunity to manage the river over a 40-year time span. This longer interval will allow you to become familiar with slow changes in the amount of groundwater stored in the Idagon aquifer. You'll discover that you can influence the amount of water stored in the aquifer, and thereby influence the aquifer discharge flow. The spring flow rejoins the river and becomes part of the surface-water system. The interconnections between the surface-water system and the groundwater system make the Idagon a particularly challenging system.

The name *Idagon* is taken from Idaho and Oregon, two states in the American West. Like the real rivers in the West, the Idagon is used heavily for irrigation. Its flows are diverted to irrigate millions of acres, and irrigators produce crops that would not otherwise be possible in a region with so little rainfall. The Idagon's flows also spin the turbines at four dams, generating thousands of megawatts of electric power. Power production and crop production combine to give an "Idagon economic product" of nearly $1 billion per year. The Idagon's flows support environmental goals as well. The flows support quality habitats in sensitive reaches of the river, and they are crucial to the success of the salmon smolts' spring migration.

The computer model has been constructed to serve as a "management flight simulator." It permits highly interactive experiments in the same spirit as that of the flight simulators described in chapters 20 and 21. But the Idagon is considerably more complex than the feebate and Daisyworld systems in those chapters. A description of all of its components and their interconnections would fill many chapters. It makes better sense to learn about the Idagon using the home page and clicking on the Idagon link. You'll then see an image similar to the one shown in figure K.1.

The Idagon home page begins with an aerial view of the river and a collection of links to separate pages for more information. You can bring up information on any of the rivers or reservoirs by using the conventional links at the bottom of the screen. Or you can pass the cursor across the aerial view. If the finger appears, you know you have found another link to the same information. In figure K.1, for example, the finger points at American Lake, located in the northeast corner of the region. You can click on this invisible link to learn more about the role of this reservoir in generating electricity, in serving irrigation demands, and in providing sufficient flows for the wildlife habitat below the dam.

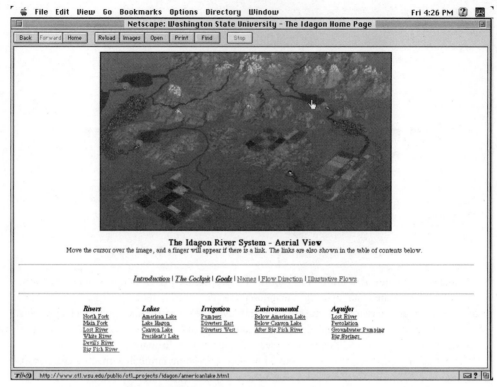

Figure K.1. Opening screen of the Idagon home page.

As you browse the home page, you'll learn that nature provides the region with huge runoff each and every year. You'll learn that the water is put to many uses during its journey to the ocean, and that the region has several unserved uses that could be satisfied if nature were to provide more water. You'll read that the water proceeds swiftly in its journey in the surface-water system, but the water that enters the groundwater system is slowed considerably. You'll read that the huge Idagon aquifer is crucial to the long-term behavior of the system. The aquifer is fed by flow from the Lost River and by percolation flows from the irrigation fields in the eastern region. The aquifer discharge is at Big Springs. (The spring flow is visible as a white dot in the south center of the aerial view in figure K.1.)

The best way to test your knowledge of the river is to answer the questions in the "Driver's Test" at the end of the home page. Passing the test will confirm that you've acquired a basic understanding of the water flows, the units of measure, the names and places, and the physical interconnections in the system. You would then be qualified to take on a more difficult challenge—learning how the river works as a dynamic system.

The Flight Simulator

Figure K.2 shows the opening screen of the Idagon Flight Simulator with instructions in the scrolling field. The river is depicted in the main panel along with navigation buttons to move to separate screens for status reports on the different parts of the system. The opening screen also provides a collection of five buttons that enable you to jump to separate screens where the model inputs can be controlled. The first set of controls involve your priorities for the river. You'll read that there are five goals for the river, and you'll appreciate that there is some merit in each of the goals. They involve increasing the Idagon economic product, sustaining a land-based economy, improving wildlife habitat in the sensitive reaches, providing high spring flows for the salmon smolts' migration, and sustaining a strong flow at Big Springs. Your first decision will be to judge the relative importance of these goals and assign importance "weights" to each goal. The model accepts your weights for purposes of "keeping score" during a simulation.

You can't control the amount of water that nature gives the region each year, but you can shape the river flows by the minimum flow requirements specified at each of the dams. Also, you are given considerable control over the agricultural activity in the region. For example, you can expand or retire the land developed for irrigation in all three of the irrigated areas. You can also change the efficiency of the delivery canals that bring water to irrigation fields, and you can change the efficiency with which the delivered water is used to irrigate the crops.

If you look closely at the northeast portion of the sketch in figure K.2, you'll see that the finger is pointed at the American Lake button. Clicking on this button moves you to a screen like the one shown in figure K.3. Simulation results for American Lake are displayed over a 4-year time span, enough time for you to experience the seasonal changes in the system. The top chart shows the flows into and out of the reservoir. You can shape the outflow at the dam by the minimum flow requirement slider. For example, you might want to set the minimum flow at 3 MAF/yr, which is the flow needed to maintain the quality of the wildlife habitat below American Lake. The first 2 years of the simulation in figure K.3 were conducted with 3 MAF/yr, so that particular environmental goal would have been satisfied.

The second half of the simulation in figure K.3 was conducted with the minimum flow

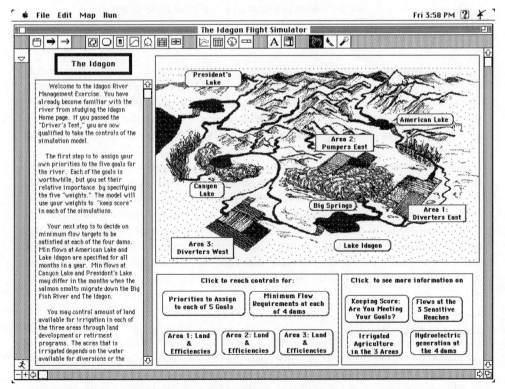

Figure K.2. Opening screen of the Idagon flight simulator. (You can download the flight simulator from the home page. It uses Stella, ver. 5.0.)

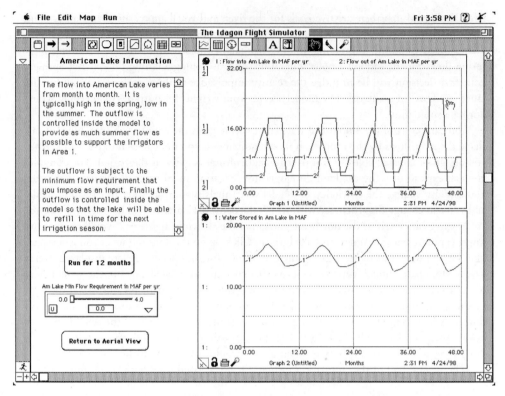

Figure K.3. Illustrative results on the American Lake screen.

requirement reduced to zero. This permits a higher outflow during the summer irrigation season, so more water reaches the diversion gates to the 1 million acres known as Area 1: Diverters East. You'll learn that the higher flows allow nearly all of the land in Area 1 to be irrigated, so crop production is increased. Unfortunately, the increase in crop production is not achieved without sacrificing water quality in the wildlife habitat located below American Lake.

This illustration portrays one of the lessons to be learned from experimenting with the Idagon. In this example, we see a conflict between the use of water for agriculture and the use of water to support environmental quality in the northeast corner of the region. You'll see several conflicts arise in your experiments with the river. There may be conflicts between irrigators (as when groundwater pumpers increase their crop production at the expense of irrigators downstream from the aquifer), and there may be conflicts between hydroelectric generators, irrigators, and the environment. Finally, there may be conflicts between improving the Idagon's performance in the short run at the expense of poor performance in the long run.

Focus of the Idagon: Conflict or Complexity?

Conflict over water dates back to the early years of water development in the American West, so the many sources of conflict in the Idagon confirm that the model incorporates some of the difficult challenges in the West. But the main purpose of the model is not to resolve conflicts between multiple uses of an over-appropriated river. Rather, the main purpose is to help us understand the river as a dynamic, complex system.

The Idagon is powered by huge flows that return year after year as the snow pack melts from the surrounding mountains. Some of the flows can be shaped by the controls at each reservoir. Other flows can be shaped by expanding or reducing the irrigated land or by changing the efficiency of irrigation. And finally, we can shape the groundwater flows by extent and efficiency of the agricultural activity over the aquifer. With all these controls, the Idagon has the potential to be quite a complicated system. Certainly, it is more complicated than the simple "pie chart" that seems to dominate many arguments over water. There are usually three slices in the pie—my water, your water, and their water—and it is commonly believed that there is no way to expand one slice of the pie without shrinking one of the other slices. Therefore, debates over water policy degrade into futile arguments over the relative value of the purpose for "my water" versus the purpose for "your water." Positions are hardened as various parties extol their purposes and belittle the competing purposes.

There is no need to become trapped in such futile arguments when you use the Idagon. You will set your own priorities for managing the river, and there is no requirement that your values must be the same as your classmates' values. You will then search for a combination of policies that allows the river to best serve your goals. Your classmates will do the same. When you have all found a way to improve the river's long-term performance, take the time to compare policies. Perhaps you will find common ground for improving the river.

Further Reading

- Reisner's (1986) *Cadillac Desert* provides an excellent description of water issues in the West. Current events are covered by *Western Water,* the news magazine of the Water Education Foundation, Sacramento, California.
- The Idagon was created to expand on our experiences with a flight simulator of the Snake River in southern Idaho (Ford 1996). You can learn more about the Snake River from Palmer (1991).

References

AAI. 1986. *Aluminum statistical review for 1986.* Aluminum Association, Inc. 900 19th Street NW, Washington, DC 20006.

AES. 1993. *An overview of the ideas model,* The AES Corporation, 1001 North 19th Street, Arlington, VA 22209.

Alfeld, Louis. 1995. Urban dynamics—The first fifty years. *System Dynamics Review* 11, no. 3 (fall): 199–217.

Alfeld, Louis, and Graham, Alan. 1976. *Introduction to urban dynamics.* Walthan, MA: Pegasus Communications.

Andersen, David. 1988. Foreword to the special issue on chaos. *System Dynamics Review* 4, no. 1–2: 3–13.

Anderson, Virginia, and Johnson, Lauren. 1997. *Systems thinking basics: From concepts to causal loops.* Cambridge, MA: Pegasus Communications, Inc.

Andrewartha, H. G. 1970. *Introduction to the study of animal populations.* London: Methuen.

Armstrong, David. 1987. *Rocky Mountain mammals.* Niwot, CO: Colorado Associated University Press.

Arquitt, Steve. 1995. *A system dynamics study of a commodity production system and its natural resource base: A case study of shrimp aquaculture in Thailand.* Bangkok, Thailand: Asian Institute of Technology.

Backus, George, and Amlin, Jeff. 1985. "Combined multidimentional simulation language, database manager and sensitivity/confidence analysis package for system dynamics modeling," *Proceedings of the 1985 International Conference of the System Dynamics Society.*

Barlas, Yaman. 1996. Formal aspects of model validity and validation in system dynamics. *System Dynamics Review* 12, no. 3 (fall): 183–210.

Barlas, Yaman, and Carpenter, Stanley. 1990. Philosophical roots of model validation: Two paradigms, *System Dynamics Review* 6, no. 2 (summer): 148–166.

Barney, Gerald O. 1974. Understanding urban dynamics. Chap. 3 in *Readings in urban dynamics,* vol. 1, edited by Nathaniel Mass. Walthan, MA: Pegasus Communications.

Bass, Frank. 1969. A new product growth model for consumer durables, *Management Science* 15 (January): 215–227.

Begon, Michael; Mortimer, Martin; and Thompson, David. 1996. *Population Ecology.* 3rd edition. Oxford, UK: Blackwell Science.

Berggren, Thomas, and Filardo, Margaret. 1991. An analysis of variables influencing the migration of juvenile salmonids in the Columbia River Basin. Fish Passage Center, 2501 SW First Ave., Suite 230, Portland, OR 97201-4752.

Berk, Rhea; Lax, Howard; Prast, William; and Scott, Jack. 1982. *Aluminum: Profile of the industry.* New York: McGraw-Hill Publications.

Bernstein, Dan; Richardson, George; and Stewart, Thomas. 1994. "A pocket model of global warming for policy and scientific debate," *Proceedings of the 1994 International System Dynamics Conference.*

Berryman, Alan. 1993. Food web connectance and feedback dominance, or does everything really depend on everything else? *Oikos* 68, no. 1: 183–185.

Bjornn, T.C. 1987. A model for predicting production and yield of Tucannon River salmon and steelhead stocks in relation to land management practices. Technical Report 98-1 of the Idaho Cooperative Fish and Wildlife Research Unit, University of Idaho, Moscow, ID 83843.

Bodily, Samuel. 1986. Spreadsheet modeling as a stepping stone. *Interfaces* 16, no. 5 (Sept.–Oct.): 34–52.

Botkin, Daniel. 1990. *Discordant harmonies.* New York: Oxford University Press.

Botkin, Daniel; Broecker, Wallace; Everett, Lorne; Shapiro, Joseph; and Wiens, John. 1988. *The Future of Mono Lake.* Report no. 68, Water Resources Center, University of California, Riverside.

Botkin, Daniel, and Keller, Edward. 1995. *Environmental Science.* New York: John Wiley.

Boyce, Stephen. 1991. *Models for managers in natural resources.* Published by Stephen Boyce, 27 Moytoy Lane, Brevard, NC 28712.

BPA. 1986. *The magnificent journey,* October. (Available from the Bonneville Power Administration Public Involvement Office, PO Box 3621, Portland, OR 97208.)

Bunch, David; Bradley, Mark; Golob, Thomas; Kitamura; Ryuichi; and Occhiuzzo, Gareth. 1992. Demand for clean fuel personal vehicles in California: A discrete choice stated preference survey. March 20. Institute of Transporation Studies, University of California, Irvine, CA 92717.

Bunn, Derek; Dyner, Isaac; and Larsen, Erik. 1997. Modelling latent market power across gas and electricity markets. *System Dynamics Review* 13, no. 4 (winter): 271–288.

Bush, James; Schneider, Alan; Wachtel, Thomas; and Brimm, John. 1985. Fluid therapy in acute large area burns. *System Dynamics Review* 1, no. 1 (summer): 20–41.

Cannon, Walter. 1932. *The wisdom of the body.* New York: W.W. Norton.

Capra, Fritjof. 1996. *The web of life.* New York: Doubleday

Carson, Rachel. 1962. *Silent spring.* Boston: Houghton Mifflin.

Caughley, Graeme. 1970. Eruption of ungulate populations, with emphasis on Himalayan thar in New Zealand. *Ecology* 51, no. 1 (winter): 53–72.

Clark, Colin. 1985. *Bioeconomic modelling and fisheries management.* New York: John Wiley.

Clemen, Robert. 1989. *Making hard decisions: An introduction to decision analysis.* College of Business Administration, University of Oregon.

Clutton-Brock, T., and Albon, S. 1992. Trial and error in the highlands. *Nature* 358 (July 2): 11.

Costanza, R.; Sklar, F.; and White, M. 1990. Modeling coastal landscape dynamics. *BioScience* 40: 91–107.

Coyle, Geoffrey. 1977. *Management system dynamics.* New York: John Wiley.

———. 1996. *System dynamics modelling: A practical approach.* New York: Chapman and Hall.

CRA. 1971. An economic analysis of the aluminum industry. (Charles River Associates, 16 Garden Street, Cambridge, MA.)

Dawkins, Richard. 1982. *The extended phenotype.* New York: Oxford University Press.

———. 1986. *The blind watchmaker.* New York: W.W. Norton.

DeCicco, John; Geller, Howard; and Morrill, John. 1993. Feebates for fuel economy. May. American Council for an Energy Efficient Economy, 1001 Connecticut Avenue NW, Suite 801, Washington, DC 20036.

DeCicco, John, and Thomas, Martin. 1998. *Green guide to cars & trucks: Model year 1998.* American Council for an Energy-Efficient Economy, 1001 Connecticut Avenue, NW, Suite 801, Washington, DC 20036.

de Geus, A. P. 1988. Planning as learning. *Harvard Business Review* (March/April): 70–74.

de Geus, Arie. 1997. *The living company.* Santa Rosa, CA: Nicholas Brealey.

Diamant, Adam, and Wiley, Zach. 1995. Water for salmon: An economic analysis of salmon recovery alternatives in the Lower Snake and Columbia Rivers. Report of the Environmental Defense Fund, prepared for the Northwest Power Planning Council, April.

Diehl, Ernst. 1994. Managerial microworlds as learning support tools. In *Modeling for learning organizations,* edited by J. Morecroft and J. Sterman. Walthan, MA: Pegasus Communications.

Doolittle, W. F. 1981. Is nature really motherly? *CoEvolution Quarterly* (spring): 58.

Draper, F., and Swanson, M. 1990. Learner-directed systems education: A successful example. *System Dynamics Review* 6, no. 2: 209–312.

Duncan, Angus. 1994. Northwest Power Planning Council. A proposal for a Columbia Basin Watershed Planning Council, August.

Eberlein, Robert. 1989. Simplification and understanding of models. *System Dynamics Review* 5, no. 1 (winter): 51–68.

Edwards, Ward. 1977. How to use multi-attribute utility measurement for social decision making. *IEEE Systems, Man and Cybernetics,* SMC-7, May.

Elton, Charles. 1933. The Canadian snowshoe rabbit enquiry, 1931–1932. *Canadian Field Naturalist* 47: 63–86.

EPRI. 1981. Case study comparison of utility corporate models. Report EA-2025. (Electric Power Research Institute, 3412 Hillview Avenue, Palo Alto, CA 94304.)

————. 1996. Balancing risk and return in an uncertain future. Power Markets and Resource Management Division. (Electric Power Research Institute, 3412 Hillview Ave, Palo Alto, CA 94304.)

Espinosa, Jess, editor. 1996. *Metal statistics 1996.* American Metal Market, 825 Seventh Avenue, New York, NY 10019.

Few, Arthur. 1996. *System behavior and system modeling.* Sausalito, CA: University Science Books.

Fiddamann, Thomas. 1997. Feedback complexity in integrated climate-economy models. Unpublished Ph.D. dissertation, MIT Sloan School of Management, Cambridge, MA.

Forbes, Stephen A. 1887. The lake as a microcosm. First appeared in the *Bulletin of the Peoria Scientific Association.* Reprinted in *Readings in ecology,* edited by Edward Kormondy. Englewood Cliffs, NJ: Prentice-Hall, 1965.

Ford, Andrew. 1980. A new look at small power plants. *Environment* 22, no. 2 (March): 25–33.

————. 1990. Estimating the impact of efficiency standards on the uncertainty of the northwest electric system. *Operations Research* 38, no. 4: 580–597.

————. 1992. The impact of electric vehicles on the Southern California Edison system. Final report for the California Institute for Energy Efficiency, July.

————. 1994a. Electric vehicles and the electric utility company. *Energy Policy* 22, no. 7: 555–570.

————. 1994b. Simulating the controllability of feebates. *System Dynamics Review* 11, no. 1 (spring).

————. 1995. The impacts of large scale use of electric vehicles in Southern California. *Energy and Buildings* 22: 207–218.

————. 1996a. Electric vehicles: The case for and against incentives. *Public Utilities Fortnightly* (April 15).

————. 1996b. Testing the Snake River explorer. *System Dynamics Review* 12, no. 4 (winter): 305–329.

————. 1997. System dynamics and the electric power industry. *System Dynamics Review* 13, no. 1 (spring): 57–85.

Ford, Andrew, and Bull, Michael. 1989. Using system dynamics for conservation policy analysis in the Pacific Northwest. *System Dynamics Review* 5, no. 1: 1–16.

Ford, Andrew; Bull, Michael; and Naill, Roger. 1987. Bonneville's conservation policy analysis models. *Energy Policy* (April): 109–124.

Ford, Andrew, and Mann, Greg. 1982. Summary of the workshop on regulatory-financial models of the U.S. electric utility industry. Report LA-9815-C. Los Alamos National Laboratory.

Ford, Andrew, and McKay, Michael. 1985. Quantifying uncertainty in energy model forecasts. *Energy Systems and Policy* 9, no. 3: 217–247.

Ford, Andrew, and Sun, Hojun. 1995. Maintaining control of a feebate system. *Simulation* 62, no. 4 (April): 228–242

Ford, Andrew, and Youngblood, Annette. 1983. Simulating the spiral of impossibility in the U.S. electric utility industry. *Energy Policy* (March): 19–38.

Forrester, Jay. 1961. *Industrial dynamics.* Walthan, MA: Pegasus Communications.

————. 1968. *Principles of Systems.* Walthan, MA: Pegasus Communications.

————. 1969. *Urban Dynamics.* Walthan, MA: Pegasus Communications..

————. 1972. *World Dynamics.* Walthan, MA: Pegasus Communications.

————. 1973. Counterintuitive behavior of social systems. Chap. 1 in *Toward global equilibrium,* edited by Dennis Meadows and Donella Meadows. Walthan, MA: Pegasus Communications.

————. 1975. Market growth as influenced by capital investment. *Collected papers of Jay W. Forrester.* Walthan, MA: Pegasus Communications.

————. 1980. Information sources for modeling the national economy. *Journal of the American Statistical Association* 75, no. 371: 555–566.

Forrester, Jay, and Senge, Peter. 1980. Tests for building confidence in system dynamics models. *TIMS studies in the management sciences,* vol. 14, edited by A. Legasto, Jr., J. Forrester, and J. Lyneis. Amsterdam: North Holland Press.

Gallaher, Edward. 1996. Biological system dynamics: from personal discovery to universal application. *Simulation* (April): 243–257.

Gardiner, Peter, and Ford, Andrew. 1980. Which policy run is best, and who says so? In *TIMS studies in the management sciences* 14: 241–257. Amsterdam: North Holland Press.

Gleick, James. 1988. *Chaos: Making a new science.* New York: Viking Penguin.

Goodman, Michael. 1974. *Study notes in system dynamics.* Walthan, MA: Pegasus Communications.

Goodman, Michael; Kemeny, Jennifer; and Roberts, Charlotte. The language of systems thinking: 'links and loops.'" Chap. 17 in *The fifth discipline fieldbook.* New York: Doubleday Currency.

Gordon, Deborah. 1991. *Steering a new course: Transportation, energy and the environment.* Washington, DC: Island Press.

Gordon, H. 1954. The economic theory of a common property resource: The fishery. *Journal of Political Economy* 62 (April).

Graham, Alan. 1980. Parameter estimation in system dynamics modeling. In *Elements of the system dynamics method,* edited by Jorgen Randers. Walthan, MA: Pegasus Communications.

Greenberger, Martin; Crenson, Matthew; and Crissey, Brian. 1976. *Models in the policy process.* New York: Russell Sage Foundation.

Gregory, R. L. 1988. *Eye and brain: The psychology of seeing.* New York: Oxford University Press.

Hannon, Bruce, and Ruth, Matthias. 1994. *Dynamic Modeling.* New York: Springer-Verlag.

———. 1997. *Modeling dynamic biological systems.* New York: Springer-Verlag.

Hansen, Jan, and Bie, Peter. 1987. Distribution of body fluids, plasma protein and sodium in dogs. *System Dynamics Review* 3, no. 2 (summer): 116–135.

Hardin, G. 1968. The tragedy of the commons. *Science* 162.

Harrison, John. 1992. Tackling the Tucannon. *Northwest Energy News* March–April. (Northwest Power Planning Council, 851 SW Sixth Avenue, Portland, OR 97204.)

Hart, John. 1996. *Storm over Mono: The Mono Lake battle and the California water future.* Berkeley: University of California Press.

Harte, John. 1988. *Consider a spherical cow.* Sausalito, CA: University Science Books.

Hass, Jerome; Mitchell, Edward; and Stone, Bernell. 1974. *Financing the energy transition.* Cambridge, MA: Ballinger Publishing.

Hastings, Alan. 1997. *Population biology: Concepts and models.* New York: Springer-Verlag.

Holling, Crawford. 1966. The strategy of building models of complex ecological systems. In *Systems analysis in ecology,* edited by Kenneth Watt. New York: Academic Press.

———. 1976. Myths of ecology and energy. Proceedings of the Symposium on Future Strategies for Energy Development. Oak Ridge, TN: Oak Ridge National Laboratory.

Homer, Jack. 1993. A system dynamics model of national cocaine prevalence. *System Dynamics Review* 9, no. 1 (winter): 49–78.

———. 1996. Why we iterate: Scientific modeling in theory and practice. *System Dynamics Review* 12, no. 1 (spring): 1–19.

———. 1997. Structure, data and compelling conclusions: Notes from the field. *System Dynamics Review* 13, no. 4 (winter): 293–309.

Horgan, John. 1995. From complexity to perplexity. *Scientific American* (June).

House, Peter, and McLeod, John. 1977. *Large scale models for policy evaluation.* New York: John Wiley.

Howe, Charles. 1979. *Natural resource economimcs.* New York: John Wiley.

HPS. 1992. *Stella II: An introduction to systems thinking.* (High Performance Systems, Inc., 45 Lyme Road, Hanover, NH 03755).

———. 1993. *Stella II: Technical documentation.* (High Performance Systems, Inc., 45 Lyme Road, Hanover, NH 03755).

Hubbert, M. King. 1969. Energy resources. In *Resources and Man.* Washington, DC: National Academy of Sciences; New York: W. H. Freeman.

Huffaker, C. B. 1958. Experimental studies on predation: Dispersion factors and predator-prey oscillations. *Hilgardia* 27: 343–383.

Huggett, Richard. 1993. *Modelling the human impact on nature.* New York: Oxford University Press.

Jacobsen, Chanoch, and Bronson, Richard. 1987. Defining sociological concepts as variables for system dynamics modeling. *System Dynamics Review* 3, no. 1 (winter): 1–7.

Johnston, J. 1972. *Econometric methods.* New York: McGraw-Hill.

Jones and Stokes Associates, Inc. 1993. *Draft environmental impact report for the review of Mono Basin water rights of the City of Los Angeles.* Prepared for the California State Water Resources Control Board, 901 P Street, Sacramento, CA 95814.

Jongkaewwattana, Sakda. 1995. *Systems simulation and modeling.* (Available from the Multiple Cropping Center, Faculty of Agriculture, Chiang Mai University, Chiang Mai 50200, Thailand.)

Jordao, Luis; Antunes, Paula; Santos, Rui; Videira, Nuno; and Sandra Martinho. 1997. Hydrological and ecological economic simulation to support watershed management: linking SD and geographical information systems. *Proceedings of the 15th International System Dynamics Conference.*

Joseph, Lawrence. 1990. *Gaia: The growth of an Idea.* New York: St. Martin's Press.

Kalman, Rudolf. 1960. A new approach to linear filtering and prediction problems. *Journal of Basic Engineering,* series D, vol. 82.

Kaufmann, Thomas. 1983. Aluminum industry prospects 1983–93. *Mineral & Energy Resources* 26, no. 5 (September).

Keeney, Ralph, and Raiffa, Howard. 1976. *Decisions with multiple objectives: Preferences and value trade-offs.* New York: John Wiley.

Kirchner, James. 1989. The Gaia Hypothesis: Can it be tested? *Reviews of Geophysics* 27, no. 2 (May): 223–235.

Kirkwood, Craig. 1992. An overview of methods for applied decision analysis. *Interfaces* 22, no. 6 (November): 28–39.

———. 1995. *Vensim tutorial.* (Department of Decision and Information Systems, Arizona State University, Tempe, AZ 85287-4206.)

Kitching, R. L. 1983. *Systems ecology: An introduction to ecological modelling.* Saint Lucia: University of Queensland Press.

Knight-Ridder. 1993. *Commodity Yearbook, 1993.*

Kormondy, Edward. 1976. *Concepts of ecology.* Englewood Cliffs, NJ: Prentice-Hall.

Kreith, Kurth. 1994. Look, Ma—No Calculus! *Quantum* (November–December): 15–22.

———. 1997. The limits to growth revisited. *Quantum* (September–October): 5–12.

Lack, David. 1954. *The natural regulation of animal numbers.* Oxford: Oxford University Press.

LADWP. 1987. *Mono Basin geology and hydrology.* Prepared by the Aqueduct Division, Los Angeles Department of Water and Power, PO Box 111, Los Angeles, CA 90051.

———. 1988a. *Mono Basin.* Available from the Public Affairs Division, Los Angeles Department of Water and Power, PO Box 111, Los Angeles, CA 90051.

———. 1988b. *Mono Lake report.* Available from the Public Affairs Division, Los Angeles Department of Water and Power, PO Box 111, Los Angeles, CA 90051.

———. 1995. *Draft urban water management plan for the City of Los Angeles.* Los Angeles Department of Water and Power, 111 North Hope Street, Room 1348, Los Angeles, CA 90012.

Lane, D. C. 1992. Modelling as learning: A consultancy methodology for enhancing learning in management teams. *European Journal of Operational Research* 59: 64–84.

Lane, David, and Smart, Chris. 1996. Reinterpreting generic structure. *System Dynamic Review* 12, no. 2 (summer): 87–120.

Larkin, P. A. 1988. Pacific salmon. Chap. 7 in *Fish population dynamics,* 2nd ed., edited by J. A. Gulland. New York: John Wiley.

Leopold, Aldo. 1943. Deer Irruptions. *Wisconsin Conservation Bulletin,* publication 321, August.

Levine, Laurence. 1993. GAIA: Goddess and idea. *BioSystems* 31: 85–92.

Levins, Richard. 1966. The strategy of modeling building in population biology. *American Scientist* 54, no. 4: 421–431.

Lotka, A. J. 1925. *Elements of physical biology.* Baltimore: Williams & Wilkins.

Lovelock, James. 1988. *The ages of Gaia: A biography of our living earth.* New York: W.W. Norton.

———. 1990. Hands up for the Gaia Hypothesis. *Nature* 344 (March): 100–102.

———. 1991. *Healing Gaia.* New York: Harmony Books.

———. 1995. *Gaia: A new look at life on earth.* New York: Oxford University Press.

Lovelock, James, and Margulis, Lynn. 1974. Atmospheric homeostasis: The Gaia Hypothesis. *Tellus* 26: 1–10.

Lovins, Amory. 1991. *Supercars: The coming light vehicle revolution.* Report of the Rocky Mountain Institute, 1739 Snowmass Creek Road, Snowmass, CO 81654-9199.

Lovins, Amory, and Lovins, Hunter. 1995. Reinventing the wheels. *Atlantic Monthly* (January).

Luoma, Jon. 1991. Gazing into our greenhouse future. *Audubon* (March).

Lyneis, James. 1982. *Corporate planning and policy design: A system dynamics approach.* Cambridge, MA: MIT Press. (Available from Pugh-Roberts Associates, 41 Linskey Way, Cambridge, MA 02142.)

Lyneis, James; Reichelt, Kimberly; and Sjoblom, Todd. 1994. Professional dynamo: Simulation software to facilitate management learning and decision making. In *Modeling for learning organizations,* edited by J. Morecroft and J. Sterman. Walthan, MA: Pegasus Communications.

Margulis, Lynn, and Lovelock, James. 1989. Gaia and geognosy. Chap. 1 of *Global ecology,* edited by Mitchell Rambler, Lynn Margulis, and Rene Fester. Orlando, FL: Academic Press.

Marmorek, D., and Peters, C., editors. 1996. *PATH—Plan for analyzing and testing hypotheses, conclusions of FY96 retrospective analyses.* ESSA Technologies Ltd., Vancouver, B.C., December 10.

Mashayekhi, Ali. 1990. Rangelands destruction under population growth: the case of Iran. *System Dynamics Review* 6, no. 2 (summer): 167–193.

Mass, Nathaniel. 1991. Diagnosing surprise model behavior. *System Dynamics Review* 7, no. 1 (winter): 68–86.

————, editor. 1974. *Readings in urban dynamics,* vol. 1. Walthan, MA: Pegasus Communications.

Mass, Nathaniel, and Senge, Peter. 1980. Alternative tests for selecting model variables. In *Elements of the system dynamics method,* edited by Jorgen Randers. Walthan, MA: Pegasus Communications.

Matson, Pamela, and Berryman, Alan, editors. 1992. Special feature: Predator-prey theory. *Ecology* 73, no. 5 (October).

McKay, M.; Beckman, R.; and Conover, W. 1979. A comparison of three methods for selecting values of input variables in the analysis of output from a computer code. *Technometrics* 21, no. 2 (May): 239–245.

McKinney, Michael, and Schoch, Robert. 1998. *Environmental science.* Sudbury, MA: Jones and Bartlett Publishers.

Meadows, Dennis. 1970. *Dynamics of commodity production cycles.* Walthan, MA: Pegasus Communications.

Meadows, Dennis, and Meadows, Donella, editors. 1973. *Toward global equilibrium: Collected papers.* Walthan, MA: Pegasus Communications.

Meadows, D. H., and Robinson, J. M. 1985. *The electronic oracle: Computer models and social decisions.* New York: John Wiley.

Meadows, Dennis; Behrens, William; Meadows, Donella; Naill, Roger; Randers, Jorgen; and Zahn, Erich. 1974. *Dynamics of growth in a finite world.* Walthan, MA: Pegasus Communications.

Meadows, Dennis; Fiddaman, Thomas; and Shannon, Diana. 1989. *Fish Banks, Ltd.* Institute for Policy and Social Science Research, Hood House, University of New Hampshire, Durham, NH 03824.

Meadows, Donella; Meadows, Dennis; and Randers, Jorgen. 1992. *Beyond the limits.* Chelsea Green Publishing.

Meadows, Donella; Meadows, Dennis; Randers, Jorgen; and Behrens, William. 1972. *The Limits to Growth.* Universe Books.

Mech, David. 1966. *The wolves of Isle Royale,* Fauna Series 7. Washington, DC: National Park Service, U.S. Department of the Interior.

Miller, G. Tyler, Jr. 1988. *Living in the environment.* Belmont, CA: Wadsworth Publishing.

————. 1997. *Environmental science.* Belmont, CA: Wadsworth Publishing.

Milsum, John. 1966. *Biological control systems analysis.* New York: McGraw-Hill.

Mohapatra, P., and Sharma, S. 1985. Synthetic design of policy decisions in system dynamics models: A modal control theoretical approach. *System Dynamics Review* 1, no. 1 (summer): 63–80.

Mono Lake Committee. 1989. *Mono Lake: Endangered oasis. Position paper of the Mono Lake Committee,* PO Box 29, Lee Vining, CA 93541.

————. 1997. *Mono Lake Newsletter.* Quarterly publication of the Mono Lake Committee, PO Box 29, Lee Vining, CA 93541.

Morecroft, John. 1988. System dynamics and microworlds for policymakers. *European Journal of Operational Research* 35: 301–320.

Morecroft, J. D. W. 1992. Executive knowledge, models and learning. *European Journal of Operational Research* 59: 9–27.

Morecroft, John, and Sterman, John. 1994. *Modeling for learning organizations* Walthan, MA: Pegasus Communications.

Mosekilde, Erik; Aracil, Javier; and Allen, Peter. 1988. Instabilities and chaos in nonlinear dynamic systems. *System Dynamics Review* 4, no. 1–2: 14–55.

Mosekilde, Erik, and Mosekilde, Lis, editors. 1991. *Complexity, chaos and biological evolution.* New York: Plenum Press.

Moxnes, Erling. 1996. Mismanagement of renewable resources. Working Paper #1/1996, ISSN 0803-4028, Centre for Research in Economics and Business Administration, Norwegian School of Economics and Business Administration, University of Oslo, Bergen, Norway.

Mundy, Phillip. 1994. *Transportation of juvenile salmonids from hydroelectric projects in the Columbia River Basin: An independent peer review,* May 16. Portland, OR: U.S. Fish and Wildlife Service.

Naill, Roger. 1973. The discovery life cycle of a finite resource: A case study of U.S. natural gas. In *Toward global equilibrium,* edited by Dennis Meadows and Donella Meadows. Walthan, MA: Pegasus Communications.

————. 1992. A system dynamics model for national energy policy planning. *System Dynamics Review* 8, no. 1 (winter).

Naill, Roger; Belanger, Sharon; Klinger, Adam; and Petersen, Eric. 1992. An analysis of the cost effectiveness of U.S. energy policies to mitigate global warming. *System Dynamics Review* 8, no. 2 (summer).

Nisbet, R. M., and Gurney, W. S. C. 1982. *Modelling fluctuating populations.* New York: John Wiley.

NPPC (Northwest Power Planning Council). 1987. *Columbia River Basin Fish and Wildlife Program.* Portland, OR: Northwest Power Planning Council.

NRC (National Research Council). 1987. *The Mono Basin ecosystem: Effects of changing lake level.* Washington, DC: National Academy Press.

Odum, Eugene. 1971. *Fundamentals of ecology,* 3rd ed. Philadelphia: Saunders College Publishing.

OECD (Organization for Economic Co-operation and Development). 1992. *The urban electric vehicle.* Proceedings of an International Conference, Stockholm, May. (OECD, 2 rue Andre Pascal, 75775 Paris Cedex 16, France.)

Olsen, Darryll. 1992. *The Idaho Fish Manager,* Ver. 1.0, August. Northwest Irrigation Utilities, 825 Multnomah, Portland, OR 97232.

Paich, Mark, and Sterman, John. 1993. Boom, bust and failures to learn in experimental markets. *Management Science* 39, no. 12 (December): 1439–1458.

Palisade Corporation 1988. *@Risk: Risk analysis and modeling for the PC.* Palisade Corporation, 2189 Elmira Road, Newfield, NY 14867.

Palmer, Tim. 1991. *The Snake River.* Washington, DC: Island Press.

Paulik, G., and Greenough, J. 1966. Management analysis for a salmon resource system. In *Systems analysis in ecology,* edited by Kenneth Watt. New York: Academic Press.

Peck, Merton, editor. 1988. *The world aluminum industry in a changing energy era.* Washington, DC: Resources for the Future.

Peterson, David. 1975. *Hypothesis, estimation and validation of dynamic social models.* Ph.D. dissertation, Department of Electrical Engineering, MIT, Cambridge, MA.

———. 1980. Statistical tools for system dynamics. In *Elements of the system dynamics method,* edited by Jorgen Randers. Walthan, MA: Pegasus Communications.

Peterson, David, and Eberlein, Robert. 1994. Reality check: A bridge between systems thinking and system dynamics. *System Dynamics Review* 10, nos. 2–3 (summer-fall): 159–174.

Peterson, Steve. 1994. Software for model building and simulation: An illustration of design philosophy. In *Modeling for learning organizations,* edited by John Morecroft and John Sterman. Walthan, MA: Pegasus Communications.

Pimentel, David. 1968. Population regulation and genetic feedback. *Science* 159: 1432–1437.

Porter, Michael. 1980. *Competitive strategy.* New York: Free Press.

Powersim Corporation. 1996. *Powersim 2.5 reference manual.* Powersim Corporation Inc., 1175 Herndon Parkway, Herndon, VA 20170.

Pratt, Carl. 1995. *Ecology.* Applied Science Review, Springhouse, PA: Springhouse Corporation.

Pugh-Roberts Associates, Inc. 1986. *Professional Dynamo reference manual.* Pugh-Roberts Associates, 41 William Linskey Way, Cambridge, MA 02142.

Radzicki, Michael. 1988. Institutional dynamics: An extension of the institutionalist approach to socioeconomic analysis. *Journal of Economic Issues* 22: 633–666.

———. 1990. Methodologia oeconomiae et systematis dynamis. *System Dynamics Review* 6, no. 2 (summer): 123–147.

Randers, Jorgen. 1973. DDT movement in the global environment. In *Toward global equilibrium,* edited by Dennis Meadows and Donella Meadows. Walthan, MA: Pegasus Communications.

———. 1980. Guidelines for model conceptualization. In *Elements of the system dynamics method,* edited by Jorgen Randers. Walthan, MA: Pegasus Communications.

Rasmussen, D. 1941. Biotic communities of Kaibab Plateau, Arizona. *Ecological Monographs* 3: 229–275.

Rasmussen, Steen; Mosekilde, Erik; and Sterman, John. 1985. Bifurcations and chaotic behavior in a simple model of the economic long wave. *System Dynamics Review* 1, no. 1 (summer): 92–110.

Reilly, J.; Edmonds, J.; Garder, R.; and Brenkert, A. 1987. Uncertainty analysis of the IEA/ORAU carbon dioxide emissions model. *The Energy Journal* (July).

Reisner, Marc. 1986. *Cadillac desert.* New York: Viking-Penguin.

Richardson, George. 1986. Problems with causal-loop diagrams. *System Dynamics Review* 2, no. 2 (summer): 158–170.

———. 1991. *Feedback thought in social science and systems theory.* Philadelphia: University of Pennsylvania Press.

———, editor, 1996. *Modelling for management: Simulation in support of systems thinking.* Brattleboro, VT: Dartmouth Publishing.

Richardson, George, and Andersen, David. 1995. Teamwork in group modeling building. *System Dynamics Review* 11, no. 2: 113–138.

Richardson, George, and Pugh, Alexander. 1981. *Introduction to system dynamics modeling with Dynamo.* Walthan, MA: Pegasus Communications.

Ricker, W. E. 1975. Computation and interpretation of biological statistics of fish populations. *Bulletin 191.* Ottawa, Canada: Department of Environment.

Ricklefs, Robert. 1990. *Ecology,* 3rd ed. New York: W.H. Freeman and Company.

Riggs, Douglas. 1963. *The mathematical approach to physiological problems.* Baltimore: Williams & Wilkins.

———. 1970. *Control theory and physiological feedback mechanisms.* Baltimore: Williams & Wilkins.

Roberts, Edward, editor. 1978. *Managerial applications of system dynamics.* Walthan, MA: Pegasus Communications.

Robinson, Jennifer. 1980. Managerial sketches of the steps of modeling. In *Elements of the system dynamics method,* edited by Jorgen Randers. Walthan, MA: Pegasus Communications.

Romesburg, H. Charles. Wildlife science: Gaining reliable knowledge. *Journal of Wildlife Management* 45(2).

Russo, John. 1970. *The Kaibab North Deer Herd.* Wildlife Bulletin no. 7, State of Arizona Game and Fish Department, Phoenix, 2nd printing.

Ruth, Matthias, and Pieper, Frederick. 1994. Modeling spatial dynamics of sea level rise in a coastal area. *System Dynamics Review* 10, no. 4 (winter): 375–389.

Saeed, Khalid. 1996. Sustainable development: Old conundrums, new discords. *System Dynamics Review* 12, no. 1 (spring): 59–80.

———. 1998. *Toward sustainable development,* 2nd ed. Brattleboro, VT: Ashgate Publishing.

Safina, Carl. 1995. The world's imperiled fish. *Scientific American* (November): 46–53.

Sancar, F. H., and Allenstein, S. 1989. System dynamics simulation of spatial character. In *Computer-based management of complex systems.* Proceedings of the 1989 International Conference of the System Dynamics Society, Peter Milling and Erich Zahn, editors. New York: Springer-Verlag.

SCAQMD. 1991. *1991 Air Quality Management Plan.* Draft final report, May. (South Coast Air Quality Management District, 21865 E. Copley Drive, Diamond Bar, CA 91765-4182.)

Schneider, Stephen, and Boston, Penelope, editors. 1991. *Scientists on Gaia.* Cambridge, MA: MIT Press.

Schroeder, Walter, III, and Strongman, John. 1974. Adapting urban dynamics to Lowell. Chap. 16 in *Readings in urban dynamics,* vol. 1, edited by Nathaniel Mass. Walthan, MA: Pegasus Communications.

Schroeder, Walter, III; Sweeney, Robert; and Alfeld, Louis, editors. 1975. *Readings in urban dynamics,* vol. 2. Walthan, MA: Pegasus Communications.

Schweppe, Fred. 1973. *Uncertain dynamic systems.* Englewood Cliffs, NJ: Prentice-Hall.

Senge, Peter. 1977. Statistical estimation of feedback models. *Simulation* (June): 177–184.

———. 1990. *The fifth discipline.* New York: Doubleday Currency.

Senge, Peter; Kleiner, Art; Roberts, Charlotte; Ross, Richard; and Smith, Bryan. 1994. *The fifth discipline fieldbook.* New York: Doubleday Currency.

Shampine, L., and Gear, C. A user's view of solving stiff ordinary differential equations. *SIAM Review* 21, no. 1 (January).

Slobodkin, Lawrence. 1980. *Growth and regulation of animal populations,* 2nd ed. New York: Dover Publications.

Smith, George David. 1988. *From monopoly to competition: The transformation of Alcoa, 1888–1986.* Cambridge, England: Cambridge University Press.

Smith, Kimberly. 1996. Computer simulation of bone remodeling and osteoporosis as a tool for medical education. M.S. thesis, University of Georgia, Athens, GA.

Soltzberg, Leonard. 1996. *The dynamic environment: Computer models to accompany 'consider a spherical cow.'* Sausalito, CA: University Science Books.

Sperling, Daniel. 1988. *New transportation fuels.* Berkeley: University of California Press.

———. 1995. *Future drive.* Washington, DC: Island Press.

Standard & Poors. 1994. Metals–nonferrous current analysis. *Standard & Poors Industry Surveys* 162, no. 31 (August): sec. 1.

Sterman, John. 1989. Modeling managerial behavior: Misperceptions of feedback in a dynamic decision making experiment. *Management Science* 35, no. 3: 321–339.

———. 1992. Teaching takes off: Flight simulators for management education. *OR/MS Today* (October).

———. 1994. Learning in and about complex systems. *System Dynamics Review* 10, no. 2–3 (summer–fall): 291–330.

———. Forthcoming. *Business dynamics.* New York: Irwin/McGraw-Hill.

Sterman, John, and Richardson, George. 1985. An experiment to evalulate methods for estimating fossil fuel resources. *Journal of Forecasting* 4, no. 2: 197–226.

Sturis, Jeppe; Polonsky, Kenneth; Mosekilde, Erik; and van Cauter, Eve. 1991. Computer model for mechanisms underlying ultradian oscillations of insulin and glucose. *American Journal of Physiology* 260.

Swart, Johan. 1990. A system dynamics approach to predator prey modeling. *System Dynamics Review* 6, no. 1 (winter): 94–98.

Taylor, Robert J. 1984. *Predation.* New York: Chapman and Hall.

Theobald, D., and Gross, M. 1994. EML: A modeling environment for exploring landscape dynamics. *Computers, Environment and Urban Systems* 18: 193–204.

Timmerman, P. 1986. Mythology and surprise in the sustainable development of the bioshpere. Chap. 16 in *Sustainable development of the biosphere,* edited by W. Clark and R. Munn. Laxenburg, Austria: International Institute for Applied Systems Analysis.

Turoff, M. 1970. The design of a policy delphi. *Technological Forecasting and Social Change* 2: 149.

University of Washington. 1993. The Columbia River salmon passage model manual, CRiSP 1.4, March. University of Washington.

U.S. Army Corps of Engineers, Bonneville Power Administration, and Bureau of Reclamation. 1992. *Columbia River salmon flow measures options analysis/EIS.* Walla Walla, WA: Department of the Army.

Vallentine, John. 1990. *Grazing management.* San Diego: Academic Press.

Vennard, John, and Street, Robert. 1976. *Elementary fluid mechanics.* New York: John Wiley.

Vennix, J. 1990. Mental models and computer models. Doctoral thesis, Department of Methodology, University of Nijmegen, 6500 HE Nijmegen, The Netherlands.

Ventana Systems. 1995. *Vensim user's guide,* Ver. 1.62. Ventana Systems, Inc., 149 Waverley Street, Belmont, MA 02178.

———. 1996. *Vensim Personal Learning Edition, User's Guide,* Ver. 1.62. Ventana Systems, Inc.,149 Waverley Street, Belmont, MA 02178.

Verburgh, Luc. 1994. *Participative policy modelling: Applied to the health care insurance industry,* Doctoral thesis, Department of Methodology, University of Nijmegen, 6500 HE Nijmegen, The Netherlands.

Volterra, V. 1926. Variations and fluctuations of the numbers of individuals in animal species living together. Reprinted 1931 in R. N. Chapman, *Animal ecology.* New York: McGraw-Hill.

Volti, Rudi. 1990. Why internal combustion? *Invention & Technology* 6, no. 2 (fall).

Vorster, Peter. 1985. *A water balance forecast model for Mono Lake, California.* Earth Resources Monograph, U.S. Forest Service, Region 5,Western Forest Information System, Berkeley Service Center, Box 245, Berkeley, CA 94201.

Watson, A. J., and Lovelock, J. E. 1983. Biological homeostasis of the global environment: The parable of daisyworld. *Tellus* Series B, 35: 284–289.

Watt, Kenneth E. F., editor. 1966. *Systems analysis in ecology.* New York: Academic Press.

Watt, Kenneth E. F. 1968. *Ecology and resource management: A quantitative approach.* New York: McGraw-Hill.

———. 1982. *Understanding the environment.* New York: Allyn and Bacon.

Waugh, Geoffrey. 1984. *Fisheries management.* Boulder, CO: Westview Press.

Weil, Henry. 1980. The evolution of an approach for achieving implemented results from system dynamics projects. In *Elements of the system dynamics method,* edited by Jorgen Randers. Walthan, MA: Pegasus Communications.

White, I. D.; Mottershead, D. N.; and Harrison, S. J. 1992. *Environmental systems: An introductory text,* 2nd ed. New York: Chapman and Hall.

Wilber, Charles, and Harrison, Robert. 1978. The methodological basis of institutional economics: Pattern model, storytelling and holism. *Journal of Economic Issues* XII, no. 1: 61–89.

Williams, Richard N. 1996. *Return to the river: Restoration of salmonid fishes in the Columbia River ecosystem,* September 10. Portland, OR: Northwest Power Planning Council.

Winkler, David, editor. 1977. *An ecological study of Mono Lake, California.* Institutute of Ecology Publication no. 12. Davis: University of California.

Wolstenholme, Eric. 1990. *System enquiry: A system dynamics approach.* New York: John Wiley.

Zaraza, Ron, and Fisher, Diana. 1997. Introducing system dynamics into the traditional secondary curriculum. *Proceedings of the 15th International System Dynamics Conference,* August.

Index